# MUSLIM INSIDER CHRIST FOLLOWERS

This study is what is most needed today in the debate over what are called insider movements—a study of the actual theological and missional beliefs and practices of 26 indigenous leaders of these movements in Asia and Africa. These deal with such topics as views of God and Jesus, varied relationships with traditional churches, development of biblical understanding over time, and suffering from Muslims and traditional Christians. The author finds them generally more orthodox than commonly portrayed. It certainly moves the discussion forward.

—J. Dudley Woodberry
Dean Emeritus and Senior Professor of Islamic Studies
Fuller Theological Seminary

The research developed and presented in Henk Prenger's groundbreaking work is both unique and important. The uniqueness is not only found in the fact that he has interviewed both "alongsiders" as well as "insiders" but that he has investigated the theological convictions and presuppositions that underlie their praxis in mission. This, in turn, is also why his work is so important: his findings challenge a good deal of the presuppositions about so-called insider movements and their theological underpinnings. I hope many will read this crucial work, and I pray that these results may in part serve to reframe how discussion and debate concerning insider movements takes place in the future.

—Kevin Higgins
International Director, Global Teams International

We are greatly in debt to Henk Prenger both for what he studied and how he did it. His research topic is one many have wondered about: what actually is the missiology and theology of Muslims who follow Jesus? Through meticulously researching the views of 26 leaders of insider movements in seven parts of the world, he has gone a long way in helping us answer these questions. How he carried out this massive research project is also noteworthy. A long-term field person himself, Henk established trust with both alongsiders and insiders, assuring them that their stories would be told, but in ways that guarded anonymity and safety for them and the movements. Without such trusted relationships and safe protocols, research of this nature could put people in harm's way. This is truly a landmark study; no other field research on the convictions of insider movement leaders has gone to this level of depth, detail, and analysis.

—John J. Travis
Missiologist, Affiliate Faculty, Fuller Theological Seminary

It's helpful to hear how outsiders view contextualization within a Muslim insider movement. More helpful, however, is hearing the voices of those within the movement. Henk Prenger's grounded-theory study of Muslim insider movements does just that by giving voice to central figures within the movement.

—Tom Steffen
Professor Emeritus, Biola University

Prenger's careful and detailed thesis offers answers we have sought over the last few years. It chronicles the reply to key theological questions by new Christ followers among Muslim peoples. We may not like all the answers—we usually like things to be clearly and carefully delineated. You will likely be challenged by some of the material, but I hope you will also see newer believers who are in the process of "working out their salvation."

—Greg Parsons
Global Director, Frontier Ventures (formerly U.S. Center for World Mission)

Theologies of Islam are neither the preserve of theologians nor of professional missionaries or missiologists. Such theologies are helpful as signs of deeply inspired Christian concerns about making sense of Islam, but a genuine theology of Islam that promises to move beyond the traditional Islamic positions can only emerge from among the "insiders." Henk Prenger's work demonstrates that this is not merely wishful; Islam and Muslims are not static entities and Islamic dynamism is not necessarily oppositional. Insider movements furnish one with a solid evidence of a vibrantly natural re-conception of Islam from within; the insiders' radical experiences are already coalescing into emerging theologies that remain as yet truly uncontrived. This work underlines the sadly forgotten traditions of Christian thought which saw Muslims and Islam in genuinely relational terms. They saw Islam as a context for the operation of "the spirit of Jesus" and Muslims as kinsfolks worthy of love, hospitality, and sacrificial substitution.

—David Singh
Research Tutor in Islamic studies, Oxford Centre for Mission Studies

This book contributes an important voice to an ongoing controversy in Western mission communities with regard to the emergence of so-called insider movements. The theological and communal preferences of communities which describe themselves as Muslim but follow Christ have been hotly debated in a variety of venues during the past years. Full of extensive quotes gleaned from interviews with leaders of some of these groups, Prenger has given them voice in a way which will be of great interest to people engaged in these debates.
—KATHRYN KRAFT
Sociologist, author of *Searching for Heaven in the Real World*

# MUSLIM INSIDER CHRIST FOLLOWERS

THEIR THEOLOGICAL AND MISSIONAL FRAMES

**JAN HENDRIK PRENGER**

*Muslim Insider Christ Followers: Their Theological and Missional Frames*
Copyright ©2017 by Jan Hendrik Prenger
All rights reserved.

No part of this book may be reproduced, stored in a retrieval system, or transmitted in any form or by any means—electronic, mechanical, photocopy, recording, or otherwise—without prior written permission of the publisher, except brief quotations used in connection with reviews in magazines or newspapers.

Published by William Carey Library, an imprint of William Carey Publishing
10 W. Dry Creek Circle
Littleton, CO 80120 | www.missionbooks.org

Melissa Hughes, editor
Andrew Levin, copyeditor

William Carey Library is a ministry of Frontier Ventures
Pasadena, CA 91104 | www.frontierventures.org

23 22 21 20 19 Printed for Worldwide Distribution

---

Library of Congress Cataloging-in-Publication Data

Names: Prenger, Jan Hendrik, author.
Title: Muslim insider Christ followers : their theological and missional frames / Jan Hendrik Prenger.
Description: Pasadena, CA : William Carey Library, 2017. | Includes bibliographical references.
Identifiers: LCCN 2017003540 (print) | LCCN 2017005378 (ebook) | ISBN13: 9780878084982 (pbk.) | ISBN10: 0878084983 (pbk.) | ISBN 9780878086559 (eBook)
Subjects: LCSH: Insider movements. | Christianity and other religions--Islam. | Islam--Relations--Christianity.
Classification: LCC BP172 .P735 2017 (print) | LCC BP172 (ebook) | DDC 261.2/7--dc23
LC record available at https://lccn.loc.gov/2017003540

# CONTENTS

**INTRODUCTION** ............................................... xix

**CHAPTER ONE**
Introducing the Debate ........................................ 1

**CHAPTER TWO**
Literature Review ............................................. 9

**CHAPTER THREE**
Research Summary ........................................... 25

**CHAPTER FOUR**
Views on Allah and Isa al Masih ............................. 31

**CHAPTER FIVE**
Insider Movements and the Theologizing Process ........... 239

**CHAPTER SIX**
Conclusions and Recommendations ........................ 305

**REFERENCES** ................................................. 315

**APPENDIX A**
Interview Guide ............................................. 319

**APPENDIX B**
Summary M-Framework Plots by Context Variable .......... 323

**APPENDIX C**
Additional works consulted ................................. 329

**APPENDIX D**
Additional M-Framework figures ............................ 333

# LIST OF FIGURES

**FIGURE 1** Four elements in first two research sub-questions. . . . . . . . . . . . . 32

**FIGURE 2** Theology code map for what Allah is like . . . . . . . . . . . . . . . . . . . . . 37

**FIGURE 3** Creation code map for Allah's plans and purposes for this world and heaven . . . . . . . . . . . . . . . . . . . . . . . . . . . . . . . . . . . . . . . . . . 43

**FIGURE 4** The Qur'an versus the Bible . . . . . . . . . . . . . . . . . . . . . . . . . . . . . . . . 73

**FIGURE 5** The foundation of the four paradigms of the M-Framework . . . . 121

**FIGURE 6** M-Framework plot for Lucas. . . . . . . . . . . . . . . . . . . . . . . . . . . . . . . 128

**FIGURE 7** M-Framework plot for Zach . . . . . . . . . . . . . . . . . . . . . . . . . . . . . . . 130

**FIGURE 8** M-Framework plot for Ian . . . . . . . . . . . . . . . . . . . . . . . . . . . . . . . . . 132

**FIGURE 9** M-Framework plot for Phil. . . . . . . . . . . . . . . . . . . . . . . . . . . . . . . . . 133

**FIGURE 10** M-Framework plot for Monty . . . . . . . . . . . . . . . . . . . . . . . . . . . . . . 135

**FIGURE 11** M-Framework plot for Silas. . . . . . . . . . . . . . . . . . . . . . . . . . . . . . . . 136

**FIGURE 12** M-Framework plot for Kent. . . . . . . . . . . . . . . . . . . . . . . . . . . . . . . . 137

**FIGURE 13** M-Framework plot for Stuart . . . . . . . . . . . . . . . . . . . . . . . . . . . . . . 138

**FIGURE 14** M-Framework plot for Drew . . . . . . . . . . . . . . . . . . . . . . . . . . . . . . . 140

**FIGURE 15** M-Framework plot for Ross . . . . . . . . . . . . . . . . . . . . . . . . . . . . . . . 143

**FIGURE 16** M-Framework plot for Ray . . . . . . . . . . . . . . . . . . . . . . . . . . . . . . . . 145

**FIGURE 17** M-Framework plot for Josh . . . . . . . . . . . . . . . . . . . . . . . . . . . . . . . 149

**FIGURE 18** M-Framework plot for Tyler . . . . . . . . . . . . . . . . . . . . . . . . . . . . . . . 150

**FIGURE 19** M-Framework plot for Andy. . . . . . . . . . . . . . . . . . . . . . . . . . . . . . . 155

**FIGURE 20** M-Framework plot for Howard . . . . . . . . . . . . . . . . . . . . . . . . . . . . 158

**FIGURE 21** M-Framework plot for Kevin. .................................160

**FIGURE 22** M-Framework plot for Mitch ................................165

**FIGURE 23** M-Framework plot for Axel. .................................167

**FIGURE 24** M-Framework plot for Angus. ..............................169

**FIGURE 25** M-Framework plot for Frank. ...............................171

**FIGURE 26** M-Framework plot for Arthur. ..............................174

**FIGURE 27** M-Framework plot for Paxton ..............................181

**FIGURE 28** M-Framework plot for Wilbur. ..............................186

**FIGURE 29** M-Framework plot for Julius ...............................193

**FIGURE 30** M-Framework plot for Gus .................................195

**FIGURE 31** M-Framework plot for Jason ...............................197

**FIGURE 32** M-Framework plot for Arnold ..............................200

**FIGURE 33** M-Framework plot for Oliver ...............................204

**FIGURE 34** M-Framework plot for Homer ..............................209

**FIGURE 35** M-Framework plot for Brad .................................211

**FIGURE 36** M-Framework plot for Melvin. ..............................217

**FIGURE 37** The summary plot of Monty's theological and missional understanding. .................................................220

**FIGURE 38** The summary plots of the theological and missional understandings of 26 IM leaders and five alongsiders ...............220

**FIGURE 39** Showing regional plots for the frame Religions and 26 IM leader plots, indicating Religions as an outlier frame ..........223

**FIGURE 40** Showing regional plots for the frame The Qur'an and 26 IM leader plots, indicating The Qur'an as an outlier frame .........224

**FIGURE 41** Seven IM leaders who adhere to Christology paradigm 3 or 4. .................................................229

**FIGURE 42** M-Framework summary plots of IM leaders with Christian religious education. .................................................233

**FIGURE 43** M-Framework summary plots of IM leaders with Islamic religious education...............................................234

**FIGURE 44** The connection between the M-Framework and the main research question and sub-questions 1 and 2 ......................235

**FIGURE 45** The 26 IM leaders came from seven regions ................241

**FIGURE 46** The 26 IM leaders came from 15 groupings..................242

**FIGURE 47** Five alongsiders in seven regions..........................242

**FIGURE 48** Relationship between insider identity and movement secrecy levels, and influencing factors. ..............................266

**FIGURE 49** Three main aspects of IM as context for the processes that lead to the development of theological and missional frames ........277

**FIGURE 50** The main processes that lead to the development of theological and missional frames ...................................301

**FIGURE 51** IM leaders with Christian background ......................323

**FIGURE 52** IM leaders who never connected with a traditional church ....324

**FIGURE 53** IM leaders still connected with a traditional church ..........324

**FIGURE 54** IM leaders with Christian religious education.................324

**FIGURE 55** IM leaders with only Christian religious education ...........325

**FIGURE 56** IM leaders with Islamic religious education ..................325

**FIGURE 57** IM leaders with both Christian and Islamic religious education...............................................325

**FIGURE 58** IM leaders without formal religious education................326

**FIGURE 59** IM leaders in a movement < 100............................326

**FIGURE 60** IM leaders in movement between 100 and 1,000 ............326

**FIGURE 61** IM leaders in movement > 1,000............................327

# LIST OF TABLES

**TABLE 1** 26 IM Leaders and five alongsiders . . . . . . . . . . . . . . . . . . . . . . . . . . . . 27

**TABLE 2** Number of codes in code sets . . . . . . . . . . . . . . . . . . . . . . . . . . . . . . . . 29

**TABLE 3** Four interview guide sections and code clusters . . . . . . . . . . . . . . . 32

**TABLE 4** 12 Segments coded with "compassionate and gracious" . . . . . . . . 34

**TABLE 5** Lexical search for "merciful" . . . . . . . . . . . . . . . . . . . . . . . . . . . . . . . . 35

**TABLE 6** Lexical search for "the Fall" . . . . . . . . . . . . . . . . . . . . . . . . . . . . . . . . . 39

**TABLE 7** Unfamiliar with the concept of salvation of the world . . . . . . . . . . . 41

**TABLE 8** Is Allah interested in just and healthy societies? . . . . . . . . . . . . . . . . 43

**TABLE 9** Restored relationship between man and God . . . . . . . . . . . . . . . . . . 44

**TABLE 10** Heaven bound . . . . . . . . . . . . . . . . . . . . . . . . . . . . . . . . . . . . . . . . . . . . 46

**TABLE 11** Two paths . . . . . . . . . . . . . . . . . . . . . . . . . . . . . . . . . . . . . . . . . . . . . . . 47

**TABLE 12** Love others . . . . . . . . . . . . . . . . . . . . . . . . . . . . . . . . . . . . . . . . . . . . . . 49

**TABLE 13** Faith in action . . . . . . . . . . . . . . . . . . . . . . . . . . . . . . . . . . . . . . . . . . . . 51

**TABLE 14** Hell forever . . . . . . . . . . . . . . . . . . . . . . . . . . . . . . . . . . . . . . . . . . . . . . 55

**TABLE 15** Most people to hell . . . . . . . . . . . . . . . . . . . . . . . . . . . . . . . . . . . . . . . 59

**TABLE 16** Connection between this world and heaven . . . . . . . . . . . . . . . . . . 60

**TABLE 17** Heaven now and later . . . . . . . . . . . . . . . . . . . . . . . . . . . . . . . . . . . . . 61

**TABLE 18** Mohammed . . . . . . . . . . . . . . . . . . . . . . . . . . . . . . . . . . . . . . . . . . . . . 65

**TABLE 19** The Scriptures as a guide . . . . . . . . . . . . . . . . . . . . . . . . . . . . . . . . . . 71

**TABLE 20** Qur'an compatible with Bible . . . . . . . . . . . . . . . . . . . . . . . . . . . . . . . 74

**TABLE 21** Follow Isa, not religion . . . . . . . . . . . . . . . . . . . . . . . . . . . . . . . . . . . . 79

| | | |
|---|---|---|
| **TABLE 22** | Ross on static nature of Islam | 82 |
| **TABLE 23** | Jesus did not start Christianity | 84 |
| **TABLE 24** | High Christology | 86 |
| **TABLE 25** | Isa as the Word of God | 89 |
| **TABLE 26** | Low Christology | 92 |
| **TABLE 27** | The meaning of "al Masih" | 93 |
| **TABLE 28** | Son of God as metaphor | 94 |
| **TABLE 29** | Isa's actions: God's love in action liberating people | 99 |
| **TABLE 30** | Isa's actions: our model for faith in action | 101 |
| **TABLE 31** | Isa's actions: God's power and authority | 102 |
| **TABLE 32** | Our sins and the cross | 105 |
| **TABLE 33** | Allah's plans, Isa's submission, and the cross | 107 |
| **TABLE 34** | The cross as God's love sacrifice | 113 |
| **TABLE 35** | Good news–Satan is defeated | 115 |
| **TABLE 36** | M-Framework for Allah–Theology | 122 |
| **TABLE 37** | M-Framework for Allah–Missio Dei | 123 |
| **TABLE 38** | M-Framework for Isa al Masih–Christology | 126 |
| **TABLE 39** | M-Framework for Isa al Masih–Missio Christi | 126 |
| **TABLE 40** | Identity and Christology frames | 225 |
| **TABLE 41** | IM Leaders' background and connection to traditional church | 230 |
| **TABLE 42** | IM Leaders' religious education and movement size | 231 |
| **TABLE 43** | Number of codes for "Movement" and "Theologizing" | 241 |
| **TABLE 44** | Why insider movements? | 245 |
| **TABLE 45** | Individual religions paradigms | 274 |
| **TABLE 46** | Progressive Christology | 278 |
| **TABLE 47** | Bible-centered | 284 |

**TABLE 48**  Different viewpoints are acceptable..........................290
**TABLE 49**  Unity on basic beliefs.......................................293
**TABLE 50**  What is Allah like?..........................................309

# INTRODUCTION

The purpose of this book is to give voice to the voiceless—namely, the Muslim insider Christ followers who are leaders of insider movements (IM).[1] The debate on insider movements, which sometimes are also referred to as Jesus movements, has a theological overtone and applies directly to missiology. The discussion mostly takes place between Western theologians and missiologists, without participation from the real stakeholders, the Muslim insider Christ followers themselves. I decided to research the theological and missional views of these insiders, as part of my doctor of missiology studies at Biola University. The pages that follow are by and large my dissertation without the full research design chapter and appendices. I also moved and summarized some content as footnotes. The full version of my dissertation can be found in ProQuest.

I interviewed 26 insider movement leaders and asked them to share their views on what we could call theology-proper topics such as God, man, the cross, Jesus, election, salvation, heaven, hell, the gospel, and our mandate. By publishing my research in this format I hope that the voices of Muslim insider Christ followers will become part of the debate we are having about them.

As with every dissertation, chapter 1 is the introduction of the problem, and chapter 2 is a literature review on the topic at hand. Chapter 3 presents a summary of the research design.

Chapter 4 is the core of the book, as it addresses the research question: what are the theological and missional frames (views/understandings) of IM leaders? I recommend looking at the interview guide first, which you

---

1. There are many insider movements, not just one, but the topic or phenomenon of insider movements is singular. The acronym "IM" in this book refers to a singular movement, to insider movements (plural), or to the general topic of insider movements.

find in appendix A, in order to appreciate the flow of information. The first part of chapter 4 is a long review of each theological and missional topic/code. I am directly quoting the IM leaders extensively on each topic, introducing the reader to the voices of the Muslim insider Christ followers, the emic data.

I introduce the M-Framework in the second part of chapter 4 and analyze sections of each interview that speak to the theological and missional understandings of the interviewees. The M stands for mission, *missio Dei*, or *missio hominis*. The M-Framework defines four theological paradigms for Christianity by listing the range of views on 21 theological topics across these four paradigms. I found the M-Framework a very useful tool to plot someone's theological and missional views. It can be used in any setting.

Chapter 5 presents my analysis of more general information about insider movements, based on comments made by the interviewees. This general setting is of interest, because it is the context in which the theological and missional views of insider movement leaders develop. You find my overall research conclusions and recommendations for further inquiry in chapter 6.

This book presents the findings of qualitative research on the views of others—namely, 26 insider movement leaders—and as such, my personal opinions are not in focus or relevant. This has been challenging, since everyone has opinions on theological and missional matters. The interviews were not debates but listening sessions for me. I found myself disagreeing with the views expressed many times, but my opinions were not the research topic. Even though I conducted my research in an objective way, it may help the reader to understand my circumstances and general views.

I was a member of Wycliffe Bible Translators, USA, and one of the SIL International directors who was named in an online petition in early 2011 against our organizational best practices for the translation of *Son of God* when it refers to Jesus, and of *Father* when it refers to God, in the various Bible translation projects that SIL served in Muslim contexts. Being the director over a region where these projects occurred, I was deeply involved in explaining and promoting SIL's policies, and in the ensuing debate, which also is known as the Divine Familial Terms (DFT) controversy. I observed that the critics of SIL's practices by and large used theological argumentation over points of concern related to linguistic or translation principles. I also noted that those who oppose dynamic translations of *Son of God*, which was SIL's policy at the time, saw the DFT translation and insider movements as very closely related, if not the same. The critics of both SIL's past best practices for translating DFTs in a Muslim context and of insider movements in that same context mostly seem to be evangelical conservatives or fundamentalists.[2] For example, a high view of the Scriptures means for some that literal word-for-word translations are better than dynamic ones. High Calvinism may lead to a view on election that leaves little room for the need to contextualize, as does a high view of the Holy Spirit choosing to fill some but not others. Furthermore, a strong felt need to differentiate the religion of Christianity from Islam can lead to intentionally defining clear, impenetrable doctrinal boundaries, one being that the phrase *Son of God* is a reference to the Second Person of the Trinity, and to the archetypal ontological sonship of Jesus to the Father. Such a view, combined with the conviction that the good news (gospel) is fully and solely defined as our adoption as sons and daughters, makes a dynamic translation or a nuanced view of the word *son* unacceptable. These are just a few examples of theological argumentations by fundamentalists against dynamic DFT translations and IM, which are two separate and unique topics that tend to draw criticism from the same groups. These critics see insiders as dangerously liberal or as heretics. I disagree with the critics of IM fundamentally, on a theological basis. We have the liberty to disagree in the West, and that itself is not an issue. However, I was fascinated by the observation that certain theological views automatically lead to either a support of, or an opposition to, insider movements. With that, I became very interested and motivated to research what the actual theological views of the insiders themselves are. These views have been missing data points in the IM debate.

Back to the DFT debate and to Wycliffe and SIL: The issue was "resolved" by an arbiter, a panel of scholars chartered by the World Evangelical Alliance. They set boundaries for theologically acceptable translation methodology in Muslim contexts, and particularly for DFTs.

---

2. Fundamentalists adhere to a set of fundamentals as developed in the early twentieth century. The M-Framework defines the theological views on 21 topics for four paradigms. I named the first paradigm "Fundamental." See this framework for my expanded definition of the views of fundamentalists.

Their report came out in May 2013. The panel critiqued SIL's dynamic translation practices for DFTs and mandated the most direct (literal) translation for the DFT word *son*, to carry the meaning "son by nature." Wycliffe and SIL accepted the panel's report, which ended the funding crisis caused by the online petition. I stepped down from leadership out of principle, and I have since resigned from Wycliffe and SIL. I still highly respect my colleagues in SIL who are carrying on with a new and more restrictive set of DFT translation standards and policies.

The M-Framework has four theological paradigms. Fundamentalists and today's conservative evangelicals fit in paradigm 1. My personal views aligned with paradigm 1 many years ago, as I was maturing in the faith, attended seminary, and moved into mission work. Over the last 10 years, however, my views have moved to paradigm 4. I understand and can appreciate each of the four paradigms, since I have been part of each one. This personal theological experience and journey helped me in the analysis of the interview transcripts. As the IM leaders were sharing certain words, phrases, and concepts, I was able to associate those alternately with paradigm 1, 2, 3, or 4.

One of the research findings is that most of the 26 interviewed IM leaders hold paradigm 1 and 2 views. As such, they have the same theological convictions as their critics. Some have asked me whether I am disappointed in not finding more IM leaders who are theologically aligned with my own views of paradigm 4. I am not, for several reasons. Basically, I found a range of views, including those belonging in paradigms 3 and 4, among IM leaders, as well as among the five Western IM-supporting alongsiders. We see this kind of range in the West, where people have the freedom to explore, innovate, and progress theologically. It is encouraging to me that I also found this range in insider movements, which in some sense are theological incubators, protected from an influx of Western neatly packaged theological answers. There is of course an exposure to Islamic concepts, such as a heavy emphasis on heaven and hell, which may explain the leaning towards paradigms 1 and 2, but in general, the context of these movements allows for fresh, innovative, and insightful theologizing based solely on the Scriptures and on their own faith journey. I think that this will lead to a shift towards paradigms 3 and 4, and beyond, over time. This healthy shift is happening in the West, where there is far more freedom of belief, and can also happen in insider movements. In a way, the debate on the four paradigms is more important to the church, or the body of Christ, and to the kingdom of God than discussions on a specific application of that kingdom in insider movements. I would label paradigm 4 not as dangerously liberal but as sincerely orthodox. An open and honest conversation about the paradigms can result in a dramatic reforming of our view of what God is like, and of the gospel, which in turn can result in transformative orthopraxy that truly marshals in the kingdom of God on earth. The IM debate brings out our theological differences, but in a sense it is only the catalyst for a bigger, very exciting emerging debate on our foundational doctrines as represented in the M-Framework.

In the meantime, it is my hope and prayer that insider movements continue, and that the rest of the global body of Jesus followers increasingly stand in awe of what God is doing in them. May we encourage and wisely support these movements, and may we all eagerly learn from the sacrificial faith and theological insights of Muslim insider Christ followers, as presented in this book.

# CHAPTER ONE
## INTRODUCING THE DEBATE

He introduced himself as Abdullah. "I am a Muslim follower of Jesus," he said. "I am a completed Muslim." I spent a whole evening with Abdullah and one of his friends. A colleague of mine, who works with them on a regular basis, introduced them to me. Abdullah's testimony of how he had come to faith in Jesus Christ was amazing, and the testimony of his friend was even more remarkable. They were humble and polite men, but they were on fire for the Lord. Abdullah and his friend are believers in Christ who have decided to remain in their socioreligious community, and who retain their identity as members of that community, which makes them by definition Muslim insiders, according to Rebecca Lewis (2007). They are cultural and socioreligious insiders of their community of birth.

John Travis (pen name) developed the now well-known C1–C6 Spectrum in 1998 in which the *C* stands for "Christ-centered communities." With the exception of C6, which refers to a secret/underground community of believers, the higher the number on the C-scale, the more aspects of the language, culture, and socioreligious elements of the local Muslim population (the people on the inside) are an integral part of this Christ-centered community (Travis, 1998). In principle, every person who is part of a local community is an insider of that community.

I will refer to Muslim insiders as followers of Jesus who remain inside their socioreligious Muslim community (C5). Insider movements (IM) can be briefly defined as movements to obedient faith in Christ that remain integrated with or *inside* their natural community (Lewis, 2009). The definition section below provides a more detailed definition of IM.

The hotly debated topic of IM in Muslim contexts seems to lie at the center of the contextualization debate, which is related to the concept of *missio Dei* and the theology of religions. Well-known leaders such as John Piper speak out against insider strategies (Piper & Taylor, 2007), while the Lausanne Theology Working Group recently recognized God's church in many different cultures and forms, "including those that are strange and even disturbing to us." This working group confesses that we often fail to recognize the whole church, and it specifically identifies insider movements as part of God's church "whose contribution may be undervalued, diminished, overlooked, or even prevented." Referring to insiders, the group says, "This phenomenon of following Jesus within diverse religio-cultural traditions needs careful biblical, theological and missiological evaluation" (Lausanne Theological Working Group, 2010).

A topic related to IM is the current debate on how to best translate so-called Divine Familial Terms (DFT) such as *Son of God* when it refers to Jesus and *Father* when it refers to God, in Bible translation projects in Muslim contexts. Wycliffe Bible Translators and SIL International use the meaning-based or functional equivalent approach to translation rather than a literal or formal equivalent one, based on their core value of accurate, natural, and communicative translations. This practice led in some cases to translating DFTs in other than the literal or commonly used words for *son* and *father* in certain languages of majority-Muslim communities, to correct misconceptions and avoid inaccuracy. They would use words and phrases that show respect and honor and that could be used in family circles, but that would not exclusively communicate a biological or siring relationship, in order to not perpetuate a misconception among many Muslims: that Christians believe that Allah had sex with Mary to have a son, Jesus.

This translation practice has been discussed with increasing intensity in journals and at conferences. The Presbyterian Church in America (PCA) and the Assemblies of God (AoG) denominations in the US gave clear indications to Wycliffe and SIL in 2011 of plans to separate from them, based on DFT misalignment. I review some of their documents in the literature review. In 2012 Wycliffe and SIL International called for a global consultation and asked the World Evangelical Alliance (WEA) to establish a panel to independently review their translations of *God the Father* and *Son of God*. WEA agreed in March 2012 and established a panel of twelve members in September 2012, under the leadership of Dr. Robert E. Cooley.[1] This panel submitted its findings and report by

---

1. WEA to Form Independent Review Panel on Wycliffe and SIL Bible Translation. (2012, March 12). Retrieved from http://www.worldea.org/news/3934

April 2013 to SIL and Wycliffe, who had pledged beforehand to abide by the panel's recommendations, which had ended their funding crisis with AoG and PCA. The WEA panel report calls for translators to always use the most direct (i.e., common, literal) word for *son* and *father* in the target language that communicates "by nature." Wycliffe and SIL have changed their practices accordingly.

In late 2011, i2 Ministries published a book entitled *Chrislam: How Missionaries Are Promoting an Islamized Gospel*, edited by Joshua Lingel, Jeff Morton, and Bill Nikides. According to the i2 Ministries website,[2] this organization engages in ongoing studies of Islam and the arguments Islamic apologists use in continuing to propagate Islam worldwide. They seek to develop tools that Christians in Islamic societies can use in their evangelism efforts to counter the arguments of Islamic apologists and bring the truth of the Bible and of Jesus to Muslims in each nation. They oppose IM: i2's founder and president makes the following statement on the Biblical Missiology website: "The Insider Movements (IM) methodology needs to be discussed and assessed until IM is no longer an Evangelical option for Christian missions to Muslims" (Lingel, 2010).

Journals and magazines such as *Mission Frontiers* (MF), *Evangelical Missions Quarterly* (EMQ), the *International Journal of Frontier Missiology* (IJFM), the *St. Francis Magazine*, *International Bulletin of Mission Research* (IBMR), *Missiology: An International Review*, the Evangelical Missiological Society's *Occasional Bulletin*, and *Christianity Today* frequently feature articles on IM, both in support of and critical of these movements.

For example, the February 2011 issue of *Christianity Today* was largely devoted to IM and the idiom *Son of God* for Muslims. Collin Hansen mentions the success among Muslims of Bible translations that avoid the phrase *Son of God* but also identifies the concerns from some missionaries and scholars (Hansen, 2011). The *St. Francis Magazine* issues from August 2009 and December 2009 have multiple articles on IM, and in their April 2012 issue Bradford Greer (pen name) writes about the DFT controversy (Greer, 2012). *IJFM* devoted the July–September 2011 issue to this topic as well. I review a sample of the main articles in the literature review.

The four cover stories in the January/February 2013 issue of *Christianity Today* are on IM. The title of the main article is "Worshipping Jesus in

---

2. www.i2ministries.org

the Mosque," by Gene Daniels (pen name), in which he interviews a Muslim follower of Isa (Daniels, 2013, pp. 23–27). Timothy Tennent reviews the hidden history of IM in the second cover story. He thinks that the current debate about C5 believers centers on five key issues: the biblical precedent of Acts 15; the relationship between personal salvation and identification with the larger church and historical Christian doctrines; the ethical question about encouraging insiders to retain a Muslim identity; IM as a new phenomenon or something coming from issues in the Protestant Reformation; and C5 being a permanent movement or transitional bridge (Tennent, 2013, pp. 28–29). John Travis wrote the third cover story, titled "Jesus Saves, Religion Doesn't," in which he shares his own experience in witnessing the start of an IM (Travis, 2013, p. 30). Phil Parshall authored the fourth cover story on IM, supporting C4 insiders but questioning C5 movements (Parshall, 2013).

Bradford Greer wrote a review in the Winter 2011 issue of *IJFM* on a book by Doug Coleman (pen name) titled *A Theological Analysis of the Insider Movement Paradigm from Four Perspectives: Theology of Religions, Revelation, Soteriology and Ecclesiology* (Coleman, 2011). Greer writes, "The title led me to assume that Doug Coleman was going to provide a theological analysis of insider movements. Many missiologists are eagerly awaiting studies of this nature" (Greer, 2011, p. 204). He goes on noting that Coleman did not do field research but only analyzed articles written primarily by Western authors (mostly articles by Kevin Higgins) who have written in favor of insider movements. I distinguish my study from Coleman's in that this study includes field research and has a focus on theology and missiology from an insider's perspective. According to Greer, missiologists are eagerly awaiting this study.

I trace the theological and missional frames, or paradigms, in the literature review in chapter 2 by identifying which frames and underlying assumptions typically lead to support of IM or to an opposing stance towards these movements. The literature review helped me design the research and formulate the initial and basic research questions. This study is a response to the call from Lausanne for further evaluation of IM. I researched the theological and missional frames of Muslim IM leaders, and the IM communal theologizing processes, and as such demonstrate their kind of Christ following.

## PROBLEM STATEMENT

The church today is debating the validity of IM, often without knowing the theological and/or missional frames of IM leaders and their communal theologizing processes. Are Muslim insiders part of the body of Christ or a sect of Islam? Is IM a prescription of an approach or a description of what God is doing? How do leaders of IM and supporting practitioners know which theologizing processes are biblical? What are the theological and missional frames of IM leaders? The church often lacks theological and/or missional insights gained from solid research among insiders to conduct constructive dialogue on IM, and to apply biblical theologizing processes within IM. The voices of IM leaders should be heard, but they are lacking.

## PURPOSE STATEMENT

The purpose of this grounded-theory study is to understand and explain the theological and missional frames of IM leaders (i.e., their view of God and his mission). The outcome of this study will lead to deeper insights and enrich the church's understanding of IM, making possible more informed and constructive dialogue on IM.

## RESEARCH QUESTIONS

The central research question is, What are the theological and missional frames of IM leaders?

The sub-questions include:
1. How do Muslim insider leaders understand Allah and his plans and purposes?
2. How do Muslim insider leaders understand Isa al Masih and his role and identity?
3. How do Muslim insiders study the Tawrat, Zabur, and Injil and apply insights gained within IM?
4. How do IM leaders develop theological and missional frames within their communal context?

## DEFINITIONS

*Theological frame* The foundational understanding of God's being or essence, which includes a perception of his main characteristics and typical behavior.

*Missional frame* The foundational understanding of God's mission and purposes, which includes a perception of his main actions in history, today and in the future, as part of his overall intentions and ultimate goals.

*Divine Familial Terms (DFT)* Terms that express divine familial relationships, as in God the *Father* and in Jesus the *Son of God*.

*Insider movement* Any movement to faith in Christ where (a) the gospel flows through pre-existing communities and social networks, and where (b) believing families, as valid expressions of the body of Christ, remain inside their socioreligious communities, retaining their identity as members of that community while living under the lordship of Jesus Christ and the authority of the Bible. (Lewis, 2007)

## DELIMITATIONS

The main delimitation of the field research is its focus on a finite set of Muslim insiders. In addition, the focus is on an insider's understanding of God and his mission (theology proper), and the study describes these insider understandings in church terminology. Also, the study does not delve into church-planting strategies among Muslims and related language development activities. The study will not delve into linguistic or detailed exegetical issues related to Bible translation. The geographical area of focus is limited to parts of Asia and Africa.

## LIMITATIONS

The potential weakness of this research lies in collecting data from a limited number of IM leaders. Participants selected for this study cannot be considered a representative sample of the whole population of insiders or even IM leaders. I followed leads to connect with 26 IM leaders from various contexts and with a range of maturity. This sample presents a limited view of the theological and missional frames of IM leaders. However, purposefully selecting insiders from different regions helped mitigate the potential shortcoming of not being able to take a representative sample of the whole.

Another limitation is my translation of insider expressions and viewpoints into commonly understood church idiom, making these views accessible to the wider church but limiting the induction of new idiom and emphases within the domain of theology proper.

## SIGNIFICANCE

This study directly applies to the ongoing heated debate within the church about IM. It is a response to the call from Lausanne III for more research in this area. The significance of this study lies in its uniqueness and breadth. This is one of the first efforts to identify and articulate the theological and missional views of insiders, moving beyond studies of their identities, social challenges, and religious practices. The breadth comes from doing research at the theological and missional level, bringing in a variety of viewpoints within Christianity throughout history and in today's church in a globalizing world with pluralistic societies. Theologians, missiologists, and the body of Christ as a whole will gain needed insights into the many questions surrounding IM.

Evangelists, pastors, church planters, and Bible translators in Muslim contexts will use the additional knowledge gained by this study in their daily ministries and long-term strategies. The academic community at large will gain by seeing how grounded-theory field research can inform hotly debated topics such as IM. On the global scene this research will help inform discussions on contextualization and enculturation, which can lead to more unity, with diversity, within the church, as new and emerging theological and missional frames mature and transform Christianity.

# CHAPTER TWO
## LITERATURE REVIEW

In this chapter I review a sample of some of the main documents and publications that represent the current heated debate on IM.

It is interesting to note that Kenneth Cragg, an Anglican bishop with six decades of writing on Muslim-Christian issues, and seen by some as the dean of Christian Islamicists, supported sincere dialogue between Christians and Muslims, but he did not speak out specifically on the IM topic.

On the other hand, Phil Parshall entered the IM debate quite early. Parshall worked as a missionary in Bangladesh and the Philippines for over three decades, authored many books, and has published various articles in *EMQ*, *Missiology*, and other journals. Parshall pioneered contextualized approaches but critiqued IM for the first time in his article titled "Danger! New Directions in Contextualization," in October 1998. He contends that a new believer in Christ has a transitional period in which he would stay "on the inside" and still attend a mosque on occasion, but he places John Travis' C5 Muslim completely in the syncretism category.

> But now I am the one to protest the "slide," not by our team, but by others who are ministering in various parts of the Muslim world. This slide is incremental and can be insidiously deceptive, especially when led by people of highest motivation. Now, it seems to me, we need to bring these issues before our theologians, missiologists, and administrators. Let us critique them before we suddenly find that we have arrived at a point which is indisputably sub-Christian. (Parshall, 1998, p. 1)

This study critiques and researches IM, as Parshall suggests. Is IM indeed indisputably sub-Christian, or sub-biblical, theologically and missional, as Parshall claims?

Paul Gordon-Chandler wrote *Pilgrims of Christ on the Muslim Road*, in which he describes the life and experiences of insider Mazhar Mallouhi, a Syrian from Muslim background, who calls himself a "Muslim follower of Christ." Mallouhi's views of Islam and Christianity are unorthodox for most evangelicals. He suggests that Islam could be viewed as originally an Arab contextualization of the monotheism of the Jews and the Christians (Chandler, 2007, p. 103). Being a Muslim is the normal, cultural identity of every Arab. To these Arabs, an Arab Christian is someone who is deculturated and who has shamed his or her family and community.

Mallouhi sees Islam as his heritage and Christ as his inheritance. He actually tried leaving his Muslim identity and taking on a Christian one, but when he did so he felt he had completely lost his identity. So he decided to go back to his roots. He did not go back as an insider in order to be more effective in sharing Christ with his fellow Muslim brothers and sisters. "For him it is not a means to an end, but rather a coming to rest in his true identity, discovering who he really is, a finding of his way home" (p. 107). Is IM mostly a strategy for success and expansion or the natural home for insiders?

I mentioned the various journals that frequently publish articles on IM in chapter 1. Frontier Ventures, formerly the U.S. Center for World Mission (USCWM), continues to support IM through their bimonthly magazine, *Mission Frontiers*. The September/October 2005 edition is entitled "Can We Trust Insider Movements?" and has supporting articles by Frank Decker, Charles Kraft, John and Anna Travis (C1–C6 Spectrum), and Donald McGavran. In their January/February 2006 issue John Piper and Gary Corwin expressed their disappointment about the articles in the September/October 2005 edition. Gary Corwin is associate editor of *EMQ* and missiologist-at-large for Arab World Ministries. In the July/August 2008 edition of *MF*, which is called "Rethinking Our Approach to Muslim Peoples," Don Allen, Paul-Gordon Chandler, and Rick Brown wrote articles in favor of contextualization and IM. In the March/April 2010 issue, with the interesting title, "Loving Bin Laden: What Does Jesus Expect Us to Do?," Rick Wood, Carl Medearis, Darrell Dorr, Ted Dekker, and others present ways to truly love Muslims without fearing Islam. *MF* devoted the May/June 2011 issue to IM under the title "Jesus Movements." In an article in this issue Rebecca Lewis (2011) pleads for discernment as she writes:

> It is our turn to be shocked, like Peter, that God would bestow His Spirit on those outside of our acceptable religion. It was inconceivable to him that pagan households, like Cornelius', could receive God's Holy Spirit (even while uncircumcised and as yet unbaptized!). Likewise, we cannot fathom that God would have "no favorites" today and bestow His Spirit on Muslims, Buddhists, Hindus and, in fact, all who through meeting a living Jesus "fear Him and do what is right." But His Kingdom is breaking out of the boxes we try to keep it in, again, and He seems to be inviting the least-expected people to His banquet, without our permission. (p. 15)

Are Muslim insiders outside our kingdom box, or are they a sect of Islam?

*IJFM*, also an arm of Frontier Ventures, publishes articles in support of IM on a regular basis. Several of the same authors who write articles for *MF* also publish in *IJFM*.

The *St. Francis Magazine* is mainly a forum for those critical of IM, although authors such as Kevin Higgins publish articles in favor of these contextualized approaches among Muslims, which he did in their August 2009 edition (Higgins, 2009). Bill Nikides critiqued Higgins in the same edition (Nikides, 2009).

Insiders prefer translations of the Scriptures that render the true meaning of the text in a way that is understandable and clear to a Muslim and in which DFT renderings are terms that they perceive as honorable expressions. Lamin Sanneh sees the translatability of the Word of God in the vernacular (local language) as the biggest strength of Christianity. He speaks of indigenous discovery of Christianity rather than the Christian discovery of indigenous societies. He gives priority to indigenous response and local appropriation over against missionary transmission and direction (Sanneh, 2003, p. 10).

For example, Sanneh advocates that translators pick a local name for God, as they "pioneer a strategic alliance with local conceptions of religion" (p. 11). Sanneh calls this "indigenous theological domestication" similar to the Hellenization of theology in the early church (p. 11). He shows that in Africa the spread of Christianity went hand-in-hand with the national awakening after colonialism. With vernacular translation came cultural renewal. He especially notes that this expansion only really happened where people had preserved the indigenous name for God. He also observes that Africans responded to Christianity positively where indigenous religions were the strongest, *suggesting a degree of indigenous compatibility with the gospel.* Is IM an example of the "indigenous theological domestication" that Sanneh discusses?

Interestingly, Sanneh observes the opposite response to Islam. Muslim expansion was strongest where indigenous religions were subjugated and where people hardly remembered their name for God. Sanneh notes that the colonizing of African countries often weakened indigenous religions and introduced secularism. As such, the secularizing effect of colonialism by European Christian nations actually helped advance the Muslim cause in Africa (pp. 18, 19).

The term *God* comes with a concept that contains ideas of personhood, economic life, and social/cultural identity. Sanneh sees African religions as conveyers of the names of God as *relevant anticipations of Christianity*. Indigenizing the translations helped Africans to become renewed Africans, not remade Europeans (p. 43). Sanneh defines syncretism as the unresolved, unassimilated mixing of Christian ideas with local customs and ritual that scarcely results in fulfilling conversion and church membership. He sees it everywhere and finds it an unhelpful topic for criticism of others. He suggests that unless we refer to syncretism in our own Western Christianity, we had better just drop the term (p. 44).

Rick Brown, a close SIL colleague, has a similar view of syncretism, attributing it to under-contextualizing. The notion is that you can never indigenize (Sanneh) or contextualize (Brown, 2006) too much. Brown also is known for his articles in journals such as *IJFM* and *MF* about Bible translation for Muslim audiences. His 2005 article on the term *Son of God* is widely shared but also widely critiqued. Brown explains how the term *Son of God* often is the biggest obstacle for Muslims to reading the Gospels. For Muslims the term only has one meaning— namely, God's offspring by sexual union (Brown, 2005).

Brown published an article in *EMQ* in 2007 in which he explores four ways in which translations circumvent this taboo. First, a translation could use expressions that are as near as possible to the original meaning, such as "God's beloved people," "God's Beloved Christ," "God's Beloved," or "God's Eternal Word." Second, he notes that some translations may retain the sonship image in the text but change the metaphor into a simile to avoid using the taboo term, such as "the Christ whom God loves as a Father loves his Son." Third, some translations retain the sonship image but use a wording that is not a simile but differs enough in other ways from the taboo term that it is not regarded as a blasphemy. Examples include "spiritual son(s) of God," "the Spiritual Son of God," "the Son from God," "the Prince of God," and "the Beloved Son who comes from God." And lastly, Brown notes that a few translations have used the original Hebrew phrase, *ben elohim* ("son of God"), either in one or two passages or as the normal translation of the term (Brown, 2007).

In the July–September 2011 issue of *IJFM*, which is dedicated to IM, Rick Brown and Leith and Andrea Gray expand and partially correct Brown's earlier view from 2005 and 2007. "A New Look at Translating Familial Biblical Terms" makes a distinction between social and biological kinship terms in languages and says that strictly biological DFT renderings in Bible translations "are inaccurate because they add a procreative meaning that was absent from the original" (Brown et al., 2011, p. 108). Defending the use of nonliteral renderings for DFT in translations based on the goal to produce accurate, natural, clear, and communicative translations, they write:

> This highlights the fact that translators are not trying to remove original meanings from the translation that might offend the audience. On the contrary, their concern is to avoid incorrect meanings that fail to communicate the informational content, feelings, and attitudes of the original inspired text. (Brown et al., 2011, p. 109)

Brown et al. recommend the third approach as mentioned above to express the divine familial sonship of Jesus, and the second and third approaches to express the sonship of believers. They present the multiple and complex meanings of DFT in the biblical text and in dogma, and comment on the distinction between the immanent/ontological and economic Trinity. They observe, "No term in a target language can encode all of these components of meaning. . . . most will need to be explained in the paratext." Brown et al. support expressing the familial components of the meaning in the text instead of in the paratext. Regarding the translation of *Son of God*, they write:

> We now believe it is ideal that terms like "Christ/Messiah" should be used only to translate *Christos/Meshiach* and should not be used to translate huios/ben. We would discourage anyone from doing this. (Brown et al., 2011, p. 116)

In June 2011 the General Assembly of the PCA published "A Call to Faithful Witness,"[3] which contains a motion that established a study group on the topic of IM, and includes the following statement:

> The Assembly declares as unfaithful to God's revealed Word, Insider Movement or any other translations of the Bible that remove from the text references to God as "Father" (pater) or Jesus as "Son" (huios), because such removals compromise doctrines of the Trinity, the person and work of Jesus Christ, and Scripture.

In order to respond more comprehensively to critics, SIL convened a conference on the DFT topic in August 2011 in Istanbul, where theologians, biblical scholars, translation consultants, and missiologists came together and defined SIL's "best practices." The full so-called "Istanbul statement" and commentary are available on the SIL public website at http://www.sil.org/translation/divine_familial_terms_commentary_full.pdf (SIL International, 2012). The multi-page document touches on the various dynamics of a translation project. On the actual translation of DFT, it describes in item 1.5 a guided process to work through the rendering options using the following steps:

1. Consider the literal rendering for the text and add necessary paratext, then test (text + paratext) in the local community, and evaluate the strength and weaknesses.
2. Consider clearly familial, but non-literal options for the text (e.g. "God's one-and-only" [son implied]) and find several options. For each of these add the necessary paratext, test with community, and evaluate the strengths and weaknesses.

---

3. http://biblicalmissiology.org/wp-content/uploads/2012/01/Faithful-Witness-PCA-2011.pdf

3. Review all options from steps 1 & 2 and then choose the one which is most effective in communicating meaning, is most economical, and respects the preference of the intended audience of the translation product.
4. If no possible option has been identified through this process, non-literal options for the text may be considered which conserve as much of the familial meaning as possible, provided that the paratext includes the literal form.

> From the commentary with 1.5: "One of the main outcomes from Istanbul is that there was agreement that neither Messiah nor Word of God adequately convey the necessary relational components of meaning" (SIL International, 2012).

On January 6, 2012, Biblical Missiology posted an online petition against Wycliffe, SIL, and Frontiers, all involved in Bible translation in Muslim contexts. Biblical Missiology is a network of individuals representing dozens of organizations who discuss, according to their website (http://biblicalmissiology.org), "the application of biblical missiology" under a leadership team that includes Georges Houssney, Scott Seaton, Adam Simnowitz, Bill Nikides, Elijah Abraham, Jeff Morton, and Joshua Lingel. The petition is posted at http://www.change.org/petitions/lost-in-translation-keep-father-son-in-the-bible and is titled *Lost in Translation: Keep "Father" & "Son" in the Bible*. It was very successful in that many people, especially in the US, responded and were upset about these alleged false translations.

The PCA Committee on IM published part one (of two) of their report in June 2012, entitled *Like Father, Like Son: Divine Familial Language in Bible Translation*, which is available on various websites, including http://bible-researcher.com/pca.mit.report1.pdf. The report is a well-structured document that makes a reasoned case for the need to use common, biological familial terms for *Father* and *Son of God*, based on interpretations of Reformed theology (Calvinism) and confessional (creedal) orthodoxy. The authors seek translations that faithfully present the Triune God—Father, Son, and Holy Spirit—and they defend the use of biological sonship terms because those reflect better the eternal begottenness and incarnate sonship.

> Replacement with functional/social words creates critical theological problems. . . .
>
> Contra some MIT [Muslim Idiom Translation] advocates' assertions, the original Greek terms *pater* and *huios* are strongly biological, as are "begetting" terms of the historic Christian creeds, such as *natum* and *genn thenta,* in the Latin and Greek versions of the Nicene Creed, respectively. (PCA General Assembly, 2012, p. 12)

The report says that biological terms add the concept of shared nature and identity, over and beyond the notion of protection and affection from social terms (p. 12). Is there confusion in the IM debate about the difference between the biblical text and dogma?

The PCA report states that translators are not trained in theology, resulting in unfaithful translations. It speaks out against meaning-based translation (functional equivalence) and for the traditional formal equivalence approach. MIT is seen as a postmodern approach that lets the reader determine the meaning of the text. The authors seem to hold to the position that the meaning of the text is known and defined in orthodoxy. There is no need for self-theologizing or a discovery of new indigenous understanding of the text. On the contrary, the report calls for Bible translators to produce non-expository translations, so that pastors and church leaders can provide the proper theological exposition. Is this view of already having a known and defined orthodoxy a major contentious point in the IM debate?

The PCA report understandably reflects Reformed theology (pp. 51–53). It is not surprising to find the report stating that the Bible is a covenantal document solely for the elect. The Bible is for the church, the elect people of God, according to the report.

> Divine purpose includes Scripture's recipients. . . . The proper frame of reference for translation method is Scripture's divine purpose to its appointed hearers, and to preserve the integrity of this thoroughly divine and theological revelation, formally equivalent translation of key biblical terms like "Son of God" and "Father" should prevail. . . . Methods of Scripture translation ought not be driven or shaped primarily by evangelistic zeal. . . .

> Redemptive understanding [of translations] of the divine
> Word is a divine gift, delivered successfully not by theo-
> logically weakened translation but by the Spirit's power
> in applying divine redeeming grace. (pp. 50–52)

The report further states that translators should not yield to the "temptation of ungodly over-reliance upon anthropological, cultural, and linguistic analysis" (p. 52). Is someone's view about IM directly related to that person's understanding of the doctrines of election and the inspiration of the Scriptures?

Finally, the PCA report discusses at length the perceived link between human biological begetting and the Trinity.

> Only the biological terms of human familial identity
> adequately carry the contours of meaning revealed from
> God about his Tri-unity. . . . We note, however, that the
> begotten-ness relating the First and Second Persons of the
> Trinity to each other resembles biological sonship much
> more than social sonship. (pp. 57, 65)

This part of the PCA report seems to be in direct response to the 2011 article by Brown et al. mentioned above, in which they state that procreative meaning is absent from the original (Brown et al., 2011). Procreative meaning is offensive to Muslim insiders. To what degree do these convictions about the original meaning affect someone's opinion about IM?

The AoG USA denomination also disagrees with SIL's best practices for the translation of DFT. A group of AoG scholars wrote a report in May 2011 titled "The Necessity for Retaining Father and Son Terminology in Scripture Translations for Muslims," which is posted at http://www.fatherson.ag.org/. AoG's stated concern is "promotion of heterodox views regarding the nature of God, the deity of Jesus, and the Trinity." Their main point of argument stems from AoG's commitment to the doctrine of inerrancy, including verbal inspiration. Their doctrinal statement includes the sentence, "We conceive the Bible to be in actuality the very Word of God" (AoG World Missions, 2012, p. 4). AoG's website adds that this inerrancy applies to revelational inerrancy and to factual inerrancy. For AoG, to remove Father and Son terminology from Scripture is to deny its verbal-plenary inspiration (AoG World Missions, 2012).

They also state that possessing eternal life is contingent on the belief, acceptance, and confession of Jesus Christ as the Son of God. Basically, they believe that divinely inspired terms, which are not mere metaphors to AoG, can only be accurate when literally translated. To AoG the literal term *Son of God* is necessary to retain and prove Jesus' divinity. "Or is He simply the Beloved Messiah?" AoG asks (AoG World Missions, 2012, p. 11). They insist that "none of the 'equivalents' for Son indicate Jesus' deity" (p. 12). They see two contributing factors to these, in their view, inaccurate translations: postmodernism and syncretistic accommodation in Muslim evangelism (leading to C5 communities). Here is another indication of a link between someone's doctrine on the inspiration of the Scriptures and their view of IM. Is IM syncretistic? Does it deny the divinity of Jesus?

According to the i2 Ministries website (www.i2ministries.org), IM is not an evangelical option for Christian missions to Muslims. Individuals such as Ravi Zacharias, Josh McDowell, and J. P. Moreland have endorsed this organization. Their *Chrislam* book is dedicated "to our Christian brothers and sisters who have courageously come out of Islam . . . and with prayers for those who want to." This is hinting at the often-heard claim that followers of Jesus who stay on the inside of Islam do this to avoid persecution and therefore are not courageous.

The book *Chrislam* has 25 chapters written by various authors, most of whom are well-known in the contextualization debates. It engages the question that every Muslim who comes to believe in Jesus faces: "How much can and should he stay connected to his Muslim heritage?" The authors of *Chrislam* all have the same main concern. "Insider movements risk underestimating the impact of failing to differentiate enough in translation and practice between Christianity and Islam" (Lingel, Morton, & Nikides, 2011, p. i). Creating more differentiation between Christianity and Islam together with well-grounded apologetics is the foundational strategy of i2 Ministries. They organize conferences to critically assess IM, whereas the organization Common Ground Consultants (http://comgro.org/) has been organizing consultations for practitioners promoting an incarnational and kingdom-building ministry model that supports contextualized and insider approaches. Their motto is, "Building Bridges of Trust That Bear the Weight of Truth."

The *Chrislam* authors recognize that Lausanne III in Cape Town in 2010 validated IM, and they realize that opponents have the opportunity to publish articles in journals such as the *St. Francis Magazine*, sponsored by Arab Vision and Interserve. They saw a need, however, for a concerted effort to speak out against IM in addition to writing articles in journals, hence the book *Chrislam*.

Those opposing IM seem to think of themselves as promoting the historical approach, and in that sense they are "traditionalists" who promote traditional church doctrines and creeds as the Great Tradition and the Third Testament. *Chrislam's* editors draw a parallel between IM and the emergent church. "What the emergent church is to the church in the United States, IM is to the Church at large" (Lingel et al., 2011, p. 3). Both the emergent theology and IM challenge traditions within the church and missions. Do Muslim insiders hold to emergent theology?

The book *Chrislam* supports the views of Gerald McDermott, professor of religion and philosophy at Roanoke College in Salem, Virginia. He places today's evangelicals in two camps: the Meliorists and the Traditionalists. The latter are presented as the defenders of historical and traditional beliefs and creeds, standing on the Scriptures, and "believing the *forms* of Church and office are not culturally conditioned options, but necessary for God's people" (Lingel et al., 2011, p. 4). Reformed traditions fit within the Traditionalist camp.

McDermott includes the emergent church in the Meliorist camp. This is not a common term, but the basic meaning of Meliorism is that people can make a difference in a society and improve it. McDermott seems to refer to the idea of the social gospel when he speaks of Meliorists. He assumes that these Meliorists look at the Traditionalists either as simple-minded biblicists or paleo-orthodox. *Paleo* refers to "old," and as such paleo-orthodoxy goes back to the creeds and doctrines of the fourth and fifth century (Nicene/Chalcedonian).

> For many Meliorists, biblical inspiration means the authors of Scripture were inspired, but the words were not. The logic of the Meliorists leads them to proclaim Scripture's authority while rejecting the Church's historical understanding of it, making a theologian "just another culture-bound interpreter of spiritual existence." Out go the theologians; in come the anthropologists. (Lingel et al., 2011, p. 5)

In McDermott's article, posted on *First Things*, he wonders whether the Meliorists or Traditionalists will prove to be more influential over time.

> Which will now prevail in this most recent division within evangelicalism? The answer depends on whether evangelical leaders and theologians will follow mainline Protestantism in its Meliorist accommodation to culture or Roman Catholicism in its Traditionist insistence on the priority of the Christian tradition. (McDermott, 2011)

McDermott especially critiques Roger Olson, a professor of theology at Truett Theological Seminary (at Baylor University). Olson dialogued with McDermott (Olson, 2011) and posted an article entitled "The New Fundamentalism" on his blog in March 2011. He makes some interesting observations about the neo-fundamentalists. In summary, he mentions the following distinguishing features of neo-fundamentalism:

> [There is a] certain militancy in defense of perceived evangelical doctrinal tradition. . . . pointing out heresy or heterodoxy where it has not yet been recognized. Their practice of theology is almost exclusively critical; they see no value in constructive or reconstructive theology even if it is based on fresh and faithful biblical research. They are militant defenders and promoters of something they call "the received evangelical tradition" (or by another name). . . .
>
> [They have] a tendency to fill up the "essentials" (dogmas) category of Christian beliefs with non-essentials. For example, many neo-fundamentalists are claiming that substitutionary atonement is an essential of Christian faith.
>
> A new version of separationism [is appearing]. Neo-fundamentalists don't often practice secondary separation. But it is beginning to raise its ugly head among them. (Olson, 2011)

Is the critique on IM mostly coming from the neo-fundamentalists? Are various views on the doctrine of substitutionary atonement influencing the IM debate? Are convictions about evangelism versus social gospel/kingdom-building behind the opposing views on IM?

D. A. Carson, well-known author, Reformed evangelical theologian, and professor of the New Testament, wrote the book *Jesus the Son of God: A Christological Title Often Overlooked, Sometimes Misunderstood, and Currently Disputed* (Carson, 2012). The book originated from three lectures delivered at Reformed Theological Seminary in Jackson, Mississippi, on March 5–6, 2012. In the preface, Carson makes an interesting point on the difference between doctrines and the biblical text.

> For some time I have been thinking through the hiatus between careful exegesis and doctrinal formulations. We need both, of course, but unless the latter are finally controlled by the former, and seen to be controlled by the former, both are weakened. The "Son of God" theme has become one of several test cases in my own mind. (p. 11)

In chapter 1, Carson evaluates the phrase *Son of God* as a Christological title. In chapter 2 the author exegetes two passages (Hebrews 1 and John 5:16–30), and in the third and final chapter, Carson addresses the question of how to translate the phrase *Son of God* for a majority-Muslim language community. He first identifies the larger issues, which to him are limited to the C5 and IM debate and to the recent history of the translation controversy involving Wycliffe, SIL, and Frontiers. He describes the C5 communities critically by saying that these people have accepted Jesus as Lord, as they understand him, and reject a pretty short list of elements of Islam that they think are completely incompatible with the Bible—insinuating that their understanding of Jesus as Lord is wrong, and that their list of incompatible elements in Islam is too short. He identifies the ferment (agitation) around the IM topic and identifies the DFT debate as part of that same ferment.

Carson uses the phrase "avoid using Father/Son language" as something C5 supporters likely favor in the new translations (p. 88). He reflects a perception, similar to other critics, that IM and new translations are Western impositions on Muslim-background believers in their own context (p. 91). Is IM about avoiding Father/Son language? Is it something imported by Westerners? In the last eighteen pages of the book

Carson highlights six critical evaluations of these new translations, summarized as follows:

1. The term *Son of God* should be rendered directly, perhaps with explanatory notes.
2. The use in a translation of diverse forms for *Son of God* that are not exactly synonymous with respect to referent, but also with respect to association and connotation, results in a systematically unfaithful translation.
3. The use of a reader-response theory is domesticating the Scriptures and a recipe for disaster.
4. The consistent use of the expression *Son of God* itself is needed to hold the thematic linking and trajectories together and to cross-pollinate its distinctive uses.
5. SIL/Wycliffe members approach translation challenges atomistically because of their lack of training in exegesis, biblical theology, or systematic theology.
6. It is not good that insiders are cut off from the universal church, that Westerners are imposing new translations on local churches, and that new translations are being pushed ahead in communities where there are no missionaries or pastors. (pp. 91–109)

Carson does not support SIL's best practices. He calls SIL's four steps in the DFT translation process "a wee bit slippery" (p. 99). If, according to Carson, receptor-focused translations (i.e., those that use a reader-response theory) are recipes for disaster, what is the role of the receptor-audience in key term translation decisions? Is IM an imposition from the West? Would a genuine indigenous movement be acceptable?

The January 2013 edition of *Christianity Today* includes several articles about IM by Daniels, Tennent, Travis, and Parshall. Gene Daniels reports on an exclusive interview conducted in 2011 with Abu Jaz, a Muslim IM leader in eastern Africa. Both names are pseudonyms. Reflecting on Isa al Masih appearing to Abu Jaz in a dream, after he had witnessed a miracle the day before, Abu Jaz shares, "He [Isa] didn't talk to me about any complicated theological issues. He only told me that if I followed him, he would multiply my life" (Daniels, 2013, p. 24). After a challenging two years for Abu Jaz of adjusting to a Christian culture and after attending Bible college, he felt a calling and a joy in restoring his former Islamic cultural identity so that he could express himself and his faith in God more naturally. "Then I rejoiced that God is just" (p. 25). He considers the church creeds as answers the church fathers found for their own problems, in their own contexts, and he calls those now working among Muslims to find answers in the Word of God for those contexts. Abu Jaz promotes starting with general revelation and with recognizing *Allah* as a term for God when sharing the gospel with Muslims.

> If we say that the one they know as Allah is not God, we are not [speaking] against the religion of Islam, or Muhammad or Qur'an, but against the doctrine of general revelation. The missionary must first receive the name of the Creator God from the people, and then they have heavenly authority to give the people the name of the Savior, Isa al Masih. (p. 25)

In this article Abu Jaz further explains how Muslims start with an Islamic Christology and move towards higher Christology over time. He promotes Muslim-focused church-planting strategies that use terms and forms from the local Muslim communities.

As mentioned in the Introduction, Timothy Tennent contributed an article to this same edition of *Christianity Today*, as did John Travis, who recounted how a Jesus movement started in the neighborhood where they had lived for many years when they were out of the country. A woman called "Fatimah," who had been reading the New Testament for nearly 10 years and had seen miraculous answers to her prayers, assumed that she could not become a Jesus follower because she was a Muslim. An Asian pastor finally told her that she could receive Jesus because he saves, not religion (Travis, 2013, p. 30).

Travis observed that Jesus-centered groups began to form, comprised of individuals who had accepted Jesus as their Savior and in whom there was clear evidence of the work of the Holy Spirit. He considers them spiritually and biblically part of the body of Christ, or the church universal. "They affirm most aspects of their Muslim heritage, simply seeing it as their natural identity. Yet they clearly reform certain teachings and practices that are not in line with the New Testament" (2013, p. 30). This last characteristic makes these Jesus followers different in their communities, and many have endured much suffering. Travis calls evangelicals to respond to IM by praising God and by praying for these insiders. He cautions against criticism. "We should be careful. We could find ourselves opposing what God is doing, when God moves in ways we do not expect" (p. 30).

The fourth article is by Phil Parshall and is titled "Too Much Context May Harm." Even though in the 1970s he was involved in Bangladesh to contextualize their ministry to the Muslim context, which bore much fruit, he has significant concerns about IM. Specifically, Parshall does not promote Muslim followers of Jesus still remaining in the mosque, reciting the Muslim creed, and identifying themselves as Muslims (Parshall, 2013).

The aforementioned WEA Panel that reviewed Wycliffe and SIL's best practices for translating DFTs published their report on the WEA website in May 2013 (WEA, 2013). The Panel cites as its mandate to set boundaries for theologically acceptable translation methodology, particularly in a Muslim context, and to suggest how to practically implement these recommendations. Their report recommends that "when the words for 'father' and 'son' refer to God the Father and to the Son of God, these words should always be translated with the most directly equivalent familial words within the given linguistic and cultural context of the recipients" (WEA, 2013, p. 6). This recommendation has satisfied many critics of Wycliffe and SIL's previous practices, and is restricting these organizations now to this new standard for translating DFTs.

This brief literature review raises many questions that are theological and missional in nature. Other scholars have contributed to the debate on IM and DFT and could have been quoted, but ultimately, the major stakeholders—who are mostly still missing from the scene of the investigation—are the insiders themselves. This study will address many of the questions raised in the IM debate by giving Muslim insider leaders a voice, to discover their theological and missional frames.

# CHAPTER THREE
## RESEARCH SUMMARY

This chapter is a brief summary of the "Methods and Procedures" chapter in my dissertation, as published in ProQuest. This grounded-theory study used a qualitative approach to collect and analyze data. IM is widely discussed, but it still is a fairly new topic without well-developed theories. In addition, the voices from insiders themselves are underrepresented. Their perspectives should be heard and understood before outsiders can formulate well-informed theories on IM. To date, the topic lacks structure and outsiders are expressing their opinion on (or personal experience with) IM in a variety of ways. IM is better understood from an insider's perspective. Thus far, little research has been done with an emic approach.

In this inductive study I learned from IM leaders by interviewing them and by analyzing the transcripts. These interviews were guided, informal interactions with many open-ended questions in order to solicit as much qualitative data from the insiders as possible. I collected and analyzed these data and found general themes and principles.

This study used the grounded-theory approach. I sought to learn and derive patterns, themes, and generalizations leading to a substantive theory or framework that is grounded in the views of the participants. After my analysis of the empirical data I considered the literature on the current IM debate and developed a framework with four paradigms. I applied a social constructivist philosophical worldview to the research. Insiders seek understanding of the world and of the Muslim society they live in as followers of Christ. They develop subjective meanings of their experiences negotiated socially and historically (Creswell, 2009, p. 8). This description fits the insider very well.

There is a touch of advocacy in this research in that I purposed to give a voice to insiders. This group is potentially very misunderstood, and in some areas indeed persecuted, by some parts of the church. I value basic incarnational approaches and the unique inculturation of the gospel in each context, and as such I have a bias towards contextualization. However, I did not come to this research with a predetermined agenda that must be advocated. I was open-minded about the outcomes of the data analysis.

The purposeful sampling of participants for interviews was done with much care, since insiders in a Muslim context often remain "on the inside." They do not want to be characterized and exposed within their context as special cases, and they certainly do not want to be seen closely associating with foreigners. My sampling was therefore very selective, and the process of finding participants involved checking references and using a network of personal contacts. The sampling was at times opportunistic in that a contact with one participant led to finding another. My sampling was selective and purposeful in that I sought out insiders who are representative of an IM in a certain language group or region. In other words, the participants are leaders of an IM in their own region.

The security of these insiders is, of course, very important. I met IM leaders only after we were introduced by a trusted contact, and in settings that did not compromise the participant's role and profile. We never met in villages or the countryside, where foreigners are rarely seen. We met in cities, in places such as a public park, a mall area, an office at a seminary, and hotel rooms.

I connected with insiders from seven countries in Asia and four in Africa. All IM leaders I interviewed appeared very knowledgeable and aware of their unique status. Several have master's degrees and a few are in PhD programs. All are ministering in a Muslim context now, and there is a wide range of experience among them with traditional church settings. In addition to collecting interview data from 26 insiders, I interviewed five expatriate workers who have close relationships with insiders and their ministries. These five alongsiders are well known in their areas of ministry, and two of them are widely published. Their input served as support to my analysis of the primary data from IM leaders.

The interviews were guided conversations to explore the theological and missional views of IM leaders and the communal processes within their movement that develop those views. I asked open-ended questions using an interview guide, and encouraged the participant to feel free to respond openly and in a way they themselves desired. The interviews were "open-ended but directed, shaped yet emergent, and paced yet flexible" (Charmaz, 2006, p. 28).

I developed the interview guide with the Muslim context in mind and with a focus on theology proper, because the majority of the critique of IM falls within that domain. Regarding sensitivities to the Muslim context, I intentionally used, for example, *Allah* instead of *God,* and *Isa al Masih* instead of *Jesus (the) Christ.* During the research process I adjusted the interview guide slightly to make sure that I would address the main questions in the most logical or natural flow. Appendix A has the final version of the interview guide that I used the most. Without interpretation each interview lasted at least one hour. With interpretation each interview lasted two hours or more.

These interviewees are typical Muslim followers of Jesus who have spent some time "on the Christian side" but have for various reasons decided to cross back over to their Muslim communities. These individuals are also called "cross-overs." I collected interview data from 26 IM leaders and five alongsiders. In order to protect the anonymity of those interviewed and their exact locations, I used the following names and identifiers for the general region, the local IM leaders, and the five associated foreign alongsiders (Table 1).

**Table 1:** 26 IM Leaders and five alongsiders

| Region | IM Leader | Alongsider |
|---|---|---|
| SE Asia | Lucas | Tyler |
| | Zach | |
| | Ian | |
| | Phil | |
| | Monty | |
| | Silas | |
| | Kent | |
| | Stuart | |
| | Drew | |
| | Ross | Josh |
| | Ray | |
| South Asia A | Andy | Kevin |
| | Howard | |
| South Asia B | Mitch | |
| South Asia C | Axel | |

| Region | IM Leader | Alongsider |
|---|---|---|
| South Asia D | Angus | Wilbur |
| | Frank | |
| | Arthur | |
| | Paxton | |
| Central Asia | Julius | |
| | Ted | |
| | Gus | |
| | Jason | |
| Africa | Arnold | Melvin |
| | Oliver | |
| | Homer | |
| | Brad | |

All interviews were audio-recorded with the exception of one session, per Gus' request. This resulted in 57.3 hours of recorded conversations. I transcribed these recordings verbatim, and combined with my notes from Gus' interview, this gave me an amount of text to analyze that is equivalent to 360 pages (single-spaced), or 236,000 words. I distilled this text to about 57,000 words in the form of interview summaries, retaining the most pertinent comments from the participants. Chapter 4 contains sections of these interview summaries that relate to the theological and missional views of the interviewees.

Using the coding procedures is especially recommended in a grounded-theory approach. I used the MAXQDA (MQ) qualitative data analysis computer software. The first and most crucial step of coding was the open coding procedure in which I named and categorized each part of the data through close examination. I started with an initial set of 66 codes based on the categories in the interview guide. I went through each part of the interview transcripts and made comparisons between them to find similarities and differences. The MQ software tool facilitated this process very well. Using the open coding process I increased the initial set to a final set of 654 codes, and coded 2,390 references in the 41 documents that comprised the interview transcripts.

The first two sub-questions under the overall research questions are, "How do Muslim insider leaders understand Allah and his plans and purposes?" and "How do Muslim insider leaders understand Isa al Masih and his role and identity?" In both the initial and final code sets these two sub-questions represent two of the four top-level codes: Allah and Isa al Masih. Similarly, sub-questions three and four represent the top-level codes: Movement and Theologizing. Table 2 shows the total number of codes for each set.

**Table 2:** Number of codes in code sets

| Top-level Code | Initial Set | Final Set |
| --- | --- | --- |
| Allah | 24 | 266 |
| Isa al Masih | 18 | 116 |
| Movement | 15 | 179 |
| Theologizing | 09 | 93 |
| Total: | 66 | 654 |

The coding process resulted in an extensive structured and layered final code set that gave much insight into the theological and missional frames of IM leaders, as presented in the first part of chapter 4. I followed the code structure in that analysis and identified the range of views among the IM leaders for each code or code cluster. In order to be able to also analyze the data by following the list of interviewees versus the codes, I created a model, or framework, that can capture the range of theological and missional views on a variety of topics reflected in the codes. The framework has four columns (paradigms) and 21 rows (frames) and forms a higher level of abstraction to the 654 codes. I "framed" each interviewee in the framework by analyzing the data (interview transcripts) again and plotting someone's comments and answers in one of the four paradigms, for each of the 21 topics (frames). This process created for each interviewee a scatter plot that I further analyzed by comparing the various plots by region. I also was able to identify some frames in the framework as outliers because IM leaders consistently expressed views on those topics that fell in a different paradigm than most of their other frames.

In general, the framework was a very helpful data analysis tool in addition to the set of codes and the coding process. The second part of chapter 4 describes the framework and my data analysis using this tool.

# CHAPTER FOUR
## VIEWS ON ALLAH AND ISA AL MASIH

### INTRODUCTION

The central research question is, What are the theological and missional frames of IM leaders? Based on data analysis, the central understanding or ground theory is that there is a spread of theological and missional understanding among IM leaders, but that most of them adhere to basic evangelical views summarized by the titles *Fundamental* and *Ecumenical*. A minority of the IM leaders hold views associated with the kingdom of God on earth, new perspectives on Paul, liberation theology, and the emerging church, summarized by the titles *Integral* and *Global*. These four titles are the four paradigms in the M-Framework, which is an analysis tool that I developed for this study.

The first two research sub-questions are on the topic of Allah and Isa al Masih. Sub-questions three and four address the general context of IMs and their internal processes that lead to understandings about Allah and Isa al Masih. Chapter 4 presents the analysis of the interview data on sub-questions one and two, and chapter 5 does the same for sub-questions three and four. The first two sub-questions are:

1. How do Muslim insider leaders understand Allah and his plans and purposes?
2. How do Muslim insider leaders understand Isa al Masih and his role and identity?

This chapter documents the analysis of the interview data to answer these two questions. Figure 1 shows the four elements in the first two research sub-questions that form the structure for the code set related to these questions.

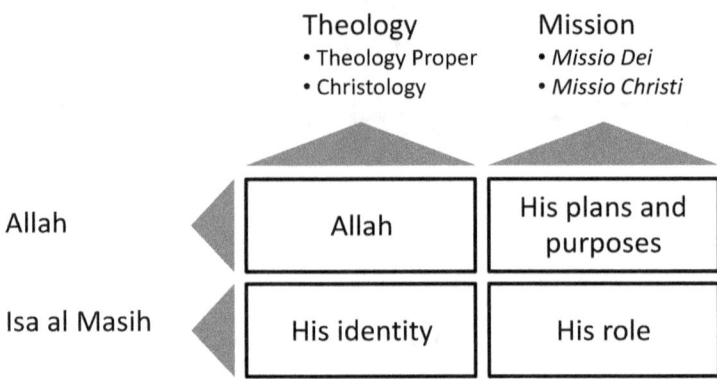

**Figure 1:** Four elements in first two research sub-questions

In order to discern the theological and missional frames of IM leaders, the interview guide included a section on Allah and one on Isa al Masih, with questions about theology and the mission of God and Jesus Christ. Table 3 depicts a portion of the final code set related to the first two research sub-questions and to the four elements in Figure 1.

**Table 3:** Four interview guide sections and code clusters

| Four Elements | Related High-level Code Clusters |
|---|---|
| Allah—Theology | Essence |
| | First Creation |
| | Problem |
| Allah—Missio Dei | Plans and Purposes |
| | Revelation |
| | Religions |
| Isa al Masih—Christology | High |
| | Other |
| | Low |
| | Al Masih |
| | Son of God |
| Isa al Masih—Missio Christi | Actions |
| | Message |
| | Cross and Resurrection |
| | Good News |

In the "Initial Observations" section of this chapter I followed the code structure and made some first observations from the interview text segments in each code category. This section is an analysis by topic. I present the range of views among IM leaders on each topic. I also present comments from the five alongsiders, as clarification and secondary information. Unless otherwise indicated, a name of an interviewee refers to one of the 26 IM leaders. When I present comments from interviewees in table format, those from the alongsiders are always listed last, separated from the primary comments by IM leaders with a horizontal line.

The initial observation of the various viewpoints on each theological and missional topic led to the need and desire to also analyze the same interview data by interviewee and region. To this end I developed an M-Framework that captures the full range of theological and missional understandings, or frames, among the interviewees. The M stands for *missio Dei*, because someone's description of God's mission seems central and influences all aspects of theological and missional understanding.

The final step in the analysis process was using this M-Framework to compare and contrast IM leaders and alongsiders, IM leaders from the various regions, etc. I made an M-Framework plot for each interviewee and created integrated M-Framework plots to assist in this full analysis. Finally, I drew some initial conclusions from these plots that answer the first two research sub-questions.

## INITIAL OBSERVATIONS

In this section I analyze the coded segments in the interview transcripts related to Allah/Theology, Allah/*Missio Dei*, Isa al Masih/Christology, Isa al Masih/*Missio Christi*, and the initial frame development for these topics. I make extensive use of tables to present as many direct quotes from the IM leaders on certain topics as possible. The direct quotes by alongsiders appear at the bottom of the tables as secondary and clarifying data.

### Allah—Theology—Essence and Beginnings

The main question in the interview guide addressing the theology of Allah was the first question: "How would you describe what Allah is like? What are his main characteristics?" This question addresses God's essence or his typical behavior patterns. The rest of the questions in the interview guide about Allah are related to his mission, the *missio Dei*, or the "missiology" of Allah.

The answers to this first question varied widely, from a reluctance to describe what Allah was like to the full narrative of creation, the Fall, and redemption. I placed the comments about the theology of Allah in three groups titled Essence, First Creation, and Problem.

## Essence

Interviewees most commonly described Allah as the Creator. I used that code 18 times. A close second was some indication that Allah loves. I named the code for the third most mentioned description of Allah "compassionate and gracious" (Table 4), but it is noteworthy that the words "merciful" and "mercy" appeared more often in the replies than "grace" or "gracious."

**Table 4:** 12 Segments coded with "compassionate and gracious"

| IM Leader | Direct Quote |
| --- | --- |
| S-Asia-C\Axel | He is especially merciful. |
| C-Asia\Gus | He is merciful. He delights to forgive. |
| Africa\Arnold | He is the gracious one. He is the merciful one. |
| Africa\Homer | He is very caring and merciful to me. |
| S-Asia-D\Frank | God is merciful and he does good. |
| SE Asia\Ross | He is the most compassionate and loving. |
| SE Asia\Zach | He is full of grace and mercy. |
| SE Asia\Silas | He is generous and patient. |
| SE Asia\Kent | He is a compassionate one. |
| SE Asia\Stuart | He is all merciful, all compassionate. |
| Alongsider\Kevin | The first two words that come to mind are merciful and compassionate. |
| Alongsider\Wilbur | He is also tender and compassionate. |

A lexical search of all interview transcripts of IM leaders showed a preference for "merciful" and "mercy" over "gracious" and "grace" (Table 5).

**Table 5:** Lexical search for "merciful"

| Lexical Search | # of Hits/Documents |
|---|---|
| Mercy, merciful | 48/18 |
| Compassionate, compassion | 9/6 |
| Gracious, grace | 33/11 |

In addition to these first three categories/codes for Allah's essence, the interviewees mentioned various other characteristics such as relational, powerful, sovereign, one, holy, etc. Referencing Islam, Julius mentioned that Allah has 99 beautiful names. Ross is identifying in Islam what he calls agnosticism.

> We are dealing with fear cultures controlled by wicked kings, influenced by Satan. The holy Qur'an says, "God, show me your face." I do not know why, but in the Muslim world, and especially in Arabized regions, this phrase is often translated as, "God, show me your will." God is sitting on a throne and we are in his right hand, but we have become Hellenistic. To describe God is sinful now. That is not in the holy Qur'an; it is not in the Tawrat; it is not in the Zabur; it is not in the Injil. We have become agnostic. In the mosque the agnostic beliefs are very strong. God cannot be described. God does not sit, he does not have hands, he does not have a face, he does not have a word, and he does not have a son. That is what I call agnostic or Hellenistic. Muslims are agnostic. This is for Greek philosophers, but it is not where human beings would like to be.

It is interesting to note that only three IM leaders mentioned the negative image they used to have of Allah as Muslims before coming to faith in Isa al Masih. Andy described this previous Allah as a big and scary giant who punishes people, and Howard shared how his concept of Allah was that of an angry God who he somehow had to make happy. Jason believes that the God of the Qur'an is not loving or merciful, and not interested in people. All other interviewees made no mention of a distinction between the Allah of the Qur'an and the God of the Bible. Paxton specifically mentioned that the Qur'an has a word for love that is ascribed to Allah, but this concept was not developed in later Islam. He makes another general observation about what Allah is like from the Qur'an and the Bible.

> To me what God is like is all very positive. It has no negative connotations whatsoever. There may be some statements in the Qur'an or other places that can be used to come to a concept that is somewhat different, but in the same way it could also be argued that way against the Old Testament. In the Old Testament God acts in such a way that most Christians don't like. But certainly they do not just reject him. When people had advanced to a certain revelation and understanding, then he came at the proper time. This is no problem for me.

The answer to the question, "What is Allah like?" is the foundation of someone's theological and missional framework and needs to be informed by more than just a list of characteristics. It is linked to a person's view of Allah's plans and purposes, the identity and role of Isa al Masih, the meaning of the cross, heaven and hell, other religions, etc. Figure 2 illustrates this point and is a code map with the codes other than the "Essence" one that inform this question, "What is Allah like?"

### First Creation

The interview guide did not have a specific question about the first creation, but in the course of the conversation several interviewees made mention of it that is worth noting. Arnold and Axel specifically said that Allah created us to be close to him and to relate to him. Many others implied this initial purpose of the first creation when they stated that God's current plans and purposes are to restore that first relationship between mankind and himself. Gus said that the word "relationship" as a way to describe the connection between man and Allah is difficult, because in his Muslim context all types of "relationships" are socially well-defined as connections between humans. "So what is my relationship with Isa? What kind of relationship is that?" he asked.

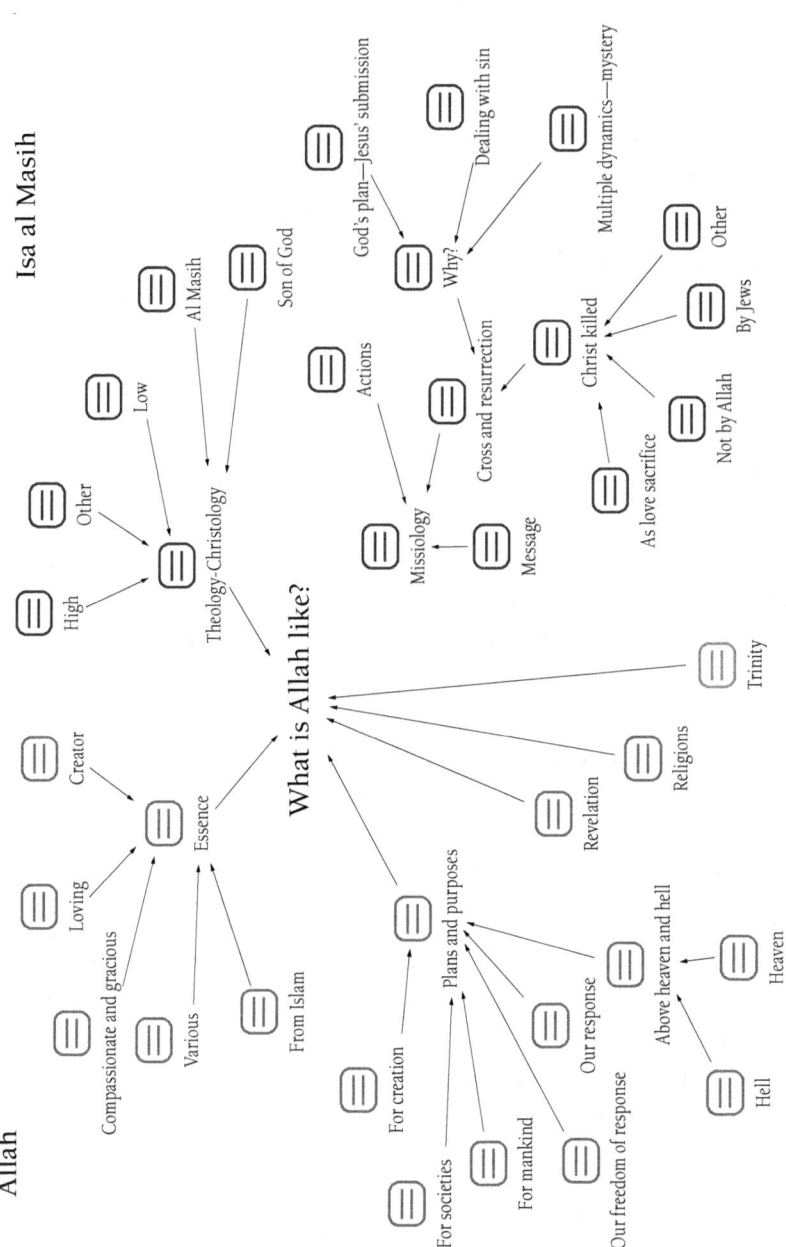

**Figure 2:** Theology code map for what Allah is like

Two of the alongsiders, Wilbur and Melvin, referred to a harmonious creation living in peace and happiness as the metanarrative and purpose of the first creation, while Oliver, Lucas, Zach, and Silas emphasized the worship of God and our obedience to him as the main purpose.

> Coming from a Muslim background and as a Muslim, Allah created people, especially when he created Adam and Hawa [Eve], for them to obey him, to submit to him. I think that was the first purpose of creation. Because he created them in his image and he wanted people to obey him. There is no other thing than to obey him, and to pray to him. I understand that to be the main purpose of his creation.

Both Arthur and alongsider Tyler mentioned that humans are the pinnacle of creation and function as Allah's vice-regents, acting in this world on his behalf. Phil, Angus, and Tyler made note of the fact that we are created in God's image and as such are called to reflect his grace as we effect positive change in this world. Several referred to Allah's care for his creation as a craftsman. Kent said, "God planned for the goodness of creation."

The garden of Eden came up a few times in the interviews even though it was not a topic in focus. Most seem to assume that this was part of the initial creation here on earth, but Andy and Howard believe that the garden of Eden was in heaven, and that living on earth is mankind's punishment for the sin of Adam and Eve. Andy said, "The punishment was that God threw them out of heaven and we are all suffering because of this first sin. Still God wants us to go back and restore us to the same place where he created us." Oliver described this earth as a testing ground. "Allah brought us to earth even though he had a promise for us, and he is testing us in our faith, and it is agreed that whoever has faith will go to heaven."

## The Problem

As with the topic of the first creation, I did not specifically ask what the problems are with creation. Both topics came up as part of the answer to the question, "What are Allah's plans and purposes for his creation and mankind?" Some phrased those plans and purposes as reactions to a specific problem in the past, while others saw Allah's plans and purposes more in the light of current ongoing challenges to live the right way, on the right path.

The concept of "the fall" of mankind into sin was only mentioned by that name by one alongsider and seven IM leaders (Table 6), but others implied it in different words. For example, Axel said that because of Adam's sin mankind is going away from the right path. Alongsider Melvin talked about our depraved hearts, and Arnold referred to the mistake of man that makes us fall short of having a relationship as originally planned. Oliver said that we have fallen into sin and Arthur talked about human beings making a mistake, while Ray and Stuart talked about our separation from God because of Adam.

**Table 6:** Lexical search for "the Fall"

| IM Leader | Direct Quote |
|---|---|
| C-Asia\Jason | Other people think that God wants to restore his creation as it was before the Fall. |
| S-Asia-B\Mitch | This is the restoration of the fellowship and relationship that Adam had before the Fall. |
| Africa\Brad | It starts at the Fall, I mean at creation, and it ends with the restoration of the relationship between Allah and humans. |
| SE Asia\Phil | Since the fall of man, God's plan for creation was not the destruction of mankind, but a good plan. |
| SE Asia\Monty | One of the results of the Fall and sin was the separation of mankind from God, but also from that perfect environment that God had provided for them. |
| SE Asia\Lucas | But because of the fall of man, mankind lost its glory. |
| SE Asia\Ray | After the fall of Adam, Allah can reveal himself through dreams, like to Joseph, or through his voice, or through someone's heart. |
| Alongsider\Tyler | To me, the restoration issue comes out of the Fall. |

Not primarily the fall of man but Satan is the problem, according to Andy, Oliver, Arnold, Angus, Phil, and alongsider Wilbur. The original sin is attributed to Satan. Andy said, "Adam and Eve were in heaven and enjoying that, but Satan destroyed their life." Angus pointed out the ongoing problems because of Satan. "In a father's house there can be children that go the right way, but others go astray. Satan brainwashes them and uses them for his purposes and turns them against their father." Oliver talked about Satan keeping us from the right path. "We are still not on the right path. We are trying to be on the right path but the devil is trapping us out. He is taking us from the right path."

The perennial nature of the problem with creation was attributed to mankind in general in various ways. Gus said that we currently are incompatible with God. Ross mentioned pollution, wars, gossip, and our love to shame others instead of covering their wickedness. Monty and Zach also attributed the problem to people's sin, rather than to Satan, and Ken referred to that as people choosing their own way.

## Allah–*Missio Dei*

The first question in the interview asked for a description of God. The conversations touched on his essence, his general way of interacting with his creation, and the initial as well as ongoing problems with creation. Given that background, the next topic was God's mission. What has God been doing, what is he still doing, and what will he do? These types of metanarrative questions set the stage in the first part of each interview. What are God's plans and purposes, and how do concepts of heaven and hell fit within them? How has God revealed himself and how do religions play a role in all of this? The answers and comments by the interviewees revealed much about their theological and missional understandings.

### Plans and Purposes

The second question in practically all interviews was, "What are Allah's plans and purposes for his creation and mankind?" This question triggered either a long response that summarized all of the Scriptures or a brief answer at a conceptual level. Answers to the follow-up and clarification questions in either case demonstrated the basic views of each interviewee on Allah's plans and purposes. I grouped those views in six code clusters:

1. For creation
2. For societies
3. For mankind
4. Our response
5. Our freedom of response
6. About heaven and hell

FOR CREATION

What are Allah's plans and purposes for his creation, for this world in general, including all of nature? Subsequent sections look at subsets of creation—namely, mankind and societies—but this first section covers all of creation in general. During the interview I typically pressed for specifics by asking a version of the following question:

> Some say that Allah's plans and purposes are to establish and restore all of his creation to what it should be. The focus is on this world, people, societies, nature, etc. The focus is on the salvation of the world. Others say that Allah's plans and purposes are to save people away from this world for heaven. He gave up on this world and is saving people away from it. Is Allah about populating heaven or about saving all of his creation? What are your views on this?

My first observation was that many times there seemed to be unfamiliarity with the concepts represented in the question. Table 7 gives a sample of some initial reactions from the interviewees.

Others were quite specific about the finality of this world. Jason sees sin and corruption growing and believes that this world will be burned up. Arnold talked about heaven as plan B so that we are not destroyed and wiped out like the earth. Homer expressed it in terms of the world being desolate. Angus believes that Jesus did not value the physical world. "He did not give any importance to the world." Stuart likewise sees this world going in the direction of destruction. Alongsider Wilbur said that this earth has a shelf life and is not our eternal home.

**Table 7:** Unfamiliar with the concept of salvation of the world

| IM Leader | Direct Quote |
| --- | --- |
| S-Asia-A\Andy | I don't follow those two concepts. Both are not representing fully what God's plan is. |
| S-Asia-A\Howard | This is the first time I'm hearing about a group that you are talking about, that is thinking about this world. |
| S-Asia-C\Axel | I do not understand the question. |
| C-Asia\Jason | I have not heard a lot about that. About the restoration of this world, I am not sure about that. |

| IM Leader | Direct Quote |
|---|---|
| C-Asia\Jason | My understanding is that God of course wants to save people and get them to heaven. That is kind of strange why people think another way. Does that happen more within the Muslim world? |
| Africa\Brad | Basically, what I heard regarding this topic is what some believers from some Christian background, particularly the Jehovah's Witnesses, teach. Other than that I did not hear about these two views within the church, particularly salvation just on this earth. |

Others added some nuance to their response. Alongsider Wilbur, for example, uses as his metanarrative the creative mandate for man to take care of creation, which due to the Fall now takes second place to the redemptive mandate to evangelize the world, which is heading towards destruction. Nevertheless, we should not have an "abandon ship mentality," according to Wilbur.

> Where the redemptive mandate is extended, then we embrace the creative mandate again and we care very much about things like stewardship about all the resources God has given us including a beautiful temporary home on the earth.

Zach looks at the restoration of this world and heaven as two sides of the same coin. Phil referred to Allah working on the restorative process now as a way towards peace all the way through into heaven. Ray connects the two concepts by seeing Allah as King of his life now on earth and also after he dies when he has a spiritual body. Both alongsider Josh and Zach spoke of the kingdom of God impacting things on earth, reflecting the fruit of the Spirit and supreme justice. Many of the IM leaders, such as Julius, Gus, Brad, Arthur, Phil, Monty, and Ray, mentioned that God's purpose is a full restoration to the original creation, highlighting his love and care for his own creation.

The total picture of Allah's plans and purposes for creation only becomes clear when we also consider someone's views of heaven and hell, as illustrated in Figure 3. Is heaven a restored or completed earth, or another created place separate from this world? Paxton promotes the former. "I think logically that if God is really interested in taking human beings to heaven, first of all he must bring heaven to earth. If he cannot do that, he should not expect us to go to heaven."

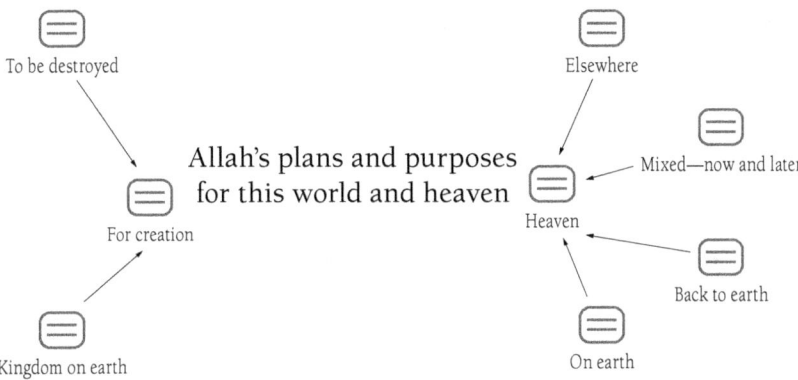

**Figure 3:** Creation code map for Allah's plans and purposes for this world and heaven

## For Societies

The question of whether Allah is interested in just and healthy societies was somewhat rhetorical. It would be somewhat strange to say no to that question. Many gave a full-hearted affirmative response. Table 8 gives a sample of those types of responses. Others answered the question with the individual in focus versus society as a whole. To them God is interested in the individual believer living a just and healthy life, and as a society has more believers, society as a whole naturally will reflect more of God's justice and righteousness. Lucas adheres to this view. "If an individual stops stealing or stops committing adultery, and if this is all determined by their faith in God and by their worship of God, the results are changed and transformed lives, which then affects society."

**Table 8:** Is Allah interested in just and healthy societies?

| IM Leader | Direct Quote |
| --- | --- |
| S-Asia-C\Axel | Allah wants us and our societies to be righteous. |
| C-Asia\Gus | Yes, I would say that Allah is concerned about injustice in societies and that he wants to see more just and righteous societies. Absolutely. |
| C-Asia\Jason | I think he does. The people who know Jesus are not to run away from this world or flee from this world, but to be in this world and to influence it. |

| IM Leader | Direct Quote |
|---|---|
| Africa\Oliver | Yes, Allah likes justice. He wants people to have justice and dignity. |
| SE Asia\Phil | The longing of God is for all society to live godly and righteously. |
| SE Asia\Ray | Yes, I think so. |
| SE Asia\Kent | Of course, God will pay attention to a way of living in a community that does not destroy one another. |
| Alongsiders\Kevin | I would say that, yes. |
| Alongsiders\Melvin | Absolutely. I would say that is the main goal. I see an eschatological salvation and a salvation here and now. |

The interesting point on this question was that I asked it right after our conversation about Allah's plans and purposes for this world, as I purposefully tried to make a connection between God's plans for each individual, for this world, and then for societies. Those who had just stated that God's plans for this world are for total destruction did not apply those plans to societies. In later analysis I show that these interviewees stayed consistent with those plans for the end of the world when it comes to individuals, as they believe that the plans for each individual are heaven or hell, away from this world. Their expression of support for just and healthy societies appeared somewhat inconsistent with their belief that God is about heaven and bringing people there.

For Mankind

Allah's plan and purposes for mankind tended to come up during the interviews at various points, but an often-repeated theme was the restoration of the relationship between Allah and man as it was in the beginning. Table 9 shows this theme.

**Table 9:** Restored relationship between man and God

| IM Leader | Direct Quote |
|---|---|
| S-Asia-A\Andy | Still God wants us to go back. He wants to restore us and that is why he sent Jesus. |
| S-Asia-C\Axel | Allah has one purpose, for everyone to be with him. |

| IM Leader | Direct Quote |
|---|---|
| C-Asia\Jason | My understanding is that Allah first of all wants to bring people into a relationship. This is the main purpose. |
| S-Asia-B\Mitch | His purpose is that mankind glorifies him, bringing glory and praise to him alone. He does not like to share his glory with any other human being, or any other creation. He sent Jesus to give his life, so that we can be restored and brought back to him. This is the plan. Now that Jesus has done the work and went up to heaven, the plan is that people know this, the saving work of God, so people can come back and join him. |
| Africa\Arnold | The solution for mankind is the redemption that Allah has provided for us through Isa al Masih. Isa al Masih is the solution to put back this relationship that man lost when he sinned originally. |
| Africa\Brad | Particularly when we come to mankind, Allah wants to restore his relationship with them and also wants to take them to heaven, so that they can enjoy eternal life. He did that by taking the initiative before we humans took initiative, to save us by sending Isa al Masih. |
| Africa\Brad | It is the plan that God has prepared to save humans from sin. It starts at the Fall, I mean at creation, and it ends with the restoration of the relationship between Allah and humans. |
| SE Asia\Phil | Regarding the purpose of God, he created man in his image, and he is seeking to restore that image and the relationship with himself, so that there will be a reunion and a uniting with God. |
| SE Asia\Phil | What are God's purposes for mankind? The need of man is to welcome and receive the provision of God and to be restored in oneness, and then being able to reflect more fully the image of God. |
| SE Asia\Lucas | The final objective from God's point of view, the final objective of redemption, is to return to the former condition of our relationship with God. Restored as they formerly were. There is a restoration aspect towards God and there is a restoration aspect to mankind and one another. |
| SE Asia\Ray | This is mentioned in the Qur'an and also in previous books like in the Tawrat, in Genesis, and also in the Injil. Allah created and had good relationships with humans, but humans rebelled against his will and his command, which broke the relationship between Allah and humans. But Allah is still trying to relate to humans as mentioned in Genesis. Allah was looking for Adam even though Adam had disobeyed. Allah is still trying to get in touch with humans. |

| IM Leader | Direct Quote |
| --- | --- |
| SE Asia\Silas | Isa wants to return mankind to the pure state at the beginning of history when mankind was created, to an obedient state as it was in the beginning. |
| SE Asia\Stuart | God has a plan to return mankind, or to restore his people so that they become close once again and return in closeness to God. |

Another set of comments from the interviewees shows that God's plans and purposes for mankind are heaven bound. Table 10 has text segments that reflect this belief that God's purpose for us is to come to heaven.

**Table 10:** Heaven bound

| IM Leader | Direct Quote |
| --- | --- |
| S-Asia-A\Andy | Still God wants us to go back and restore us to the same place where he created us. He wants us back to heaven. That is his kingdom place. |
| S-Asia-A\Howard | What we believe about heaven: God sent his Son for our sins, that he should come here and save us from our sins. There is a day of judgment and heaven. Jesus himself is saying that if you declare yourself a follower of me in this world, you will have many problems, but if you will be my witness, then on the day of judgment I will be your witness and I will take you to heaven. |
| C-Asia\Julius | There is Allah's kingdom and there is Satan's kingdom. His plan is to save people and redeem people so that they can escape hell and enter heaven. |
| C-Asia\Jason | My understanding is that God of course wants to save people and get them to heaven. That is kind of strange why people think another way. |
| S-Asia-D\Frank | In the time of Jesus, the Jewish leaders brought accusations against him to the Roman officials, saying that Jesus claimed to be above the Sharia. Jesus is beyond and above the Jewish Sharia, and this is part of God's plan. The Sharia of Moses was related to our physical bodies, but the Sharia of Jesus relates to our spirits and souls. |
| SE Asia\Stuart | God centers his purposes upon heavenly life because this world is full of sin. His purpose for mankind in this world is to remember heavenly life so that they are not tripped up by this worldly life that goes in the direction of destruction. |

| IM Leader | Direct Quote |
|---|---|
| Alongsiders\Josh | I think it is clear that one of the most important reasons Jesus came was to provide a way for people to spend eternity in heaven. |
| Alongsiders\Wilbur | Of course the incarnation and the whole gospel ministry come about as part of this—what looks to us as a detour in God's original purposes. He is bringing about a great restoration and culmination and completion of that original purpose in creation through this redemptive phase of everything. We look forward to a day when that redemptive phase is completed and we'll get on with plan A, which in the end will be a great deal richer in terms of our own appreciation of him and our own love response to him, because we did time on the other side of all this. That's how I understand his purposes. |

The concept of there being two eternal states for man, and two pathways to those states, comes through in many of the interviews. The phrases "the path," "the right path," or "the straight path" are used 50 times in all interviews combined, and just the word "path" over 100 times. The segments in Table 11 show this emphasis on two paths. One goes to heaven and the other to hell.

**Table 11:** Two paths

| IM Leader | Direct Quote |
|---|---|
| C-Asia\Julius | There is Allah's kingdom and there is Satan's kingdom. His plan is to save people and redeem people so that they can escape hell and enter heaven. |
| Africa\Oliver | You can choose to follow the wrong path, and you can choose to follow the right path. That is a personal choice. It is up to an individual. Whoever chooses the right path goes to heaven and whoever chooses the wrong path goes to hell. I think it is very clear. |
| S-Asia-D\Frank | All the time there are two paths in front of people. God's plan and will is that all people be saved, of every nationality and language group. Both ways are clear. The way of Satan and the way of God: God has shown us the results of both paths, and therefore we can choose. If a person repents and comes on the right path, he will be forgiven and will receive heaven. If this person does not repent but continues to go against God and off the path, then it is obvious that he is under the control of Satan and once he dies he will go to hell. |

| IM Leader | Direct Quote |
|---|---|
| Alongsiders\Wilbur | I think, for instance, even in the teachings of Jesus Christ there is so much material on the contrasting eternal states, that the only way to embrace a different view would entail a different doctrine of Scripture than is tenable, because I see that distinction [between two eternal states] there in the earliest textual witnesses. It is the only way to understand his teachings. |

God's actions in response to his plans and purposes for mankind are motivated by his love for all. This concept was mentioned repeatedly in all interviews. Alongsider Melvin framed God's actions as part of a conflict between good and evil. He said, "God's main aim and purpose is to bring good back to earth. That will only happen through extreme goodness, and he wins the conflict between good and evil through goodness." Arthur also highlighted the love of God over his wrath.

> I am very clear on these two different ideas. Of course God Almighty has the intrinsic attribute of mercy and love. Love is more highlighted than wrath. Also, as far as Islam is concerned, it has clearly said that God's mercy has won the race against his wrath. He is more most-merciful than most-wrathful. In Christianity there quite clearly are these aspects of the Lord. His mercy is vast, wide and extensive. So I don't think that the wrath is highlighted in Christianity. It is based on love.

Other types of actions on the part of God with regard to his plans and purposes for mankind are patiently and frequently showing the way, and the provision of a sacrifice. For example, Monty mentioned how a human sacrifice was needed to redeem humans, and that God provided this sacrifice in Isa. Lucas referred to the Old Testament sacrificial system as a picture of reconciliation that was climaxed in the sacrifice of Jesus. Others saw God's actions towards man more in the realm of providing instruction and models. Oliver mentioned the sending of many prophets and Isa al Masih himself. Frank noted that God's Sharia teaches us, and Paxton refers to Isa as God's provision of a model. "Some model was required," he said. "Someone was needed to whom we could refer under all these circumstances." Paxton sees God's love for mankind lived out in very practical ways in Jesus, and not just through the cross. He believes that Isa's life was a living protest to how things were going in this world. "He protested against diseases, evil spirits, and all those kinds of things. All the evils found in the world, he practically fought against them." To Paxton, Isa al Masih is our model to follow to fight against evil in this world.

OUR RESPONSE

People's response to God's plans and purposes for mankind depend, of course, on what someone believes those plans and purposes to be. The two categories of response represented in the interviews were for man to believe and submit, and for man to put faith into action. Monty represented the idea of believing and of submitting and surrendering to God.

> Man is called to the hard work of surrendering ourselves and becoming committed to him. It is only through that kind of surrendering and commitment of loyalty to Isa al Masih that mankind and others will be able to come back and enjoy that garden of God.

Man's response through faith in action by loving others is the topic in these comments in Table 12.

**Table 12:** Love others

| IM Leader | Direct Quote |
|---|---|
| S-Asia-D\Angus | He was merciful and gracious. Jesus told people to forgive each other, but we will not forgive but kill each other. "He is not a Jew, so kill him." But Jesus said, forgive. Forgive your enemies. Just as I forgive you, you forgive others. |
| S-Asia-D\Arthur | Pauline Christianity is presenting that you only need faith, and you will be saved. But actually, Paul is not saying that. Some Christians are saying that. The first step is faith. And then you are liable and duty bound to act according to your faith, to be a person so polite and so useful to society. There is the love of God, and the next thing is the love for your neighbor. Neighbor does not mean the person living next to you or relatives, but any human being. |

| IM Leader | Direct Quote |
|---|---|
| S-Asia-D\Paxton | If you follow the belief that Jesus saved me, and that everything is finished, and therefore I don't have to do anything, then definitely you don't have any ethical Christians in the world. But I think that is imperative of the truth that he loved me and saved me, that I love other people. I have to show that love, which he demonstrated in a certain way, within my means. If you stop with the narrative of what he did, then it is not following what the Bible presents as the complete picture. If God loved me so much then I have to show by my own actions that God's decision was justified. I have to respond to that love. |
| SE Asia\Ross | The purposes of Allah are for us to cover our brothers when they are weak. Do not expose their nakedness. The test is, love your enemies. |
| SE Asia\Lucas | You need to love others as yourself (paralleling that with doing the will of God). |
| Alongsiders\Wilbur | On the global scale the majority of the world is living on a moralistic basis, and not living lives of love of the type that were both commanded by Christ, exemplified by Christ, and ultimately made feasible by Christ through the whole gospel package. |

Additional faith-in-action comments were dealing with ethical living, serving your community, caring for nature, and transforming cultures. Table 13 gives a sample of those types of responses.

It is noteworthy that several of the interviewees mentioned Allah's law and his command to obey this law. Oliver mentioned the need to be righteous.

> Most of the Christians say that we are under grace, which doesn't make a lot of sense either. As a Muslim I am under the law, which I need to protect. He told me not to kill and all those things in his commandments, which are part of the law. It talks about loving your neighbor which is something that Jesus said also. And the way we think about justice can be found in the commandments of God. If you become righteous to your neighbor and righteous to your friend and righteous to your people, God will help you and he will give you his paradise. But if you do injustice to people that is a big sin.

**Table 13:** Faith in action

| IM Leader | Direct Quote |
|---|---|
| S-Asia-D\Paxton | This world has to change, not that we should be taken out of it but living in it here, transforming it in such a way that when we go over there, it suddenly does not feel alien to us, like going to a different culture that we do not understand. |
| SE Asia\Ian | We must bring influence. We must reduce the descent of moral degradation all around us in Muslim communities. |
| S-Asia-D\Angus | Producing fruit is our job and duty in front of God. Good fruit really shows that we are following God. If our deeds are not producing fruit, it shows that we are lying and not following God. |
| SE Asia\Phil | But man still has the image of God and is able to do well. Within this setting man has freedom of choice to move forward. This does not mean that man has the capacity to save ourselves from the consequences of sin, but we have the capacity to see something as good and to determine what is good and what is bad, and to move towards that. |
| SE Asia\Monty-1 | Everyone should follow the prophets' example, not just their words but also their lives. |
| SE Asia\Zach | Jesus did things with gentleness, full of love, without complaint. He went throughout the region and gave the message about the kingdom of heaven. He also performed works that met the needs of the people in the community. He showed his power to expel Satan. These categories of things are models for us for what we should be doing. |
| SE Asia\Ray | I think Isa is the best model for us. We can apply or adopt his ethics in our lives. He has very good and deep ethics, even better than those in the Torah. We can adopt his ethics to relate to our neighbors. I hope we can be a good person when we adopt his ethics and values. |
| SE Asia\Ross | We love our community, and the community feels loved by us. But our river is still polluted; people are still polluted even with their seemingly Islamic and religious slogan. There are still drugs and drug users. There is pornography. We are to be reformers. We want to live sacrificially for this. |

| IM Leader | Direct Quote |
|---|---|
| SE Asia\Zach | This free will has to be served to God. In the ideal sense, this takes self-sacrifice and surrender, so we do not get pulled off to the way of exercising free will as the world sees it. We have to wage a war against our flesh, as Paul called it. |
| S-Asia-D\Arthur | But Christianity is a faith, and then according to your faith you have actions and words. Your words need to testify of your faith. If you are injuring God's creation, you are not keeping faith in God. |
| Alongsiders\Melvin | I would say that is the main metanarrative of what his purpose is, how he brings that about in creation, and to mankind finally fully submitting to his will, and learning to live a life of full submission to him, and understanding the principles laid out in Matthew 5, 6, and 7, and to a greater extent across the Bible. As mankind fully submits to that we will see things happening like we see in Revelation, the whole earth is lightened with his glory as we learn to follow the Lamb wherever he goes. |

Arthur made an interesting comment about faith in action versus just believing.

> The Jewish emphasis was on actions and acts. And the Christian emphasis is on faith. It is untrue. The Christians and Jews and Muslims actually all should focus on faith, and then on action according to your faith, to prove that you are really faithful. For example, when people accused Jesus of changing the law, he said that he was there to complete the law, not to abolish it. We have this from Jesus. Then how in the world can someone say to just believe and then go to heaven. It has nothing to do with that.

## Our Freedom of Choice

The question of how an individual's freedom of choice relates to Allah's plans and purposes for that individual brought out the fact that all of the IM leaders believe that man has a choice in his response to God. We have a free will and, with that, the full responsibility to choose God or not, according to all. Brad's reply was characteristic of all others as he pointed out that Allah does not force people in their choice to follow him or not.

> Yes [we have freedom of choice], because Allah does not force anybody to choose even the right thing. In fact, Allah never forces people to choose the wrong thing. He gives them the choice, he shows them the path, and then asks them with love to follow his path, so that they can be saved. Otherwise every person has his or her own choice whether to follow that or not.

Only a few interviewees had some additional comments. Axel mentioned that Allah is sovereign and all-powerful, and if he wanted to, he could "turn people on the right path." I explained that some people believe that Allah does that. Allah determines who will go to heaven and who will go to hell, and we do not have free will, according to that viewpoint. Axel replied, "I cannot say that. That is like a *kafir*, blaspheming God, that he is playing with us, and that we are nothing and can do nothing. He gave us free will to choose the right or wrong path." Gus (an IM leader from Central Asia) was the only one who included theological labels. He said, "I am Arminian. I have a big problem with Calvinism. People have a free will and a choice."

Ross made a comment about God deciding what happens to us now and into eternity, but that was in the context of God loving us all before we were born and after we die.

> God has decided to love us even before we were in the womb of our mothers. Eternity means that we are in God's plan. He has decided before we were in the womb of our mothers. Now we must reflect God's plan. [What happens to us] after we die also is [in] God's plan.

Andy was the one person who came the closest to expressing a doctrine of election, but more with the idea of being chosen or elected to be a blessing to others versus chosen in the soteriological sense.

> Well, with God's choosing, when I came to the Lord I never knew that I am the one. I am the first believer from my language community. But now I believe that God chose me to be a witness for my people. Not only is my household saved, my brothers and sisters and mother, etc., as in being the chosen one, but we should bless people.

> God chose us, like the Jewish concept for today. They are the chosen people, but God loves everyone, which is why he sent Jesus. God chose one person or one group to bless everyone around them.

Only two of the IM leaders indicated some tension between man's freedom of choice and God's sovereignty when it comes to personal salvation. Jason accepted that there is a contradiction in concepts, and Lucas resolved the tension by referring to God's foreknowledge about who from all people throughout the ages would be the ones to be saved.

Mitch believes in man's freedom of choice but pointed out some cultural aspects of that personal freedom. He has seen that in the movement, people are coming to faith in groups. They are following the practice that everyone who gets baptized is asked to make the decision to follow Isa al Masih personally as well. Mitch further shared that freedom of choice is a relative term for women in their culture. He said that in a Muslim family, if the wife goes against the decision of the husband, she would not be considered a good person. Women are dependent on the men.

> Especially in Muslim families the wives are not that free or independent. No matter how strongly, how nicely, how simply we teach them, I have found no wife that says, "My husband wants to follow Isa al Masih, but I am not." Culturally this is difficult. Even in the educated families this is difficult. Our women depend 100 percent on men.

Among the five alongsiders, Josh, Melvin, and Tyler expressed a clear view in support of man's freedom of choice to trust in God or not. Kevin and Wilbur keep man's free will and God's sovereignty a mystery. Kevin said, "This is one of those places where I think the Bible is very clearly Reformed and very clearly also Wesleyan, all at once." Wilbur commented on the observation that most insiders are Wesleyan, to use Kevin's term—that from an Islamic worldview they would have no difficulty with the double predestination position, but upon reflection as they consider the spiritual condition of basically everyone they know, they land in the Wesleyan camp. Wilbur commented on their emotional and intellectual process.

It is inconceivable to them that the only difference between them and everyone else they know is an eternal decree that is specific to the individual level. That is emotionally untenable if not also equally a stumbling block intellectually for them. I think they are much more likely, upon reflection, to come out at a different place, one that favors free will over the decreeing of individuals' destinies.

About Heaven and Hell

The discussion about heaven and hell was an interesting and revealing part of the interview. I introduced the topic with the question, "How does your understanding of heaven and hell fit within the bigger picture of Allah's plans and purposes?" I was especially interested in their viewpoints on hell. Is it an actual place somewhere? Does it last forever? Who goes there? When is that decision final?

The comments about hell in Table 14 are representative of the belief among the majority of interviewees that hell is a real place somewhere that lasts forever.

**Table 14:** Hell forever

| IM Leader | Direct Quote |
|---|---|
| S-Asia-A\Andy | This world is the punishment area that God placed Adam in, and heaven will be the kingdom of God. This here is the kingdom of humans; we are living in the kingdom of humans, so this concept of heaven and hell being experienced in the here and now is different and does not make sense. |
| S-Asia-A\Howard | I don't know where Jesus is talking about that kind of heaven and hell in the Bible. Muslims do think about heaven and hell in this world. They think that when you get punishment, this means that you are in hell, in this world. Likewise, when you are happy, you are in heaven. But as a follower of Jesus we don't have that concept. |
| C-Asia\Julius | Yes, in our Muslim concept, heaven and hell are eternal places. |
| C-Asia\Jason | This is a place where God is not present and there is eternal torture. There is punishment without a time limit. It is for eternity. You cannot stop it. It is a very scary place and people do not want to be there. |

| IM Leader | Direct Quote |
|---|---|
| S-Asia-B\Mitch | In our teaching hell is forever. Once I am there, there is no way to come out. |
| Africa\Arnold | He who chooses to follow Satan here on earth will ultimately follow him in hell. |
| Africa\Oliver | My basic understanding is that both heaven and hell are existing. They are there. And God created them for a purpose. Both are everlasting. |
| S-Asia-D\Frank | We see hell along with heaven. The two go together. The people that do not follow God's plan and do not follow Jesus obviously are going to hell, which is forever. |
| S-Asia-D\Paxton | I personally believe that if someone decides to go to hell, then God respects that person's decision, and he sends him to that place where he wants to go. Perhaps it is not the duration that matters but the kind of sin or crime we have committed. If that sin is against the holy nature of God, and he exists from eternity, then we have to be deprived through eternity from his presence. I don't find any injustice in that concept. |
| SE Asia\Monty-1 | Those who reject him are also rejected by God in the end days, so they have to have a separate place. |
| SE Asia\Lucas | I see hell as the judgment of God on those who do not believe and receive that provision of God. |
| SE Asia\Silas | At this time, mankind is tested to determine the way, or the street, for life in the coming age. |
| SE Asia\Kent | Death is a transitional period from life to the other world, and it is a transition into eternity. |
| SE Asia\Stuart | Hell is pictured as a place where there is fire which continuously flames without stopping. |
| S-Asia-C\Axel | And if you are not with God, that is hell for you, forever. |
| C-Asia\Gus | I used to believe that when believers die, or unbelievers, that they go to a storage area called heaven or hell. Now I believe that these are not storage/waiting areas but eternal ones. |
| S-Asia-D\Angus | People who do not accept Jesus and who do not follow his teaching will go there. Yes, hell lasts forever. People will scream and gnash their teeth in the fire. They will remember their previous life and say, I wish. The place of punishment that God has prepared, we may call hell or the unending fire, which is definitely there. |
| SE Asia\Ray | Is hell forever? Of course forever. Yes. |

| IM Leader | Direct Quote |
|---|---|
| Alongsiders\Wilbur | Yes, hell is forever, as I understand the language of Scripture, the eyewitnesses' report, Jesus speaking of it. Yes, I have looked carefully at some of these other nuances on this, whether there is annihilation. I don't think we get there exegetically. I think that that becomes attractive to us, or that becomes possible for us by means other than exegetical ones. |
| Alongsiders\Josh-1 | From what I see in Scripture, it looks like hell is an actual place. |

There were several alternative views about hell. Four interviewees (Paxton, Phil, Zach, and Ray) made reference to the concept of hell being experienced here on earth already. Ray said, "Hell here means that there is no joy, and there is no peace, and they always fight each other. In families without God's will, we can see that they live in trouble."

Arthur does not see hell as a place out there somewhere but as a human condition of sorrow in this world.

> Actually heaven and hell are both our names for happiness or sorrow. If you lose the soul and have no faith, no satisfaction, not anything you rely on, then you are infected with perplexity, perturbed, and you have no peace or serenity in your mind, heart, and body. Hell is sorrow that a human being gets in this world. I do not believe it is a place somewhere in space where some people go.

Alongsider Kevin still is wrestling with the concept of hell. "I tend to see that as the state of being for those of us who simply continue to elect to not cooperate with what God is trying to do," he said. He does not believe in a literal house of punishment, and he also does not believe hell is an existence absent from God, because he is convinced that any created being would simply cease to exist without God. Kevin concluded, "The absence of his relational presence and what that means for being alive in the true sense of that term—that to me is hell."

The last alternative view of hell is held by Homer, Brad, and alongsider Melvin, who see hell as a future event here on earth but not as a place of punishment that lasts forever. They believe that the cleansing of the earth by fire is God's termination of all evil including Satan, demons, and all unbelievers. Brad said, "For sinners, I understand that this fire will consume them, and they cease to exist." This annihilation also applies to Satan and demons. Alongsider Melvin connects this view with the triumph of God's love.

> I don't see an eternal hellfire being consistent with the love of God. It does not fit within my framework and understanding of the immense love God has for us, to have a place where people would be tortured forever and ever and ever. If you look at Revelation and the fire and torment going forever and ever, I see this as metaphorical language saying that sin is no more, evil is no more. There is a triumph of God's love. This is how I would see most of those eternal texts. It is metaphorically saying, it is over, it is done.

Who goes to hell or experiences hell? The following terms were used for those who are heading for hell. People who:

- are not followers of Isa al Masih
- oppose Isa al Masih
- do not believe in Isa al Masih
- reject the sacrifice of Jesus as the Lamb as the only way to come to salvation
- die outside Jesus
- follow Satan and demons
- disobey
- do not follow God's plan and Jesus
- go down the wrong path or way
- do not put their faith in Christ
- do not take the mercy from Allah and Isa
- are not named in the book of life

Several people gave some additional qualifiers. For example, Andy mentioned that God will count those people who never heard about Jesus and how to be saved as innocent, and that they will not go to hell. He added, "I am not saying that they will go to the kingdom of God, but I don't know where they will go." To him heaven and hell are for us who have heard of the good news. Monty likewise believes that hell is for those who knowingly do not follow Isa. He commented, "We realize that from the religion of Christianity many will end up in hell when they die, as will be the case of many people from Islam."

Phil defended his view of the existence of hell as fitting with the justice of God. He said, "God is fair and just. It is not that any one of us deserves heaven, we all deserve hell." Five people explicitly said that they believe that most people will suffer punishment in hell, as indicated in Table 15.

**Table 15:** Most people to hell

| IM Leader | Direct Quote |
|---|---|
| C-Asia\Julius | From my view, it seems that a lot of people do not follow Isa al Masih. But, I do not know. |
| C-Asia\Jason | I would say so, that most people will go to hell, and that is why we need to call all Christians to spread the good news. |
| Africa\Oliver | Those who don't obey God, those who don't follow him, those who do evil things, those who shed blood, those who are against God and his people will go to hell. Even the Qur'an says that most of the Jews, Christians, and Muslims are wrong. I understand that the majority will inherit hell instead of heaven. |
| Africa\Brad | Most people will be part of the punishment, and fewer people will be part of heaven, according to my understanding of the Scriptures. |
| Alongsiders\Wilbur | I would fully expect that he will make sure that everyone knows that they are invited to the party. It is also very clear that many will decline the offer. The majority of the people in the world will go to hell. I don't see the majority of people living today on planet earth living lives of love. I take that as an indication again that many have been called, but few have been saved, at least as I look at the world scene. |

Regarding heaven, most interviewees expressed a belief in heaven as a place where believers and followers of Isa al Masih go forever, as expressed by Homer.

> I think God is in heaven. God lives in heaven. His seat is in heaven. His throne is in heaven. I believe that God has prepared heaven as a good place where all those who are committed to him and are faithful to him will go and be with Jesus.

As with hell, several interviewees expressed some alternative views about heaven. Angus emphasized that heaven is only spiritual because God does not place importance on physical things here on earth, proven according to Angus by the fact that David was not allowed to build a temple for God. Paxton, who looks to Jesus as our model to follow here on earth, looks for heaven on earth and considers it in part as our responsibility as we work out the salvation of this world.

> God must bring heaven to earth. If he cannot do that, he should not expect us to go to heaven. If that situation is not created in this world, and a whole person with all his emotions and sentiments, his feelings, and everything has to be fulfilled in him; I'm not in favor of saving the souls and losing the bodies, but in saving the whole person, whatever he is composed of. To me going to heaven is not the ideal thing. What is ideal is that God is omnipresent, he is working in this world, and he wants to change this world into an ideal state. If the main thing is that you have to get out of this world, then in that way, Jesus cannot be my model, I am very sorry to say. Let us hope something, which certainly does not seem to be attainable, that it is our responsibility to work out the salvation of the world in a practical manner. At the same time we also have to look at history, what we've done so far. We have failed miserably. So you cannot expect without the help of God that we will be able to achieve that, although it is a very good purpose. We need some kind of divine intervention.

**Table 16:** Connection between this world and heaven

| Alongsider | Direct Quote |
| --- | --- |
| Alongsiders\Josh-1 | I think of course that God is on the side of goodness. God is on the side of virtue. He works to see the best things happen because he loves us now and he loves us later. He loves his creation now, and he loves it into eternity. |

| Alongsider | Direct Quote |
|---|---|
| Alongsiders\Kevin | I probably lean towards some kind of transformation of what we now know as the world. There will be some kind of connection with it, but I'm not sure if it's just the making a lot better of what we already see. It seems to me that the whole idea of heaven and the long-term future is somehow more than just the gradual transformation and sanctification of what we see. For me it is somewhere in between the long gradual transformation and the sudden dramatic breaking in of something totally other. Somewhere in between, or maybe a mix of both of those. |
| Alongsiders\Tyler | In other places, like at the end of Revelation, heaven seems to be a physical place in a different sense, because the earth is re-burned, it is almost like the earth is re-cleaned around it—instead of with the flood, this time with fire. It is a new heaven and a new earth, but it has a connectedness with the old somehow. It has been re-purified. |

In table 16, three of the alongsiders expressed some connection between this world and heaven.

Others preferred to express heaven as something that we can experience now partially here on earth and more fully once we get there. Table 17 shows those comments.

**Table 17:** Heaven now and later

| IM Leader | Direct Quote |
|---|---|
| S-Asia-D\Paxton | Yes, some bring heaven and hell into the present, but at the same time we cannot bring it completely. That is the problem. We have to wait for something. |
| SE Asia\Phil | In one sense heaven and hell are in the future, as locations, but in another sense they already are beginning to be an experience in the current day. |
| SE Asia\Lucas | Heaven is the place but also the condition of enjoying a restored fellowship with God after having been made holy. |
| SE Asia\Zach | A person does not become perfect immediately, but there is a process of him growing, becoming more and more perfect during your lifetime, being transformed. In that process the concept of heaven is not just something in the future that starts later, but in a sense colors our experiences now. |

| IM Leader | Direct Quote |
|---|---|
| SE Asia\Ray | In the Injil we read Jesus saying, "The kingdom of God is at hand." He also teaches his followers to pray, "Let your kingdom come on earth as it is in heaven," so I think there are two aspects, physical and spiritual. To go to the spiritual kingdom, we have to go through a physical kingdom. The physical kingdom means that we have to follow his teaching while living on the earth. In other words, the kingdom of God is accessible now but it is not perfect yet. Later, when we are face-to-face with him, we can feel the kingdom of God perfectly. |
| Alongsiders\Josh-1 | Heaven is wherever people come under the lordship of Christ and the reign of God, so it has no physical location. It is in part present now, when people know Jesus, and it will be more complete at the end of time. |
| Alongsiders\Melvin | I would say that having healthy societies is the main goal. I see an eschatological salvation and a salvation here and now. |

Who will be part of heaven? Everyone said that believers or followers of Isa al Masih will be part of heaven. The following additional terms were used for those who will be part of heaven. People who:

- accepted Isa and pleased God
- follow Jesus
- live according to the light that they know, whether they have heard of the name of Christ or not
- never had a chance to hear about Isa al Masih
- accept Jesus as their only Savior and Messiah
- receive Jesus and become sons and daughters of God
- are obedient
- are called the holy ones
- find a way to Jesus
- take the mercy of Allah, who take Isa as Redeemer
- live according to the good path
- follow God

Mitch and Paxton believe that apostasy is possible. Mitch said that once you accept Jesus as your Savior and Lord, you have to remain in that faith every day. He specified, "You can fall out, if you want. You can reject Jesus and go out somewhere." Paxton admitted that, theoretically speaking, individuals can lose their salvation. He finds that adherence to the phrase "once saved, always saved" produces a type of Jesus follower who thinks that it does not matter what kind of life they live. I did not specifically ask the question about possible apostasy to everyone, so I do not know whether the views of Mitch and Paxton on this topic are representative.

Howard gave a hint that maybe all will be part of heaven when he said, "I know that Jesus will come again. When he comes again, God will have a big plan again for how he will save all human beings." Arthur believes that all will receive God's mercy—maybe even Lucifer.

> Isa al Masih will come back, and he will fill the world with justice and peace and love. At that time my heart says, I have no evidence, the Lord will forgive all. Hallelujah. Until this last judgment we are all still in process. We will all be there. And all may get the blessing, and mercy and grace. Even Lucifer will get it, maybe. It is abundant, abundant! A great sea of mercy.

I was able to ask most interviewees whether they thought that a person's point of death is the last possibility to affect the eternal destiny for that person. Is our death the fork in the road? Practically everyone answered this question in the affirmative, meaning that we need to make our choice for God and Isa al Masih before we die, otherwise hell is our punishment. Paxton thinks that a second-chance notion will only corrupt people. "Once we die we have missed the boat. Then no other chance can be given to us." Alongsider Wilbur does not support an alternative view because it would undermine the urgency of the redemptive mandate.

> The Scripture utterly precludes the possibility that because God's magnanimity is going to overwhelm even the most calloused and rebellious heart, it is more or less no big deal what we do with the redemptive mandate. There is no support in Scripture for that position. Quite the contrary, I think there is a tremendous urgency.

On the other hand, Ross emphasized the power of Jesus over the living and the dead. He believes that a message that if you did not accept Jesus before you died, Jesus' hands are tied is a weak message. "After you die, Jesus is not Lord anymore? He is powerless if he does not have power after you die," according to Ross. Arthur believes that death is the beginning of hope for everyone as they experience Allah's abundant mercy. Alongsider Kevin also has some openness to the possibility of repentance and change after death.

> It seems that most of Scripture would push one to have to conclude that there is not an ongoing choice that can be made, but I see things like in the book of Revelation, the tree whose leaves are for the healing of the nations. If everything is all done, and everything is finalized, then why is there a need for a tree whose leaves are for the healing of the nations? I wonder if there are hints there of some kind of ongoing process that continues. I am a little bit more open-minded about that than I used to be. I think there may very well be some ongoing opportunity for repentance and change.

## Revelation

Part of the interview guide was focused on God's revelation to his creation. I asked about prophets, the Scriptures, the Qur'an, and how God is revealing himself to the interviewee today.

### Prophets

The question about how Allah reveals himself through the prophets resulted in some basic responses. Most interviewees said that prophets revealed Allah through words and miracles after Allah first revealed himself to them. "They reveal what they know about God," Lucas said. They often had a message to correct or rebuke people. "God chose people whose lives are holy to be used by God to rebuke mankind," Kent said. Alongsider Kevin refers to prophets as people who somehow grasp the character of God at a deep, visceral, gut-feeling level and see the world as God perhaps sees it, and then reflect that in what they say or in their own life experiences. Paxton described prophets as God's mouthpiece, but not in the sense of a tape recorder. Andy mentioned, "Prophets can commit sins because they are humans like us." Basically prophets were sent by Allah out of mercy, to correct us back to the right path, according to Axel. Arnold mentioned the contextual aspect of each prophet. "These people wrote in their own culture what they understood this thought inspiration from Allah to be." He does not believe that their writing is perfect. "Maybe it is a perfect message written in an imperfect language of human beings," he added. I did not ask specifically about Mohammed but Phil mentioned that it is important to share the chronology of the prophets with Muslims, ending in God's revelation of himself in Jesus. This will bring up the question in their mind what would be the purpose of yet another prophet.

Andy was the only one that explicitly said in response to the question about prophets in general that he believes that Mohammed was not a prophet. Since I did not ask interviewees specifically how they see Mohammed, I cannot make any further inferences from that comment for the rest of the interviewees, but it is interesting to observe how Mohammed was spoken about throughout the interviews. A lexical search of the transcripts reveals that the word *Mohammed* was used 127 times. Most of them occur in their sharing of personal testimonies. Table 18 includes various statements about Mohammed that relate to the current theological or missional understanding of the interviewee with regard to Mohammed. Almost all have a positive view of Mohammed.

**Table 18:** Mohammed

| IM Leader | Direct Quote |
|---|---|
| S-Asia-A\Andy | I think Mohammed was influenced by some of the Catholic people. Then he wrote the guidebook, but he was using many understandings from the Bible. |
| S-Asia-A\Howard | I do not believe that the Qur'an is a holy book. It is written by Mohammed, and he was not a prophet in my concept. He was a man and he had Christian and Jewish friends from whom he learned. He was mixing all this information and made his own law that controls the Arabs and Muslims. |
| S-Asia-C\Axel | As an insider it means that I can go to the mosque and pray with them. I like the way they pray, not the way we pray in church. I used to go to church, but I don't go now. I don't want to recite the same things that I used to recite before. I don't want to repeat again and again that I believe Mohammed is the prophet and so on. I don't want to worship like that. I don't have any problem going to the mosque, but I don't believe that is the only way to worship. |

| IM Leader | Direct Quote |
|---|---|
| Africa\Oliver | Even according to Islam, the majority of the Islamic scholars say that Islam is not a religion but a message. Islam is listening to the message of God and the Word of God, hearing him and obeying him. But after Mohammed died, peace be upon him, his disciples also changed. There was conflict, like the way the Catholics and Reformed Church had a conflict, we have Shiite and Sunni. |
| Africa\Oliver | Every culture will misinterpret the text in the way they want to understand it. The Qur'an is like that as well. It is written in Arabic. The message was revealed through Mohammed, *Aleh Salam*, and he gave it to his people. |
| Africa\Homer | God revealed himself to the prophets, and the prophets reveal to us who God is. The prophet Mohammed, in a contextual manner when I share with Muslims, I have to recognize him. The Bible says, all truth is God's truth, so whatever truth is in the Qur'an that can lead to the knowledge of God, we determine it as God's truth. Even Mohammed himself could not have placed that truth in the Qur'an without God's knowledge. It was God's work to have that truth in there, to make those people finally see the right way of God. |
| Africa\Homer | God might have used Mohammed in whatever he preached to his people. He might have used him. |
| Africa\Homer | The prophet Mohammed is asked by God to follow the faith of Abraham. All Muslims are being called to be followers of Abraham. Therefore we teach them that they have to follow all the Scriptures and all the prophets. |
| Africa\Homer | I told you about those who have not accepted baptism. That is a theological matter. They say that the prophet Mohammed did not do baptisms; therefore we do not perform baptisms either. We follow the Scriptures because the prophet Mohammed also followed all previous Scriptures, but since he was not baptized, they don't believe in baptism either. |

| IM Leader | Direct Quote |
|---|---|
| S-Asia-D\Frank | There are no problems as we continue to learn together and teach each other and welcome outsiders as well, but as the broader society starts to learn more about us and what we teach, and how our theology is different—for example, they say there's God, Mohammed, and all the prophets, and we say there is God, Jesus, and nothing else—then there will be more problems of different sorts as this becomes more public knowledge. A lot of people ask us, "Do you accept Mohammed?" And we say, yes, we accept him, but he himself never said that he was a savior, a salvation giver. There are all sorts of prophets and gurus and this is just another one. There are thousands of them. But he never said that he was a savior. |
| S-Asia-D\Arthur | In the end, from Jordan, King Abdullah II started the Common Word and I joined that. I said, "The Prophet's prodigy, 41 generations later, king of Jordan, the only kingdom on earth that belonged to the prophet Mohammed, peace be upon him, I am with him. If he says that interfaith is good, then I will say that it is good." |
| S-Asia-D\Arthur | I cannot understand the Qur'an without the Injil because it is referenced in the Qur'an. The Tawrat is referenced in the Qur'an as well. If I don't read those books and if I believe that those books are lost in no man's land, then where did Mohammed, peace be upon him, get these references? We have to be realistic. |
| S-Asia-D\Arthur | I believe that the Qur'an is pro-Christ. Mohammed, peace be upon him, was pro-Christ. This means that he was a supporter of the Christ. In another way, I am actually going to prove that Muslims are pro-Christ Muslims. Early Jews could be Christian, so how can Muslims who came 600 years later not be pro-Christ Muslims as well? The Qur'an is debating about Christ, and there is a continuous train of memoirs of Jesus Christ from the beginning to the end. That proves that Mohammed, peace be upon him, was mending his own community, Arabia, who were fixed in a quagmire of polytheism, taking them to the oneness of God, which was the brief from the Christians and the Jews. But unfortunately, it has been hijacked. |
| SE Asia\Ian | Mohammed said, "I and Isa are close friends." By saying things like that we can get people to have a greater interest in meditating on Scripture reading, and it will begin to take power in their lives. |

| IM Leader | Direct Quote |
|---|---|
| SE Asia\Drew | When people compare Jesus with Mohammed I think we are underestimating Jesus. We are decreasing his status as the Son of God to Mohammed's level. I think that if these two people would live together at this time, they would not fight together. When Christians ask me about what I feel about Mohammed I say, obviously I did not start out being a university student. We all need to go through elementary and secondary school first. I am a university student now and Jesus is my professor, but when I was in elementary school Mohammed was my teacher, yet I don't find any of his teaching contradicting the teachings of Jesus. Jesus explains more about what Mohammed is talking about but they're not contradicting. There's nothing wrong with believing in Mohammed because it does not affect your salvation. At the same time, there is no obligation for Christians to believe in Mohammed. If you don't want to believe Mohammed, that is okay since you already have Jesus. Yes, there are some Muslims who convert to Christianity and who hate Mohammed, but for me, I want to serve my friends and I want to respect their beliefs, and a central figure of Islam is Mohammed. I don't find that this goes against the teachings of Jesus. |
| SE Asia\Ross | The prophet Mohammed, a sinner chosen by God, wrote to confirm that the Tawrat, Zabur, and Injil are guidance from God and light from God. Mohammed points to God's plan that is not coming through because of the rebellion of man. The solution to carry out his plans is sending Jesus Christ, his Son, the Son of God. This is very normal, that God sent his Son to remind his deviating children to go home. |
| SE Asia\Ross | The prophet Mohammed points to Jesus. Today people say that the prophet Mohammed only points to himself, but this is distorted. There is a difference between a distorted Islamic community and an idealistic Islamic community, the way it should be. The holy Quran says that this community should be looking forward to the second coming of Jesus. |

| IM Leader | Direct Quote |
|---|---|
| SE Asia\Monty | Mohammed says that there is no god but God, moving away from polytheism and paganism to monotheism. The Qur'an calls people back to the monotheism of the former days of Adam. The one thing that Mohammed did not understand was the concept of *Kalaam*, or the word. But in the Qur'an he actually talks about the Word of God coming forth in the form of a man. He didn't tell this to the people of God because there were two things that were worrisome. The first is that the Jews rejected Jesus as the Messiah. God could not come as a man. And the second thing is that this man who came was not the kind of Messiah they were waiting for. These two misconceptions of the Jews also had influence on Mohammed. Even though there was a revelation of Jesus as a miracle worker, a prophet, and apostle, there is no additional higher Christology in the Qur'an, because of these two misconceptions of the Jews. These two things still remain as some of the biggest obstacles. When we come with the story of Jesus, it takes a long time for a Muslim to accept that. We must ask for special powers of Christ to bring about this effect. |
| SE Asia\Monty-2 | One of our principles is to never insult the prophet Mohammed. |
| SE Asia\Zach | Mohammed was a type of missionary to the Arab world with his teaching. |
| SE Asia\Stuart | The Qur'an is a revelation of God given to the prophet Mohammed [he gives SAW at the end, respectfully— *sallallahu alayhi wasallam*, or "peace be upon him"]. |
| Alongsiders\Josh-1 | I would believe too, though, that even if it [the Qur'an] were not inspired by God in a sense that he was speaking these words to Mohammed, I think it could be that God in his sovereignty and mercy made sure that certain things were in there as a record of himself. This is kind of the redemptive analogy idea. |
| Alongsiders\Josh-2 | As they read the Bible and do self-theologizing, they are revaluing or marginalizing certain things. By revaluing I mean, and this is the most obvious one, the place of Mohammed and the place of the Qur'an; they could never be Muslims and outright reject the Qur'an or Mohammed. They would never speak ill of Mohammed. I can hear it in my mind's eye people saying, "Yeah, Mohammed is good, yeah, yeah," but then they get quickly talking about some of the other prophets, including Jesus. |

| IM Leader | Direct Quote |
|---|---|
| Alongsiders\Kevin | I see the Qur'an as a communication that continues to participate in that narrative. I would put it and Mohammed in a very similar category in a sense that I think that there are clearly places where he seems to have spoken out of a deep experience of the character of God, and he is participating in the biblical narrative, particularly where he is retelling biblical stories with a view towards applying them in his context and environment, and in some cases in his personal life. I think he is very much participating in that same process. |
| Alongsiders\Kevin | We began to talk about the prophethood of Mohammed among the leaders. This seems to be one of those areas where there are leaders with different views within the movement. |
| Alongsiders\Kevin | Andy and Howard have a pretty negative view of Mohammed, and of the potential for seeing him as a prophet. The kinds of views these two hold about Mohammed are never going to be accepted as a Muslim movement, if that is what they are teaching. But, what they have said is that this is not what they are teaching others. To me this is an open question for the self-theologizing process. |
| Alongsiders\Tyler | Both Mohammed and the Qur'an had a positive role towards monotheism. |
| Alongsiders\Tyler | They have an internal lingo that they develop between them that is quite beautiful and innovative, to preserve the faithful core of individuals and of groups. That's why they never talk negatively about Mohammed or the Qur'an. I cannot see anything positive to be gained from it. |

THE SCRIPTURES

The lead question on the Scriptures was, "How would you describe the status of the Scriptures?" and an additional clarifying question was, "Are the Scriptures a rule book or God's narrative story, or something else?" Most replied that the Scriptures primarily are God's narrative story. Arnold's reply is representative of these responses. He said, "I think it is kind of a narrative story of God telling us about God's relationship with human beings throughout history. It is not a kind of, do this and do that, don't do this and don't do that." Others added some qualifiers. Alongsider Melvin sees the Scriptures as a casebook, and Frank said that the Bible is full of stories, and that some of them are not necessarily complete, but that they are in there as much as is necessary for us the reader. Ross likes to think of the Bible as a set of love letters and not as a rule book or a constitution that must be obeyed.

As Table 19 shows, thirteen IM leaders mentioned that the Scriptures are a guide for right living on the right path.

**Table 19:** The Scriptures as a guide

| IM Leader | Direct Quote |
|---|---|
| S-Asia-A\Andy | The whole book is the Word of God, about how God wants us to be and how he wants this world to be. |
| S-Asia-A\Howard | The Word of God is a guide. It is giving explanations about how to live. |
| Africa\Oliver | Allah and his prophets and the text show us the righteous things we're supposed to do. |
| Africa\Brad | I believe that the holy Scripture, meaning the Bible, is the true Word of God that guides us. |
| S-Asia-D\Frank | It is God's word. There are also God's commands and God's Sharia, and the path of salvation. |
| SE Asia\Ross | The Scriptures contain what God says, his guidance. It is not low. I cannot put the Scriptures on the ground. It is our guidance to be what God wants us to be. It is a source for guidance. |
| SE Asia\Ross | So I see the Scriptures not as my doctrine. The book of God has the power to guide. |
| SE Asia\Phil | These are the words of God that are written. It is the guide that brings people in the way of salvation. It is the only guide. |
| SE Asia\Phil | It is a book that includes pointers towards the way, towards traveling the right way to God. It is not only about the future perspective, about where we end up, but it is about the process of following that way all the way forward from now. |
| SE Asia\Monty-1 | We have a view of the Scriptures as a guide for us, so that we can know how to get close to God. We can hear his voice, and then our faith can grow from the Scriptures. |
| SE Asia\Lucas | In a bigger sense I view it as a guide and a teacher. The best term to use is thinking of it as a guide for our lives. |
| SE Asia\Ray | It is guidance from God for humans. |
| SE Asia\Stuart | The holy book is the Word of God that guides mankind to pursue goodness. |

Others highlighted the fact that the messages in the Bible were given in a given cultural context at a specific time in history, and that not each word but the meaning in context is the inspired message. Ray's response is an example of this group of responses.

> I think that Allah revealed himself to humans by using human culture. He used human language. We have to understand the words and what they meant at the time they were spoken. We cannot generalize it through many centuries. Also we cannot generalize across cultures. We have to understand the meaning of the term when God revealed it in that context.

Paxton added the comment, "The message is infallible to the extent any language can be infallible." Angus also focused on the meaning of a passage over the words when he said, "It is not like a mantra. There is no value in just reading the words." Homer pointed out that the text is not straight from heaven. "In time I came to learn that these were not the original words but that God inspired people to write, and therefore it may not be 100 percent."

Silas, Lucas, and Kent all used the phrase "breathed out by God" in reference to the Scriptures. Silas said, "The holy book, or books, is a book of which its content is revealed and breathed out by God." Other comments that interviewees made about the Bible were that it is thought-inspired, reliable, truthful, metaphorical, and for all of humanity. Oliver makes an interesting observation about the status of the Word of God beyond words to read.

> In the Qur'an it talks about the fact that no one can change the Word of God. The Word of God is everlasting. I do understand that it is not just a written thing. It is faith in Allah. It does not matter whether you read or not, it is faith. Abraham was there not reading but just listening to God in faith. I think our faith is very important over just reading a book or a text or whatever it is.

### The Qur'an

After discussing the status of the Tawrat, Zabur, and Injil, the next question in the interview always was, "What status do you give to the Qur'an?" The responses can be grouped in three categories, as illustrated in Figure 4.

Most find the Qur'an compatible with the Bible. Many expressed this compatibility by saying that there are pointer in the Qur'an back to the previous books and Jesus. A few responders included a cautionary note about the Qur'an.

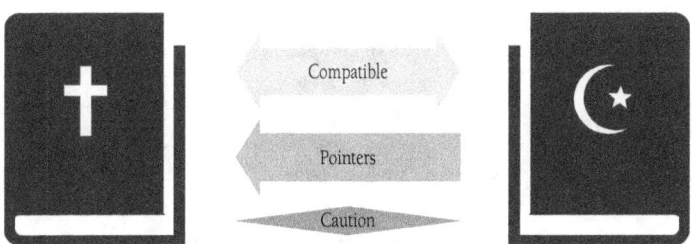

**Figure 4:** The Qur'an versus the Bible

"I believe the Qur'an is a book that Allah has revealed," Axel said. He sees it as a good book, and he also said that the Qur'an and Allah are not against anything, implying that they are not against the Scriptures. Arthur promotes the Qur'an as a record from the people in Arabia when they were thinking about Judaism and Christianity. "Why should we destroy it or hate it?" he said. He supports an interpretation of the Qur'an that brings God's people near to one another for the good of humanity and culture. Ray sees the Bible and the Qur'an as very similar. He said, "Some will say that the Qur'an is different from the Tawrat, Zabur, and Injil, but for me, because of the process of canonization, the Qur'an and the Bible are similar." I asked him what he does when he perceives conflicts between the Injil and the Qur'an. He replied that he reinterprets.

> I will try to reinterpret the text. Within the Qur'an there are some contradictions. Within the Bible there are also some contradictions. Some Muslims say, "The Bible is corrupted because there are many contradictions in it." But they forget that there are many contradictions in the Qur'an as well. So, to reconcile the differences between the Bible and the Qur'an, I will reinterpret.

Ray also shared that he believes that God never said that he would stop revealing himself to humans. Stuart calls the Qur'an a revelation of

God given to the prophet Mohammed. He included the honorific *sallallahu alayhi wasallam* to show respect to Mohammed.

There were various other statements by interviewees on the compatibility between the Qur'an and the Bible. Table 20 has a representative set of comments on this compatibility.

**Table 20:** Qur'an compatible with Bible

| IM Leader | Direct Quote |
|---|---|
| S-Asia-C\Axel | My understanding is that the Quran does not contradict the Injil, if you read it in your own way, not the way taught in the madrasahs or by other teachers. |
| C-Asia\Gus | He directed or allowed Islam to come, which is mostly compatible with the Bible. Nothing in the Qur'an is blatantly against the Bible. Someone could interpret it in a way that it is against the Bible, but each sura starts with, "In the name of the most merciful and 'wishing-good' God." That is the hermeneutical theme of the Qur'an. |
| S-Asia-D\Angus | There are many things in the Quran that are mentioned, but only briefly and not fully. |
| S-Asia-D\Arthur | We need more acceptance. The Qur'an, the Injil, the Tawrat, second Tawrat, the Psalms. We should put them all together in one place. If we really want peace, we have to respect all the Scriptures. We need a preaching system not by a father [i.e., pastor, priest] but by a mullah, who takes the Qur'an and speaks openly, holding the Qur'an in one hand and the Bible in the other. And I say that all are unanimous. |
| SE Asia\Ian | It does not make sense for the Qur'an, which appeared 700 years after the gospel, to merely repeat the same message. What is conveyed is only a brief summary, which gives an "amen" to the gospel and confirms what was already written in the Scriptures 700 years before. |
| SE Asia\Ray | For me as a Muslim, there is nothing wrong with the teachings of Islam, but the question becomes: which teaching? If the teaching is based on the Qur'an, there is no problem. |
| SE Asia\Monty-1 | In the process of studying the Qur'an in the Islamic institution I thought that everything that is in the Qur'an is really a retelling or summarizing of things and stories that came from the Jewish prophets. The only difference is the prophet Mohammed. The Quran gives an "amen" to what already exists. It is not that it corrects or replaces it, but it gives an "amen" to the former books. |

| IM Leader | Direct Quote |
|---|---|
| SE Asia\Lucas | It has within it truth. There are a lot of truths within it that are good for teaching and leading people. Different aspects that we find in the Bible are also found in the Qur'an. The Quran is quite fitted to the Tawrat, Zabur, and Injil, but of course not completely so. |
| Alongsiders\Kevin | Where to place the Qur'an relative to the other canonical books? I tend to see it as a collection of narratives that depend on the earlier narrative for its environment and existence. I tend to see it as secondary in that sense, but very powerful. |

Arthur seems to be the most outspoken about the value of the Qur'an. This is not surprising given his ongoing role as an Islamic leader in his region. He finds Christ throughout the book. "The Qur'an is debating about Christ, and there is a continuous train of memoirs of Jesus Christ from the beginning to the end," said Arthur. He believes that Mohammed was trying to lead his own community, which was fixed in a quagmire of polytheism, towards the oneness of God, which was the message from the Christians and the Jews at that time. Arthur calls the Qur'an "the cloak of the Lord Jesus Christ" and speaks out against any kind of banning.

> I am going to say to Terry Jones, "Do not ban the Qur'an, because you do not know about the Qur'an. If you ban the Qur'an you actually ban the cloak of the Lord Jesus Christ. You are banning the child of Mary. You are banning the sacred record of Abraham, Ishmael, Isaac, Jacob, and his 12 sons. Their record is in the Qur'an. How in the world are you going to ban it?" So, we are not going to ban the Qur'an, but we are going to highlight from the Qur'an the Lord Jesus Christ.

Many interviewees indicated that they see very helpful pointers in the Qur'an to Isa al Masih and to the former holy books. There is a range of opinions about the whole of the Qur'an beyond these pointers. Paxton explained how the Qur'an led him to Jesus Christ and faith. He is thankful for the Qur'an for that reason. He said, "Anything that has led me to Christ has a function like you find in the Old Testament, as a mentor who guides you along until you are educated, and after that its function has finished." Julius explained that the earlier three books are easier to understand, and that in his community taking the four books together can help a Muslim to more completely understand Allah. Zach explained that these pointers are helpful in themselves, without needing to exegete all of the Qur'an.

> The point of this is not to discuss whether the Qur'an is perfect. That is not really the point of this. What I am talking about is whether the Qur'an is helpful to help people better understand the grace and mercy of God, and we feel it is.

The fact that the Qur'an mentions and affirms the Tawrat, Zabur, and Injil is a helpful entry into the Scriptures. Brad, an IM leader from Africa, calls it an entering wedge that he is using for Muslims to understand more of the truth that is hidden in the Qur'an. He said, "I use the Qur'an as an entering wedge, but I use the Bible as the guiding principle and the Word of Allah." Monty sees two functions for the Qur'an. "It gives witness to the truth that was sent before, and it legitimizes the text that came before." Kent commented, "Within the Qur'an there is a pointer, a signpost, a sign which points to truth." Several interviewees talked about building bridges of understanding. Alongsider Melvin sees diamonds of truth and the footprints of God in the Qur'an and the need to build bridges from those.

> I believe that we should build bridges from those diamonds of truth and the footprints of God. I personally almost find it like a puzzle hidden within the Qur'an. It has strong evidence towards the true nature of Christ and strong evidence for the plan of salvation. It is not open by any means, but there are pieces of the puzzle that are put there.

IM leaders Axel, Oliver, Angus, Arthur, Paxton, Ray, and Ross expressed their dismay that the Qur'an is being misinterpreted today. Arthur used the expression "being hijacked." A few demonstrate this belief with some examples. Angus and Arthur talked about the aggressive language towards others in the Qur'an as only applying to the war conditions in Mohammed's time. "These verses are against warriors and not against the normal peaceful Christians and Jews," Arthur said. He also believes that the "Do not say three" comments in the Qur'an are for untrained Muslims who were misinterpreting attributes and aspects of Allah, such as used in Trinitarian formulas and in expressions in use in those days, like Mary being the mother of God. Arthur concluded, "What God Almighty is saying in the Qur'an actually is refuting the belief of those people who were untrained, and who were interpreting their own way." On the topic of Jesus not dying, Paxton interprets the saying in the Qur'an that says that "they" (the Jews) did not kill Isa as correct in that physically the Romans killed Jesus, and spiritually all of us killed Jesus because of our sins. "Every one of us is responsible for that murder. Every one of us is a God killer," Paxton said. He also believes that references in the Qur'an to "the people of the book" are not to the Christians and Jews, but to Jewish scholars and rabbis who controlled the former books and who are criticized for distorting them. Ross shared that Islam's focus on Mohammed is a misinterpretation of the Qur'an. He believes that Mohammed pointed to Jesus and not to himself. "The holy Quran says that this community should be looking forward to the second coming of Jesus," said Ross.

A few of the interviewees were more cautious or negative about the Qur'an and only saw it as a necessary tool within their context, but nothing more. Alongsider Wilbur looks at the Qur'an in the same way Paul regarded some of the Greco-Roman writings. He supports using parts of it, but just as initial bridge material. He said, "The point is to take them across that bridge to a different and distinct destination and not sort of let it all run together." Homer also is cautious. "I use it as a means to reach Muslims, but to me I don't find any value in it," he said. Jason considers the Qur'an to be an attempt by a man to write a heavenly book. "It is really mixed up," shared Jason. Frank and Angus deny that God had anything to do with the Qur'an. "It came from the prophet and his buddies," said Angus. Frank referred to the absence of any reference in the New Testament to another book coming, but he did confirm that there are good things in the Qur'an. Interestingly, Andy blamed the Christians from the time of Mohammed for not giving better instructions to him. "If they had given Mohammed a better teaching, the whole world would not suffer now," Andy said.

## Today

When asked how Allah is revealing himself to them today, many of the responses mentioned dreams and visions. Both Homer and Brad mentioned that they often have dreams about events before they happen. Oliver's response is representative of many of the comments from others. He had several visions of Jesus when he was a teenager.

> Whoever seeks to know his faith and seeks the right path, Allah reveals himself to this person. I was seeking him and I wanted to know him, so he has come down and revealed himself to me. I think that is the correct way. Whoever seeks the right things in the right faith, God reveals himself and speaks to him.

Other ways in which Allah reveals himself today that were mentioned in the interviews were answered prayers and healings. Lucas said, "There are a lot of people that have been healed through my prayers." Monty said that through all these ways people begin to see that Isa is not limited to being only a prophet, but that he is more. Others mentioned Allah revealing himself through everyday life and work. Julius said, "When I am doing practical work I can sense him giving me help to do things beyond my ability." Kent expressed his awareness of God every moment of the day. "Every breath I take is the gift of God. When we breathe, we are aware that God is with us, that he is around us, and that he is within us." Frank talked about the Holy Spirit giving him guidance today. Phil had an interesting comment about Muslims in the community coming to him for advice because they have seen in him a bright light and a sense of the presence of God. Arnold, Oliver, and Paxton said that the beauty of nature is a revelation of Allah to them. Julius feels close to God and in a sense experiences a revelation from him when he is praying or performing *salat*. He said, "Also through the Muslim prayers, the *salat*, I feel really close to Allah and honor him; I feel in awe of him, in a very special way."

### Religions

How do insiders view religions, since insiders appear to some outsiders to be part of one religion—namely, Islam—while following another one? The question in the interview was, "How do religions (Christianity and Islam) relate to your understanding of Allah and his purposes, and to your relationship with Isa al Masih?" The basic response was that it is all about following Isa al Masih and not about religions, which are man-made systems.

The responses in Table 21 are all about the need to only focus on following Isa al Masih, in a Muslim context, and not on religion.

**Table 21:** Follow Isa, not religion

| IM Leader | Direct Quote |
|---|---|
| S-Asia-A\Andy | I do not want any of our people to follow the church or any denomination. I want them to follow Jesus. That's it. |
| S-Asia-C\Axel | I am trying to reach my community, so that they can understand Isa in the right way, in the way of Allah and not of other people. Isa does not want us to believe in any religion. Allah's plans are for us to be with him, and he sent many prophets. The people created religions. I do not believe in any religion. |
| S-Asia-B\Mitch | I follow Isa al Masih. He's my Savior. That's all. We want to put less light on religion because we don't want to say, "He is a Christian and he is a Muslim." That name should not become a big part of our life. Our life is about following the teachings and instructions of Allah. If I follow Isa al Masih, I am not becoming a Christian, and I'm not becoming a Muslim. What I am is what I am. |
| Africa\Arnold | Isa did not come to plant any church or any mosque or any religion. He just came as the Savior of the world. The original plan was just to share the good news, to get people to accept Isa al Masih, and to live holy lives. |
| Africa\Oliver | I think it is very important for people with whom you are sharing your research to understand that insider movements are not a new religion. It is about seeking the truth and following Jesus without contradiction from any religion. |
| S-Asia-D\Angus | We consider ourselves to be faithful pro-Christ Muslims, so we are one in faith but different in culture. The purpose of religions is that we want to be distinct from others. That is why Jesus called the Pharisees whitewashed. But what is more important is to have faith in God. We are one *jamaat* or fellowship. Our faith is one, whether you are Chinese or whatever. |
| S-Asia-D\Arthur | The two of us can be near to one another if we believe that God has sent his Word, and we both believe that Jesus Christ was the Word of God. The Qur'an and the Injil are unanimous on that point. |

| IM Leader | Direct Quote |
|---|---|
| SE Asia\Ross | To read the Tawrat, Zabur, and Injil is illegal. We are meant to feel that way. If we break the law of the community by reading these books, we do not follow community consensus. But we want to follow the holy Qur'an and not community consensus. We are reforming our community by inserting the teachings of Jesus in our materials and compositions and in our way of life. God loves us the way we are. It is not that you have to be Christian first, and then God loves you. Do you have to be westernized first, and then God loves you? It is not like that. God loves you where you are. Muslims can respect that as well. |
| SE Asia\Zach | Our approach is that we think about how to renew their religious system so that it is really centered on the true identity and teachings of Jesus, to come back to the true foundations of the teachings of Jesus. There must be an evaluation and improvement of the system in order to come in full alignment with the teachings of Jesus. So Islam is an introduction to Jesus. The objective of that is not to get them into a church building. We want to guide them into the direction of Jesus. |
| SE Asia\Silas | I prioritize my priesthood unto Jesus Christ rather than looking at or being limited by the term *religion*. |
| Alongsiders\Josh-1 | I think religion is a bad starting point to talk about Jesus. I think he is beyond and above world religions. So, my relationship with Isa al Masih is not what puts me into a particular religion; rather, I would say, it puts me into a relationship with God and in the kingdom of Christ. |

Ross added a comment about joining the church and leaving your current community life, as he is advising new believers to stay in the mosque and their communities as reformers.

> So when people decide to go to the church, I say to them, "It is okay, and you can read the Tawrat, Zabur, and Injil in the church. But Jesus has given you the responsibility to bless the people in the mosque. You cannot convert your skin into white skin. You must not become a stumbling block to an agnostic Muslim. You must reform them in a way that is accepted by them, because you are their brothers, and you now know the truth. Don't keep it for yourself. It is a crime."

Paxton is equally focused on Jesus and mentioned that he does not like the idea of conversion from one religion to another but rather sees it as repentance from sin and a turning to Christ. That kind of conversion applies to everyone. He said, "Why don't you talk about Christians being converts? Why do you talk about us Muslims being converts only? What have we done wrong to you?" Ray and alongsider Kevin approached the relevance of religion from a kingdom perspective. "Isa is the special one sent by God to restore his kingdom. Every religion such as Judaism, Christianity, and Islam must believe that," Ray said. Kevin looks at religions as human responses to what God is doing in their midst kingdom-wise. He said, "There is kingdom stuff going on all the time in every religious system, but there's also rebellion going on in every religious system." The need to focus on Jesus also came out in a comment from Kent, who said that to him religion is just a status and a category on your identity card, but it is no indication of how well you follow what Isa al Masih taught. Ross highlights Jesus over religions because Jesus is a public figure with a public truth that the whole community needs. Jesus is not interested in being tamed by any religion, according to Ross. He said, "You cannot know Jesus within the walls of a Christian church. You cannot know Jesus within the walls of an Islamic secret sect."

Looking at religions in a more general sense, practically all interviewees mentioned that they see them as man-made systems. Julius said that religions tend to form traditional thinking and ways of behaving. Arnold also referred to religion as human forms and practices. Interestingly, Zach described religions as systems that make following Isa more difficult. He said, "From their religious system, Christians observe and then criticize efforts by other people to have a relationship with God through Isa." Other general and more positive comments about religions were that they push people to do good things and respect others. Frank referred to the Qur'an and said, "In the Qur'an it is written that Allah says that the most important religion is humanity, respecting and loving each other and human rights."

Several made some specific comments about Islam. The most negative comment about Islam came from Jason, who said that Muslims see Jesus only as a prophet. "They take away the core meaning of his death. This is the sin of Islam and I stand firm on that." Others were more accommodating towards Islam but pointed out its shortcomings. Oliver noted the many conflicts and splits within Islam.

> But after Mohammed died, peace be upon him, his disciples also changed. There was conflict. Even today, in Christianity you have many different denominations, and among Muslims also, every year there is a new sect. Every year there is a new denomination within Islam. This is growing, because every day there is conflict because of different doctrines in both Christianity and Islam. It seems that we are not listening to God.

Homer mentioned how there is fear of Allah among Muslims. "Not fear out of disrespect, but fear because if you do not follow, there are consequences either immediately or after some time." He sees God as distant in Islam, and life as a Muslim lacks personal choice. "When you are a Muslim following whatever the Qur'an says, it is as if you are burdened with things," he said. Homer also recalled how community pressure is real. "Sometimes others would come to my house saying, 'You did not come to the mosque.' So you have to go." But in the end Homer recognizes that the God of Islam is the God of Abraham, and that a veil needs to be lifted.

> There is some misunderstanding, but there is the same origin. The only thing is that there is a veil on the side of the Muslims which does not allow them to see God in all fullness. But the God that they are claiming to believe in is the God of Abraham.

Ross seeks to reform Islam with Christ and especially commented on the static nature of today's Islam. Table 22 has comments from Ross on this static nature.

**Table 22:** Ross on static nature of Islam

| IM Leader | Direct Quote |
| --- | --- |
| SE Asia\Ross | In the mosque you cannot show your emotions. |
| | To read the Tawrat, Zabur, and Injil is illegal. We are meant to feel that way. |
| | Today Islam, as a submission to God, is like a statue. |
| | You must be Arabized. You must believe in a holy language without even knowing the language. You don't have to understand the book of God. It is like a mantra. It is agnosticism. |

| IM Leader | Direct Quote |
|---|---|
| | The message in the mosque is still the same from the past. There is a book of sermons that is repeated again and again. You must be good, you must be good, you must be good, you must be good. It is preached to an audience that already has been bad. |
| | The Middle East–oriented religion says that we must have manuals, written manuals. Those who do not have written manuals don't have religion, according to them. It actually is a judgment. |
| | We are only saying in Islamic prayers how wonderful our God is. We keep repeating, "You are wonderful, you are wonderful, I worship you." |

Arthur called for more tolerance between Islam and Christianity. He pointed out that Islam recognizes eight attributes of Allah and that people use philosophy to describe the relationship between these attributes and Allah. Arthur said, "We say that these attributes of God are not God, and that they are not separated from God. They are not God and not without being God." He laughed and said, "The Christians have only three-in-one, and Muslims unfortunately have eight-in-one." He appealed not to the deliberately ignorant ones but to all those who are in search of the truth to conclude that if eight-in-one is allowed, then three-in-one is easy. Arthur further promoted tolerance by saying that all blasphemy laws should be discarded because they are political and misused. "This is the biggest sword dangling over the heads of the preachers, all preachers," Arthur said. He warns against expanding the blasphemy law to all prophets and to making it an international law. "If this happens, there will be the biggest problem in the world. Why don't they go back to before 1860 when there were no blasphemy laws?" He illustrated this by showing how the Old Testament would become blasphemous in his country on multiple accounts because it mentions many sins of various prophets.

Drew's view of Islam is positive. He recalled how he was born into a mixed family. His father was a Muslim and his mother was a Christian. He recalled how as a five-year-old boy he was asked what his religion was. His answer was that he followed Chrislam. He shared in the interview, "I still remember that event. From my childhood on I have wanted to hold on to both, because I perceive both as good."

The responses to the question about how religions fit in God's plans and purposes with regard to Christianity were by and large quite critical of this religion. Many expressed the opinion that Jesus did not start Christianity, as indicated in Table 23.

**Table 23:** Jesus did not start Christianity

| IM Leader | Direct Quote |
|---|---|
| S-Asia-A\Andy | Jesus never said to follow Christianity, or to create something like it, that only these people come and they have this sign, then they are saved. |
| S-Asia-C\Axel | Isa does not want us to believe in any religion. We made the Christian religion, etc. We can say that we all are Muslims, or we all are Christians or whatever. |
| C-Asia\Jason | People made religions, not God. |
| Africa\Arnold | Jesus never intended these things. |
| Africa\Oliver | From the beginning to now God never brought any religion. God was bringing us message after message, not a religion. |
| S-Asia-D\Frank | When it comes to religions, we cannot deny that they exist with all their philosophies and teachings, but we cannot consider them divine or from God. |
| SE Asia\Ray | During my seminary studies I realized that Jesus never asked anyone to change their religion. |
| S-Asia-D\Paxton | I don't consider the message of Jesus Christ to be a religion. |
| Alongsiders\Josh-1 | It is striking to me that Jesus did not speak of what we would call today a religion. He spoke almost entirely about a kingdom, which is here now and also has a future dimension. |
| Alongsiders\Tyler | Isa actually did not start Christianity. |

Paxton talked about religion as being a straitjacket. He said that following Isa al Masih has always been an insider movement but that something went wrong when this faith traveled west and became Christianity, made in England and in the USA. "This was a foreign Christianity that was introduced to us. We thought that this was Christianity and we had to express it in a way that a white fellow expresses it." Paxton considers Christianity to be a foreign aid and a foreign mission. It is interesting to see that Lucas compared being part of a religion to being colonized by foreigners.

Religions are constraining conditions for people similar to being colonized by foreign powers, and to living under that overlordship. People want to become free. They are trying to find some pathway to freedom from their overlordship. Is it better that we find our own pathway through their religious system to find our freedom of this overlordship from the colonizers? We will never find it that way. Or, should we give that up and instead look to Jesus to find our freedom from these colonizers?

This comment seems to apply to Islam and Christianity alike. Several interviewees commented on Christians not really following the teachings of Isa. Phil said, "I see Christianity as a group of people who claim faith in Jesus Christ, but not always do and follow the teachings of Jesus." Likewise, Andy said, "Many Christians that I have seen are not fully following Jesus, yet they say they are Christians." Alongsider Wilbur put it in more theological terms. He believes that a spirit of antinomianism reigns in Western Christianity. "I would say that Christianity is very far from its moorings, and could be broadly characterized as guilty of kind of a cheap grace reception," he shared. He believes that it is possible that God is using Islam at this time as a means to shield a billion people from the devastating effects of that cheap grace, for a future time of great hearing for the gospel.

## Isa al Masih—Theology-Christology

After talking about Allah, his characteristics and his plans and purposes for his creation, including mankind, the second main topic during the interviews was Isa al Masih. Using a series of questions from the interview guide, I asked about the identity and essence of Isa al Masih and about his mission. His essence relates to the theology of the Christ, or to Christology. I grouped the responses into the following five sections:

1. High Christology
2. Other
3. Low Christology
4. Al Masih
5. Son of God

## High Christology

The majority of the respondents indicated adherence to a high Christology. Table 24 shows that 18 interviewees see Isa al Masih as divine.

Others showed support for a high Christology in other ways. Angus described Jesus as a reflection of the light of God in this world. Paxton also sees the Messiah as God's presence on earth. "The title 'the Messiah' means that God does everything through him. He is the means through which he expresses his love and the means through which he expresses his power." Zach likewise emphasized the presence of God in Jesus.

> Many of our Muslim friends do not really know what *al Masih* means. We are defining it for them from a not-knowing starting point. I really emphasize that this means that he is now present, that Jesus is always right here, with us. To those who receive the presence of the Messiah it is really a way of describing them receiving the Savior. What is the meaning of the presence of God? It has a lot to do with the fullness of our present life. It is also a guarantee of what is to come. Then it depends on how we put faith in that.

**Table 24:** High Christology

| IM Leader | Direct Quote |
| --- | --- |
| S-Asia-A\Andy | Well, if I come through the Trinity, they are one. I think they are one. In our understanding, he sent his Son to save us, and he went back and sent his Spirit to help us. So, they are one. They have different functions but they are one. |
| S-Asia-A\Howard | Yes, I think they are one. There is no separation between God and Jesus. |
| S-Asia-C\Axel | I believe Jesus is divine. |
| C-Asia\Jason | Isa al Masih has a divine nature and a human nature. |
| S-Asia-B\Mitch | So if somebody thinks, well this relationship between Allah and Isa al Masih seems like an Allah-Allah relationship, that is fine. |
| Africa\Arnold | I personally believe, not everyone believes this, that Isa al Masih is more than just a prophet, as many people believe. I believe he is God walking with human beings. |

| IM Leader | Direct Quote |
|---|---|
| Africa\Brad | In fact, insider believers believe that Isa al Masih is divine. |
| S-Asia-D\Angus | In spite of all those burdens, to take the absence of hope far away, God became flesh. We cannot normally see God. Therefore, he came on the one hand as flesh and on the other hand still as God. |
| S-Asia-D\Frank | Jesus was both human and God. |
| SE Asia\Ross | Jesus reveals himself. Jesus reveals God, and then his disciples wrote the Injil. |
| SE Asia\Phil | The central role of Jesus is to be a continuation of the character of God, in terms of being the Savior and the Messiah. Jesus is God who took on the form of man to bring us salvation. God can do whatever he wants to do, so he could do that. If God cannot take on the form of man, he is not God. In this way God made his promises of salvation more concrete. |
| SE Asia\Zach | Some of the earlier prophets often spoke of the coming Messiah. He begins to take shape in a human form. From one angle he is seen as fully man. But we also see in the theophanies and other revelations of God in the Old Testament that this figure is also seen as divine. He is 100 percent divine within the oneness of God. Like two faces of one coin, these are inseparable. This gives us a lot of difficulty in our context here. |
| SE Asia\Silas | Isa al Masih is the Lord [a word only used for God] who revealed himself and took on the form of mankind, because the Lord longed for mankind, who is lost. Therefore, the Lord took on the form of mankind so that he can be understood by mankind and his teachings could be followed by mankind. |
| SE Asia\Kent | Jesus is Lord [a word only used for God] and therefore he is capable of defeating death. |
| SE Asia\Stuart | The word of Isa al Masih was before the world existed. He already existed. He also said, "The Father and I are one." If this is true, Isa al Masih is God. |
| Alongsiders\Wilbur | He has actively revealed himself from the beginning and then intermittently, and supremely in actually taking human form and speaking directly into the human situation. |
| Alongsiders\Melvin | I would say that his largest revelation is through Jesus Christ, Isa al Masih. We see God with the most clarity when the Word became flesh and habitated among us. |
| Alongsiders\Tyler | We find and believe the best expression (both context fitted and Bible fitted in the sense of biblical theology) is to say that the Son shares the exclusive divine identity that only belongs to the One God. |

Paxton also commented on the eternal nature of Isa. "If God is love, then it is logically possible that he loves from eternity, and therefore he must have some internal beloved, from eternity." When I asked Ray whether he thought Isa was eternal, he affirmed this partially by saying that "al Masih" was unseen in eternity past as the Word of God. He explained the eternality of Isa with a metaphor. "If I want to make a car, I have an idea in mind, or a picture. My plan cannot be seen. Later, my plan becomes real in a physical car."

Other expressions of high Christology were Isa being the image of the invisible God (Frank and alongsider Josh), Isa being God's own eternal personal communiqué of himself (alongsider Wilbur) and Isa being God's self-revelation (Monty and alongsider Tyler). Tyler also mentioned that high Christology is embraced when insiders experience the presence and power of Isa in their lives.

> For simpler people they more quickly move up the levels of Christology when they experience his touch in different ways. At that point they surrender everything, get involved deeply, and risk even their lives for Isa. So we have high percentages of believers who are mentoring others, in some places triple the participation level compared to conventional churches. This full surrender way of living is a fluent way to express their high Christology, even though when asked they may stutter and stammer and not get out the words to say it nearly as well.

### Other

Before looking at some expressions of low Christology, there were other comments about what the title "al Masih" means and what the relationship between Isa and Allah is that deserve some attention. Table 25 shows how 12 interviewees referred to the relationship between Isa al Masih and Allah primarily as one between Allah and the Word of Allah.

**Table 25:** Isa as the Word of God

| IM Leader | Direct Quote |
|---|---|
| S-Asia-B\Mitch | This is a very touchy subject, right? What I want to teach to my people, to the people in the movement, and I'm trying to go there, is that Jesus was with Allah even before creation, as *Kalaam*. Allah used his *Kalaam* to create the universe and me. How to describe this relationship, I do not know. |
| Africa\Oliver | We know that he was the Word [*Kalaam*] of God among us. My understanding as a Muslim who follows Jesus is that he was the Word of God who came to save his people. |
| Africa\Brad | The insider believers and I also believe that Allah revealed himself through Isa al Masih in the form of flesh. Isa al Masih is part of Allah. He is his Word. He is an integral part of Allah, but he also revealed Allah as his Word, taking on flesh. |
| S-Asia-D\Frank | It is the entity or person that is the Word of God. |
| S-Asia-D\Arthur | The Qur'an testifies that Jesus is the Word of God. The Word is not created. It is emanated from God. People who believe in God give this attribute the name *Son*, in their own human language, because a son comes out from the father. We are not worshiping the person who was born of Mary, but we are worshiping the Word of God that came to Mary through an angel, and we are worshiping that Word and not the body that was born of Mary. |
| SE Asia\Zach | Isa is the Word of God. We find it three times in the Qur'an referring to Jesus (Al Nisam 171; Al Imran 45, 39). The text shows that the word came from God. God is the source. This term, the Word of God, is a symbol of the power of God to create creatures with a simple word. Because of the association between the word and creation and the Creator, this is a way that is used in the Qur'an to unite the lordship character within the person of Isa al Masih. So, when we talk about him as the Son of God, it is used in the negative sense, but when we talk about the Word of God, it can be used in a very positive sense. |
| SE Asia\Ross | The Word of God became a man, a real man. His name is Jesus. |

| IM Leader | Direct Quote |
|---|---|
| SE Asia\Ray | As mentioned in the Injil and in the Qur'an, Isa is Allah's Word. In the Qur'an he is also called the Spirit of Allah. I believe Isa is the Word of Allah and the Spirit of Allah. How to explain that I do not know. There is no clear explanation about the relationship in this sense, ontologically. The Scriptures do not explain this. They only say, Isa is the Word of God, he is sent by God to redeem and save humankind, he will be reigning in the kingdom of God, but eventually he will give the kingdom back to God. That's what I know. Ontologically I do not know. |
| SE Asia\Silas | Jesus is the Word of God. Whatever Jesus spoke was the same as what God spoke. |
| SE Asia\Kent | Isa is the honored Word of God, the living Word. I am only going to do what God says through Isa al Masih. What was spoken by Isa was spoken by God. Isa came to this world and he is the same with God, and he revealed himself in this world to teach what the truth is. What is the meaning of the Word of God? The Word of God is al Masih, the Messiah. |
| Alongsiders\Kevin | I think that the whole introduction to the Gospel of John, the Word becoming flesh and dwelling among us, that is for me the most helpful description of the relationship between God and Jesus, in terms of the Word becoming flesh, the Word that was divine, the Word that was with God, the Word that was from all eternity becoming flesh in Jesus, so that what he is and says and does somehow shows us what God is and says and does in a way that is different than just a prophetic message, but it is probably different from what most Christians say when they say, "Jesus is God." I have a hard time saying that without a lot of biblical qualifications to that, because I think we tend to say it in ways that deny his humanity. |
| Alongsiders\Melvin | I see that Isa al Masih is the Word of Allah, and that relationship has implications. The story that I like to share with Muslims, just as a digression to your question but also to explain it better, is on the word *debar*. Jesus and John were probably thinking in Aramaic, when this was spoken, and the Aramaic word is *debar*. It has a very strong and double meaning. Besides just meaning "word" it had taken on the connotation of the presence of the Shekinah in the most holy place. |

As others described the relationship between Allah and Isa al Masih, some mentioned Isa as King (Angus, Ross, and Ray), or the coming Judge (Frank), and alongsider Josh referred to the relationship as a mystery. "There is some kind of unity between the two of them that I think is indescribable in human words." Frank also shared that they use an honorific for Isa that is inverted from the normal "peace be upon him" used in Islam for prophets. They use "his peace be upon us" as the honorific for Isa.

> Only we as believers use this special honorific for Jesus. Also legally, we cannot use the honorific "peace be upon him" for someone who is alive. It is only used in Islam for deceased prophets. We believe that Jesus is alive, which is another reason why we use a different honorific.

Ray prefers to describe the relationship between Isa and Allah as Isa being the mercy of God. He recognized that the Qur'an exalts Isa as a King, the Messiah, the Word of Allah, and the Spirit of Allah, and he added, "The Qur'an also says that Isa is the sign for mankind and he is the mercy from God. That for me is the most important description of Isa in the Qur'an." Ray also mentioned that in the Gospel of John we read that God so loved the world that he sent his Son. "For me," he said, "the Son of God is the mercy of God." Ray holds to a low Christology. I asked him how he reconciles references in Revelation to Isa being worshiped as the Lamb of God. He replied, "If people are worshiping him as the King or the Messiah, that is no problem. The Qur'an agrees that he is the Messiah and the King, and the one that will come back."

## Low Christology

Five insiders see the relationship between Allah and Isa al Masih in a way that reflects a low Christology. Table 26 shows how each one of them says in their own words that Jesus is not God.

**Table 26:** Low Christology

| IM Leader | Direct Quote |
|---|---|
| S-Asia-C\Axel | I do not believe that Isa and Allah are the same. The Isa that came to earth is not Allah. That is *shirk*. He was human, and you cannot say that a human is Allah. The Word that existed before, you can say that was God. But when that Word came into the flesh, you cannot believe that flesh or a human is God. Many people do not understand what the Scriptures are saying about the incarnation. Isa says that our God is one God. Love him with all your heart and with all your soul. So when the Word became flesh, is this another God? That is a Gentile understanding. They believe that there are many, many gods. Isa is a man. He is very close to Allah and he is the one that can reconcile us, so he deserves high honor, but I cannot worship Isa. That is. I only pray to and worship Almighty Allah. Isa is with me and he also can give me guidance, but I cannot worship him. That is the difference. |
| C-Asia\Julius | Isa al Masih reveals Allah and embodies Allah, but is not Allah. Allah reveals himself in Isa al Masih, and by means of the Spirit. Those are two ways he reveals himself. |
| Africa\Oliver | He had authority to give life to the dead person, to give sight to a blind person, to cast out demons, and many other things that only God can do. In my understanding, although he was not God himself, he did have the authority to do these things, because God was there. He was the one and the Spirit. There is no differentiation between God, his Word, and the Spirit. So there is a lot of confusion even when we say that he is the Son of God. He is not the Son of God. Rather, he is not God himself. In my understanding I could say he was the Word and the Spirit of God. He also did not say, "I am God." The Christians make a mistake. They call Jesus God, but he was not God. He never ever said that he was God. He always said that he was depending on his Father. He was listening to his Father. He was talking about the will of his Father. |
| SE Asia\Ross | We are learning that Jesus said that to pray you must pray, "Our Father in heaven." Jesus does not make a coup d'état. He does not say, "Father is nothing and I am greater than Father." So if you say suddenly that Jesus is God, you tell us that Father is nothing and that Jesus is greater than Father. This is false theology. Jesus is the Son of God. He represents God. |
| SE Asia\Ray | No, of course not. Isa al Masih and Allah are not the same. How can they be the same? If Isa and Allah are the same then that would mean that Allah died on the cross. How can Allah die on the cross? 1 Timothy 2:5 says that there is one mediator between God and humans, which is the human Jesus, or the human Isa. |

I asked Ray specifically whether he thought Isa al Masih is divine. He wondered what the word "divine" meant in this case and said, "If it means like in Latin 'from God,' yes, Isa is divine. If 'divine' means being the same as Allah, I do not think he is the same as Allah."

Other descriptions of or titles for Isa al Masih that fit with a low Christology were Isa's high priestly roles (alongsider Tyler), Jesus as mediator between God and his people (Oliver) and Isa as the highest prophet (Julius).

## Al Masih

From the interviews in which I specifically asked what the term "al Masih" means, eight respondents mentioned that it means "the Anointed One." This reply was given by Andy, Jason, Mitch, Frank, Ross, Lucas, Kent, and Stuart. Seven others used a variety of definitions of "al Masih" that were all close to the idea of "the chosen honored one." Table 27 shows this variety.

**Table 27:** The meaning of "al Masih"

| IM Leader | Direct Quote |
| --- | --- |
| S-Asia-A\Howard | The Son of God, the chosen. |
| S-Asia-C\Axel | He is the beloved one. He's closer than any other human. |
| Africa\Arnold | To me *al Masih* means the appointed one, the one set aside for a holy purpose. |
| S-Asia-D\Angus | In Arabic the meaning is this: the one who is important, who is really special. If the person is really a special one, then there is *al* in front of it. Quoting from the Qur'an, all the prophets are special, but Jesus is the special one. |
| SE Asia\Phil | This means the promised one, the one promised by God that would bring all the help that God had promised to deliver. |
| SE Asia\Monty-1 | I am starting with the Islamic answer. It is a much admired name. It is very deeply respected by Muslims as a name. |
| SE Asia\Silas | It means that he is the promised one. God promised someone to bring forgiveness, which is Jesus. He is the Messiah, the one that was promised by God to bring forgiveness. |

Monty added that because Muslims see Jesus as a highly honored figure, they reject the notion of him being treated like a criminal.

Monty concluded, "So we need to give them a greeting of brotherhood because of their great admiration for Jesus."

## Son of God

It is interesting to observe that all but one of the interviewees found the phrase *Son of God* challenging. Only Ross promoted the use of the father-son language because it is heartfelt.

> Not only Jesus but also the Father suffers [on the cross]. Why does the Bible use the terms Father, Son, Holy Spirit? It is heartfelt. It is not figurative. These are terms people can understand. There is a saying in my language that if a child falls into a deep well, the father will be jumping afterwards to save the child, his son. No other words can bring this story alive than father and son expressions.

All others found the phrase *Son of God* challenging. As Table 28 indicates, many see this phrase as a figure of speech or metaphor, leaving the exact meaning a mystery.

**Table 28:** Son of God as metaphor

| IM Leader | Direct Quote |
| --- | --- |
| S-Asia-C\Axel | I don't have any problem with that word if I understand it as being unlike a human relationship. If it is about a human relationship then I cannot accept the term *Son of God*. |
| C-Asia\Julius | As God's beloved chosen one, God's Anointed One. After being resurrected and raised to be with Allah, he was appointed al Masih and Lord. I understand *Son of God* to be a metaphor to express a belovedness and closeness between Isa al Masih and Allah, but not as a physical relationship, like we would think of between a son and a father. It is probably better to think of it, if we are using human terms, as "like the love between a father and a son." That is the kind of relationship between Allah and Isa al Masih. This is very helpful for Muslims to understand the term Son of God. |

## Views on Allah and Isa al Masih

| IM Leader | Direct Quote |
|---|---|
| C-Asia\Gus | Isa is fully human, like us, with a created body. He has mystical origins and he has an awareness of pre-creation time. Isa has concepts of different worlds and the spirit worlds. Is Isa God? He is God's Word that has become human. What is the relationship between a human's body and the Word of God? What is that? I don't know. |
| C-Asia\Jason | There is a close relationship between Allah and Isa, as in a father and son. This does not mean that one is higher or better. The Father-Son relationship is an example of trust between the two of them. I can have the same relationship with Allah as Jesus had. I would say that there is a close relationship between them. |
| Africa\Arnold | I try, to the extent possible, to avoid entering into a debate with anyone about Jesus being the Son of God, but what I do with my Muslim friends is that I just tell them that these terms were used back in that time, and they were very acceptable. It never meant that God had a wife who gave birth to Jesus. When you go to Christian circles, they even will deny this. It was a kind of relationship that Isa al Masih had with God. The same way in our culture we can say, this is the son of the road. The road is not the son's father or mother, or whatever. In my dialect you can say, the son of Satan. That is someone who likes fighting and things like that. So when you say "the son of God," it is someone who likes God, who is close to God, and who is always mindful of God's business. So, that is the meaning and people are okay with that. |
| Africa\Brad | He is not a biological son, but it shows a very intimate relationship between Allah and Isa al Masih. |
| S-Asia-D\Angus | It is like father and son. But not a physical thing. It is about intimacy. Intimacy as Father and Son. And it is about love, which is why he is the Son. |
| S-Asia-D\Arthur | When someone reads the Bible and comes to Christ, he first may say that Isa is the Word of God, and then say that he is the Spirit of God, and then say, coming back again, that he is the Son of God; metaphorically we can say that. If you say the first time that Isa is the Son of God, all will run away and you just stand there. This is the problem in this country. The Word is not created. It is emanated from God. People who believe in God give this attribute the name *Son*, in their own human language, because a son comes out from the father. They give this name in this metaphorical way. |

| IM Leader | Direct Quote |
|---|---|
| S-Asia-D\Paxton | But when we talk about God the Father, and the Son, we start talking about something literally and something that is ontologically true, but we don't know what it is. But Jesus was using ordinary language. The relationship between a father and son basically is a relationship of love. He talked about the one who loves, and who was sent. I consider the *Son* and *Father* terms as metaphors, revealing something that is beyond our comprehension, but at the same time talking about some kind of similarity between the way God the Father behaves and a way Jesus behaved. |
| SE Asia\Ian | To overcome their feelings that this is in opposition of Q 112:1–4, we must explain that this is a metaphorical meaning, and not a literal meaning. Jesus was born of the Spirit of God, just as the Qur'an was born of the Spirit of God. We should not reject Jesus. |
| SE Asia\Monty-2 | This one is very interesting. This of course cannot be understood as God having a biological son, and it cannot be understood as God having a wife. |
| SE Asia\Silas | The term *child of God* does not mean that God physically had a son. The term *Son of God* is not something that we should receive as the naked or raw meaning. *The Son of God* is only a term and an illustration and a picturing of the reality, so it will be more easily understood. |
| SE Asia\Kent | *Son of God* is only a term that symbolizes, or is a figure of speech. That is always how we have to start in our discipling, to move them away from a literal statement. |
| SE Asia\Stuart | At the foundation is the Word of God, which confesses and reveals that the Son of God is God himself. *The Son* does not mean a biological son. It is only a figure of speech. Isa al Masih was born by the Virgin Mary, and this pregnancy did not happen through the normal relationship between a man and a woman, but rather this pregnancy is the result of the work of the Spirit of God, which happened according to the Word of God, conveyed through the angel of God. |
| Alongsiders\Tyler | In Psalm 2 it says that God had a son. When Muslims challenge that text we say that they are guilty of shallowing the meaning. It is obviously not referring to a date of birth and sexual relationships. What could be further from the truth and more reprehensible? Don't say that. It is a figure of speech. |

Two IM leaders mentioned that the phrase *Son of God* does not give enough honor to Isa al Masih in their context. Axel said, "Allah and Isa should get more honor than a son and a father. I cannot give proper honor to him if I say that he is a son. I need to say more." Gus also is reluctant to use the word "son" for Isa because it does not show enough respect. He shared, "Some call Isa the Father because 'brother' or 'son' is not high enough, and not respectful enough." Gus also called the phrase *Son of God* a semantic paradox because a father and a son cannot be equal, yet Allah and Isa al Masih are equal. "It is a semantic paradox. Is the Son submitting to the Father? Is the Son eternally submitting to the Father or only as Isa on earth?"

Only a few mentioned that they associate Jesus' divinity with the phrase *Son of God*. Alongsider Wilbur highlighted the idea that Jesus did not have a human father. He said, "We have to repudiate anything that smacks of Jesus of Nazareth effectively starting his life and existence in Bethlehem, in the Roman period, or anything that implies a biological relationship." Brad also mentioned the divinity of Christ. "No one else was given that title in the Scriptures," he said, and then added, "Isa al Masih is Allah himself, but it is a relational title to be called the Son of God." Homer mentioned that for a while no one could convince him of the notion that Isa was the Son of God and God. "But it was God who revealed it to me, and I got satisfied, and it has never troubled me."

There were a number of other comments about the phrase *Son of God*. Alongsider Kevin has come to see the title as fully rooted in the messianic kingship concept and finds "the Word becoming flesh" a much richer reference. Alongsider Melvin sees the sonship title distinctly as not connected to divinity but as a reference to Jesus regaining the full kingly birthright, which was lost after Jacob. He said, "This is how a first-century Jew would have understood the phrase *Son of God*. They would not have put divinity to the term." IM leader Monty interprets *Son of God* as a direct reference to Isa being the Servant of God. He said, "The way he served; he had to become a child to do that, a child of mankind and also of God." Oliver believes that Isa never said that he was the Son of God, and that the current Western meaning of this phrase is a misinterpretation.

> If I call Allah 'my Father,' I am not his son in a literal way but I am his son because he created me. This is a misinterpretation from theology from the Romans and Greeks. They did not understand God very well and they

> just interpreted their own translation. Now they force other communities to believe their interpretation, which is not correct.

Several indicated a reluctance to use the phrase *Son of God* in their context. Axel uses the expression "the beloved." He said, "I don't say 'the Son'; I wouldn't mind saying that if people did not misunderstand 'the Son.'" Arthur is looking for interfaith reconciliation between Islam and Christianity and avoids the phrase *Son of God* because of misunderstandings and hardened hearts. He said, "In Arabic you cannot say that anyone is the son of God. You cannot say of anyone that he was born of God's semen." Referring to Muslims, Arthur laments that there is not more openness to true understanding. "People do not want to say this correctly, and they continue saying that this is from the Christians, and let them be in their problems." He said, "When you say 'father' or 'son' literally, they don't listen for one more word. They object violently." Arthur also shared his approach with Muslims in his context. "I say, 'See the Lord Jesus Christ as the Light of God. He is an expression of God. He is not God because he is not separate from God.'" Arthur promotes the use of the phrase *the Word of God* as common ground. "The Qur'an and the Injil are unanimous on that point. The difference is on the word *ibn*, 'son.' There is no difference on the phrase *the Word of God*."

Interestingly, Zach is minimizing the use of the phrase *Son of God* because he believes that it is an obstacle to people in his context coming to accept the divinity of Isa. Zach does not avoid using the phrase when directly asked about it. "In those situations," Zach said, "we must be brave and explain the distortions that they have in their thinking about this concept." Under different circumstances he prefers not using the phrase.

> This gives us a lot of difficulty in our context here. When we start using language of the fatherhood of God and the sonship of Jesus, that gives the concept of these not being one. There is a separation in this concept among our audience here. This kind of language really is an obstacle to them accepting the divinity of Jesus.

## Isa al Masih—*Missio Christi*

In parallel to the overall *missio Dei*, what is the specific mission of Isa al Masih? What is the *missio Christi*? I probed during the interviews into this domain with questions about the actions and message of Isa al Masih, and about his suffering, death, and resurrection.

### Actions of Isa al Masih

My leading question for this topic was, "How would you summarize the actions of Isa al Masih?" I had to clarify the question a few times by saying that I was not mainly referring to Jesus' actions on the cross and in the resurrection, and the subsequent Calvary-focused message, but to his actions during his three years of ministry. Alongsider Kevin's comment illustrates this clarification well, as he makes a distinction between the proclamation of a message about the three days from Good Friday to Easter and the following of Jesus and the full life lived by him.

> I think we have made in the West probably an unhelpful distinction between what he did, what he said, and what we say. We have turned it all into a message that we try to proclaim, rather than a person or a life that is still inviting people to follow. Western evangelicals are focusing on the last three days, and people believing this; if you believe this you are in, and if you don't you're not; this just seems to run counter to everything we see in the Gospels.

The first category of response to how to summarize the actions of Isa al Masih can be labeled "God's love in action, liberating people." The 11 comments in Table 29 demonstrate this category.

**Table 29:** Isa's actions: God's love in action liberating people

| IM Leader | Direct Quote |
|---|---|
| C-Asia\Julius | In Acts 2 we learn that Allah raised Isa al Masih from the dead and made him the Lord and al Masih, so his life on earth was also a revelation of God's love for all to see. He was the perfect sacrifice for all people as well. This is also revealed in his life. |
| C-Asia\Jason | I would say that you can describe Jesus' actions as showing people God's love, mercy, and compassion. |

| IM Leader | Direct Quote |
|---|---|
| Africa\Arnold | I think he did so many things. He helped those who were desperate to have hope. He fed those who were very hungry, both physically and spiritually. He healed many sick people that did not have hope. He did many wonderful things. |
| Africa\Homer | When Jesus came to the world, the Qur'an says that he treated the sick. He raised some of the people who were dead, according to the Qur'an. Also, he did miracles which were leading us to see Jesus as a Savior. |
| Africa\Brad | Isa performed many miracles including creating a bird, raising the dead, healing the sick, so many miracles. The insider believers believe that he performed many miracles. |
| S-Asia-D\Frank | He especially associated and spent time with people who had been rejected by society, who were on the fringe of society. |
| S-Asia-D\Paxton | I think that his actions really talk about God's love. God is showing it in a practical way. All the prophets talked about the love of God in different ways but when it came to practically showing it, many prophets unfortunately retaliated. But Jesus never did that. |
| SE Asia\Lucas | There are many other works he has done including healings. |
| SE Asia\Zach | He also performed works that met the needs of the people in the community. |
| Alongsiders\Wilbur | He especially devoted a great amount of time to liberating people who were under the more visible domination of Satan, either through demonic possession or through some sort of physical illness or malady. A deliverance and healing ministry by which he sort of directly took on the enemy's direct control over people, and the consequences of sin in this world, demonstrating his mastery over the physical and spiritual universe by the great string of miracles. |
| Alongsiders\Melvin | I see his whole life as a revelatory experience of the kingdom of God, of him becoming the King and establishing his kingdom, and the plan of salvation being acted out throughout this whole period; not just in one period but at a much larger level throughout his whole life, from birth. |

Another theme that came out in the responses is that the actions of Isa al Masih function as examples for us to follow, living a life of faith in action. Table 30 illustrates this theme.

**Table 30:** Isa's actions: our model for faith in action

| IM Leader | Direct Quote |
|---|---|
| S-Asia-A\Andy | Sometimes I run into big humanitarian NGOs and they suggest that we should help people and save their lives, but they don't think about Christianity. Do humanitarian work? I say, yes, Jesus is the biggest humanitarian worker. Why are you following this model? This is a big model for us. For me his life is how we should live and follow and act. |
| S-Asia-C\Axel | His life was perfect, and he was showing us how a person lives the right way. Don't be in bondage. Don't just follow rules and regulations, but be a good human. Don't hurt anyone. Don't do any wrong things, be a good human. He did not ask us to follow all the laws of Sharia and Moses. God wants us to live a simple life and we should not reject these laws but if these laws stand in the way of that, we are in bondage. He is asking us to live the right life, not under the bondage of religion. |
| C-Asia\Julius | God's love was revealed in his life. We can conclude that he shows us the path, the true path to Allah. In his life on earth he was an example for all people of a perfectly submitted person, a perfectly submitted man, for everyone to see what that looks like. |
| SE Asia\Zach | We have a principal, "Look and see what Jesus did, and then listen and think about what he said." I am often emphasizing this strongly, "Look and see what Jesus did." Only after that, come back and listen and see what he said. This becomes a basic and simple discipleship pattern. It is kind of a slogan repeated by many people. Among the people of God who live in these small communities, the emphasis is on what they are doing, not what they are debating. These categories of things are models for us for what we should be doing. |
| Alongsiders\Melvin | The Son actually does not see beyond the grave, but he is so committed to his mission and his love for his people is so great that he decides to lay it down, and he dies of a broken heart. I see that his actions are following the full will of his Father in heaven, and that they are revelatory of how the people in his kingdom should live. |
| Alongsiders\Josh-1 | I believe that the actions of Jesus are what God would do if he were in a body here on earth. So, healing and deliverance and treating people as he did, and all the things that he did, were done because he completely did the will of the Father. I think his actions are precisely what God wants humans to do and be. |

Seven respondents highlighted God's power and authority when summarizing the actions of Isa al Masih. In this case his actions are not necessarily seen as a model to follow or an expression of God's love, but rather as a demonstration of Allah's power and authority (Table 31).

**Table 31:** Isa's actions: God's power and authority

| IM Leader | Direct Quote |
|---|---|
| C-Asia\Julius | He came to earth with a mission for all of humanity, to reveal God's power among the people, and to attract and welcome people to seek God's kingdom, and establish God's kingdom on earth. |
| Africa\Oliver | He did a lot of miracles. He had authority to give life to the dead person, to give sight to a blind person, to cast out demons, and the many other things that only God can do. In my understanding, although he was not God himself, he did have the authority to do these things, because God was there. |
| Africa\Homer | Wherever he did miracles, people were amazed and said, "He must have God's power." |
| Africa\Brad | He has the power of Allah within himself. |
| S-Asia-D\Frank | He had authority over all things, raising people to life and creating things. He had power and authority. In this way he is totally different from any prophet or human. |
| Alongsiders\Wilbur | I look at his actions as having a number of categories. One is just exercising all sorts of supernatural power over and against the kingdom of Satan. |
| Alongsiders\Tyler | He establishes the kingdom of God. It is a kingdom of absolute rule over all the enemies of God. |

## Message of Isa al Masih

In the flow of an interview I did not always directly ask about the message of Isa al Masih, but even in those cases the interviewee made comments that revealed his understanding of Isa's main message, which seems to link in most cases to Isa's actions during his life of ministry, instead of to his death and resurrection. The main theme in the various comments associated with the message of Isa al Masih is that of hope that all will be well, and of Isa being an example for our lives today based on his call, "Follow me." Highlighting this comprehensive gospel message,

Alongsider Kevin referred to the Gospel of Mark, which begins with, "This is the good news about Jesus the Messiah, the Son of God." Kevin concluded, "Jesus is the gospel. Everything he did and said, and not just the last three days, is the gospel." Arnold likewise took a wide-angle look at the gospel and mentioned how Jesus is the Alpha and the Omega whose message is to have hope. Everything is going to be okay. The clear message he sees is, "Have this hope that one day everything is going to be restored and we will get back this paradise that was lost right at the time of Adam and Eve."

Isa being our example to follow was something that came out in the discussions about his actions, and it also surfaced as a viewpoint when the topic of Isa's message was in focus. Gus mentioned the notion of us becoming more compatible with living in God's presence by following Isa's example. He said, "You can look at Isa as a Sufi leader who is starting a new 'race' that is compatible with him." Arnold referred to helping other people as a way we should follow Isa. "He has commissioned us to go and help other people. When we do that we are helping the kingdom to expand. We need to be actively involved," according to Arnold. He also said, "Either we do this in this insider way or we can participate in a different way." Stuart also looks at Isa al Masih as our example and said, "Isa al Masih calls us so that we would do good works."

The message of Isa al Masih is that he is the way. This is a familiar expression, and a lexical search of the interview transcripts shows that respondents collectively used the phrase "the way" over 200 times. I probed deeper with some to better understand what they meant with this phrase. I asked Julius whether he sees "the way" as a path to somewhere else or as a way of living here and now that saves the world. His response indicated the latter.

> I think of the path as a metaphor. We see this in the Qur'an and in the New Testament, regarding Isa al Masih. I see the path as a way of living, in copying Isa al Masih as the example for how to live. It is the life of submission lived out as a light to others who are not on the path.

On the theme of Jesus being the way, Zach shared that Muslims are praying five times a day asking God to show them the way, the straight and true path. "It is about a pathway for salvation. It usually is much broader than people think about," Zach said. He uses John 14:6 ("I am the way, the truth, and the light") as the summary of the message of Isa al Masih. He mentioned that the notion of *amal saleh* or doing good deeds for rewards is strong in Islam, but that Muslims still want to go beyond that frame of thinking to find this way of salvation.

> So whether we talk about someone focusing on doing good works, or someone maybe going on the Hajj pilgrimage to Mecca, they are not really defining that as the way that they are looking for. They continue to pray and ask God to show them the straight and true path. So beyond all the rituals and other things they are doing, there is still this search that is going on. When Jesus says, "I am the way," it is a gracious offer to them to provide what they are looking for.

I asked Zach whether he sees "the way" as a way of living now or as a way to reach the end of the road. He referred to Jesus' parable of the wide and the narrow road.

> Jesus talked about two roads, one is narrow and one is wide. There are just a few that want to go the narrow road, because it is a struggle. Many people like the wide road. It starts with the way of life, the way of living. Many people want an easy way of living, and then choose the wide road. They think of it as a road that does not restrict them, that allows them to do whatever they want. The second option is also a choice of life. It has to do with facing the struggles of life now, and how well we do now, but there's also a sense of peace and of this being part of our final experience with God too.

Zach continued and explained how many Muslims seek the narrow road, doing good deeds and saving money to go to Mecca, but that they also hope that it will contribute to a future and afterlife that they are longing for. He concluded that Isa's message of being the way is very relevant for all of us.

So Jesus' words are very relevant and urgent, including for our Muslim friends. It has meaning for the present struggles in life but it does not stop there. There is a continuation of that in relation to their final eternal experience.

## Cross and Resurrection

It sometimes felt like a shift in paradigms when we came to the topic of the cross. The main question was, "Why did Isa al Masih suffer and die, and who ultimately made him suffer and die?" The shift moved us from talking about daily following Isa al Masih as our example as we seek to do good in this world to topics such as sin, punishment, judgment, and atonement. I grouped the comments dealing with the "why" in three sections: our sins, Jesus' submission to God's plan, and multiple dynamics. The fourth section below addresses the "who."

### Our Sins

The most common response to the question of why Jesus suffered and died was that he did so because of our sins. Table 32 illustrates this point.

**Table 32:** Our sins and the cross

| IM Leader | Direct Quote |
|---|---|
| S-Asia-A\Andy | Why did God let him die, and how does that benefit us? Yes it benefits us, because every sinner has to go through punishment. Jesus was not a sinner. His whole life shows that he was not a sinner. But he wanted to save us, because of our sins he went through all these punishments and went all the way to death. |
| Africa\Brad | Allah cannot just simply say, "Sin is a simple matter, and I forgive." Sin is not a simple matter for Allah. It is a deadly thing and a very serious matter for Allah. The cost of sin should be known forever and ever, and it is not a small matter. Allah had to put himself in the position and bear the consequences and die for it. |
| S-Asia-D\Angus | God did everything for us. Most especially, he purchased us with his own death. He purchased our sins, he saved us from that and put the burden on himself, as predicted in Isaiah. |

| IM Leader | Direct Quote |
|---|---|
| S-Asia-D\Paxton | It was actually human beings and our sins that put him on the cross. It may be Jewish sins, Christian sins, Muslim sins, or whatever form it takes. |
| SE Asia\Phil | The "why" is us and our sins. |
| SE Asia\Silas | The one who made Isa die was because of sin, sin that belonged to mankind. |
| SE Asia\Kent | The essence of what made him die was the sin of mankind. |
| SE Asia\Stuart | What caused Jesus to die was the sins of mankind, and truly all of us should have been judged, but the Messiah, the one without sin, he was the one that bore our sins as a substitute for us. With his death on the cross as the Messiah, the sins of mankind were redeemed. |
| Alongsiders\Wilbur | He very much and by his own choice embraced this path of inevitable suffering, as he would be rejected, so he underwent a period of intense testing and physical suffering which culminated in some felt separation from his father on the cross, as the weight and the blackness of the human sin problem actually came to rest on him. He bore our sins in his own body. He took all that on himself. |
| Alongsiders\Tyler | He took on our alienation, the deepest shame and the deepest sense of distance, and it was for all of us that he cried, and he swallowed it. His mouth was big enough to swallow it. The cosmic King had big enough arms to embrace it all, for all of eternity, and to heal this cosmic wound. |

The connection between our sins and Jesus' death was sometimes implicit, while others commented explicitly about that relationship. Phil summarized a commonly understood connection by referring to the love and the justice of God. He said, "God could have snatched us out with other means, if it only were for the love of God, but that would have compromised his justice. His justice combined with love necessitated the shedding of blood." Ross also mentioned the need for God to punish sin. God became a man, and this Jesus took the punishment in God's court. Gus simply said, "Justice demands punishment." Jason and alongsider Wilbur also mentioned the justice of God but added that the wrath of God had to be satisfied. The idea that Jesus was our substitute was not always stated in those exact terms but was present nonetheless. Kent's statement is an example of this when he said, "The suffering and death of Jesus, Isa al Masih, was because he took upon himself the evil of mankind.

Mankind was the one that should have died, not Jesus. But Jesus was willing to bear it upon himself." In addition, the need for the shedding of blood was another expressed connection between our sins and Jesus' death. Axel explained that both Judaism and Islam teaches that when you do something wrong, you have to sacrifice something to God. "You have to shed blood for your sins. So Isa was the perfect sacrifice (*kurbani*) for us," he said. Howard, Homer, and Brad also mentioned the blood of Jesus as our salvation.

### Isa's Submission to Allah's Plan

Three alongsiders and 10 IM leaders simply mentioned that Isa al Masih suffered and died because it was Allah's plan. Isa submitted fully to Allah, all the way to his own death. Mentioning Allah's plans as the reason is not in and of itself explaining the underlying purpose for these plans, and I assume that the respondents were thinking of a range of underlying goals, but it seems significant that so many mentioned Isa's submission to Allah in the context of this question, realizing that the fundamental purpose for mankind in Islam is to submit and serve Allah. Table 33 shows responses saying that Allah's plans were the reason for the cross. Isa's submission is mentioned explicitly or is implicit.

**Table 33:** Allah's plans, Isa's submission, and the cross

| IM Leader | Direct Quote |
|---|---|
| C-Asia\Julius | In the end, he suffered because of Allah's plan for him to suffer, not because of his own sin but because of the sins of all of humanity. |
| C-Asia\Gus | It was not easy for him, but it was the will of God that he be crucified, so that our sins will be forgiven. |
| S-Asia-B\Mitch | Well I said before, that was the plan of God, to destroy Satan, and Jesus had to pay the price for us. God did not force him. In nature, Jesus was able to overcome and be victorious over Satan. We see this even in the beginning in the temptations. He came out victorious. To the end, he remained faithful and obedient to God, to Allah, and he did not deny going to the cross and paying the price, to give his life in a very humiliating way. That is his submission to God, to God's will. |

| IM Leader | Direct Quote |
|---|---|
| Africa\Oliver | I think it was God's plan. When Allah sent him, it was in his plan. In my human understanding, God had a purpose for Jesus to die. At that time the Jews could not see that he was the Word of God and the Spirit of God. They disobeyed him. He showed them many miracles, but they couldn't see all those things, and I think God had a plan. It was his purpose for Isa al Masih to die on the cross. |
| Africa\Homer | So he came to the world, the world of sinners, and he died for us. Sometimes people say, those people did the wrong thing killing Jesus Christ, but it was God's plan that he would die, in order to save the world. |
| S-Asia-D\Angus | It was the purpose of God's story that this should happen. It was the time of the sacrifices. That is a sign. People would understand that. The time of the Passover. |
| S-Asia-D\Frank | God's plan was fulfilled, and he used the Jewish people and the Romans to fulfill his plans. It appears that they did bad things, the Romans and the Jewish leaders, when we look at it humanly. It was wrong. But if Jesus would not have died, we would not have attained salvation, and the many prophecies would not have been fulfilled. |
| S-Asia-D\Arthur | The thief was sent away, but this man should not go. You have chosen. This shows God's plan. Otherwise those people were not corrupted people. The Jewish rabbis were not a liar people. They were not street people. They were not vulgar people. They were God's people. But God was using them to do this, and they will never be caught on this point. I'm telling you the truth. They will not be judged by God for doing this. They did it unconsciously, uncontrollably, without any intention. They were diverted towards that, and directed to that. It has nothing to do with their sin. They were part of God's plan. I believe this. People say, "Oh, the Jews killed the Christ." I say, "What nonsense you are saying. The Jews made you and me to recognize the Christ. If he is not highlighted on the cross, we will not see him." This is my belief. |
| SE Asia\Phil | Allah picked Jesus as the sacrifice. |
| SE Asia\Zach | This is his assignment for the kingdom of God, and he must realize the program of the kingdom of God. Isa is submitting to the will of God as this process is unfolding. |

| IM Leader | Direct Quote |
| --- | --- |
| Alongsiders\Josh-1 | It seems clear that his suffering and dying were part of God's will. He pleaded with God for it not to happen, and yet God still wanted it to happen. I think it is clear that Jesus was doing this in submission and obedience to God, even to death on the cross, and he gave up his spirit in the end. I think that there was a complete submission on the part of Jesus to God's will. |
| Alongsiders\Wilbur | By orchestrating his own death, he supremely was able to hold the whole world accountable to their supreme rejection of him while at the same time providing the means for their reconciliation to him. He came into the world as the Lamb of God to take away the sins of the world, and this was the chosen means, to die on a Roman cross, a very brutal death, a very painful and miserable death, as the culmination of a slightly longer suffering and rejection process. He took that on himself. |
| Alongsiders\Tyler | I believe God had this all orchestrated. |

Multiple Dynamics

Several of the interviewees responded to the "why" of the cross question by stating that to them there remains a mystery with the cross, posing that there are multiple dynamics at play. All five alongsiders had some comments along those lines. Josh said that he cannot completely understand why God required something like the sacrifice of Jesus to atone for human sin. Kevin shared that the cross is a mystery to him and that he sees the three classic theories of atonement as attempts at understanding this mystery.

> Three atonement theories: as an example for us, as victory over death and the devil, and as somehow in a substitutionary role. They all have biblical data behind them, but the fact that all three can be found in the Scripture tells me that probably none of the three exhausts what was going on there. In the end, there is something mysterious about it. The fact that this is both the result of human sin and the putting to death of an innocent man, and somehow God's plan also at the same time, that is part of that whole mystery that we were talking about earlier.

Kevin added that he thinks that the substitutionary atonement theory is overused. He said, "I think that the metaphors of taking punishment in our place, and making it as if God was the punisher, and he was a sacrifice in our place, I think that metaphor gets pushed too far sometimes." Wilbur also made a comment about the substitutionary atonement doctrine.

> Of course there are multiple things going on, on the cross. Not just what we call substitutionary atonement, otherwise we might have expected him to go lay on the altar in the temple and slit his own throat in a very ceremonial fashion, or something like that. That did not happen. Instead, it is clear that he was allowing himself to be the subject of the worst kinds of suffering and rejection and mockery that the Jews and the Romans could serve up to him at that time. This functions in other ways to actually exalt the righteousness of God in light of the suffering and rejection that he endured.

Melvin said that he sees these big metanarratives in the Scripture that help explain the cross and that he looks at many of the atonement theories as metaphors. Tyler marvels at salvation as a diamond and said, "I don't know how many faces there are to this diamond, but each one has some beauty to it. It is not just the idea of substitution in theological terms."

A few of the IM leaders mentioned the complexity of the cross as well. Paxton looked at the word *for* in the phrase that Jesus died *for* our sins and said, "And 'for' can mean on behalf of my sins or because I am a sinner, and he wanted to save me, so someone had to give his life." He prefers the latter meaning, as he added, "So it is not like you are suffering from a headache and I take an aspirin, and that helps you. It will never help you, because there is no relationship between us." Zach views the cross as a restoration of God's honor and the removal of the shame of mankind, but he is unable to follow God's logic. He said, "He defeated death and darkness, and this divine paradox is that necessary thing [the cross] from God's logic, although it does not fit within man's logic. Who are we to question the logic of God?" Ray also falls short in having all the answers. He mentioned how we are in debt to God, and how Isa is our Redeemer who paid the debt. When I asked whether Isa's life was the price he said, "I do not know the price, because the Injil does not mention the price.

The Qur'an also does not mention the price. But the one who paid was Isa through his death."

In addition to the multiplicity and mystery associated with the cross, there were some additional comments made about the relationship between our sins and the death of Jesus. For example, Melvin uses the cosmic conflict between God and Satan as one of the metanarratives of redemptive history and looks at the cross as God's victory in that conflict. Mitch likewise mentioned this victory. He said, "It was the plan of God to destroy Satan." In my interview with Paxton I summarized the doctrine of penal substitutionary atonement and he replied, "Unfortunately, I cannot accept that." He said that if God really wanted to kill Jesus, he could have done so without sending him. God sent Jesus because he so loved the world. Paxton prefers the concept of solidarity over substitution. "There is solidarity of humanity. If one suffers, all suffer. And if he was the representative of humanity, therefore he suffered the most. He had to die for them. It is the concept of solidarity." He also looks at the doctrine of original sin that way, saying that we did not inherit Adam's sin but that sin is inherent. "If one man sins, if our representative sins, we have sinned in him in a way that only the concept of solidarity can explain, but not the concept of substitution."

Oliver does not link the death of Isa al Masih to our sins but considers it proof of his superiority. He said, "Jesus died and rose again and went to heaven as evidence that he was superior to others. He was not like us, but it doesn't qualify that he died for my sins." Isa's resurrection proved his superiority to his disciples and it does the same to us, according to Oliver. He even references the Qur'an.

> It [the resurrection] gives them [his disciples] a witness that he was above all other people and human nature. Also in the Qur'an it says in sura 3:55 that whoever follows Jesus, Allah will make superior to others. Jesus was superior to all others. The controversial issue is that the rest of the prophets died, were buried and none of them are alive. Jesus is the only one and he is sitting at the right hand of God as written also in the Qur'an and the Bible. It qualifies him as having authority.

Oliver looks at the concept of Jesus dying for our sins as a teaching that may fit within a Christian culture, and he sees it used out of a desire to see Muslims follow Jesus, but he disagrees with it and attributes this teaching to mistranslations. He said, "In a Muslim context, Allah says that each individual is responsible for their own life. Each one gives an account for what they did, right or wrong." Referring to the cross, resurrection, and ascension Oliver commented, "This is evidence that he was superior to others. He was not like us, but it doesn't qualify that he died for my sins. It qualifies him for me to follow him, but I am accountable for what I do." He mentioned that God is full of mercy and love, and that God can forgive sins. He also expressed his opinion that Jesus himself never said that his death was for the sins of people and that such a notion is a misunderstanding. "They interpreted this wrongly. Jesus cannot die for my sins."

Who Killed Jesus?

My question, "Who ultimately made Isa al Masih suffer and die?" was meant to further solicit comments about what was happening at the cross. The vast majority referred to Isa's suffering and death as a love sacrifice by God himself. Table 34 shows comments from 13 respondents to that effect.

During this part of the interview several indicated explicitly that Allah did not kill Isa al Masih. Paxton laughed at this notion, Mitch and Axel rejected the idea, and Melvin said that this does not fit within the paradigm he sees in the Bible. When I presented the viewpoint held by some that God placed the sins of the world on Isa al Masih and satisfied his wrath for these sins by killing Isa (or by letting him be killed), Arthur said, "This is a new thing I hear from you, but I would say I have an answer from my heart in my mind." He appealed to God's justice.

> How can God Almighty be unjust? When he is using the Christ to put all the sins of the world on him to bring all of creation to its mandate, then he is doing this himself and blaming the Christ? God would make Christ responsible for the sins of the world? He is not responsible for the sins of the world. He is a merciful and kind person. I don't believe that this idea is convincing to me. No. It is impossible, because whatever he was doing, it was actually the plan of God himself.

**Table 34:** The cross as God's love sacrifice

| IM Leader | Direct Quote |
|---|---|
| S-Asia-C\Axel | I believe that he gave his life as a sacrifice on behalf of people who are not on the right path. |
| S-Asia-B\Mitch | This is Allah's sacrificial love for his creation, for mankind, to open the way, a door, for people to come back to him. Jesus could've said no. If it were a punishment, there is no freedom to say no. Jesus said that the Son of Man must suffer and give his life and then come alive again. This was his mission. His willingness and submission was involved in this. |
| Africa\Brad | But we believe that Allah is not only his Word, but also the Holy Spirit, and Allah himself was in heaven and looking at it, but he was in a way sacrificing himself, because it was his Word that was being sacrificed. |
| S-Asia-D\Angus | No, no, no, God did not kill Jesus because all the sins were on him. God himself took our burden. |
| S-Asia-D\Frank | Since a perfect human being was needed, God allowed Jesus to be that perfect sacrifice. |
| S-Asia-D\Paxton | And so it is not the death of Jesus Christ that saves you but the way you interpret that death. If it is a sacrifice on his part, then it can save you. Love requires some kind of sacrifice. It goes through trouble and suffering. If he really loves us, then he has to suffer. And it is not only he who suffers, but if you read the Old Testament you see that God also suffers. He had to die. There was no other alternative left for him, because he loves, and love always requires some kind of sacrifice by the person who loves. And if you love to the utmost, then you suffer to the utmost. There is no other way. |
| SE Asia\Ross | God punishes and suffers. Not only Jesus, but also the Father suffers. He paid our debt. When you pay, you suffer. |
| SE Asia\Phil | It is not that Allah killed Jesus, but it was his sacrifice. God prepared the sacrifice. It is the sacrifice of God in light of the need for a substitute for the demands on humans, because of the justice of God. This is a symbol of the greatness of God's love for us. |
| SE Asia\Monty-1 | He chose to offer himself. |
| SE Asia\Lucas | One of his central works was his self-sacrifice on the cross. The biggest work was his own surrender of his life. |
| SE Asia\Stuart | As a means, he became the sacrifice in order to put into harmony mankind with God. |

| IM Leader | Direct Quote |
|---|---|
| Alongsiders\Josh-1 | I would see this most likely as God weeping when Jesus is on the cross. Not punishing as it were, but allowing him to go through a necessary sacrifice. I'm not saying that God died on the cross. I don't think that the Scriptures teach that God died on the cross, and I also don't think that the Scriptures teach that God was punishing Jesus in the sense that he was ever angry with him. He allowed this thing to happen for a larger purpose. |
| Alongsiders\Melvin | He gave up his life. He says, "No one can take my life, unless I lay it down." Isa al Masih decided to lay down his life. He wins the battle over all odds, but he dies of a broken heart. He lays down his life for his people. |

There were a few other comments on who killed Isa. Andy, Howard, Lucas, and Zach identified the Jewish leaders as the killers. Zach also mentioned Satan as the killer. He said, "Satan himself is also present in this. You can think of a cooperative effort where Satan is using humans to try to cause the plan of God to fail." Frank noted that it was not God who died on the cross but only Jesus' body. He said, "If in this scene we kill God, everything is destroyed. God is a spirit and does not have a body, and therefore cannot die. In the form of Jesus, God sent a perfect person for the salvation of humankind." Finally, three interviewees—namely, Arnold, Homer, and Ross—explicitly mentioned that all of us collectively killed Isa because of our sin. Many implied this same answer in their comments.

## *Good News*

Depending on the flow of the interview and on the information shared already, I sometimes probed further into the scene of the cross and asked, "How is Isa al Masih's death and resurrection good news?" There were a variety of responses. Ross gave a list of reasons why this is good news. He started out by saying, "The good news is that there is a solution from God, for our forgetfulness, for our sinfulness, for our dirtiness, for our debt." He also sees as good news that Isa is the true al Masih, that Allah will comfort and bless you when you are poor in spirit and feel like crying, that Isa did not get rid of the law of Moses but tells us to keep the Ten Commandments, and that he can forgive the ones who hurt him. "This is because of the sacrificial life of Jesus, by the true life of Jesus, by the examples of Jesus."

Several mentioned the victory over Satan and evil as the good news. Table 35 shows those types of responses.

**Table 35:** Good news—Satan is defeated

| IM Leader | Direct Quote |
|---|---|
| C-Asia\Jason | This shows that he was not just a good teacher but that he really had the power and still has the power. |
| SE Asia\Phil | We are gripped by sin, but behind that is that Satan has a grip on mankind. God prepared a way for mankind to be restored and renewed. This is in the context of still being tempted to sin by the evil one. There is a war, a cosmic conflict, between this restoring and tempting. And wherever there is a war, there is the shedding of blood. The resurrection is the proof that God defeated Satan. This is the way God designed the freeing of the captives. |
| SE Asia\Zach | The first aspect of why this was good is that Jesus fully submitted to the will of God. Secondly, the plan of Satan failed because of Jesus' faithfulness. The third good news is that the power of the darkness, which I associate with hell, was defeated, because it was unable to shake the plan of God. |
| SE Asia\Silas | The death and resurrection of Jesus is good news because if Jesus did not rise from the dead it would mean that mankind remains in the power of Satan, and Jesus is only a regular person. But because he was raised, the power of Satan was destroyed, and this makes it good news. |
| SE Asia\Kent | The death and resurrection of Jesus is proof that evil and sin and Satan [a strong Islamic term is used here] have been defeated, because Jesus is Lord [this is a direct reference to God] and therefore he is capable of defeating death. |
| Alongsiders\Wilbur | In terms of the spiritual conflict issues: where the deliverance from that sort of chronic supernatural harassment is experienced and is very profound—whether it is sort of the night terrors, or whether it is possession, or whatever that is—it is good news in that way. |
| Alongsiders\Melvin | The biggest part of this good news is that Christ in his death has overpowered the powers of evil. This is how many of the Muslims live it out. As these powers have been conquered, they have no more power over me in Jesus' name, as long as I have faith in him. |

Several others, such as Julius, Homer, and Monty, mentioned the forgiveness of our sins as the good news. Stuart called it "salvation free of charge."

Gus, Mitch, and Lucas referred specifically to the restored relationship between God and us as good news. Mitch said, "Now God does not see my sin, but he sees the sacrifice made by Jesus, and because of that I am right to him." A few IM leaders highlighted the resurrection as the good news; it gives us hope that we also will be resurrected. Jason said, "No prophet was resurrected. This means that Isa has power over death. For us it is good news because if we believe that he is a substitute, we also will be resurrected." Monty sees the resurrection as our foundation. He said, "If he was not raised, this whole thing is futile. It is the foundation for all of our faith. The faith of Islam without having heard about Isa is a faith that is incomplete."

There were a few other responses to the question of why the death and resurrection of Jesus is good news. Alongsider Wilbur mentioned the fact that believers avoid hell as being good news. He said, "They are personally no longer on death row, so to speak. The offer of amnesty to the prodigals is sincere and substantial." Applying the good news more to this life, Zach said that the death and resurrection of Jesus increases his conviction and his faith in what Jesus did and said. Monty likewise considers the way of life here on earth and said, "We now know what the right way is and what the wrong way is." Alongsider Melvin mentioned the inauguration of God's kingdom on earth as the good news. Overall, the replies to this question about the good news added to the responses to the other questions and helped give a fuller picture of a respondent's theological and missional understandings about Allah, his plans and purposes, and Isa al Masih.

## M-FRAMEWORK DEVELOPMENT

We all use a grid or framework through which we understand our world and God. The M-Framework is a communications and analysis tool that is centered on the mission (M) of God. In this section I present the development and foundation of this framework and the framework itself.

### Introduction and M-Framework Foundation

The literature shows that the range of viewpoints and opinions about IM among outsiders mainly comes from the variety of theological convictions among the opponents and proponents of IM. This research basically looks at the theological convictions of insiders themselves. Based on the literature and research data, I developed a framework that gives some structure to this overall theological picture, which includes our basic understanding of God (theology) and Christ (Christology), and the missional aspect of God (*missio Dei*) and Christ (*missio Christi*). My framework has 21 topics, or frames:

Allah—Theology
1. Essence
2. The Problem
3. Satan
4. Man

Allah—*Missio Dei*
1. Gospel
2. This World
3. Our Mandate
4. Healthy Societies
5. Religions
6. Election
7. Hell
8. Heaven
9. The Bible
10. The Qur'an

Isa al Masih—Christology
1. Identity
2. Christology

Isa al Masih—*Missio Christi*
1. His Life
2. On the Cross
3. The Cross
4. The Resurrection
5. The Future

Ultimately it seems that it is our understanding of the mission of God, and within that our understanding of the mission of Jesus Christ, that gives us a framework to interpret what God is like, what he is doing, who we are, and what we are called to do. I call this framework the M-Framework. The *M* stands for *missio Dei* or "mission." This framework is not a one-dimensional scale, like the C-scale, but a matrix that consists of 21 one-dimensional scales (rows), each with four levels (columns). Basically, I described the range of understanding on each of the 21 topics listed above. Each range has four entries (columns). I tried to align these entries for a specific column to represent an M paradigm, or a basic understanding someone may have of Christianity as a whole. As such, the M-Framework has four M paradigms.

As the M-Framework took shape, it became clear that the four paradigms fall into two camps. In summary, the first camp (paradigms 1 and 2) defines the gospel as a restoration of our relationship with God when we believe in Jesus. Salvation is having your personal destiny in heaven, away from this world that is evil and will be destroyed. Certain points in church history form the historic framework for this camp, which has a low view of creation. In contrast, the second camp (paradigms 3 and 4) defines the gospel as the full culmination of God's creation on earth that will come about when we accept Jesus as Lord and follow his example. Salvation is salvation *of* the world, not *away from* the world. This world will transform into God's kingdom on earth. Creation, covenants, messianic fulfillment, and the kingdom on earth form the framework for this camp, which has a high view of creation.

The development of the M-Framework was an iterative process as I went back and forth between the available literature on IM and my research data. At the end of that process I titled the four paradigms as follows:

1. Fundamental (Crucicentric)
2. Ecumenical (Ecclesiocentric)
3. Integral (Christocentric)
4. Global (Creation-centric)

The first two paradigms represent camp A, in which God is in focus and in which it is all about God. God elects or double elects. God seeks to be glorified. God is conflicted between his love and his need to punish injustice, and the cross solves God's problem. God needs to be believed in before he accepts you into heaven. God is in a cosmic conflict with Satan. It is God's fight. In this camp, man is totality depraved. Man is helpless, a victim of Satan, and unable to do any good. Salvation is upwards to heaven. Paradigm 1 represents the fundamentalist views in which the gospel centers on the cross and resurrection (crucicentric). High Calvinism, dispensationalism, and general conservative Reformed beliefs fit within this paradigm. Paradigm 2 has similar foundations as paradigm 1 but embraces a wider set of views including modernist theology and Arminianism, and as such is ecumenical and ecclesiocentric.

Paradigms 3 and 4 represent camp B, in which man is in focus and in which it is all about man. Man was created with a mandate to take care of and rule this world wisely and justly, reflecting as God's vice-regents his love into the world, and in the opposite direction reflecting the world's praises and love back to God. Man is responsible for his own sin and this world's state of affairs. Man is called to repent of forfeiting his mandate, and man is once again called into action in this world by following the example of Jesus Christ of overcoming evil with self-sacrificial love. Man is able to do good. Salvation comes downward to earth. Paradigm 3 integrates proclamation and demonstration of the gospel and looks for holistic transformation of cultures and societies. Liberation theology fits in this paradigm. It centers on Christ as the promised Messiah and seeks to apply the Sermon on the Mount on earth today as its salvation, striving for justice and peace on earth while helping the weak. Paradigm 4 also seeks to establish God's kingdom on earth through self-sacrificial love, following Jesus' example, bringing all of creation, globally, into Christ. Emergent theology belongs in this paradigm.

Figure 5 depicts the foundation of the four paradigms. It presents for each paradigm a definition of the gospel; the foundational driver; the historic framework; the views on redemption in history, this world, the end times (eschatology), and creation; and the approach to humanity. There is a sense that the gospel enlarges and becomes more encompassing as one moves from paradigm 1 to paradigm 4. Another observation is that the major shift of focus between camps A and B, from the salvation *away from* this world to the salvation *of* this world, impacts all frames and related doctrines. I defined the frames for the four paradigms in such a way as to create cohesion and alignment within each paradigm, realizing that individual theological and missional beliefs may not always logically and perfectly align within one frame.

|  | 1. Fundamental Crucicentric | 2. Ecumenical Ecclesiocentric | 3. Integral Christocentric | 4. Global Creation-centric |
|---|---|---|---|---|
| Gospel | **Restoration of Relationship; to Heaven**  Jesus Christ, as the 2nd Person of the Trinity, took your sins and endured the wrath of God on the cross as your substitute. He rose bodily on the 3rd day as proof that God the Father has accepted this payment. **Believe** this and you will go to heaven when you die. | **Restoration of Relationship; to Heaven**  Jesus Christ died for the sins of the world and rose victorious on the third day. **Believe** this and you will go to heaven when you die. | **Culmination of Creation on Earth**  Jesus was Israel's promised Messiah and he is the Savior of this world, by modeling through all his actions how to love God and others. He overcame evil with love on the cross and in the resurrection. **Follow** Jesus as Lord, be liberated from bad bondages and participate in the redemption and cleansing of this world. | **Culmination of Creation on Earth**  Jesus was Israel's promised Messiah and he is the Savior of this world, by modeling through all his actions how to love God and others. His death and resurrection shows Gods sacrificial love, abundant grace, for all and ongoing commitment to bring all of his creation to fullness in love, righteousness and justice. **Follow** Jesus as Lord, be liberated from bad bondages and participate in the cleansing of this world and the establishment of a loving, righteous and just world. |
| Foundation | Doctrinal; fundamental doctrines | Conciliar; first seven world councils | Apostolic; 1st Century church | Kingdom now; OT and Gospels |

| | 1. Fundamental Crucicentric | 2. Ecumenical Ecclesiocentric | 3. Integral Christocentric | 4. Global Creation-centric |
|---|---|---|---|---|
| **Historic Framework** | Reformation | Church Councils | Covenants & Messianic fulfillment | Creation and Kingdom on earth |
| **Redemption: This world; Eschatology** | Ahistorical; this world is getting worse; God will destroy it; timeless existence in heaven or hell. | Ahistorical; this world is getting worse; God will destroy it; while here try to make a positive impact for live on this earth; timeless existence in heaven or hell. | Historical; this world is getting better; God will transform it into his Kingdom on earth; Preach liberation in Christ and participate in the transformation of this world. | Historical; this world is getting better; we are called, with God's help and with Christ as our model, to manage this creation and evolve it into his Kingdom on earth. |
| **View of Creation** | Low view of creation. | Low but caring view of creation. | High view of creation. | High view of creation. |
| **Approach to Humanity** | Divide humanity between heaven-bound and hell-bound. | Divide humanity between heaven-bound and hell-bound. | Unite humanity through interfaith initiatives for the good of mankind. | Unite humanity through initiatives in multiple domains for the good of this world. |

**Figure 5:** The foundation of the four paradigms of the M-Framework

## The M-Framework

The M-Framework has an entry for each of the 21 frames (rows) in each of the four paradigms (columns), totaling 84 entries. The 21 frames form four clusters:

- Allah—Theology (frames 1–4)
- Allah—*Missio Dei* (frames 5–14)
- Isa al Masih—Christology (frames 15–16)
- Isa al Masih—*Missio Christi* (frames 17–21)

Table 36 shows the M-Framework for the Allah—Theology cluster, and Table 37 for the Allah—Missio Dei cluster.

**Table 36:** M-Framework for Allah—Theology

| Frame | Paradigm | | | |
|---|---|---|---|---|
| | 1. Fundamental | 2. Ecumenical | 3. Integral | 4. Global |
| Essence | Truth; just but also loving; judgment: eternal damnation for most and eternal life for some | Teacher; loving but also just; judgment: eternal damnation for some and eternal life for others | Merciful; loving, guiding, and correcting; seeking righteousness and justice; eternal life for most and eternal damnation for none | Love; enabling, guiding, and correcting; seeking righteousness and justice; eternal life for all |
| The Problem | Satan's rebellion and the Fall; broken relationship between God and man | The Fall and man giving in to Satan's temptations; broken relationship between God and man | Man's forfeit of the Creation Mandate; strife among men and corruption | Man's forfeit of the Creation Mandate; chaos and pollution |

|       | Paradigm |  |  |  |
| Frame | 1. Fundamental | 2. Ecumenical | 3. Integral | 4. Global |
| Satan | Main figure; responsible for sin and suffering; in a cosmic war with God | Tempts man off the right path | Not a major figure; part of a multiplicity of things that cause man to lose his way | Minor or no figure; man is responsible for sin and sufferings |
| Man | Totally depraved and unable to respond to God | Fully fallen and sinful but able to choose Christ as Savior | Able to follow Christ and impact societies for him | Fully capable of responding to God and doing good in this world |

**Table 37:** M-Framework for Allah—Missio Dei

|       | Paradigm |  |  |  |
| Frame | 1. Fundamental | 2. Ecumenical | 3. Integral | 4. Global |
| Gospel | God provided a way for your relationship with him to be restored through the substitutionary death of Jesus Christ on the cross and through his resurrection. Believe this and you will go to heaven when you die. | God provided a way for your relationship with him to be restored through the atoning death of Jesus Christ on the cross and through his resurrection. Believe this and you will go to heaven when you die. | God is full of mercy and love for all and is committed to the culmination of creation on earth. Follow Jesus Christ and you will be liberated from bondages and participate in establishing his kingdom on earth. | God is full of mercy and love for all and is committed to the culmination of creation on earth. Follow Jesus Christ and you will be fully human and help bring about his kingdom on earth. |

| Frame | Paradigm | | | |
|---|---|---|---|---|
| | 1. Fundamental | 2. Ecumenical | 3. Integral | 4. Global |
| This World | Created by God; doomed to total destruction; our testing ground | Created by God but doomed; will be replaced with a new heaven and a new earth | God's good creation being restored and purged from injustice towards the age to come | God's good creation, heading towards the fullness of his shalom over time |
| Our Mandate | Evangelism; save people out of this world; Jesus is our Savior away from this world; salvation | Discipleship; save people out of this world and obey God's commandments; impact societies through individual righteous living; sanctification | Missional; meet people's needs; work for systemic justice in societies in this world; liberation | Ubiquitous (omnipresent); manage this world; overcome evil with love; Jesus is our model for saving this world; shalom |
| Healthy Societies | Not in focus and secondary to personal salvation | Come about through individual righteous living | Establish by addressing systemic injustice | The core of man's mandate and the gospel |
| Religions | Christianity is the one true religion and in conflict with all others; conversion to Christianity is the goal | Christianity is the one true religion; there is some truth in other religions that can be used as bridges towards conversion | Seek interfaith dialogue and understanding towards harmony and peace | Irrelevant and sometimes an obstruction to the message of God and to following Jesus Christ |
| Election | Double election: God elects some for heaven and others for hell | A mystery between God's sovereignty and man's free choice that leads to heaven or hell | God's special appointment of certain people to be a blessing to others in this world | God's special appointment of certain people, and in a sense of everyone, to be a blessing to others in this world |

# Views on Allah and Isa al Masih

| Frame | Paradigm 1. Fundamental | 2. Ecumenical | 3. Integral | 4. Global |
|---|---|---|---|---|
| Hell | A place created by God for everlasting suffering for Satan, demons and all unbelievers (most people) | A place created by God for everlasting suffering for Satan, demons and all who openly reject God | Not a major theme in God's redemptive history; a man-made experience or a future event created by God to annihilate Satan, demons and all unbelievers | A man-made experience now and later as long as we reject God's love |
| Heaven | A place created by God for everlasting joy in his presence for all true believers (the elected few) | A place created by God for everlasting joy in his presence for all who positively respond to God's revelation to them | Man's joyful experience with God in societies now and in his kingdom on earth in the age to come | Man's joyful experience with God and in all of creation now and in his kingdom on earth over time |
| The Bible | The inerrant Word of God; without error in every domain; our authority; transcultural; truth; teaching; *sola scriptura*; biblicism; for the elect | The infallible Word of God; reveals God and matters of faith without failure; to be read in doctrinal context; our truth; for the church | Inspired record of God's dealings with his creation throughout redemptive history; to be read in historical context; our framework; for all faith communities | A record of communication between God and man; used by God to continue the communication; our guidance; context-shaped; learning; for all of mankind |
| The Qur'an | A satanic book; never use it | A dangerous book; only to be used as a one-way bridge to the Bible and Christ | A book with many truths from God | A record of communication between God and man; used by God to continue the communication |

Table 38 and Table 39 present the M-Framework for Isa al Masih on the Christology and *Missio Christi* clusters, respectively.

**Table 38:** M-Framework for Isa al Masih—Christology

| Frame | Paradigm | | | |
|---|---|---|---|---|
| | 1. Fundamental | 2. Ecumenical | 3. Integral | 4. Global |
| Identity | The Second Person of the Trinity; the eternal and divine Son of God; our Savior | God incarnate; the mediator between God and man | The promised Messiah and Redeemer of all of creation | The Word of God in human form; our model as the perfect servant, fully submitted to God |
| Christology | High Christology is the only true Christology | Process from low Christology to the goal of high Christology | High and low Christology are both vital elements of a wholistic Christology | Wholistic Christology with some emphasis on low Christology |

**Table 39:** M-Framework for Isa al Masih—Missio Christi

| Frame | Paradigm | | | |
|---|---|---|---|---|
| | 1. Fundamental | 2. Ecumenical | 3. Integral | 4. Global |
| His Life | Establishing his divinity through miracles | Establishing his divinity through miracles | The promised Messiah; correcting Judaism, renewing the law, and embracing others; liberating people from bondage | The Son of Man; protecting the weak, liberating people from bondage, exposing injustice |

| Frame | Paradigm | | | |
|---|---|---|---|---|
| | 1. Fundamental | 2. Ecumenical | 3. Integral | 4. Global |
| On the Cross | The Son of God, carrying the sins of the world | The Lamb of God, atoning for the sins of man | The Messiah, redeeming Israel and showing the way to bless the nations through self-sacrifice and love | The Son of Man, in full submission, reveals and overcomes evil with love |
| The Cross | Sin; justice; wrath; penal substitutionary atonement | Sin; justice and love; atonement for mankind | Lostness; love; mercy; solidarity with mankind; the way | Lostness; love; mercy; solidarity with mankind; the way |
| The Resurrection | Proof of his divinity and of God's wrath satisfied | Proof of the atonement accepted and of God's victory over Satan and death | Proof of his Messiahship and God's appointment of him as Lord of all | Proof of his special anointing and of God's commitment to his creation |
| The Future | Second Coming as Judge: destroy the earth; throw Satan, demons, and unbelievers in lake of fire; and bring believers into a new heaven and earth | Second Coming as Judge: destroy the earth; throw Satan, demons, and unbelievers in lake of fire; and bring believers into a new heaven and earth | The coming King, cleansing the earth from injustice and transforming this world into his kingdom for all; or annihilation of Satan, demons, and unbelievers | Presently at work as King towards the culmination of creation on earth |

Appendix D has additional M-Framework depictions for further reference.

# DATA ANALYSIS WITH M-FRAMEWORK

## Introduction to M-Framework Plots

Using the M-Framework as a tool, I reviewed the full transcripts of the 31 interviews and analyzed the responses and comments with this framework in mind. I associated the answers or comments from each interviewee on a specific frame/topic with one of the four paradigms: Fundamental, Ecumenical, Integral, or Global. This resulted in 31 individual M-Framework plots, 26 for the IM leaders and five for the IM alongsiders.

Some general initial observations are that most individuals seem to favor one or two paradigms. A person may find all four brief paradigm definitions acceptable for a given frame, but one or two of these definitions will have priority over the others. In my assessment of the interview transcripts I looked for that priority preference for each frame.

In the sections below I first present interview summaries related to the theological and missional views of the interviewee. I group these summaries by region, and I show the individual M-Framework plots for each IM leader and alongsider. These plots are based on my full transcripts of the interviews. Next, I introduce the individual summary plot concept and analyze the M-Framework summary plots by region. Last, I look at cross-cutting themes.

## Southeast Asia M-Framework Plots

### Lucas

Lucas described Allah as very holy and full of love and as having endearing feelings for humans. "God is glorious, and what he created was also glorious, but because of the fall of man, mankind lost its glory." He sees that Allah has taken the initiative to create a way for man back to him, and Jesus is the way. "Reconciliation with God was already prefigured in the Tawrat in the sacrificial system and climaxed in the sacrifice of Jesus," Lucas said. His central theological framework is faith and obedience. "The doing of his will is to do good to others."

| Theology Proper | 1 | 2 | 3 | 4 |
|---|---|---|---|---|
| Essence | Ls | | | |
| The Problem | | Ls | | |
| Satan | | Ls | | |
| Man | | Ls | | |
| **Missio Dei** | **1** | **2** | **3** | **4** |
| Gospel | Ls | | | |
| This World | | Ls | | |
| Our Mandate | Ls | | | |
| Healthy Societies | | Ls | | |
| Religions | | Ls | | |
| Election | | Ls | | |
| Hell | | Ls | | |
| Heaven | | Ls | | |
| The Bible | | Ls | | |
| The Qur'an | | | Ls | |
| **Isa al Masih** | **1** | **2** | **3** | **4** |
| Identity | | Ls | | |
| Christology | | Ls | | |
| His Life | Ls | | | |
| On the Cross | | Ls | | |
| The Cross | | Ls | | |
| The Resurrection | | Ls | | |
| The Future | Ls | | | |

**Figure 6:** M-Framework plot for Lucas

He sees as the purpose of Allah's plans to restore the former condition of our relationship with God. Regarding the Scriptures, Lucas considers them as "breathed out by God" and he views them "as a guide and teacher." He shared that in his life he has experienced many miracles of healings and of God's provision.

The central work of Isa al Masih is his self-sacrifice on the cross, as he surrendered his life to save us, according to Lucas. Who killed him? "The killers are the Jews." Regarding the relationship between Isa al Masih and Allah, Lucas said that the oneness is the central element. When asked about religions, he recognized that they push people to do the right thing, but he also sees them as constraining.

> Religions are like people who have been colonized by foreign powers. They are living under that overlordship, and they want to become free. They are trying to find some pathway to freedom from their overlordship. Yes, Jesus is the only one that can provide that salvation pathway.

In their small groups, called *jamaats*, they study the Scriptures inductively. Lucas explained, "There is a lot of theologizing from the passages that they are reading. They progressively understand the superiority of Jesus." Regarding the Trinity, some accept it while others don't.

They use the Qur'an in their sharing and studies. Lucas pointed out that there are a lot of truths within it that are good for teaching and leading people.

## Zach

Allah is full of grace and mercy and is the source of his life, according to Zach. Allah created this world to praise and respect him, and the issue of sin must be taken care of first so that through our transformation we are given a new realization that we need to worship Allah, according to Zach. He described hell as "a place for those who have not come to a realization and response to the grace and mercy of Allah." Regarding heaven, he shared that the concept of heaven is not just something in the future that starts later, but in a sense colors our experiences now. He prefers to see God's plan to restore and redeem this world on the one hand and his plans to get people to heaven on the other hand as two sides of the same coin.

Man has a free will to reject Allah, but once someone understands the grace and mercy of Allah, Zach stated, "this free will has to be served to Allah. This takes self-sacrifice and surrender, so we do not get pulled off to the way of exercising free will as the world sees it." Zach sees the Scriptures as a revelation of Allah, inspired by the Spirit of Allah, and as the story of Allah. He looks at the Qur'an as inspired by human teachers of Mohammed, which included Christians and Muslims. He described Mohammed as a type of missionary to the Arabs, to bring them to monotheism. Zach said that "the Qur'an is helpful to help people better understand the grace and mercy of Allah," and he uses the Qur'an as a doorway to the former books.

| Theology Proper | 1 | 2 | 3 | 4 |
|---|---|---|---|---|
| Essence | | Zh | | |
| The Problem | | | Zh | |
| Satan | | Zh | | |
| Man | | | Zh | |
| **Missio Dei** | **1** | **2** | **3** | **4** |
| Gospel | | | Zh | |
| This World | | | Zh | |
| Our Mandate | | | Zh | |
| Healthy Societies | | Zh | | |
| Religions | | | | Zh |
| Election | | Zh | | |
| Hell | | Zh | | |
| Heaven | | Zh | | |
| The Bible | | | Zh | |
| The Qur'an | | | Zh | |
| **Isa al Masih** | **1** | **2** | **3** | **4** |
| Identity | | | Zh | |
| Christology | | | Zh | |
| His Life | | | Zh | |
| On the Cross | | Zh | | |
| The Cross | | Zh | | |
| The Resurrection | | Zh | | |
| The Future | | | Zh | |

**Figure 7:** M-Framework plot for Zach

Zach mentioned that in their discipleship pattern they have a strong focus on Jesus' actions and use the slogan, "Look and see what Jesus did, and then listen and think about what he said." Their emphasis is on doing rather than debating. What did Isa do?

When explaining al Masih to Muslims, Zach said that he emphasizes the presence of God. He said,

> Al Masih means that he is now present, that Jesus is always right here, with us. What is good about Isa's death and resurrection? The first aspect of why this was good is that Jesus fully submitted to the will of God. Secondly, the plan of Satan failed because of Jesus' faithfulness. The third good news is that the power of the darkness, which I associate with hell, was defeated, because it was unable to shake the plan of God.

Zach explained how they use John 14:6 ("I am the way, the truth, and the life") much with Muslims, because every day they are praying multiple times to Allah to show them the way, the true path, which is not encompassed in good works such as going on pilgrimage. When I asked Zach whether he sees this "way" as a way of life on earth today or as a road to heaven elsewhere, Zach mentioned the two roads that Isa is talking about. "There are just a few that want to go the narrow road, because it is a struggle. Many people like the wide road. It starts with the way of life, the way of living." Jesus' way gives meaning to the present struggles, but it does not stop there. There is a continuation of that in relation to their final eternal experience, according to Zach.

On the relationship between Allah and Isa al Masih, Zach acknowledged Isa's divinity but highlighted the oneness of Allah, and regarding the phrase *Son of God*, Zach mentioned that they avoid using the phrase unless directly asked:

> When we start using language of the fatherhood of God and the sonship [of Isa], it gives the concept of these not being one. There is a separation in the concept of our audience here. This kind of language really is an obstacle to them accepting the divinity of Jesus.

On the role of religion, Zach mentioned, "Our approach is that we think about how to renew their religious system so that it is really centered around the true identity and teachings of Jesus, to come back to the true foundations of the teachings of Jesus." Islam is an introduction to Isa. Zach explained that they are not trying to guide people into the direction of the traditional church.

We want people from every religion to come to some mutual understanding of Jesus, to enter into the kingdom of God. On the one hand, there is the model that people need to go into the container of the formal church first, to find out who Jesus is and to enter into the kingdom, but it is better to go direct. We want people through their own religions to discover these things and to begin being drawn towards Jesus. It is the beginning of guidance for them in their own religions.

As people come to faith in Isa, Zach explained, they encourage them to stay in their own context and to form communities of faith, "because we want them through mentoring and coaching to have a role in saving their neighbors and friends and relatives." He also said, "One of the roles of a mentor is to encourage them to be strong and to endure in suffering, and really serve as a light in the middle of that context."

## Ian

Ian is an Islamic scholar and leader who talks to gatherings of Muslims and Christians alike about Isa al Masih. He talked about the Qur'an as a book that exalts the former books. It is the confirmer of the Tawrat, Zabur, and Injil and functions as a pointer to them. Ian encourages believers to try to get Muslims to read the Scriptures, even though they hate and reject it,

| Theology Proper | 1 | 2 | 3 | 4 |
|---|---|---|---|---|
| Essence | | In | | |
| The Problem | | In | | |
| Satan | In | | | |
| Man | | In | | |
| **Missio Dei** | **1** | **2** | **3** | **4** |
| Gospel | | In | | |
| This World | | In | | |
| Our Mandate | | In | | |
| Healthy Societies | | | In | |
| Religions | | | In | |
| Election | | In | | |
| Hell | | In | | |
| Heaven | | In | | |
| The Bible | | In | | |
| The Qur'an | | | In | |
| **Isa al Masih** | **1** | **2** | **3** | **4** |
| Identity | | In | | |
| Christology | In | | | |
| His Life | | | In | |
| On the Cross | | In | | |
| The Cross | | In | | |
| The Resurrection | | In | | |
| The Future | | In | | |

**Figure 8:** M-Framework plot for Ian

so that they experience something extraordinary, as the Spirit of Allah will begin to implant the Word of Allah in them.

> What is the role of the Qur'an in relation to the good news of the gospel? It does not make sense for the Qur'an, which appeared 700 years after the gospel, to merely repeat the same message. What is conveyed is only a brief summary, which gives an *Amen* and confirms what was already written in the Gospels 700 years before.

Regarding Jesus being the Son of God, Ian sees this as a metaphorical phrase. "Jesus was born of the Spirit of God, just as the Qur'an was born of the Spirit of God. We should not reject Jesus." He highlighted the strong monotheism from Isaiah 40, which is quoted in Mark 1, as an important foundation for Muslims to see.

As a way of building on additional common ground, Ian promotes talking with Muslims about Isa's future return and about him being the coming Judge and King. Working backwards from that future truth, it is clear to Ian that Muslims need Isa now. "Seventy percent of all Muslim families are families in trouble. They need heart transformation." Ian calls for a reduction of the descent of moral degradation all around us through Scripture memorization, "so that we can more often and more deeply apply it in our lives, so that truly heart transformation will occur."

## Phil

Regarding the plans and purposes of Allah since the fall of man, "Allah did not reject his first creation and start over, but he is repairing what is broken and restoring the consequences of the broken order. Forgiveness is part of the restoring of the consequences of sin," Phil said. He sees Allah working his plans now, "all the way through into heaven." Phil added, "In one sense heaven and hell are in the future, as locations, but in another sense they already are beginning to be an experience in the current day." Phil sees hell as for those who by their own choice do not put their faith in al Masih. "God is fair and just. It is not that anyone of us deserves heaven; we all deserve hell. God is preparing an alternative that has to be welcomed and received."

Phil considers the prophets as ambassadors and messengers of Allah. "Eventually God himself came down in the form of Jesus to give the final revelation." In sharing with Muslims he stresses using the chronological presentation of all the prophets, down to Jesus, so they will come to the question, "What then is the purpose of yet another prophet?" Phil likes this approach because it reasons rather than argues about Mohammed not being a prophet.

| Theology Proper | 1 | 2 | 3 | 4 |
|---|---|---|---|---|
| Essence | PI | | | |
| The Problem | | PI | | |
| Satan | | PI | | |
| Man | | | PI | |
| **Missio Dei** | **1** | **2** | **3** | **4** |
| Gospel | | PI | | |
| This World | | PI | | |
| Our Mandate | PI | | | |
| Healthy Societies | | PI | | |
| Religions | | PI | | |
| Election | | PI | | |
| Hell | PI | | | |
| Heaven | | PI | | |
| The Bible | | | PI | |
| The Qur'an | | PI | | |
| **Isa al Masih** | **1** | **2** | **3** | **4** |
| Identity | | PI | | |
| Christology | PI | | | |
| His Life | PI | | | |
| On the Cross | | PI | | |
| The Cross | | PI | | |
| The Resurrection | | PI | | |
| The Future | | PI | | |

**Figure 9:** M-Framework plot for Phil

The Scriptures are the words of God written as a guide for people. "They include pointers towards the way, towards traveling the right way to God," Phil said. He mentioned that *the way* is not only about a future perspective, "but it is about the process of following that way all the way forward from now."

Phil mentioned our sins as the reason for the death and resurrection of Isa. Allah picked Isa as the sacrifice. "Wherever there is a war, there is the shedding of blood. The resurrection is the proof that God defeated Satan," Phil said. "His justice combined with love necessitated the shedding of blood."

## Monty

What is Allah like? "All the fullness of Allah is revealed in Isa. And this is something very new to Muslims," shared Monty. He appreciates that Mohammed said that there is no god but God, but laments his underdevelopment of *Kalaam*, or the Word. Monty attributes this to the Jewish view of Isa. They rejected him as al Masih. "God could not come as a man." Second, the Jews were expecting a different kind of Masih.

> These two misconceptions of the Jews also had influence on Mohammed. Even though there was a revelation of Jesus as a miracle worker, a prophet, and apostle, there is no additional higher Christology in the Qur'an, because of these two misconceptions of the Jews. These two things still remain as some of the biggest obstacles. When we come with the story of Jesus, it takes a long time for a Muslim to accept that.

When asked about the plans and purposes of Allah, Monty said, "The teaching of Islam is that all of creation must submit and praise God, and give all of its life and surrender to God, until everyone knows God." Everything must come back to the beauty of the original creation. Heaven and hell are part of these plans, according to Monty. "One of the purposes of the last days is to differentiate out those who have rejected God all of their lives. There has to be a separate place for them." Monty does not see this as a religious differentiation. "We realize that from the religion of Christianity many will end up in hell when they die, as will be the case for many people from Islam." He further pointed out,

"Muslims have a very strong belief that there is a heaven and a hell, even before they come to faith in Jesus." Monty believes that man has freedom of choice to accept or reject Allah, although Allah does not want anyone to make the wrong choice.

Monty believes that the very words of the Scriptures have power when a reader or listener responds to them. He also considers the Scriptures as a guide for us to get close to God. Regarding the Qur'an, he said, "Thirty-eight percent of the Qur'an is a retelling of the Jewish prophets—a retelling and summarizing. Sixty-two percent is associated with having its own agenda and importance related to the prophet Mohammed."

| Theology Proper | 1 | 2 | 3 | 4 |
|---|---|---|---|---|
| Essence |  | My |  |  |
| The Problem | My |  |  |  |
| Satan | My |  |  |  |
| Man |  | My |  |  |
| **Missio Dei** | **1** | **2** | **3** | **4** |
| Gospel | My |  |  |  |
| This World |  | My |  |  |
| Our Mandate | My |  |  |  |
| Healthy Societies |  | My |  |  |
| Religions |  |  |  | My |
| Election |  | My |  |  |
| Hell | My |  |  |  |
| Heaven |  | My |  |  |
| The Bible |  | My |  |  |
| The Qur'an |  |  | My |  |
| **Isa al Masih** | **1** | **2** | **3** | **4** |
| Identity |  | My |  |  |
| Christology |  | My |  |  |
| His Life | My |  |  |  |
| On the Cross |  | My |  |  |
| The Cross |  | My |  |  |
| The Resurrection |  | My |  |  |
| The Future | My |  |  |  |

**Figure 10:** M-Framework plot for Monty

Monty sees the Qur'an giving witness to the truth that was sent before. In his words, "It legitimizes the text that came before." Later on Monty shared that the Qur'an defends Isa in saying that he did not die, because they had a great deal of admiration for him, the holy one. "So we need to give Muslims a greeting of brotherhood because of their great admiration for Jesus," said Monty.

Regarding the death and resurrection of Jesus, Monty sees Isa as the only suitable sacrifice. He died because he offered himself for mankind. What is good about this? "Mankind can know what is right and what is good. The good news came from heaven. We now know what the right way is and what the wrong way is." Monty considers Islam without Isa's death and resurrection incomplete. We are called to the hard work of surrendering ourselves and becoming committed to Isa al Masih.

When asked about the relationship between Isa al Masih and Allah, Monty highlights their oneness in spirit.

It is difficult to separate Isa al Masih from God because they are spirit. If you try to do it, it often ends up creating a separation that is wide between Isa al Masih and Allah. We cannot really picture Isa in a sense as a mathematical formula that is neatly structured and boxed up. They are spirit, which is the same, and Isa is God revealing himself as mankind. I want to emphasize the oneness of spirit and not of place or individual.

He considers the phrase *Son of God* to be a metaphor. It is a term that honors and signifies that he has come from Allah, according to Monty. "All of this is necessary in order for him to enter into the servanthood role, the servant of Allah."

## Silas

Silas described Allah as the Creator, generous and patient. "Allah's plan and objective is to make man obedient to his Creator and to make Allah the center of worship." Regarding this life and the age to come, Silas said, "At this time, mankind is tested to determine the way, or the street, for life in the coming age." He talked about a man receiving a reward of some kind, or a return on his life in the coming age. "In the present age, if he takes the wrong way or street (roadway), then in the coming age it will be *salaka*—it is like a terrible wreck." He described heaven as a place full of pleasure and grace (a qur'anic statement) from Allah, and a place where Allah is present. On the other hand, his description of hell is a place of torture because of the anger of Allah (two Islamic and Arabic words) for those people who do not live obedient unto Allah in this age.

| Theology Proper | 1 | 2 | 3 | 4 |
|---|---|---|---|---|
| Essence | Ss | | | |
| The Problem | | | Ss | |
| Satan | | Ss | | |
| Man | | Ss | | |
| **Missio Dei** | **1** | **2** | **3** | **4** |
| Gospel | | Ss | | |
| This World | Ss | | | |
| Our Mandate | | Ss | | |
| Healthy Societies | | Ss | | |
| Religions | | | | Ss |
| Election | | Ss | | |
| Hell | Ss | | | |
| Heaven | | Ss | | |
| The Bible | | | Ss | |
| The Qur'an | | | Ss | |
| **Isa al Masih** | **1** | **2** | **3** | **4** |
| Identity | | Ss | | |
| Christology | | Ss | | |
| His Life | | | Ss | |
| On the Cross | | Ss | | |
| The Cross | | Ss | | |
| The Resurrection | | Ss | | |
| The Future | Ss | | | |

**Figure 11:** M-Framework plot for Silas

Silas sees Isa al Masih as the Lord. "The Lord longed for mankind who is lost. Therefore, the Lord took on the form of mankind so that he can be understood by mankind and his teachings could be followed by mankind." Silas shared that Isa al Masih is the sacrifice for the sin of mankind. Silas sees the death and resurrection of Isa as good news because without it, "mankind remains in the power of Satan, and Jesus is only a regular person. But, because he was raised, the power of Satan was destroyed, and this makes it good news." Explaining the relationship between Isa and Allah, Silas said, "Isa is the Word of Allah. Whatever Isa spoke was the same as what Allah spoke. Isa is Lord." This word for "Lord" is only used for Allah, according to Tyler.

As a brief personal testimony, Silas shared that a person told him the story of Isa al Masih in a way that was not directly linked with Christianity. "So I studied this first of all from my holy book (the Qur'an), and lo and behold, I found that Isa al Masih is the straight and true pathway that I had been looking for, for a long time." He now is not limited by religion, but rather puts priority on his "priesthood unto Isa al Masih." Silas explained how he was fanatical in a legalistic way before, but that he now is "much more submissive to Allah, just like Isa previously obeyed and submitted unto the purposes of Allah."

## Kent

Kent described Allah as powerful over all creation, and full of love, righteousness, and compassion. The plans of Allah are for his creation "to do good deeds and follow the model and example of Allah." He calls us into obedience, according to Kent. In the age to come "we will receive rewards or punishments fitted to our deeds. If we live in this present age according to a good path,

| Theology Proper | 1 | 2 | 3 | 4 |
|---|---|---|---|---|
| Essence | Kt | | | |
| The Problem | | | Kt | |
| Satan | | Kt | | |
| Man | | | Kt | |
| **Missio Dei** | **1** | **2** | **3** | **4** |
| Gospel | Kt | | | |
| This World | Kt | | | |
| Our Mandate | | | Kt | |
| Healthy Societies | | | Kt | |
| Religions | | | | Kt |
| Election | | | Kt | |
| Hell | Kt | | | |
| Heaven | | | Kt | |
| The Bible | | | Kt | |
| The Qur'an | | | | Kt |
| **Isa al Masih** | **1** | **2** | **3** | **4** |
| Identity | | | | Kt |
| Christology | | | Kt | |
| His Life | | | Kt | |
| On the Cross | Kt | | | |
| The Cross | Kt | | | |
| The Resurrection | | | Kt | |
| The Future | Kt | | | |

**Figure 12:** M-Framework plot for Kent

then we will receive good rewards in heaven." Kent describes heaven as a place of peace for the followers of Allah where there is goodness and pleasure of Allah. Hell, however, is seen as the place of torture. "It is very terrifying for one who has been rebellious, for the followers of Satan and demons," Kent said. He believes that Allah gives man the freedom to choose. Allah has revealed himself through prophets to rebuke mankind "when they were blinded by the persuasiveness of Satan such that their lives turned from the right path." In addition, Kent believes that Allah revealed himself in the Scriptures (the holy books), which are "overfilled with the teachings and commands of God." He also considers the Scriptures "the narrative about Allah and about his greatness." Kent considers the Qur'an to be a valuable pointer or sign that points to the truth in the Tawrat, Zabur, and Injil.

Isa al Masih is the honored Word of Allah. "What was spoken by Isa was spoken by Allah. Isa came to this world as he was with Allah, and he revealed himself in this world to teach the truth," Kent said. Isa died because of the sin of mankind. "His resurrection is proof that evil, sin, and Satan have been defeated, because Jesus is Lord and therefore he is capable of defeating death." Kent expressed his relationship with Isa as a personal commitment to only follow the teachings of Isa al Masih. Later on he put it in terms of "uniting first with him." Kent does not put too much weight on religious affiliation.

When asked about the phrase *Son of God*, Kent said that he only sees it as a symbol and figure of speech. He leaves the exact meaning a mystery. How did he first hear about this Son of God, or Isa al Masih? Kent shared how his interest was piqued when a friend said that the Isa al Masih spoken of in

| Theology Proper | 1 | 2 | 3 | 4 |
|---|---|---|---|---|
| Essence | St | | | |
| The Problem | | St | | |
| Satan | | St | | |
| Man | | St | | |
| **Missio Dei** | **1** | **2** | **3** | **4** |
| Gospel | St | | | |
| This World | St | | | |
| Our Mandate | St | | | |
| Healthy Societies | | St | | |
| Religions | | St | | |
| Election | | St | | |
| Hell | St | | | |
| Heaven | St | | | |
| The Bible | | St | | |
| The Qur'an | | | | St |
| **Isa al Masih** | **1** | **2** | **3** | **4** |
| Identity | | | | St |
| Christology | St | | | |
| His Life | | | St | |
| On the Cross | St | | | |
| The Cross | St | | | |
| The Resurrection | St | | | |
| The Future | St | | | |

**Figure 13:** M-Framework plot for Stuart

the Qur'an is the same as the one spoken of in the Injil. "After that, I began truly to study and question various people who understood about who Isa al Masih is."

## Stuart

Allah is the Creator of all and is all-powerful, all-seeing, all-righteous, all-merciful, and all-compassionate, according to Stuart. Tyler indicated that Stuart used Arabic expressions for these characteristics. Stuart believes that Allah's plans are to return mankind, or to restore his people, "so that they become close once again and return in closeness to God." Mankind has been separated from Allah because of sin. "Allah centers his purposes upon heavenly life because this world is full of sin," Stuart said. In this life man is to remember this heavenly life and the promises of Allah, "so that they are not tripped up by this worldly life that goes in the direction of destruction." He described heaven as a place that is comfortable and without sadness, and he pictured hell as a place where there is fire that continuously flames without stopping. "Every person whose name is not noted in the book of life is intended to go to hell, which is also the place for the angels that rebelled against God." Stuart believes that man fell into sin but he also said, "Man has good characteristics, that is, he can still choose what is true or that which is wrong."

"The Word of Allah tells of his power and character and contains guidance that we must obey," said Stuart. He presented the Qur'an as "a revelation of God given to the prophet Mohammed, SAW." He gives Mohammed the honorific SAW, which in Arabic stands for *sallallahu alayhi wasallam*. The English equivalent is "peace be upon him" (PBUH). Stuart further commented about the Qur'an saying, "We just accept it for what it is."

On the topic of Isa al Masih, Stuart believes that Isa came to the world because he loves mankind. He gives us a good example and calls us to good works. Isa al Masih was without sin and bore our sin, as our substitute, according to Stuart. "He became the sacrifice in order to put mankind into harmony with God." Stuart believes that Isa calls us to be close to him, so that we grow and produce fruit. Stuart described the relationship between Isa al Masih and Allah as follows: "The Word of Isa al Masih was before the world existed. He already existed. Isa also said, 'The Father and I are one.' If this is true, Isa al Masih is God."

Stuart believes that the phrase *Son of God* is only a figure of speech and that the pregnancy is the result of the Spirit of Allah. Stuart also stated, "At the foundation is the Word of God which confesses and reveals that the Son of God is God himself."

## Drew

| Theology Proper | 1 | 2 | 3 | 4 |
|---|---|---|---|---|
| Essence | | | Dw | |
| The Problem | | | Dw | |
| Satan | | | | Dw |
| Man | | | | Dw |
| **Missio Dei** | **1** | **2** | **3** | **4** |
| Gospel | | | Dw | |
| This World | | Dw | | |
| Our Mandate | | | | Dw |
| Healthy Societies | | | Dw | |
| Religions | | | | Dw |
| Election | | | Dw | |
| Hell | | | Dw | |
| Heaven | | | Dw | |
| The Bible | | | | Dw |
| The Qur'an | | | | Dw |
| **Isa al Masih** | **1** | **2** | **3** | **4** |
| Identity | | | | Dw |
| Christology | | Dw | | |
| His Life | | | | Dw |
| On the Cross | | | | Dw |
| The Cross | | | Dw | |
| The Resurrection | | | Dw | |
| The Future | | | Dw | |

**Figure 14:** M-Framework plot for Drew

Drew grew up as the child of a "mixed marriage," with his father being Muslim and his mother Christian. As a very young child he used to go to the mosque on Fridays and to church on Sundays. He attended an Islamic elementary school, and by the fourth grade he refused to call himself Christian anymore. As he grew up Drew got very involved in Islam. One of his motivations was to convert his mother one day. He joined the most fundamental sect, but when he started seeing hypocrisy and corruption there he left it, which was a difficult process. At that point he decided to become a freethinker and agnostic. Being lost and without friends, he felt that he needed to go back to the church, where a peaceful feeling came over him and a desire to know Isa al Masih. He bargained with Allah, saying that if he found any corruption in Isa he would disassociate with Christianity immediately. "Now, five years later, I have not found anything wrong with this Isa and the teachings of the Bible. I am falling in love more and more with Isa. He is the truth, and I have no doubt about him." Drew submitted his own plots in the M-Framework.

Drew shared how from the very beginning of his walk with Isa, his identity was still Muslim. He recalled that after he got baptized and arrived home, he did the regular *salat* (prayers) as an expression of thankfulness to Allah. At that point he had never heard about contextualization and insider movements. He talked about his views of Christianity and his desire to separate religion from the action to follow Isa al Masih.

> I was a radical Muslim, so Christianity to me was associated with the West, which is America, which is a country that wants to destroy Islam. That is a common belief, but we have to separate Jesus from the Christianity that we know. The spiritual matters are beyond any religion. I think that my mother and other Christians miss this point, that somehow following Jesus means needing to be registered in a church and attending their weekly worship service. But Jesus is telling me to make disciples. It is an action.

Drew looks at Mohammed as a good elementary school teacher. He now has Isa as his professor, but he finds the two compatible.

> I don't find any of his [Mohammed's] teaching contradicting the teachings of Isa. Isa explains more about what Mohammed is talking about but they're not contradicting. There's nothing wrong with believing in Mohammed, because it does not affect your salvation. At the same time, there is no obligation for Christians to believe in Mohammed.

Drew pointed out that it is a mistake to compare Isa al Masih with Mohammed. "When people compare Isa with Mohammed I think we are underestimating Isa. We are decreasing his status as the Son of God to Mohammed's level." He also added, "If these two people would live together at this time, they would not fight together." Drew focuses on the need for transformation. "Sometimes Christians think that we need to share the information about Jesus dying on the cross for our sins, but his dying transforms us first." In his interactions with Muslims he uses the Qur'an because many verses relate to the Bible.

## Ross

Before we started on the questions, Ross shared a little on the topic of suffering. He was fairly clear in his views. "If you follow Allah but you are not interested in suffering, you are not following Allah. From Egypt to the

Promised Land is a desert. It is a desert here." He also added the aspect of struggling with Allah in our life of faith, recounting how Jacob wrestled with Allah, who respected Jacob for it. "Then God gave Jacob a new name, Israel. It means, 'You struggle with God. You need me and you desire me.' We all need to be Israel."

Ross described Allah as the Creator and as the most compassionate and loving one. Allah's purposes for us as his creation are that we would be submissive to him, glorify him, and love and honor all people and things that Allah created. Ross shared that the Qur'an addresses pollution. "If a river in front of your house is polluted, you cannot say that you are submissive to Allah, because you are polluting what God has created." Ross pointed to the sin in the world.

> The problem is that our rivers are polluted. There are wars. We gossip about the wickedness of others, instead of covering the wickedness of others. We love to shame people. The purposes of Allah are for us to cover them when our brothers are weak. Do not expose their nakedness. We deviated from the plan of God. We are lost. We are dirty like in the story of the lost child, the Prodigal Son.

God sacrificed to give us a clean shirt, according to Ross. Isa is God's sacrifice, the Lamb from the sky. He compared Allah to a rich king. "If you go to the bank to get a loan, you do not bring a friend who is also a debtor as a guarantee. You bring a very rich man, a king. The king is sacrificial to help the person in debt." We should accept Isa so that we are not afraid of death, Ross shared. When asked whether it is needed for someone to accept Isa before that person dies, he expressed his views on the good plans of Allah and the power of Isa al Masih as Lord. "Eternity means that we are in Allah's plan. He has decided before we were in the womb of our mothers. Now we must reflect Allah's plan; what happens after we die also is in Allah's plan." The implication that all are in Allah's plans and all are saved came out when Ross added, "Of course I do not say, 'Well it is okay, do whatever you want.' I hope that people will experience the love of Allah." He added, "If we say that Isa is the Lord of life and that if you do not accept Isa before you die, it is too late, Isa cannot do anything," Ross laughed. "Jesus cannot do anything after death? He is not Lord anymore after death?" He shared how he believes in the gospel, which says that Isa is Lord of the living and the dead. He noted that Western Christians do not seem to discuss or believe in the power of Isa after death.

As we dialogued about eternity, heaven, and hell, Ross kept bringing heaven to earth. "This life is part of eternity, it is part of heaven. If we accept Jesus, everything we do in this life is part of heaven."

Ross sees prophets as sinners chosen by Allah to remind mankind, which tends to forget and deviate from the path, to come back to Allah. He identifies Moses and David and their books, and calls Jesus the one who reveals Allah. "Then the prophet Mohammed, a sinner chosen by God, wrote to confirm that the Tawrat, Zabur, and Injil are guidance from God and light from God."

| Theology Proper | 1 | 2 | 3 | 4 |
|---|---|---|---|---|
| Essence | | | | Rs |
| The Problem | | | | Rs |
| Satan | | Rs | | |
| Man | | | Rs | |
| **Missio Dei** | **1** | **2** | **3** | **4** |
| Gospel | | | Rs | |
| This World | | | Rs | |
| Our Mandate | | | | Rs |
| Healthy Societies | | | | Rs |
| Religions | | | | Rs |
| Election | | | Rs | |
| Hell | | | | Rs |
| Heaven | | | | Rs |
| The Bible | | | Rs | |
| The Qur'an | | | | Rs |
| **Isa al Masih** | **1** | **2** | **3** | **4** |
| Identity | | Rs | | |
| Christology | | | | |
| His Life | | | Rs | |
| On the Cross | | Rs | | Rs |
| The Cross | | Rs | | |
| The Resurrection | | Rs | | |
| The Future | | | Rs | |

**Figure 15:** M-Framework plot for Ross

We talked some about the anger of Allah. Ross shared, "Yes, I believe that. God has feelings. He has a right to be angry. When your loved ones abandon you, what do you feel?" He blames the agnostics for keeping Allah at a distance, without feelings, which can lead to a view of Allah as not being interested in us. But to Ross, Allah has real feelings and he is very interested in and close to us. "Jesus not only saves us, but he saves God as well. He saves God from being angry. He saves God from being brutally angry."

To Ross the good news is that Isa is the true Masih who saves us and who is coming again. "Because of the sacrificial life of Isa and by his example, I can forgive the ones that hurt us and I can embrace someone that formerly I could not." Ross is convinced that the prophet Mohammed points to Isa. "Today people say that the prophet Mohammed only points to himself, but this is distorted. There is a difference between a distorted Islamic community and an idealistic Islamic community." Ross seeks to be a reformer within Islam and in his community. "I was born here with this identity, and I must reform my community. This is my responsibility."

On the topic of religions, Ross calls himself a Muslim because of the color of his skin and the language he speaks. The gospel is for those who are heavy laden and burdened to come to Isa al Masih. That is for everyone and can be done by everyone, including Muslims, according to Ross.

> So when people decide to go to the church, I say to them, "It is okay, and you can read the Tawrat, Zabur, and Injil in the church. But Jesus has given you the responsibility to bless the people in the mosque. You cannot convert your skin into white skin. You must not become a stumbling block to an agnostic Muslim. You must reform them in a way that is accepted by them, because you are their brother, and you now know the truth. Don't keep it for yourself. It is a crime."

On the topic of theologizing, Ross shared his views on doctrines. "The group that is joining the Christian church likes to teach us about doctrines of the church. For example, Isa is Allah. We do not read that in the Bible, but suddenly they teach us that Isa is Allah. This is a Christian doctrine." He pointed to the passage where Isa teaches us to pray to our Father. Isa glorifies the Father. "So if you say suddenly that Isa is Allah, you tell us that Father is nothing and that Isa is greater than Father. This is false theology." Ross views Isa as the Son of God who represents Allah, and he is Father-centered. Ross expanded on that and said, "Which one is greater, the Father or Isa? Both must be respected. That is what they mean with being one. Isa and the Father are one. This means they must be respected." Ross added, "If I do not respect your child, I do not respect you." He also said, "Jesus being the Son of God is very serious. He is God. He is God." He continued on the oneness of Allah and reasoned that actually Allah cannot be counted. It is sinful to say that Allah is 1,000, 99, three, or one. Ross concluded, "'God is one' means God is first, not one as in a number. God is first."

## Ray

Ray described Allah as Creator. "There is no god but Allah." He sees him as both near to us and immanent. Ray believes that Allah created everything, including mankind, in order to relate to it. He mentioned the rebellion of humans, which broke the relationship between Allah and mankind. "But Allah is still trying to relate to humans, just as is mentioned in Genesis, where Allah is looking for Adam even though Adam had disobeyed." According to Ray, heaven or paradise is the place for those who obey, and hell for those who disobey. Both last forever. He believes that Allah has given man the freedom of choice to follow him or not. Each person's point of death marks the last opportunity to follow Allah, since mankind does not have a will anymore in heaven or hell, according to Ray.

The Scriptures are a special revelation from Allah to mankind, and they are guidance from God to humans, per Ray's description. He said that we should interpret the text from the context in which it was given. "We cannot generalize it through many centuries. Also we cannot generalize across cultures. We have to understand the meaning of the text when God revealed it in that context." Ray puts the Qur'an at the same level as the Bible. "The Bible has problems in canonization and so does the Qur'an. I cannot make a double standard. If I say, the Qur'an is lower than the Bible, what would be the reason?" Ray believes that Allah can reveal himself to mankind whenever and however. He sees contradictions within both books, and he said, "To reconcile the differences between the Bible and the Qur'an, I will reinterpret. If both come from God, as his revelation, I need to realize that God does not change his plans from time to time." Ray sees nothing wrong with the Qur'an and the original Islam. "If the foundation is the Qur'an, there's nothing wrong. Most Muslims today do not follow qur'anic teaching, but rather the teachings of the Islamic scholars. That is the problem today." Ray has no

| Theology Proper | 1 | 2 | 3 | 4 |
|---|---|---|---|---|
| Essence | Ry | | | |
| The Problem | | Ry | | |
| Satan | | Ry | | |
| Man | | Ry | | |
| Missio Dei | 1 | 2 | 3 | 4 |
| Gospel | | Ry | | |
| This World | | Ry | | |
| Our Mandate | Ry | | | |
| Healthy Societies | | Ry | | |
| Religions | | | | Ry |
| Election | | Ry | | |
| Hell | | Ry | | |
| Heaven | | Ry | | |
| The Bible | | Ry | | |
| The Qur'an | | | | Ry |
| Isa al Masih | 1 | 2 | 3 | 4 |
| Identity | | | | Ry |
| Christology | | | | Ry |
| His Life | Ry | | | |
| On the Cross | | Ry | | |
| The Cross | | Ry | | |
| The Resurrection | | | | |
| The Future | Ry | | | |

**Figure 16:** M-Framework plot for Ray

problem with passages in the Scriptures that imply Jesus being worshiped. "The Qur'an exults Isa as a King, as the Messiah. If people are worshiping him as the King or the Messiah, that is no problem." Ray shared various other titles for Isa in the Qur'an. The one he likes best is Isa being the Mercy of Allah who was sent because Allah so loved the world.

Isa al Masih is the best revelation from Allah, according to Ray, because through him we can reach paradise. How does that happen? "This is my understanding through the Qur'an and also through the Injil: he must die as Redeemer." Ray explained that the Redeemer paid the debt that we as mankind owe to Allah. When I asked whether the price was Isa's life, Ray said, "I do not know the price, because the Injil does not mention the price. The Qur'an also does not mention the price. But the one who paid was Isa, through his death."

The relationship between Isa al Masih and Allah is mentioned in the Injil and in the Qur'an as Isa being Allah's Word, according to Ray. He added, "There is no clear explanation about the relationship in this sense, ontologically. The Scriptures do not explain it." When I asked whether he believes that Isa al Masih and Allah are the same, he answered, "No, of course not. How can they be the same? If Isa and Allah are the same then that would mean that Allah died on the cross. How can Allah die on the cross?" I asked whether Isa al Masih is divine. "What does 'divine' mean in this case? If it means like in Latin, "from God," yes, Isa is divine. If 'divine' means being the same as Allah, I do not think he is the same as Allah," Ray replied.

Regarding Christian doctrine, Ray believes that the doctrine of the Trinity is not based on the Bible. He talked about how Muslims always ridicule Christians for worshiping a god with split personalities. Not too long ago there was a conference at a university with various speakers from different religions, including a Christian speaker. He tried to explain to the students that Christians don't worship three gods but one God, with three personalities. The students all laughed. Ray said, "This was stupid, and I left the venue where there were 700 Muslim students. This speaker didn't do anything for evangelism. He should have used just the Bible."

Isa was sent to restore God's kingdom, which has a spiritual and a physical dimension, according to Ray. "The physical kingdom means that we have to follow his teaching while living on the earth." Ray sees Isa as our best model. "He has very good and deep ethics, even better than those of the Torah." Ray applies these ethics to all of creation. "We should try to keep our environment clean. We should promote peace not only in human relationships but also in nature."

Regarding theology, Ray first explained how this term is understood differently between Christians and Muslims. "Theology in Christianity is not only about how God revealed himself and what he is planning for humanity, but also how to make a systematic understanding about many things." This is complicated for Muslims, especially for uneducated groups. These insiders just read something, dialogue on the meaning, and then apply it, according to Ray. "On the theology side, all we need to know is who God is and who Isa is, and that's all. We don't have to systematize all these things," said Ray. This all happens at the local level, where everyone is equal.

Ray sees the concern about different theologies within the movement as an outsider issue. "Among insiders, what is the problem? We don't have that problem about theology. The problem is always seen by the outsider." Ray shared that differences are simply tolerated and accepted. "I see some fellowships not following Islamic traditions. Some eat pork because they are influenced by Christians. That is not a problem." Ray said that this tolerance extends to the doctrine of the Trinity.

> Our understanding of God can also be different. Some eventually believe in the Trinity. They finally believe that Isa is Allah. For me I will not blame them. They have their own experience and understanding. He is the only way to God. There is no compromise with that.

Ray's identity is Muslim, and he does not like the term "Muslim follower of Isa." "What does that mean for people who lived before Mohammed's time?" Ray prefers the term "Muslim who understands Isa as the Redeemer."

## Josh

Josh is an alongsider for Ray and to some extent for Ross as well. In addition, Josh has connections with other movements within the SE Asia region.
Allah is sovereign and cares for humanity, according to Josh. "Looking at his 99 names, Allah is all-knowing, all-powerful, wise, good, and reigns over all creation," Josh added. The purposes of God are to have fellowship

with humans and to establish the kingdom. "It will be a place where there is supreme justice, and Jesus Christ will be the King of this kingdom, and the way into that kingdom is through him." Josh further explained that this kingdom has no physical location. "It is wherever people come under the lordship of Christ and the reign of God, which means it is in part present now and will be more complete at the end of time." Josh thinks that God wants to see all that is good restored here and now, and he wants people spending eternity with him. Whether things will be getting worse here over time and then Jesus returns, or this world will improve and get restored as the kingdom expands, Josh is not sure in which camp he falls.

> I think of course that God is on the side of goodness. God is on the side of virtue. He works to see the best things happen because he loves us now and he loves us later. He loves his creation now, and he loves it into eternity.

When asked about how heaven and hell fit with God's plans and purposes, Josh said that one of the most important reasons Jesus came was to provide a way for people to spend eternity in heaven. He believes that both heaven and hell are actual places and that those who follow Jesus will go to heaven. Josh does not commit to an inverse statement about who will go to hell. "But your question was, 'How does this fit in God's purpose?' I think heaven fits within his purpose, but I don't exactly know how hell fits within his purpose." Josh does not know whether hell is forever, and he prefers not to dwell on the other side of eternal life. He likewise remained noncommittal to any position on whether a person's point of death is the final fork in the road for someone who was not following Jesus. "I don't know if God in his mercy has any other kind of plan for that person." Josh does believe in man having the freedom of choice to follow God or not. "In having that ability to choose there is true virtue and true goodness, and also true love."

Josh regards the Scriptures not so much as a rule book but as a narrative about God.

> What I would say is that it is a written record of how God was interacting with humans at given places and given times. They wrote this down for their people to know it, but not just for their people but for all of humanity. That

writing that was being done by humans is in fact inspired by God.

The Qur'an is not an inspired book, according to Josh. "I don't think it is from God. I think that humans were trying their very best to piece together what they thought that message was of what they heard of the Tawrat, Zabur, and Injil." God may have been involved in that process. "I think it could be that God in his sovereignty and mercy made sure that certain things were in there as a record of himself. This is kind of the redemptive analogy idea." Josh fully supports using the Qur'an as a reference point with Muslims.

Religions are a bad starting point to talk about Jesus, said Josh. "It is striking to me that Jesus did not speak of what we would call today a religion. He spoke almost entirely about a kingdom." Josh sees religions as human creations that are added to the things of God, but believes that there is truth in lots of world religions. Related to Isa al Masih, Josh places him beyond and above world religions. "So, my relationship with Isa al Masih, that is not what puts me into a particular religion, rather I would say it puts me into a relationship with God and the kingdom of Christ."

| Theology Proper | 1 | 2 | 3 | 4 |
|---|---|---|---|---|
| Essence | | Jh | | |
| The Problem | | Jh | | |
| Satan | | | Jh | |
| Man | | Jh | | |
| Missio Dei | 1 | 2 | 3 | 4 |
| Gospel | | Jh | | |
| This World | | | Jh | |
| Our Mandate | | Jh | | |
| Healthy Societies | | Jh | | |
| Religions | | | | Jh |
| Election | | Jh | | |
| Hell | | Jh | | |
| Heaven | | | Jh | |
| The Bible | | | | Jh |
| The Qur'an | | | Jh | |
| Isa al Masih | 1 | 2 | 3 | 4 |
| Identity | | Jh | | |
| Christology | | Jh | | |
| His Life | | | | Jh |
| On the Cross | | | | Jh |
| The Cross | | Jh | | |
| The Resurrection | | Jh | | |
| The Future | | | Jh | |

**Figure 17:** M-Framework plot for Josh

Josh summarizes the actions of Isa al Masih as what God would do if he were in a body here on earth, healing and delivering and treating people as he did. His suffering and dying was part of God's plan. "He pleaded with God for it not to happen, and yet God still wanted it to happen." Josh believes that his death paid the price we would be paying for our sins, and it opens the way for us to have eternal life. Josh painted the picture of God weeping as Jesus was on the cross. There is no sense or element of God being angry or punishing Jesus. Josh also noted that perhaps Jesus did not realize all that was happening, but that he was doing this in full submission and obedience to God.

"The relationship between Isa al Masih and Allah represents some kind of unity that is indescribable in human words," Josh explained. Jesus is the image of the invisible God, and the relationship is described in other ways in the Scriptures, but Josh believes that human attempts to describe it sound to most people more like polytheism.

On the topic of Christology, Josh thinks that the insider's view is simple and primitive. The main picture they have of Isa is as their Savior. "A common thing they say in the movement is, 'Praise God, I now have a Savior!' They see his saving in both this world and the world to come as very important." Other aspects of Christology important to them are Isa as Lord of their lives and as miracle worker, according to Josh. "But, ideas of Trinity, they are not thinking three-person kind of language, or something like that."

## Tyler

Tyler was instrumental in facilitating and interpreting many of my interviews in the SE Asia region where he has lived for many years. He is the alongsider for Lucas, Zach, Ian, Phil, and Monty, and more from a distance for Silas, Kent, and Stuart.

In describing what God is like, Tyler uses four categories: glorious, all-powerful, his coming nearness, and his oneness. "God's plans and purposes are related to the beginning of Genesis and the end of Revelation, seeing the beauty in the garden and the restoration of all of creation," Tyler said. "God has put man as

| Theology Proper | 1 | 2 | 3 | 4 |
|---|---|---|---|---|
| Essence |  | Tr |  |  |
| The Problem |  | Tr |  |  |
| Satan |  | Tr |  |  |
| Man |  |  | Tr |  |
| **Missio Dei** | 1 | 2 | 3 | 4 |
| Gospel |  |  | Tr |  |
| This World |  |  | Tr |  |
| Our Mandate |  | Tr |  |  |
| Healthy Societies |  | Tr |  |  |
| Religions |  |  | Tr |  |
| Election |  | Tr |  |  |
| Hell |  | Tr |  |  |
| Heaven |  |  | Tr |  |
| The Bible |  |  | Tr |  |
| The Qur'an |  |  | Tr |  |
| **Isa al Masih** | 1 | 2 | 3 | 4 |
| Identity |  | Tr |  |  |
| Christology |  | Tr |  |  |
| His Life |  | Tr |  |  |
| On the Cross |  | Tr |  |  |
| The Cross |  | Tr |  |  |
| The Resurrection |  | Tr |  |  |
| The Future |  |  | Tr |  |

**Figure 18:** M-Framework plot for Tyler

the pinnacle over all of creation. And he puts Messiah as the pinnacle of the pinnacle. I think God's purpose for mankind is to reflect his grace." He sees salvation as more than a point in time when we make a decision. "It is all kinds of transformations that happen in us individually and in us communally, in our families, and communities." When asked about what he means with the restoration of all of creation, Tyler mentioned a restoration of four conflicts: between man and the satanic world, between man and God, between man and creation, and between man and man.

On the question about heaven and hell, Tyler first acknowledged that this question is harder than it seems, biblically. From Luke 16 he concludes that there are boundaries to both heaven and hell, and that we are still able to think when we are there, even though there is finality to it. "In spite of the finality of both, which were decided at the point of death in the finality sense, there still is a gracious God behind it," Tyler said. From Revelation he sees heaven as a re-purified earth. "It has a connectedness with the old somehow." These pictures of heaven should impact our lives today, Tyler shared. On whether heaven and hell last forever and ever, Tyler leaves the backdoor open, especially when it comes to hell. "Does him (Satan) burning in the fire mean the end, or is it part of an ongoing hell?" Tyler does not specifically answer the question on who will go to hell. He leaves that up to God. "What he decides, and how many will come, and how many are already in the kingdom, I don't feel these are my questions."

Regarding the status of the Scriptures, Tyler recounted some of the process described in Acts 15 that resulted in certain teachings being accepted and others rejected, based on people's experiences. This resulted in specific choices in the canonization process. He sees the Scriptures coming from God and as God's narrative. It has a certain additive element to it as people get exposed to it and experience it, according to Tyler.

> They begin to experience the truthfulness of it. They come to a point of saying, "This has to be true." They feel it. They come from the religion of Islam, surrender, and then the quickness of surrender to the Lord sometimes is remarkable.

Tyler praises Mohammed for bringing his people back to monotheism and recognizes that the Qur'an connects to the former people who followed one God. Tyler recommends using the Qur'an and pointed out that connection.

> You see this in the first letter of the Qur'an, that the grace was given to a former people who were given the pathway. I think that the skilled person in using the Qur'an can connect this desire for a straight and true path to a former monotheistic people and interpret it through the lens of the Old Testament and the gospel that came before.

Tyler does not believe that the Qur'an is inspired, but he does acknowledge that God is using the Qur'an to bring people to himself, at least initially, to point them to the former books.

When asked about religions, Tyler pointed out that Jesus actually did not start Christianity. "His followers were still Jews and he wanted them to be agents to bring a renewal, and this continued after his death, to bring them back to true religion before God." Tyler makes a distinction between religions and renewal movements within them. He hinted at insider movements being part of the latter as Muslims who follow Isa al Masih work out their identity.

> They don't necessarily say that they are other than Islam, but if pressed by Christians they might not also say they are other than Christian. They are creating for themselves a collective identity that is strong in allegiance to Jesus and the Word, and they are trying to work out what that means in their context.

Could insiders be seen as agents that bring renewal to Islam? Tyler admitted that this is very much true, but it depends on how you define renewal and restoration, and from what context. "They (insiders) have an internal lingo that they develop between them that is quite beautiful and innovative, to preserve the faithful core of individuals and of groups." They need to have bridge-builders' hearts. Tyler shared that this becomes more challenging in the subsequent generations. "What we are finding is that the second and third generations are greener, more thickly culturally Islam, than those at the higher and first-level generations." They are finding that more conflicts are happening down into the third or fourth generations. "These are almost like schisms or earthquakes happening between the lands, as they bring Scripture down into the cultural norms." This requires special skills of IM leaders in those generations, Tyler said. "They have to have special peacemaking skills."

Tyler explained the reason for the cross as God's plan of perfecting Christ to make him better suited for the King's clothes. The suffering servant is the cosmic King. It was God's will that Jesus suffered for us, according to Tyler. "He took on our alienation, the deepest shame and the deepest sense of distance, and it was for all of us that he cried, and he swallowed it." Tyler sees the cross as multidimensional.

In general, Tyler sees that the justice-of-God aspect of the gospel is not context-fitted with people whose epistemology is more deeply influenced by fear culture and honor culture than by the truth dimension of culture. "I feel a significant part of an insider movement is working on reinterpreting honor such that heaven's court is the primary court of appraisal of what is honorable."

Regarding the relationship between Jesus Christ and God, Tyler first mentioned the challenges they have with the phrase *Son of God*, which to him is a figure of speech. According to Tyler, Jesus basically reveals God on earth, plays the high priestly role, and possesses unique divine identity. He quickly added, "But we don't pop it on people at the beginning. It has to go through these seven phases of Christology." Tyler prefers expressing Jesus as sharing the divine identity of God yet not changing the oneness of God, and seeing him as the divine representative.

They are not using the term *Trinity* in the movement, even though Tyler personally thinks it is biblically based when properly situated in the historical context of those who designed those words and the questions they were addressing in that time and place. Interestingly, Tyler shared some details from a baptism booklet that they have developed for the movement. The baptismal formula in the ceremony uses the Arabic terms, which nobody in their context understands, for "in the name of the Father, Son, and Holy Spirit," and then they added the phrase "who are one." In the translated version of Matthew 28 in this booklet they decided on the wording, "I dip you in the name of the honored Father, the honored Word of Allah, and the Spirit of Allah, who is very holy."

At one point Tyler and I talked about one of the criticisms of insider movements by those who oppose them: that insiders are risk averse and are trying to avoid suffering. Tyler became a bit emotional.

> How many people have to be killed for them to be seen as brave enough? Let me introduce you to some of the people who are grieving and suffering, and let's see if you are asking that question again. I think if anything, it is the traditional model that is more fearful. They don't even really engage with anyone, and certainly not with Muslims. That is being very risk averse.

I noted that in all his comments Tyler brought in certain Scripture verses and inductively answered from those verses. He never expounded deductively to respond to questions with typical systematic theology viewpoints.

## South Asia A M-Framework Plots

### Andy

Andy shared how, before knowing Jesus as his Savior, he thought of Allah as a big giant who beats and punishes us. "I was always nervous, and I'd always wanted to study the Qur'an and wanted to do something that would make Allah happy. I always had that fear in my heart." Andy continued, "But when I experienced the Lord Jesus as my Savior, then Allah, who is the Creator of everything, was not a scary thing anymore, but he is very loving. He loves us. He loves us as a father." Andy expanded on that last statement, saying that Allah loves them even more than a father, because in their culture fathers beat their children. Andy concluded that Allah is a loving God.

On the topic of Allah's plans and purposes, Andy believes that Allah created the garden of Eden and created Adam and Eve in his image. "Then Satan destroyed their life. They disobeyed God's command." The result was that God punished them. "The punishment was that God threw them out of heaven, and we are all suffering because of this first sin." But God still loved us, according to Andy, so he sent his Son to save us. "God wants us to go back and [wants to] restore us to the same place where he created us. He wants to see us in his kingdom, back in heaven." Andy believes that God made this world so that he could send his Son be the King of the world and also of the eternal world, as he phrased it. Andy sees this world as the place created for our punishment. Satan uses false prophets to misguide us and to lead us to a different god, according to Andy, "but Allah sent different prophets to show us the direction to go back to our Father."

Regarding hell, Andy repeated that he used to be very scared about going there. "But after coming to faith in Jesus I have never thought about hell. I don't have time to think about it, because I want to enjoy my time in the Lord." Who will go to hell? Andy believes that those who have never heard how to be saved are innocent. "I would never say that Buddhist or Hindus or even extreme Muslims will go to hell, because they don't know." On the other hand, Andy shared that hell is for believers who do not follow God's law and share with others. "I think most believers will go to hell because they are not obeying the Lord's commandments. I'm afraid about Christians. Maybe we will go." Andy added, "Those who believe and know, but yet deny and don't follow him sometimes, God will punish them." He concluded that heaven and hell is for us, and we have to be careful. When I asked about the idea of us experiencing a certain degree of heaven and hell here and now, depending on whether we are in the will of God or not, Andy replied that he does not agree with that idea.

| Theology Proper | 1 | 2 | 3 | 4 |
|---|---|---|---|---|
| Essence | | Ay | | |
| The Problem | Ay | | | |
| Satan | Ay | | | |
| Man | Ay | | | |
| **Missio Dei** | **1** | **2** | **3** | **4** |
| Gospel | Ay | | | |
| This World | Ay | | | |
| Our Mandate | | Ay | | |
| Healthy Societies | | Ay | | |
| Religions | | | | Ay |
| Election | | Ay | | |
| Hell | | Ay | | |
| Heaven | | Ay | | |
| The Bible | | Ay | | |
| The Qur'an | | | Ay | |
| **Isa al Masih** | **1** | **2** | **3** | **4** |
| Identity | Ay | | | |
| Christology | Ay | | | |
| His Life | | | Ay | |
| On the Cross | Ay | | | |
| The Cross | Ay | | | |
| The Resurrection | Ay | | | |
| The Future | Ay | | | |

**Figure 19:** M-Framework plot for Andy

> That does not make sense to me, because this is the punishment area that God placed Adam in, this world, and heaven will be the kingdom of God. This here is the kingdom of humans; we are living in the kingdom of humans, so this concept of heaven and hell being experienced in the here and now is different and does not make sense.

God loves everyone but elects some to bless everyone around them, according to Andy. God supernaturally does that, but afterwards we have the freedom of choice to obey God and to be a blessing to others by giving them a choice as we share with them. Andy called it "choosing for choice."

Andy described the prophets as messengers of God who sinned like us. "Satan was strong and created some sins in their lives." These messengers brought laws from God so that we would follow God, but our sins were too great, so God sent his Son, according to Andy. "He did not want to send his Son first. He wanted to save us before that. But finally, we were very strong in our sins; we need his Son's blood to be saved."

The Scriptures are from God and contain his laws and the story of Jesus, according to Andy. "The whole book is the Word of God, about how God wants us to be and how he wants this world to be." He shared how people are stupid like sheep in that they never follow God's word. The followers of the law even killed his Son, Andy shared. He uses the Scriptures as a law book and a way of life. "I apply many of the laws that Jesus said in my tribal decisions, and that is very good and helpful. It is very easy to give them the right direction."

When it comes to the Qur'an, Andy said, "I think Mohammed was influenced by some Catholic people. Then he wrote the guidebook, but he was using many understandings from the Bible." But these Catholic people did not give Mohammed clear direction, according to Andy.

> That is why I'm saying that heaven is for us and hell is for us, if we do not give good teachings to others about our faith. If they had given Mohammed a better teaching, the whole world would not have suffered now. We have to stay accountable to God.

"Jesus is our big model," said Andy. He sees Jesus as the living Word of God. "When I talk to other people I share the Word of God with them by showing how he lived, how he suffered, and his actions." To Andy, Jesus is our model of how to serve people, how to worship God, and how to pray. "Jesus is the model for everything including humanitarian work, and social work, helping people." Andy believes that the Jews killed Jesus. "They were scared for their own thing, for their own kingdom, for their own beliefs, and for Satan. In their spirit, they were afraid." God allowed this to happen for our benefit, per Andy. "Jesus took our sins on himself to be punished so that we will be free." When I asked about the Trinity, Andy emphasized the oneness. "He sent his Son to save us, and he went back and sent his Spirit to help us. So, they are one. They have different functions but they are one."

Religions are creations of people, Andy explained. "They are signboards, but they are not from God. Jesus never said to follow Christianity, or to create something like this." He believes that many Christians need to follow Jesus more and reform their systems and churches. He said that religions can be harmful. "Religions cannot save people. They can even cause more problems."

Andy said that they have had some people in the movement disagreeing on the Trinity. "And then we did not consider them as believers." He also told me about another case of a baptized believer who had lived abroad and had now been with them for six months. "He got confused and left when we talked about the Trinity, saying that God cannot have sex with anyone." Andy mentioned that the timing was off.

> I think that it was too early for him to be thinking about the Son of God and God as Father, and about the Trinity concept. It affected his faith because he was not ready enough. Sometimes that happens, but we allow it.

Andy concluded that theology is not always helpful. "That happens when people experience God by themselves, but sometimes we are confusing them with theology, and then they get angry."

## Howard

What is Allah like? "My concept was that Allah is very angry and you have to make him happy somehow," said Howard. He added, "I thought Allah will punish me and I have to do a lot of things for him. I should do things: I should go somewhere for Allah, I should kill someone, or I should give my life for Allah." All that changed when he accepted Jesus, Howard said. Because of that change, he now prefers to refer to God using different words than *Allah*. Howard believes that the garden of Eden was in heaven, and that Adam and Eve were sent to this world as punishment. Howard shared that at first he could not understand why God had not sent his Son right away, but then saw the beauty of God's plan. "After so many mysteries

I realized that Allah had a big plan for all of us, for all human beings. Jesus came for the cleansing of all sins."

After I asked him about the view about God's plan to restore and redeem his own creation here on earth on the one hand, or God being focused on heaven and bringing people there on the other hand, Howard's first reaction was, "This is the first time I'm hearing about a group that you are talking about, that is thinking about this world." He added that those who follow Jesus but are not his witnesses will be denied by God.

| Theology Proper | 1 | 2 | 3 | 4 |
|---|---|---|---|---|
| Essence | | (Hd) | | |
| The Problem | (Hd) | | | |
| Satan | (Hd) | | | |
| Man | | (Hd) | | |
| Missio Dei | 1 | 2 | 3 | 4 |
| Gospel | (Hd) | | | |
| This World | (Hd) | | | |
| Our Mandate | (Hd) | | | |
| Healthy Societies | | (Hd) | | |
| Religions | | | | (Hd) |
| Election | | (Hd) | | |
| Hell | | (Hd) | | |
| Heaven | | (Hd) | | |
| The Bible | | (Hd) | | |
| The Qur'an | | (Hd) | | |
| Isa al Masih | 1 | 2 | 3 | 4 |
| Identity | (Hd) | | | |
| Christology | (Hd) | | | |
| His Life | | (Hd) | | |
| On the Cross | (Hd) | | | |
| The Cross | (Hd) | | | |
| The Resurrection | (Hd) | | | |
| The Future | (Hd) | | | |

**Figure 20:** M-Framework plot for Howard

Jesus himself is saying that if you declare yourself a follower of me in this world, you will have many problems, but if you will be my witness, then on the day of judgment, I will be your witness and I will take you to heaven.

Howard explained that his concept of hell totally changed when he became a follower of Jesus. He used to think about hell all the time, but not anymore. "I only think about those people for which we have responsibility to bring them into the kingdom of God. I am a little worried for them." He continued and said that he does not believe that they will go to hell. "But I am thinking to save them and to bring them into the kingdom of God, giving them that shelter." He repeated that he is thinking of hell in a very small way. "When he comes again, God will have a big plan again for how he will save all human beings." I asked Howard about the idea of experiencing heaven and hell in some sense in the here and now already, depending on whether you are in the will of God or not, and the concept that this experience will then continue in some fashion when we die. He said that those ideas are not in the Bible and added that they are what Muslims think. "Muslims do think about heaven and hell in this world. They think that when you get punishment, this means that you are in hell, in this world. Likewise, when you are happy, you are in heaven." He repeated that followers of Jesus don't have that concept.

My question about freedom of choice led Howard to comment about his life in Christ not being free. "Many others, who say that they are following Jesus and that they are Christians, think that when they start following Jesus they are free, free from our sins." Howard countered that with reference to what Jesus says in Matthew.

> Jesus says in Matthew when he is sending his disciples, "I am not here to make peace but to give you difficulties in your life. When you are accepting me you will get many difficulties. Your family members can be against you. You will be beaten and threatened. People will take you out of your house." We are not free.

Howard considers the Scriptures as a guide that gives us explanations about how to live. He does not believe that the Qur'an is a holy book or that Mohammed was a prophet. "The Qur'an was written by Mohammed, and he was not a prophet in my concept." Howard said that Mohammed mixed the things he learned from his Christian and Jewish friends and made his own law to control the Arabs and Muslims.

On the topic of Isa al Masih, Howard recounted how many prophecies Jesus fulfilled. He added another observation. "Sometimes I see Jesus' life and see him acting as three personalities. One is that he is acting like a human being. The other is as a prophet, and the third as God." Howard sees Jesus' death as a political and religious killing, as he was a challenge to the king even when Jesus was born. Ultimately Jesus was killed for our sins, Howard said. "He took our sins on his body and he gave the blood for us." Regarding the relationship between Jesus and God, Howard said that they are one. "There is no separation between God and Jesus."

Howard sees the theological debate with Muslims as less of a challenge than with Christians. "I can challenge the Muslims by saying that they are not complete Muslims if they don't believe in Jesus." On the other hand, when Christians say that we are not followers of Jesus, that is the bigger challenge, according to Howard. "But we do not care. I do not want any of our people to follow the church or any denomination. I want them to follow Jesus."

## Kevin

Kevin is the alongsider of Andy and Howard in South Asia A, and also to a large extent of Mitch in South Asia B. In addition, he is quite well connected with Axel in South Asia C.

| Theology Proper | 1 | 2 | 3 | 4 |
|---|---|---|---|---|
| Essence | | | | (KI) |
| The Problem | | | (KI) | |
| Satan | | | (KI) | |
| Man | | | (KI) | |
| **Missio Dei** | **1** | **2** | **3** | **4** |
| Gospel | | | (KI) | |
| This World | | | (KI) | |
| Our Mandate | | | | (KI) |
| Healthy Societies | | | | (KI) |
| Religions | | | (KI) | |
| Election | | (KI) | | |
| Hell | | | (KI) | |
| Heaven | | | | (KI) |
| The Bible | | | | (KI) |
| The Qur'an | | | | (KI) |
| **Isa al Masih** | **1** | **2** | **3** | **4** |
| Identity | | | (KI) | |
| Christology | | | | (KI) |
| His Life | | | (KI) | |
| On the Cross | | | | (KI) |
| The Cross | | | (KI) | |
| The Resurrection | | | (KI) | |
| The Future | | | (KI) | |

**Figure 21:** M-Framework plot for Kevin

"God is merciful and compassionate," Kevin started out. He admitted that he just had been reading the Qur'an, which highlights those characteristics. Kevin also called God sovereign, holy, and involved in his life. He described God's plans and purposes as basically bringing everything back together the way it is described in Eden, in Genesis. "Although I take that pretty much to be kind of a poetic picture of things, I see him bringing everything back into that sort of harmony and beauty and peace." On the notion of whether salvation is of this world or away from it to some other world or heaven, Kevin sees it as salvation of this world, but he is unclear about the exact eschatology.

> I probably lean towards some kind of transformation of what we now know as the world. There will be some kind of connection with it, but I'm not sure if it's just the making a lot better of what we already see. There seems to be a transition to a whole new mode of this world and way of being. I don't think it is something disconnected from the world that we now know, but I don't think it is just a new paint job, so to speak.

Pressing further on this, Kevin affirmed his belief that God is interested in healthy cultures and societies, but he struggles with how matters will move towards the long-term future per God's plan. "For me it is somewhere in between the long gradual transformation and the sudden dramatic breaking in of something totally other; somewhere in between, or maybe a mix of both of those."

On the topic of heaven and hell, Kevin sees heaven as this world transformed. "It is a transformative in-breaking, but not the total disconnection of what already is." He still is wrestling with the notion of hell. "I tend to see that as the state of being for those of us who simply continue to elect to not cooperate with what God is trying to do. They are in the place of rebellion." He doesn't see heaven or hell as actual places out there somewhere. "I don't see a literal heaven as the house of reward and here's the house of punishment kind of thing." Kevin shared that hell cannot be described as existing away from the presence of God, because he does not believe any created being could exist without God. He sees things more in relational terms. "The absence of his relational presence and what that means for being alive in the true sense of that term: that to me is hell." Is hell forever? "The orthodox part of me wants to say yes. The part of me that wonders about all of this wants to say, I don't know."

Kevin talked some more about his views about what happens the moment we die. He mentioned Paul saying that to depart and be with Christ is better. "How do I balance that with all the Scriptures that talk about some kind of final point and what seems to be a final resurrection?" Regarding chronological time, Kevin is not sure whether that category applies to the next phase of what God is doing with creation, with God's plans seemingly having a beyond-time quality to them.

> I wonder if from the perspective of someone who is in time, the dying and suddenly being in the presence of the Lord, and from an outsider's perspective watching time go by, and now suddenly there's a final point where everyone is raised from the dead—I just wonder if these are just two different experiential perspectives of the same event.

On the question of whether someone's point of death is the final opportunity to make choices that affect eternity, Kevin said that he is a little bit more open-minded about that than he used to be. He recalled the picture from Revelation of the trees whose leaves are for the healing of the nations. "I wonder if there are hints there of some kind of ongoing process that continues." Kevin concluded, "I think there may very well be some ongoing opportunity for repentance and change." On a related question about man's freedom of choice and God's sovereign will, Kevin sees that as one of the mysteries in the Bible. "This is one of those places where I think the Bible is very clearly Reformed and very clearly also Wesleyan, all at once."

Regarding God's revelation to us, Kevin thinks that prophets somehow grasp almost at a deep, visceral, gut feeling level the character of God, which then reflects in what they say or do. "For prophets it is more than somehow hearing God's word. It is experiencing God's heart, and out of that come their words and perceptions and proclamations." Kevin sees God's revelation in the Scriptures as a narrative with inspired meaning within context. "I think the meaning is inspired and is communicated in a way that is in sync with the cultural context and environment in which the revelation comes." Kevin shared his views about the Qur'an as well.

> I see the Qur'an as a communication that continues to participate in that narrative. I would put it and Mohammed in a very similar category in a sense that I think that there are clearly places where he seems to have spoken out of a deep experience of the character of God, and he is participating in the biblical narrative.

Kevin sees the Qur'an as a collection of narratives that depend on the earlier narrative for their environment and existence. He tends to see it as secondary in that sense, but very powerful.

How do religions relate to God's plans and purposes? Kevin admitted to still be struggling with that. He sees religions, including Christianity, as human attempts to organize our spiritual lives, but the kingdom is somehow different. "I see Jesus speaking of the kingdom, which seems to have a very dialectical involvement with religion, including the Jewish religion from within which he was speaking." He sees all religions as attempted human responses to what God seems to be doing in their midst kingdom-wise, but the kingdom is bigger. "I think that the kingdom is bigger than any specific religion. There is kingdom stuff going on all the time in every religious system, but there's also rebellion going on in every religious system."

On the topic of Jesus and his actions and message, Kevin lamented how the West has made an unhelpful distinction between the two, as we made it a message to proclaim instead of a life to follow.

> Western evangelicals are focusing on the last three days, and people believing this; if you believe this you are in, and if you don't you're not. This just seems to run counter to everything we see in the Gospels. I see his life, his teaching, the things he did, the way that he interacted with his disciples and with people, all of that seems to me to be the message.

Kevin described what happened on the cross as a mystery as he was recalling the main three theories: as an example for us, as victory over death and the devil, and as somehow in a substitutionary role. "I think that the metaphors of taking punishment in our place, and making it as if God was the punisher, and he [Jesus] was a sacrifice in our place, get pushed too far sometimes." He recognizes that all three classical theories are our attempts at understanding it, and all three have biblical data behind them, which means that none of them exhausts what is going on.

> In the end there is something mysterious about it. The fact that this is both the result of human sin and the putting to death of an innocent man, and somehow God's plan also at the same time, that is part of that whole mystery that we were talking about earlier.

In describing the relationship between Isa al Masih and God, Kevin finds that Christians have found ways to talk about this relationship that, unfortunately, really seem to compromise the humanity of Isa al Masih. Kevin said that he prefers seeing Jesus as the Word of God in terms of the Word becoming flesh, the Word that was divine, the Word that was with God, the Word that was from all eternity becoming flesh in Jesus, so that what he is and says and does somehow shows us what God is and says and does in a way that is different than just a prophetic message. Kevin reiterated that for him just to say "Jesus is God" is difficult without a lot of biblical qualifications to that, because he thinks we tend to say it in ways that deny Jesus' humanity.

On the related topic of the Trinity, Kevin said that he is comfortable talking about God as Father, Son, and Spirit, or as Father, Word, and Spirit, but that he is more and more realizing that the fundamental reality is the unity.

> I'm realizing how much my normal Christian thinking and practice prior to this was pretty tri-theist, and I think that most Christians probably are functionally tri-theists. I'm trying to figure out the primacy of the One God, and then make sense of Trinity out of that.

## South Asia B M-Framework Plots

### Mitch

Mitch described his view of Allah as the Creator who is sovereign, all-powerful, all-knowing, and supreme. He loves his creation. "He cares so much for his creation that he can do anything to safeguard his creation." Mitch sees Allah not as a distant God but one who loves to have fellowship with his creation and his people. Allah's purposes for mankind are to bring glory and praise to Allah alone, according to Mitch. "He sent Jesus to give his life, so that we can be restored and brought back to him." Our plan now is to make sure people know this, Mitch said.

On the topic of heaven and hell, Mitch sees heaven as a certain place where we will be going, but he connects it to the kingdom, which exists here and there, and which you enter by accepting Jesus as your Savior and Messiah. Mitch believes that faith needs to be active and can be lost.

> Once you accept Jesus as your Savior and Lord, that is not everything. You have to remain, confess your faith every day, and remain with him every day. You can fall out, if you want. You can reject Jesus and go out somewhere.

Hell is forever, according to Mitch, and man determines his destiny while he is alive. "Once he is outside, after his death, there is no way to come back." Is every man free to choose? Mitch believes that there is a certain age under which you are not free. Also, in his culture people are coming to faith as groups, but he thinks that each person has to make that decision personal. Mitch further pointed out that in Muslim families the wives are not free or independent. He said, "I have found no wife that says, 'My husband wants to follow Isa al Masih, but I am not.' Culturally this is difficult. Even in the educated families this is difficult. Our women depend 100 percent on men." Mitch shared that if the wife goes against the decision of the husband, she would not be considered a good person.

The Scriptures are holy to Mitch. He promotes looking at all scriptures as a whole, as one book, even though some passages, especially in the Old Testament, are difficult. "This is not meant to make me afraid of him, but it is to help me to imagine how big he is. I cannot even imagine it." He sees it as God's narrative story to reveal himself and to show us how we should live. Regarding the Qur'an, Mitch said,

| Theology Proper | 1 | 2 | 3 | 4 |
|---|---|---|---|---|
| Essence |  | Mh |  |  |
| The Problem |  | Mh |  |  |
| Satan |  | Mh |  |  |
| Man |  | Mh |  |  |
| **Missio Dei** | **1** | **2** | **3** | **4** |
| Gospel |  | Mh |  |  |
| This World |  | Mh |  |  |
| Our Mandate |  | Mh |  |  |
| Healthy Societies |  | Mh |  |  |
| Religions |  |  |  | Mh |
| Election |  | Mh |  |  |
| Hell | Mh |  |  |  |
| Heaven |  | Mh |  |  |
| The Bible |  | Mh |  |  |
| The Qur'an |  |  | Mh |  |
| **Isa al Masih** | **1** | **2** | **3** | **4** |
| Identity |  |  |  | Mh |
| Christology |  | Mh |  |  |
| His Life | Mh |  |  |  |
| On the Cross |  |  |  | Mh |
| The Cross |  | Mh |  |  |
| The Resurrection |  | Mh |  |  |
| The Future |  | Mh |  |  |

**Figure 22:** M-Framework plot for Mitch

"The Qur'an has some passages here and there that are the Word of God, but as a whole it does not have the same status as the other books." He added that not all leaders in the movement see it this way. "We are behind. That is why I talk about teaching every year, and training people. And this is the last bit that you teach."

Regarding Isa al Masih, he revealed the nature of God to us, according to Mitch. He was anointed to have victory over Satan and to save the creation by giving his life, and when the kingdom is fully restored we will see him ruling as King. Mitch mentioned that Isa gave his life in full submission to God. "Because of that, God restored him (in Romans 4). He became the equal with God. He proved that he was equal with God." Mitch also commented on Allah's role in the crucifixion. "I don't think Allah punished him or Allah killed him. This is Allah's sacrificial love for his creation, for mankind, to open the way, a door, for people to come back to him." On the question about the relationship between Isa al Masih and Allah, Mitch talked about the *Kalaam*.

> What I want to teach to my people, to the people in the movement, and I'm trying to go there, that Jesus was with Allah even before creation, as *Kalaam*. Allah used his *Kalaam* to create the universe and me. How to describe this relationship? I do not know. But I want our people to believe and accept that the *Kalaam* that Allah used to create this universe was Isa al Masih.

Mitch concluded, "So if somebody thinks, well this relationship seems like an Allah-Allah relationship, that is fine."

How do religions relate to Allah's purposes? Mitch believes that religious identity should not be important. "We want to put less light on religion because we don't want to say, 'He is a Christian' and 'He is a Muslim.' That name should not become a big part of our life." He said that our lives are about following the teachings and instructions of Allah, about following Isa al Masih. When it comes to religion, Mitch said, "What I am is what I am."

## South Asia C M-Framework Plots

### Axel

Axel described Allah as almighty, omnipresent, and all-knowing. He is especially merciful and loving, and he wants us to be with him. Allah's plans and purposes are for us to be close to him, according to Axel. He talked about the sin, or mistake, of Adam, and mankind going away from the right path, Allah sending messengers, and finally sending his beloved, for us to be close to him. To Axel, heaven is when you are with God. "And if you are not with God, that is hell for you, forever. Not the understanding that you go there when you die, and you get punishment there; I do not understand that." Who will go to heaven? Axel replied, "If you die and God was pleased with you or according to his plan you accept Isa, then you will be with him. Isa is the mediator to reconcile between Allah and humans." He also shared that if someone does not believe in Isa, he cannot be with Allah. When I asked the question whether Allah's plans are to redeem and restore all of creation or to populate heaven, Axel replied that he did not understand the question. He repeated that Allah has one purpose, and that is for everyone to be with him. Does Allah determine who will be with him and who will not be with him? Axel replied, "I cannot say that. That is like a *kafir*, blaspheming God, that he is playing with us, and that we are nothing and can do nothing. He gave us free will to choose the right or wrong path."

The Scriptures are God's word given to mankind at a certain time in history and in a specific language. Axel focuses on the ideas in the Scriptures, not the words. He referred to the Qur'an as a good book. "You can find many good things in there, also about Jesus." He also finds the book very helpful to him to understand the whole of Scripture. Axel added, "I believe the Qur'an is a book that Allah has revealed. The Qur'an and Allah are not against anything." Axel does not believe that the Qur'an in its correct interpretation contradicts the Injil.

| Theology Proper | 1 | 2 | 3 | 4 |
|---|---|---|---|---|
| Essence | | Al | | |
| The Problem | | Al | | |
| Satan | | | Al | |
| Man | | Al | | |
| **Missio Dei** | 1 | 2 | 3 | 4 |
| Gospel | | Al | | |
| This World | | Al | | |
| Our Mandate | Al | | | |
| Healthy Societies | | Al | | |
| Religions | | | | Al |
| Election | | Al | | |
| Hell | | Al | | |
| Heaven | | Al | | |
| The Bible | | | Al | |
| The Qur'an | | | | Al |
| **Isa al Masih** | 1 | 2 | 3 | 4 |
| Identity | | Al | | |
| Christology | | | | Al |
| His Life | | | Al | |
| On the Cross | | Al | | |
| The Cross | | Al | | |
| The Resurrection | | Al | | |
| The Future | | Al | | |

**Figure 23:** M-Framework plot for Axel

On the topic of Isa al Masih, Axel sees him as the perfect sacrifice for the things we did wrong. Regarding the scene on the cross, Axel said, "I believe that he gave his life as a sacrifice on behalf of people who are not on the right path. I cannot say that Allah killed him. I cannot say that about Allah." The relationship between Isa al Masih and Allah is very close, according to Axel. "Are they the same?" I asked.

> I do not believe that. The Isa that came to earth is not Allah. That is *shirk*. We would be making someone like Allah. He was human and you cannot say that a human is Allah. You can say that the Word that existed before

> was God. But when that Word came into the flesh, you cannot believe that flesh or a human is God. If you believe that a human is God, that is *shirk*. I cannot believe that.

He added that Allah is one, and that Isa says that as well. "So when the Word became flesh, is this another god? It looks to me that Allah is sitting on the throne and he is sending another god to the world." Axel also added that he does not understand the Trinity. "I can say that God has many characteristics, but he is one being. You cannot say that there are three beings." Axel prays to and worships Almighty Allah, not Isa. Doing otherwise would be having two gods, Axel said. He does not mind the phrase *Son of God* if it is not misunderstood. He does not like to use regular family terms for Allah or Isa. "Allah and Isa should get more honor than a Son, and also more honor than a Father. I cannot give proper honor to him if I say he is a Son. I need to say more."

Regarding religions, Axel said that these are created by people, but that Isa does not want us to believe in any religion. Allah's plans are just for us to be with him, Axel repeated. "I do not believe in any religion. Islam is like my culture. I was born into it, so I follow it."

## South Asia D M-Framework Plots

### Angus

Angus shared that we cannot know what Allah is like from his creation. We cannot know what God is like without Jesus. He came to the world as a reflection of the light of God, according to Angus. "Through Jesus we see that God really loves us." He compared Allah's plans and purposes with a craftsman making something with a purpose. "He wants everyone's good. Just like a mechanic who may build something and does not want it to be destroyed." Angus added that our job and duty before Allah is to produce fruit, otherwise we are under judgment and put in the fire. Angus recalled his former ways.

> The confusion I had in my former life was just as the apostle Paul, when he was fighting believers. I was thinking that I was doing good works for God's cause. But God's love told him to not do that and to stop; what you are

doing is not true; this is not proper. Then I realized what true Islam and true love is. My life totally turned around.

Angus said that God's presence in heaven is spiritual, as will be ours. "Our spirit will be in the presence of Allah," Angus said. Allah did everything for us. "Most especially, he purchased us with his own death. He purchased our sins, he saved us from that and put the burden on himself. And because of this we are his." Angus believes that Allah took the burden of the religious regulations away from us. He took the burden from everyone. Angus added, "But God's children need to respond." This physical world and our physical bodies are not important to Allah, according to Angus. "If God would place importance on physical things in this world, he would not have stopped David from building a house for him."

Angus describes hell as a real place, in the spiritual sense, and as an everlasting place. "People will scream and gnash their teeth in the fire. They will remember their previous life and say, 'I wish.' The place of punishment that God has prepared, we may call hell or the unending fire." Angus also said, "People who do not accept Jesus and who do not follow his teaching will go there." He had specific comments about heaven as well. "It is not correct that there will be fruit there and trees there, because if that is the case, then it is just like a playground." He believes that Jesus was not focusing on this physical world but on spiritual matters. "He did not give any importance to the world. He did not say, 'You should look for independence from Rome.' Rather he said, 'You should look for freedom from Satan.'"

The Scriptures are God's story, according to Angus. "When we go through the Scriptures, when we tell the story from beginning to end, then we understand who

| Theology Proper | 1 | 2 | 3 | 4 |
|---|---|---|---|---|
| Essence | As | | | |
| The Problem | | As | | |
| Satan | | As | | |
| Man | | As | | |
| **Missio Dei** | **1** | **2** | **3** | **4** |
| Gospel | As | | | |
| This World | As | | | |
| Our Mandate | As | | | |
| Healthy Societies | | As | | |
| Religions | | | | As |
| Election | | | | |
| Hell | As | | | |
| Heaven | As | | | |
| The Bible | | As | | |
| The Qur'an | | | As | |
| **Isa al Masih** | **1** | **2** | **3** | **4** |
| Identity | | As | | |
| Christology | | As | | |
| His Life | | As | | |
| On the Cross | As | | | |
| The Cross | As | | | |
| The Resurrection | | As | | |
| The Future | As | | | |

**Figure 24:** M-Framework plot for Angus

God is, what God is, and what we have to do." God is using human language, so we need to look for the meaning in the passages, Angus said. He uses the Qur'an by pointing to references in it to the gospel. "There are many things in the Qur'an that are mentioned, but only briefly and not fully." Angus believes that the Qur'an came from Mohammed and his friends and not from Allah. "We can read the Qur'an in light of the earlier Scriptures and the completed Islam," Angus added.

What happened at the cross? I asked whether Allah killed Isa because all the sins were on him. Angus replied, "No, no, no, Allah himself took the burden. God, as he is, cannot come in front of us, so he came in human form and then he took our sins. So on the one side he was human to fulfill the plans, and on the other side he was himself." Angus said that Allah and Isa are like father and son, but not in a physical sense. It is about love. He compared Allah giving authority to Isa with Pharaoh giving authority to Joseph. "So when you see Joseph's story, you see a little of God's plans. It is just an example or an illustration. That is why we love to tell the story of Joseph to people first," Angus explained.

Regarding religions, they are made by humans, Angus said. He recounted that the Jews thought that they were Allah's beloved. The Arabs copied them and think the same thing—being chosen by Allah, and anyone else is God's enemy. Believers divide into sects and divisions, and each group has special traditions and clothes. Angus concluded, "So the purpose of religions is that we want to be distinct from others. That is why Jesus called the Pharisees whitewashed." What is more important is to have faith in Allah, Angus said. "We are one *jamaat* or fellowship. Our faith is one, whether you are Chinese or whatever. Religion is our culture. That is why we are pro-Christ Muslims," Angus said.

## Frank

Frank described Allah as without limits, without partners, and as one. He added, "At the same time, when we look at the attributes, we see the Trinity, which includes the Holy Spirit and Isa." The interpreter noted that the word Frank used for Isa is difficult to translate. It is like the image or reflection of Allah. I asked which of the many attributes of Allah he would consider the main ones. Frank repeated the Trinity, which he called the three pillars on which their faith is built. He also sees Allah as merciful, and through Isa he helps us on the way. Allah's plan and will is that all people be saved, Frank said. "He desires that everyone has faith in Isa, because there is no other way to get to heaven besides Isa." Frank looks at human attempts as futile. "Certainly humankind has tried through all kinds of means, through science and philosophy, to make paths to God, but each attempt by mankind to get to God is like bribing or coercing God." Frank sees that there are two paths in front of people, and that Allah desires that all people have faith in Isa to receive salvation and go to heaven. He shared how Allah is holy and that there is none holy like Allah among humans. "You need a perfect human to fix the problem and bring salvation, but only God is perfect."

Hell is a place that lasts forever, according to Frank. "The people that do not follow God's plan and do not follow Jesus obviously are going to hell," he said. Frank affirmed that at the point of a person's death the direction is fixed. On whether he thinks that most people will go to hell, Frank said, "Allah does not want anyone to go to hell, but Satan is trying as hard as he can to get everyone to go to hell. In the end the

| Theology Proper | 1 | 2 | 3 | 4 |
|---|---|---|---|---|
| Essence | Fk | | | |
| The Problem | | Fk | | |
| Satan | Fk | | | |
| Man | | Fk | | |
| **Missio Dei** | **1** | **2** | **3** | **4** |
| Gospel | Fk | | | |
| This World | Fk | | | |
| Our Mandate | Fk | | | |
| Healthy Societies | Fk | | | |
| Religions | | Fk | | |
| Election | | Fk | | |
| Hell | Fk | | | |
| Heaven | Fk | | | |
| The Bible | | Fk | | |
| The Qur'an | | | Fk | |
| **Isa al Masih** | **1** | **2** | **3** | **4** |
| Identity | Fk | | | |
| Christology | Fk | | | |
| His Life | Fk | | | |
| On the Cross | Fk | | | |
| The Cross | | Fk | | |
| The Resurrection | | Fk | | |
| The Future | Fk | | | |

**Figure 25:** M-Framework plot for Frank

people who do not follow Isa will definitely end up in hell." Frank believes that we have a freedom of choice. "Both ways are clear: the way of Satan and the way of Allah. Allah has shown us the results of both paths, and therefore we can choose."

Frank looks at the Scriptures as the word from Allah, which is full of stories, his commands, Allah's Sharia, and the path of salvation.

> One way we know that the Scriptures are from Allah is that in comparison to writings by humans or from other religions where only good things are written, we see in

the Bible that everything is mentioned, the good and the bad. The bad meaning the sins of prophets or kings or angels, it's all written there. It is not hidden.

Frank does not consider the Qur'an as coming from Allah, because there is no reference to it in the New Testament, but there are good things in it. He explained how they are using the Qur'an. "With new but serious people who are still on the path, but who are not complete, we use the Qur'an as a reference and show them things that are mentioned there that are also in the Bible."

On the topic of Isa al Masih, Frank said that they are using a special honorific for Isa al Masih. Instead of using the Arabic honorific "peace be upon him" which is used for all the prophets in Islam, they are using an inverted honorific for Isa that means "his peace be upon us." Frank further explained that the traditional honorific cannot be used for someone who is alive. "It is only used in Islam for deceased prophets. We believe that Jesus is alive, which is another reason why we use a different honorific." Frank considers Isa as both human and Allah, and he talked about some of the reactions by various people to Isa. "People were offended by his teachings, and their own pride and ambitions were offended. The Jewish people were waiting for someone to lead them politically and help them, but Jesus said that his kingdom was not of this world." Frank also mentioned that their focus is on our spirits and souls. "The Sharia of Moses was related to our physical bodies, but the Sharia of Jesus relates to our spirits and souls." Referring to the cross Frank said, "Allah is a spirit and does not have a body, and therefore cannot die." Allah sent his Son, his Spirit, in a human physical form, according to Frank. "By appearance he was a man, but he was very different from a man. Regarding all the things he did, his behavior, his life, he was God."

What happens when those who walk in faith make a misstep? Frank replied that if this person comes back to the path, he will be forgiven and receive heaven. "If this person does not repent but continues to go against God and off the path, then it is obvious that he is under the control of Satan, and once he dies, he will go to hell."

Good things can be found in other religions, according to Frank. "For example, in the Qur'an it is written that Allah says that the most important religion is humanity, respecting and loving each other and human rights."

Frank further said that when it comes to religions, we cannot deny that they exist with all their philosophies and teachings, but we cannot consider them divine or from Allah. We need to be witnesses and give other people an invitation to the New Testament, Frank believes.

When I asked about working on making societies healthy, Frank mentioned the need for believers to reflect what they believe so that other people notice our behavior.

## Arthur

The plans and purposes of God are quite clear, according to Arthur. He created everything and made human beings in his own image to be his vice-regents, to act in this world on God's behalf. "Then man made a mistake and became the victim of diabolic power," Arthur continued. This was unacceptable to God, who mended this wound by making a token compensation by sending his Word, according to Arthur. "God wants to save humanity from Lucifer's courts and [for humanity to] come out of the sin, and be pure and pious, so that it can be joined to God."

I probed Arthur more on God's plans for this world versus for heaven, elsewhere. He shared that God loves this world that he has created, and he wants every person to come back on the right path, to be saved, and to then be responsible for their actions.

> It is the same for us. When I make something, like a book, I do not want it to be polluted, destroyed, or burned or ignored. When this is how I think of something I create, then how can we say that God has left the world and is letting it go to hell?

Arthur shared that sometimes it looks like Pauline Christianity is presenting the notion that you only need faith, and you will be saved, but he does not believe that Paul is saying that. "Some say, 'Faith is enough,' and go. This actually is corrupt Christianity. If you are injuring God's creation, you are not keeping faith in God."

> The first step is faith, and then you are liable and duty bound to act according to your faith, to be a person very polite and very useful to society. There is the love for God, and the next thing is the love for your neighbor.

"Neighbor" does not mean the person living next to you or relatives, but any human being.

Arthur continued on this point some more by pointing out that Jesus came to complete the law, not to abolish it. "Then how in the world can someone say to just believe and then go to heaven? It has nothing to do with that." Arthur believes that man has been given the freedom of choice to believe in Jesus Christ or not. "Faith belongs to our heart and mind, not to a fist or a stick."

| Theology Proper | 1 | 2 | 3 | 4 |
|---|---|---|---|---|
| Essence | | | | Ar |
| The Problem | | | | Ar |
| Satan | | Ar | | |
| Man | | | | Ar |
| **Missio Dei** | **1** | **2** | **3** | **4** |
| Gospel | | | Ar | |
| This World | | | Ar | |
| Our Mandate | | | | Ar |
| Healthy Societies | | | | Ar |
| Religions | | | Ar | |
| Election | | | Ar | |
| Hell | | | | Ar |
| Heaven | | | | Ar |
| The Bible | | | | Ar |
| The Qur'an | | | | Ar |
| **Isa al Masih** | **1** | **2** | **3** | **4** |
| Identity | | | | Ar |
| Christology | Ar | | | |
| His Life | | | Ar | |
| On the Cross | | | Ar | |
| The Cross | | | Ar | |
| The Resurrection | | | | |
| The Future | | | Ar | |

**Figure 26:** M-Framework plot for Arthur

The cross is completely God's plan, and we should not blame the Jews for this, according to Arthur. "The Jewish rabbis were not a liar people. They were not street people. They were not vulgar people. They were God's people." I asked Arthur how he saw God in the scene of Good Friday. Was God a self-sacrificing and giving God, or was he the one killing Jesus because the sins of the world were on him? His first reaction was, "This is a new thing I hear from you." Arthur finds it impossible for God to punish Jesus for sins he did not commit. "How can God Almighty be unjust?" Jesus is merciful, and he is giving himself to save the world. Arthur said, "I don't believe that this idea is convincing to me, that God put all universal sin on him, so God hates him, and killed him. No. It is impossible." He sees Jesus as the hero and added, "God cannot hate one of his own attributes."

On the topic of heaven and hell, Arthur explained that he sees them as names for happiness and sorrow. "If you believe and are satisfied, you have salvation. You are happy in this world and you will be happy in that world as well." On the other hand he describes hell as being infected with perplexity, being perturbed, and having no peace or serenity in your mind, heart, and body. Arthur clarified that he does not believe that heaven and hell are out there somewhere, where buildings are being built for us to go and live there. "Actually, heaven or hell is sorrow and happiness that a human being gets in this world." To him, going to heaven means having no worries about what is next while being satisfied and completed in this life. "And when he goes, his spirit joins directly to the Lord." Arthur mentioned how it is difficult to even think of the existence of another world while we are here, but it is true. In this sense he sees death as the beginning of hope. He explained some of his views on heaven and hell some more. "The Lord Almighty is controlling the universe. He will put you in situations so that the same place is hell for you and paradise for me." Thinking of them as places out there somewhere is making a fool of religion, Arthur thinks. He believes that people need hope to live in this world. "How will they cope with sorrowful times? Faith is very necessary. But I don't think that we should take the word of the Scriptures literally. It is metaphorical language." I asked him about those who have not believed in Jesus Christ. He shared how his faith says that the Lord Jesus Christ will come back and will fill this world with justice, peace, and love. Justice will bring wealth, and there will be no more enmity. Love will increase, and all of nature will be restored. Goats and lions will sit together, Arthur said.

> At that time my heart says, "I have no evidence, the Lord will forgive all." Hallelujah. Until this last judgment we are all still in process. We will all be there. And all may get the blessing, and mercy and grace. Even Lucifer will get it, maybe. It is abundant, abundant! A great sea of mercy. I think this is my explanation.

Arthur added that God's intrinsic attributes of mercy and love are more highlighted than wrath. "Also, as far as Islam is concerned, it has clearly said that God's mercy has won the race against his wrath. He is more 'most merciful' than 'most wrathful.'"

I asked Arthur about the Trinity. He sees it as a philosophy.

> I say that the Trinity was actually not faith. The Trinity was not there in the first three centuries on record. But the

> First Council of Nicaea decided that since the people were differentiated about the entity of the Lord Jesus Christ, to frame this belief in the words. They said that there is one Father God, and the other is a Son, and the third is the Holy Spirit, and all three make one God. If we look into reality, then we see that every religion has its own philosophy. The Trinity is a philosophy.

Arthur's challenge is how to explain philosophy to an illiterate layperson. He continued that God Almighty is one. "The sacred Tawrat and the Gospels are unanimous on this point." He looks at the Word and the Spirit as intrinsic attributes of God that are not created but emanate from God. His words are also called metaphorically his Son, according to Arthur, and God's love is expressed as the Spirit of God. We are called to worship and respect God with all his attributes, Arthur continued. "This is the meaning when we say that someone is worshiping Allah Almighty, and then he is worshiping the Son and Holy Spirit, because they are not separated from him." Arthur goes as far as to say that if the understanding and misunderstanding of one God versus polytheism is cleared up, we are all alike. "If this problem is solved there is no difference between a Muslim and a Christian."

On the topic of the phrase *the Son of God*, Arthur is convinced that we have to solve this language problem to bring two great religions together. He explained how in Arabic the word *son* (*ibn*) means the one born of someone's semen. "You cannot say of anyone that he was born of God's semen. Still people do not want to say this correctly, and they continue saying that this is from the Christians, and let them be in their problems." Arthur also has observed reluctance on the Christian side to rectify this through the proper use of language. "When you say 'father' and 'son' literally, they don't listen for one more word. They object violently." Arthur pleaded, "The wording should be changed to be understandable. Unambiguous language should be used to express our belief." He promotes using the phrase *the Word of God*.

> It is written, first he was the Word, and the Qur'an confirms that he is the Word of God. There is no other prophet in the Qur'an mentioned as the Word of God. Then why should we not say to all Muslim brothers, "Come near us.

We are not polytheists. We are not worshiping the person who was born of Mary, but we are worshiping the Word of God that came to Mary through an angel, and we are worshiping that Word and not the body that was born of Mary." Then let's see who puts up a gulf between Muslims and Christians.

The Qur'an is clearly an important book to Arthur. He said that he has studied the Qur'an from the beginning to the end. "There are 93 verses in the holy Quran that speak directly about the Lord Jesus Christ." Arthur believes that the Quran speaks of the Lord Jesus Christ with great respect, and all his miracles are mentioned there as well. It is pro-Christ.

> I believe that this Qur'an actually is pro-Christ. Mohammed, peace be upon him, was pro-Christ. In another way, I am actually going to prove that Muslims are pro-Christ Muslims. Early Jews could be Christian, so how can Muslims who came 600 years later not be pro-Christ Muslims as well?

Arthur thinks that tribal enmity and animosity hijacked the religion of Islam so that its adherents started interpreting the Qur'an in another way. For example, Arthur explained, in the Qur'an there are some verses that say that Jews and Christians cannot be your friends, but he is convinced that this was meant to be applied to wartime only. Another thing that the Qur'an is saying is that Jesus was not killed, but that he was taken away. So what is wrong with that? Arthur asked. Was Jesus really killed? He was symbolically killed, because his spirit cannot be killed. And when the Qur'an says, "Do not say three," Arthur said, "God Almighty is actually refuting the beliefs of those people who were untrained, and who were interpreting things their own way." In other words, this is a warning to Muslims against tritheism. Arthur wants to respect and protect the Qur'an.

> I am going to say to Terry Jones, "Do not ban the Qur'an, because you do not know about the Qur'an. If you ban the Qur'an, you actually ban the cloak of the Lord Jesus Christ. You are banning the child of Mary. You are banning the sacred record of Abraham, Ishmael, Isaac, Jacob, and his 12 sons. Their record is in the Qur'an. Why in the

> world do you want to ban it? So we are not going to ban the Qur'an, but we are going to highlight from the Qur'an the Lord Jesus Christ." This is my movement.

Arthur continued, "When Arabia was thinking about Judaism and Christianity, the Qur'an is their record. Why should we lose this human record? Why should we destroy it or hate it?" He does believe that its interpretation needs to be renewed, according to the context and the history and framework of that time. Arthur recalled some of the problems on the Christian side at that time, as Christianity was very political and there was an increasing divide between East and West on philosophy and beliefs.

> And because of all these problems, the Muslim community had the chance to criticize Christianity of that time and to be separate. This was actually a sect of the Christ. That is why the Muslim emphasis is on actions and not on more beliefs. They are closer to the Jews in that aspect than to Christians.

Arthur reviewed the three Abrahamic religions and established that the theological center is Jesus Christ. Muslims believe that he did not die but was taken away. They are waiting for him to come back and fill the world with peace. Christians say that he was killed and rose up, and went to heaven. He will come back and fill the world with peace and justice and love. The Jews are still waiting for Christ to come and fill their world with peace.

> We all believe in one God, but our interpretations are different. We have to understand one another's language and philosophy and semantics, and then the problem will be solved. Otherwise, if we continue to claim that we are right and they are wrong, we never will get anywhere.

## Paxton

To Paxton, Allah is the Creator of the universe, who loves human beings very much. He shared that the Qur'an mentions the word *love* for Allah as well, even though only once. "It has not been developed in later Islam, which is unfortunate, but it is still there in the Qur'an," Paxton said. He uses the words *Allah* and *God* interchangeably in this interview. To him, God does not want to send anyone to hell, so he kept on sending different prophets and leaders so that they would be guided to the true path. Paxton believes that we can understand what God is like from what he has revealed in the Scriptures and in Jesus.

> To me what God is like is all very positive. It has no negative connotations whatsoever. There may be some statements in the Qur'an or other places that can be used to come to a concept that is somewhat different, but in the same way it could also be argued that way against the Old Testament.

God's plans and purposes have to do with his creation, Paxton said. "He created this whole universe and he wants it to be operated in a proper manner." God also knows that it is not operating properly because of some external interference, so he keeps on interfering from time to time, and he also has sent us a manual in the form of the holy books, according to Paxton. But still something went wrong. Some model was required, someone, to whom we could refer under all these circumstances, and who demonstrates the manual in a practical manner. "He had to reveal himself in such a way that we know what he wants to be done in this world."

> All these claims that God loves human beings, is there any evidence whatsoever? When I look at the universe I find out that there is so much carnage, bloodshed, and all these things. If I cannot be convinced of the love of God at all, I would become an atheist.

Paxton continued, "But when I look at Jesus and I find out that when it says that God loves you, he is showing it in a practical manner . . . To me it is clear that God still loves the world and everyone." I asked him to comment on the views in Christianity that range from a creation restoration focus as the salvation *of* this world to a view towards heaven as salvation *away from* this world. His first reply was, "If God is really interested in taking human beings to heaven, first of all, he must bring heaven to earth. If he cannot do that, he should not expect us to go to heaven." He continued describing his views.

> To me, going to heaven is not the ideal thing. What is ideal is that God is omnipresent, he is working in this world, and he wants to change this world into an ideal state. This world has to change, not that we should be taken out of it but living in it here, transforming it in such a way that when we go over there, it suddenly does not feel alien to us, like going to a different culture that we do not understand.

Paxton made a side comment about the word "eternal." "When it talks about eternal salvation and all those kinds of things, the emphasis is not on the duration of that thing, how long it will last, but with whom you will spend that." He returned to the concept of Jesus being our model. "But if the main thing is that you have to get out of this world, then in that way, Jesus cannot be my model, I am very sorry to say." Paxton noted that when Jesus came into this world, he did not concede that everything was happening according to the plan that God had for this world. "He was a living protest—a protest against diseases, evil spirits, and all those kinds of things. All the evils found in the world, he practically fought against them."

Paxton talked about how we need to be changed here on earth first to be ready for heaven. He believes that if someone decides to go to hell, God respects that person's decision. "If someone is a very evil person and God sends him to heaven without changing him completely, then he will create hell out of that heaven." Paxton repeated that God loves everyone, "but only those who respond in a practical manner towards that love, those go to heaven. People who reject it go to hell." Paxton believes that God only holds us responsible for the knowledge that we possess, when it comes to heaven and hell. He holds to the view that a person's point of physical death is the fork in the road—i.e., that there is no more hope after that for those who are lost. He also believes in the possibility of apostasy. "I see the possibility in places in Hebrews and other places." Paxton used the phrase "once saved, always saved," and commented, "A very good saying, but unfortunately it produces a kind of Christian that thinks that because they have been saved, it does not matter what kind of life they live." Paxton did not specify more things about hell other than that there will be suffering. Ultimately he does not know who goes there. "Basically I will say that it is a devaluation of the presence of God. Hell is where God is not." I presented the notion held by some that there is an ongoingness of the present into life after death, that all hope is not lost and choices can still be made. Paxton replied, "If you are generous enough to give people a second chance after death, for example, then I need justification for being honest in the present world." He believes that the second-chance notion will only corrupt people. Paxton quoted a Muslim mystic lady (Saint Rabia Basri, AD 717–801):

> God, if I love you because I want to go to heaven, then please deprive me of heaven. God, if I love you for the simple reason that I am afraid of hell, please send me to hell. But if I love you because you are loving, and I cannot but love you, then I don't care about whether I go to heaven or hell, because I know that wherever I will be, you will be with me.

God revealed himself through prophets by revealing himself first to them, according to Paxton. They were the mouthpiece of God and delivered messages about what God wanted people to do. Paxton explained how different prophets came in different situations, in different cultures and with different backgrounds. "The message may be the same, but it was expressed differently,

| Theology Proper | 1 | 2 | 3 | 4 |
|---|---|---|---|---|
| Essence | | | Pn | |
| The Problem | | | Pn | |
| Satan | | Pn | | |
| Man | | | Pn | |
| **Missio Dei** | **1** | **2** | **3** | **4** |
| Gospel | | | Pn | |
| This World | | | Pn | |
| Our Mandate | | | | Pn |
| Healthy Societies | | | | Pn |
| Religions | | | | Pn |
| Election | | | Pn | |
| Hell | | Pn | | |
| Heaven | | Pn | | |
| The Bible | | | Pn | |
| The Qur'an | | | Pn | |
| **Isa al Masih** | **1** | **2** | **3** | **4** |
| Identity | | | | Pn |
| Christology | | Pn | | |
| His Life | | | | Pn |
| On the Cross | | | | Pn |
| The Cross | | | Pn | |
| The Resurrection | | Pn | | |
| The Future | | | Pn | |

**Figure 27:** M-Framework plot for Paxton

at different places and at different times." In every case, Paxton explained, the basic message was that God is love. Paxton reflected on the world today and lamented, "Non-Christians usually do not get that message, that God is love, because they don't see any evidence whatsoever for it in nature or among the Christians." He concluded that within Islam we have to explain the love of God in different ways and in different languages, using the contextual approach the prophets used.

Regarding God's revelation through the Scriptures, Paxton realizes that language is not a perfect vehicle, but nevertheless he believes that there are no errors in the Bible. He quickly added, "That doesn't mean that everything has to be taken literally. I will not interpret each word literally, but from its historical and cultural perspective." The Qur'an has played an important role in Paxton's life since it led him to Christ, and to that extent he believes the Qur'an is inspired by God. He added that there are parts in the Qur'an that he does not agree with. "There are aspects, such as killing non-Muslims. I would say, okay, it goes to the extent of the Old Testament mentality, but it does not come up with a New Testament." Paxton added, "Basically the Mecca phase is no problem for me. It is in the Medina phase where Mohammed got power, and how he misused power sometimes, then definitely, I cannot accept that."

On the topic of Jesus and the cross, Paxton said that ultimately the sin of all human beings put him there. He believes that his death only saves us if we believe it was a sacrifice on Jesus' part. Paxton continued, "Love requires some kind of sacrifice. It goes through trouble and suffering. If he really loves us, then he has to suffer." He also said, "Love always requires some kind of sacrifice by the person who loves. And if you love to the utmost, then you suffer to the utmost. There is no other way." I summarized the doctrine of penal substitutionary atonement and asked him to comment. Paxton replied, "Unfortunately, I cannot accept that." He explained that rather than seeing the sacrifice as a substitution for humanity, he prefers seeing it as being in solidarity with humanity. He looks at Adam's sins the same way.

> I think that the Bible is not talking about the inherited sin, but it is talking about the inherent sin. Because we are part of that same humanity, therefore if one man sins, if our representative sins, we have sinned in him in a way that only the concept of solidarity can explain, but not the concept of substitution.

Paxton deduced, "So Jesus said that the Son of Man, the one who represents humanity, has to suffer with them when they suffer; not execution on the part of God." He further explained that loving someone benefits the one being loved by illustration of his mother loving him, and suffering because of it, yet he is alive because of that love. I asked him what he thought of the phrase, "Jesus paid for my sins and saved me." Paxton said, "If you stop with that, then definitely you don't have any ethical Christians in the world, if you follow the belief that Jesus saved me, and that everything is finished." He believes that the imperative of that truth is that you have to do something and love other people. He added, "What I find wanting in churches in the present is that they stop with that narrative and don't talk about the imperative." I asked whether he would say that the salvation of the world comes through the imperative, that through us acting out love, through us responding and loving self-sacrificially in this world, we are saving this world. Paxton said, "Let us hope something, which certainly does not seem to be attainable, that it is our responsibility to work out the salvation of the world in a practical manner." He admitted that we have failed miserably so far, but that it is a very good purpose. He also believes that we will need some kind of divine intervention.

On the topic of the relationship between Jesus and God, Paxton talked about the attributes of God, pointing out that many of them only apply after God has created. "But there is only one aspect that allows me to talk about the eternality of God and his attributes, and that is that he is love." Love needs to be responded to in a relationship. Paxton concluded, "So I look at it this way: that God, the lover, is the Father, and his eternal beloved is Jesus Christ, and the spirit of love that exists between the two that is very holy, is the Holy Spirit." He further added that God is one. His essence is not divided into three parts. He used the illustration of a stone, which when cut in half gives us two stones. This does not apply to human beings.

> So the more complex the unity is, the more difficult it is to divide it. If God were only a simple unity, then you could divide him into many parts. But he is a complex unity, therefore you cannot divide him. I can think about God being one and at the same time being divisible for the simple reason that he is not like a stone, which can be broken into different pieces. God is like a living entity, which cannot be divided into any parts whatsoever.

Is the phrase *the Son of God* an ectypal[4] metaphorical functional expression or an archetypal metaphysical ontological reality in the essence of God? Paxton responded that we know only the things which Jesus has revealed. It does not go beyond that. "We can talk about it until doomsday, but we will never come to any conclusion whatsoever." He also mentioned that we use limited terminology to talk about an unlimited God. "This is one of the problems that we will always face, otherwise we will invent some kind of a language that no one will understand what we are talking about." The bottom line is that Paxton sees that phrase as a metaphor revealing something that is beyond comprehension.

> If you want to know who God the Father is, or what he is, or how he works and what kind of properties he has, then we look at Jesus Christ. He is that mirror through which we see the face of God.

Regarding religions, Paxton does not consider the living message of Jesus Christ to be a religion. "Unfortunately it took the form of a religion, and definitely it has some kind of straitjacket around it, and it cannot get out of it." He said that the message of Jesus shows us how to live and die. It has to do with sin and repentance, and it applies to all of humanity, to Muslims and Christians alike. It has nothing to do with switching from one religion to another. For this reason Paxton does not like the word "convert." He has wondered whether he should present himself as a Christian or a Muslim or be two-faced about it. To him the basic question is, "How do I show and express my faith within the traditional means that are available to me?" To him this means being a Muslim, starting with the Qur'an and moving on to the prior holy books, and then ending up with Jesus Christ. Paxton shared, "The word 'Muslim' means someone who surrenders himself to the will of God. What I found to be the will of God, I surrender to that. In that sense, I am a Muslim."

## Wilbur

Wilbur is the alongsider for the movement in South Asia Region D, where he has been involved for many years.

---

4. Ectypal refers to the revealed or copied expression of the original or archetypal reality.

God, or Allah, is as Christ presents him to us, according to Wilbur. He further described God as Creator, immaterial spirit, loving, compassionate, highly relational, and perfect in every way. He cares intensely about his creation. Wilbur continued, "So he is not the watchmaker who has abandoned his watch." God's plans and purposes are part of what seem to us to be plan A and plan B, Wilbur shared. He believes that the original purpose (plan A) is the creation of the visible universe and all its inhabitants, for God's own pleasure, so that his beauty could be on display, and for his creation to be very harmonious and very happy and very integrated. "This special purpose (plan B) comes up then, when in this other category of spiritual beings that were created prior to humans, a rebellion occurs." Wilbur believes that this rebellion occurred prior to the creation of the human race and said, "God is obviously out to make a point to the rebels by his dealings with us." God created us in a position of great vulnerability, and we are complicit in the rebellion from square one, according to Wilbur.

> God is not surprised by this; rather he is undertaking, entirely out of his own infinite largeness, in his own person, to make all of that right at his own expense, with the result that again his patience, his mercy, his own superiority—ontologically and everything—is on display again to all realms visible and invisible.

Wilbur calls plan B the redemptive phase. "We look forward to a day when that redemptive phase is completed and we'll get on with plan A," Wilbur said. He calls plan A the creative mandate and believes that eventually our appreciation of and love for God will be a great deal richer because we did time on the other side of all this.

On the question whether God is about restoring his creation here on earth or about populating heaven, Wilbur explained that there is an urgency that puts the redemptive mandate, which relates to populating heaven, ahead of the creation mandate, which relates to life here on earth lived in community. Wilbur mentioned, "It is clear, of course, that this planet earth as we know it has a shelf life. We don't know what exactly that is. This physical planet is certainly not the eternal home of the people of God." Nevertheless, Wilbur said that where the redemptive mandate is extended, we should embrace the creative mandate and be good stewards of the resources that God has given us.

| Theology Proper | 1 | 2 | 3 | 4 |
|---|---|---|---|---|
| Essence | Wr | | | |
| The Problem | Wr | | | |
| Satan | Wr | | | |
| Man | | Wr | | |
| **Missio Dei** | **1** | **2** | **3** | **4** |
| Gospel | | Wr | | |
| This World | | Wr | | |
| Our Mandate | Wr | | | |
| Healthy Societies | | Wr | | |
| Religions | | Wr | | |
| Election | | Wr | | |
| Hell | Wr | | | |
| Heaven | Wr | | | |
| The Bible | | Wr | | |
| The Qur'an | | Wr | | |
| **Isa al Masih** | **1** | **2** | **3** | **4** |
| Identity | | Wr | | |
| Christology | | Wr | | |
| His Life | Wr | | | |
| On the Cross | Wr | | | |
| The Cross | | Wr | | |
| The Resurrection | | Wr | | |
| The Future | Wr | | | |

**Figure 28:** M-Framework plot for Wilbur

Regarding heaven and hell, Wilbur described hell as being a state of perpetual alienation, isolation, and broken relationship with him, which will entail suffering as it does in this present form of our existence. "Heaven on the other hand will be just the opposite. All the benefits of not being in an estranged state with him, but being in a state of nearness with him; it will be really, really good."

He expanded on this some more. "There is a value on the state of nearness to him precisely because there is an alternative, and it is ugly. There is a horror to the state of estrangement precisely because the other is possible too." Wilbur believes that God has gone the extra mile to convince us that he did the right thing. "He will make sure that everyone knows that they are invited to the party. It is also very clear that many will decline the offer." Hell is forever. The idea of annihilation may be attractive to us, but we cannot get there exegetically, according to Wilbur. An individual's physical death is the point of final decision for our eternal destination, Wilbur shared, which means to him that there is urgency with the redemptive mandate.

> The Scripture utterly precludes the possibility that because God's greatness is going to overwhelm even the most calloused and rebellious heart, that it is more or less no big deal what we do with the redemptive mandate. There is no support in Scripture for that position. Quite the contrary, I think there is a tremendous urgency.

Wilbur believes that the majority of the people in the world today actually will go to hell.

> Are the majority of people living today on planet earth living lives of love, giving evidence to the fact that they have been regenerated and are now reconciled to God, and channeling his divine love to those around them? I don't see that. I don't see that happening, so I take that as an indication again that many have been called, but few have been saved, at least as I look at the world scene.

Does each person have freedom of choice? Wilbur approached this question as something of a mystery. I mentioned, as an example, the doctrine of double election. Wilbur shared that a Muslim worldview fits well with that doctrine, but that most insider believers cannot go there emotionally, because they often are the only one in their family or community. Does this happen by eternal decree? "That is emotionally untenable if not also equally a stumbling block intellectually for them. They come out very quickly on the side that would not be predicted by what their original worldview is," Wilbur said.

God has revealed himself through the prophets. "He tells them what to say, and they say it and they do it, and there are many occupational hazards," Wilbur said. God also reveals himself through the Scriptures. Wilbur calls it a divine and human book.

> The human elements are indisputable. The divine elements are indisputable. The Scriptures are incarnational, in a way. It is the eternal Word of God breaking into human languages and human consciousness and human experience, and given to us in a very domestic flavor.

Wilbur said that the Scriptures are fully reliable. "The things that God allowed to be recorded in the Bible lead us to the correct interpretations about who God is, what he expects, and what he has done." Wilbur does not believe that we should expect a next installment. He looks at the Scriptures as both a rule book and God's narrative. He sees a great deal of rules and instructions for our lives. "Everything works best when we attend to the guidance," he said.

Regarding the Qur'an, Wilbur shared that he sees it as a book that contains a lot of truth, but he does not believe that it contains reliable revelation that is straight from the Author of our lives. It is a secondary source that can be used as bridge material, but not as destination, according to Wilbur.

> We can and we must appeal to the Qur'an, where it is a starting point. The point is to take them across that bridge to a different and distinct destination and not sort of let it all run together. Let me just flatly state it: I would not put the Qur'an in the category of revealed Scripture.

Wilbur described the actions of Jesus Christ by mentioning first that at his baptism he was clothed with power from on high. "From that moment on his actions are entirely under that direct influence and management of his father, the Creator God Allah." Wilbur mentioned that Jesus' manifold mission was right from the beginning very focused on a moment of suffering and a moment later of triumph in resurrection. "Between the baptism and those events we see him doing a ministry practicum with a handful of select companions," Wilbur said. Jesus' actions included exercising all sorts of supernatural power over and against the kingdom of Satan. He especially devoted a great amount of time to liberating people who were under the more visible domination of Satan, either through demonic possession or through some sort of physical illness or malady, according to Wilbur. Jesus also interacted with the representative power structures of the day, explained Wilbur.

> He very much and by his own choice embraced this path of inevitable suffering, as he would be rejected, so he underwent a period of intense testing and physical suffering which culminated in some felt separation from his Father on the cross, as the weight and the blackness of the human sin problem actually came to rest on him. He bore our sins in his own body. He took all that on himself.

Wilbur expressed that there were multiple things happening on the cross and not just substitutionary atonement. He believes that Jesus' suffering, rejection, and mockery function in other ways to actually exalt the righteousness of God. After the resurrection and ascension and sending of the Holy Spirit, the actions of Jesus continue in a different modus operandi. "He continues to operate, and in that way his actions continue. We are not wondering in a sort of vacuous way, like the Muslim default worldview would, what he is doing now." He is continuing the process of reconciliation, Wilbur said. When asked what the message of Isa al Masih is, Wilbur explained that it is one of repent and believe, but in a personal way. "The message is: Believe in me, receive me, attach yourself to me. By doing so, you will escape the judgment, you will escape the clutches of the rebels." Wilbur added, "If you attach yourself to me, if you have confidence in me, I will get your boat across, as they say in local idiom here. And you will have eternal life and escape eternal damnation."

Jesus willingly died on the cross to satisfy the demands of his own integrity and holiness, which require punishment for sin, according to Wilbur. It fulfilled the requirement of his own wrath, but he gave of himself.

> In his redemptive narrative his death and resurrection was the climax of a plot, which intends to overwhelmingly convince us of his righteousness, and of all his love, and of his worthiness, and at the same time move us. It is through this narrative that he woos us. It is the "We love him because he first loved us." This narrative, this passion plot, is the supreme thing that he does to appeal to us as he woos us.

Wilbur sees the death and resurrection of Jesus Christ as good news, because for those who come to feel remorse for their sins, they don't need to be on death row, so to speak. "Jesus' resurrection is in many ways paradigmatic for what becomes of us," Wilbur said.

In relation to God, Wilbur sees Jesus as a permanent incarnation into human physical form of God's self-projection, his own eternal and personal communiqué, whether you call that the image or Word, or the voice of Allah.

Regarding religions, Wilbur sees them as helpful and unhelpful to varying degrees. In general he thinks that the Christian religion is to play a mediating role in bringing about the purposes of God. He shared how he sees that much of Christianity has lost its moorings. He sees cheap grace and an antinomian spirit reigning in the so-called Christian world, with devastating effects. He thinks that it is possible that God is using the Muslim religious system as a means to temporarily shield one billion people from those effects.

> So that at an appointed time in the future a great day of hearing can actually be possible, because people's family structures will be more or less intact, and they will find talk about the holy books and the prophets and things like that to be relevant topics, because they have been sheltered in this other system.

With regard to different theological viewpoints, Wilbur said that he sees much patience with people who are still in process, but that there is very much a mood that there is a correct interpretation, and that anything that is not a correct interpretation is a false interpretation. Their backgrounds do not include the notion of a plurality of correct interpretations of anything, according to Wilbur. He added:

I think it would be very disturbing to these people if they knew the extreme variety that is held within our faith communities in a Western setting. Most of the theological discussions in the community at this point are on what we call disputable matters such as the fasting and prayer traditions. There is more freedom there, but when it comes to doctrinal topics, they are looking for one shared answer. The attitude is very much that there is a correct understanding and we have to get everybody to that correct understanding, because they will suffer in some way if they don't get to that, if they are left with something that is much more fuzzy and mixed. There has to be a definite shared understanding on essentials.

Wilbur has observed that only the top-level leaders in the movement understand that there are core doctrinal matters that we struggle to understand even with the best exegetical resources. "But those would all be advanced topics for the people that they are dealing with out in the ranks. I would say that that is not filtered down to the lower levels," Wilbur said. He thinks it is too early for that, because the needed translations are not available yet. "Too few of them have enough of the requisite resources to begin theologizing." Wilbur added that the theologizing at this point is much more charismatic, obedience oriented, relational, and conservative as part of an oral culture and community. On the question whether differences in theological viewpoints among these top leaders are acceptable,

Wilbur answered that they would hold to a set of essentials, and they would actively discourage a variety of interpretations on the person and work of Christ, or the reliability of the Scriptures. "They are not after diversity in that; they are after people 'getting it.'" These leaders work hard to mitigate there being multiple Christologies or multiple canons in their fellowship. Wilbur said that their general orthodoxy is wide, and that he would have great cause for concern if he started hearing them refer to Jesus Christ as the Second Person of the Trinity.

> That numbering is meaningful within a world and a context that is very alien to them. I would rather see them developing all sorts of new language and illustrations to help them meaningfully get their minds around a difficult topic than just sort of wholesale borrowing those that have appeared in the Western tradition.

Wilbur also shared that freethinkers such as Arthur or Paxton may get somewhat reckless at times. "They may get into metaphysical discussions that the people listening to them cannot begin to understand." Wilbur said that other people, such as Angus and Frank, who interface between him and the simpler disciples, mediate the effects of that kind of reckless theologizing.

In closing, Wilbur appealed to everyone to consider what profound things God is doing in our times in these movements.

> These are true disciples who would, for issues of survival and relevance, want to get back to a pre-Constantine expression of faith in Isa al Masih, and who also want to avoid the worldliness associated with the Western and national church bodies. I hope that others would prayerfully consider whether God might truly be blessing people like this. I am profoundly challenged by the faith and the understanding and the authenticity and the sacrifices of these people that most of my friends and associates back home would have no category for.

## Central Asia M-Framework Plots

*Julius*

Julius described Allah as one, as loving, and as one with 99 beautiful names. His plans and purposes are to save all people. Julius shared how Allah has shown this plan from the very beginning when the prophet Adam sinned. Allah also saved the prophet Noah and his family. He saved the Israelites through the prophet Moses, and he made a covenant with Abraham to save all his descendants. "It has been revealed through the prophet David and all other prophets that God wants to save sinners," Julius said. He continued and spoke about Isa in the New Testament. "The prophet Isa was God's clear plan to save, because he is the perfect sacrifice to save all people through him. Through his sacrifice, all people can be led onto the true path."

On the question whether Allah's plans are focused on the salvation and restoration of this world or on saving people away from the world for heaven, Julius said that Allah wants to save and redeem all of creation. "He wants to primarily work through people, because people are the governors of nature, under Allah's plan, according to Genesis."

On the topic of heaven and hell Julius explained, "There is Allah's kingdom and there is Satan's kingdom. His plan is to save people and redeem people, so that they can escape hell and enter heaven." I asked more about these kingdoms.

> Those who follow the true path through Isa al Masih will be the true inheritors. They will receive the inheritance of Allah. Allah's kingdom is established on earth among the people who are his inheritors. Allah's creation will be reconciled with them. At the same time, and over time, Allah's kingdom will defeat Satan's kingdom. This is a gradual process: as more and more people believe Allah and enter his kingdom, they are inheritors of his inheritance, they become his people in the kingdom, and slowly through that, Satan's kingdom is defeated.

Julius believes that heaven and hell are two places that last forever. "Those who oppose al Masih will be thrown into hell, and also those who will not accept that Isa al Masih is God's true path." Julius added that it seems like many people in the world today are not following Isa al Masih. He believes that Allah created people with free will and a choice. Regarding the people in the past and today who have not heard about Isa al Masih, Julius said, "For those people, Allah will look at those people's heart and their faith, that their faith is acceptable." When asked whether a person's heart can still change after they die, Julius said that the traditional teaching he has received in the past would say no, but he added, "I don't think I really know if people's hearts can be changed after they die."

Regarding the Scriptures, Julius sees the first three books as having authority that is higher than the Qur'an. "When I have compared the first three books with the Qur'an, I feel that those first books more completely reveal Allah to us. The revelation in the Qur'an is not complete." He believes that the verses in the Qur'an about Isa al Masih are good teachings. Julius said, "The four books taken together can help a Muslim more completely understand Allah, and to understand that Allah is the one and only." He believes that the Scriptures are inspired in the sense that the meaning is inspired, not the words themselves. He looks at the Scriptures more as God's narrative story than as his rule book.

| Theology Proper | 1 | 2 | 3 | 4 |
|---|---|---|---|---|
| Essence |  | Js |  |  |
| The Problem |  |  | Js |  |
| Satan | Js |  |  |  |
| Man |  | Js |  |  |
| **Missio Dei** | 1 | 2 | 3 | 4 |
| Gospel |  |  | Js |  |
| This World |  |  | Js |  |
| Our Mandate |  | Js |  |  |
| Healthy Societies |  |  | Js |  |
| Religions |  |  |  | Js |
| Election |  | Js |  |  |
| Hell | Js |  |  |  |
| Heaven |  | Js |  |  |
| The Bible |  |  | Js |  |
| The Qur'an |  |  | Js |  |
| **Isa al Masih** | 1 | 2 | 3 | 4 |
| Identity |  |  |  | Js |
| Christology |  |  |  | Js |
| His Life |  |  | Js |  |
| On the Cross |  | Js |  |  |
| The Cross |  | Js |  |  |
| The Resurrection |  |  | Js |  |
| The Future |  |  | Js |  |

**Figure 29:** M-Framework plot for Julius

On the topic of religions, he sees that they produce uniform teachings, but that there are aspects of a religion that often negatively influence the growth of God's kingdom. "I really think that it is important that the negative aspects of religion are discarded and that those who belong to Allah's kingdom are a blessing to all people," he said. He shared how Allah is interested in a person's heart. "Entering his kingdom is less about the external cultural aspects of religion than about the heart. Religion and the gospel are two different things."

Isa came to the world with a mission, Julius explained. "He came to reveal God's power among the people, and to attract and welcome people to seek God's kingdom, and to establish God's kingdom on earth." Julius said that Isa came to this earth via God's Word being cast into Mary, becoming Isa the prophet. In all the things Isa did, all along the way he depended on Allah's power. "In his life on earth he was an example for all people of a perfectly submitted person, a perfectly submitted man, for everyone to see what that looks like." Julius further added that we know from Acts 2 that Allah raised Isa from the dead and made him Lord and al Masih, "so his life on earth was also a revelation of God's love for all to see." He concluded that Isa shows us the true path to Allah. I asked whether the concept of the true path is about going somewhere or about a way of living that saves the world. Julius explained that he sees the path as a metaphor regarding Isa al Masih, as found in the Qur'an and the New Testament. Julius also said, "I see the path as a way of living, in copying Isa al Masih as the example for how to live. It is the life of submission lived out as a light to others who are not on the path."

Allah caused Isa al Masih to suffer because of the sin of all humanity, according to Julius, who compared Isa with Adam. "Isa became a perfect example of a submissive servant." This is good news, Julius believes, because it resolves the problem of mankind's sin, and the resurrection brings hope to people as the power of death was defeated.

Isa is Allah's Word, he is Allah's chosen prophet and highest prophet, and he is the one nearest to Allah in this world and in the world to come, according to Julius. "Isa al Masih reveals Allah and embodies Allah, but is not Allah." Julius added that Allah reveals himself in two ways: by means of the Spirit and in Isa al Masih. I asked if he experiences his faith as a relationship to Allah or to Isa al Masih. Julius said that he establishes a good relationship with Allah by following Isa al Masih. "It is not like I have a relationship with Isa al Masih that replaces my relationship with Allah. Isa al Masih is Allah's inheritor and his anointed King, but not Allah himself." Julius does not believe in the Trinity, as he finds it a confusing concept. "Understanding Allah is a mystery. I would not use this explanation or method to teach others." Julius understands the phrase *Son of God* as a metaphor that refers to Allah's chosen and anointed one.

"It expresses the belovedness and closeness between Isa al Masih and Allah, but not as a physical relationship, like we would think of between a son and a father."

## Gus

Gus said that the Allah of the Qur'an and of the Bible are the same. He has 99 names, which are all good. Gus further described Allah as the Creator, merciful and forgiving. He is completely different from his creation. Allah's plans and purposes are to restore creation, according to Gus. "There is something wrong with creation. It currently is incompatible with Allah. That is the main problem." Gus explained that he does not like the image of Allah being a judge, because Allah is not happy when people go to hell. Gus added, "His mercy is bigger than his anger, and Allah's anger is still different from human anger. I am not sure if God is emotional. He doesn't judge by emotions." Gus used to look at heaven and hell as temporary storage areas, but he now believes these to be eternal places. On the question on freedom of choice Gus said, "I am Arminian. I have a big problem with Calvinism. People have a free will and a choice."

Gus believes that it was the will of Allah for Isa to be crucified so that our sins are forgiven. Justice demands punishment. He sees Allah's purposes as being for us to become more compatible with living in his presence while we are here on earth, which he believes will be burned and then there will be a new creation. "You can look at Isa as a Sufi leader who is starting a new 'race' that is compatible with Him."

On the topic of the relationship between Isa al Masih and Allah, Gus first explained that the father-son language falls short. "It doesn't work with Muslims and it doesn't work with Christians. It is

| Theology Proper | 1 | 2 | 3 | 4 |
|---|---|---|---|---|
| Essence | | Gs | | |
| The Problem | | Gs | | |
| Satan | | | Gs | |
| Man | | Gs | | |
| Missio Dei | 1 | 2 | 3 | 4 |
| Gospel | | Gs | | |
| This World | | Gs | | |
| Our Mandate | Gs | | | |
| Healthy Societies | | Gs | | |
| Religions | | | | Gs |
| Election | | Gs | | |
| Hell | | Gs | | |
| Heaven | | Gs | | |
| The Bible | | Gs | | |
| The Qur'an | | | | Gs |
| Isa al Masih | 1 | 2 | 3 | 4 |
| Identity | | | | Gs |
| Christology | | Gs | | |
| His Life | Gs | | | |
| On the Cross | | Gs | | |
| The Cross | | Gs | | |
| The Resurrection | | Gs | | |
| The Future | Gs | | | |

**Figure 30:** M-Framework plot for Gus

a semantic paradox." Gus asked whether the Son is eternally submitting to the Father or only as Isa on earth. He said how some in his language community call Isa the Father because "brother" or "son" is not high enough, and not respectful enough. Gus believes that Isa is fully human, with a created body and mystical origins, and with an awareness of pre-creation time. Gus still has questions about the relationship between Isa al Masih and Allah. "Is Isa Allah? He is Allah's Word that has become human. What is the relationship between a human body and the Word of God? What is that? I don't know."

Regarding the role of religions, Gus sees them as faith systems that humans need for the good of a community, otherwise violence would be everywhere. He believes that Allah allowed Islam to come and rise because he knew that Christian communities would stop multiplying. He sees Islam and the Qur'an as compatible with the Bible.

> Islam is mostly compatible with the Bible. Nothing in the Qur'an is blatantly against the Bible. Someone could interpret it in a way that is against the Bible, but each sura starts with, "In the name of the most merciful and 'wishing-good' God." That is the hermeneutical theme of the Qur'an.

Gus believes that Allah is concerned about injustice in societies and that he wants to see more just and righteous societies here on earth. Gus added, "Absolutely. We need to apply the kingdom of God rules in politics now. Through the regeneration of the heart, we will see societies transformed."

### Jason

Jason does not mind using the word *Allah* or another term in their language for God. He does believe, however, that the God of the Qur'an, as he is described, is totally different from the God of the Bible. Jason described God as loving and holy. His main purpose, according to Jason, is to bring people into a relationship with him, similar to the one Adam had in paradise. God's second purpose is for all of us to understand our calling, Jason said.

> My obligation is to fit with his plan and to start moving towards it. So first there is the relationship, and second

you have to find out your calling. God has a calling for each Christian. There are no Sunday-morning Christians.

Hell is a place where God is not present and where there is eternal torture, according to Jason. "There is punishment without a time limit. It is for eternity. You cannot stop it. It is a very scary place and people do not want to be there." On the other hand, Jason sees heaven or paradise as a place where we experience eternal joy in the presence of God and Jesus himself. "There will be no tears or anything that brings sadness to you." Jason said that people who reject the sacrifice of Jesus as the Lamb, who do not believe that he is the only way to come to salvation, will go

| Theology Proper | 1 | 2 | 3 | 4 |
|---|---|---|---|---|
| Essence | Jn | | | |
| The Problem | | Jn | | |
| Satan | | Jn | | |
| Man | | Jn | | |
| **Missio Dei** | **1** | **2** | **3** | **4** |
| Gospel | Jn | | | |
| This World | | Jn | | |
| Our Mandate | Jn | | | |
| Healthy Societies | | Jn | | |
| Religions | | | | Jn |
| Election | | Jn | | |
| Hell | Jn | | | |
| Heaven | | Jn | | |
| The Bible | Jn | | | |
| The Qur'an | | Jn | | |
| **Isa al Masih** | **1** | **2** | **3** | **4** |
| Identity | Jn | | | |
| Christology | | Jn | | |
| His Life | Jn | | | |
| On the Cross | | Jn | | |
| The Cross | Jn | | | |
| The Resurrection | Jn | | | |
| The Future | Jn | | | |

**Figure 31:** M-Framework plot for Jason

to hell. He added a comment about Islam. "For Muslims, Jesus is a prophet, and that's it. They take away the core meaning of his death. This is the sin of Islam and I stand firm on that." When asked whether he thought that most people will go to hell, Jason replied, "I would say so." He shared that this motivates him to share the good news using all means possible, including the latest technologies. People need to accept the gospel before they die in order to go to heaven, according to Jason. Regarding an individual's freedom of choice to accept the gospel as it relates to God's plans and purposes, Jason said that there are different viewpoints on that, and that it is a hard question for him.

I asked Jason to comment on the view of some people that God's plans and purposes are focused on this world and on restoring his own creation to its complete fulfillment, to what it is supposed to be, compared to another view held by others who say that God's plans and purposes are focused on saving people out of this world to go to heaven. After getting the question clarified he said, "My understanding is that God of course wants to save people and get them to heaven. That is kind of strange why people think another way. Does that happen more within the Muslim world?" Jason repeated that God wants to save people by restoring our relationship with him and equipping us to follow our calling.

> About the restoration of this world, I am not sure about that. This world is going to be burned. It is being corrupted more and more. Sin is growing and people are becoming crazier. In spite of that, as the light of the world, we have to continue to shine until Jesus comes back or until you die. We have to continue doing God's job. You may be killed for Jesus.

Is God interested in just and righteous societies? Jason believes that Christians are called to be the salt of the world and to influence it to have just and healthy societies. He said that many people are suffering because of corruption and injustice.

The Bible is the eternal and inspired Word of God, according to Jason. "It is universal. It is not connected to a certain time or culture. It goes beyond culture and time. It can be applied at any time and in any culture." Jason holds that the Bible teaches high moral standards, especially in Jesus' teaching and in the Ten Commandments. He also said, "You can see from Genesis to Revelation that there is one theme in the Scriptures: the salvation of people." Regarding the Qur'an, Jason does not consider this book to be inspired by the Holy Spirit. "God had spoken to his people and finished his revelation," Jason said, adding, "and there is no prophecy in the Qur'an that points to salvation." He said that it is a dangerous topic and then shared his opinion on the Qur'an in a few more phrases.

> It is really mixed up. There is no chronology. There are many contradictions, missing the point. There is no plan of salvation. If you do this or that, then maybe Allah will have mercy on you, or maybe not. And there are no prophecies about Jesus. And there are no high moral standards, I would say. There are some rules in the Qur'an and the Hadith, but that was more for that century in Mohammed's time.

I asked Jason whether he used the Qur'an in his ministry. He said that it depends on the level of dedication by the Muslims. "Sometimes I use verses from the Qur'an to talk about Jesus and the Scriptures. With some people I use the Qur'an as equal to the Bible." Jason said that he uses the Qur'an to show that people need to open the other books and believe what they say.

Jesus Christ perfectly showed the character of God, according to Jason. He said that Jesus helping people in need shows us God's love, mercy, and compassion. "He was not just a Santa Claus allowing people whatever they wanted to do. He stood firm on his own principles. This led to his own sacrifice." When asked what the term "Messiah" means to him, Jason said that such a question is maybe more relevant to the Jews. "For me I do not pay much attention to what the term 'Messiah' means. But what Jesus has done for me is much more important than this term," Jason concluded.

The reason for the death of Christ is the bringing together of the love of God and the justice of God, according to Jason. He believes that sin separates us from God, and sin can only be forgiven through a sacrifice. Isa al Masih is the sacrificial Lamb that satisfies God's wrath through his blood. His resurrection shows that he conquered death and hell. "For us it is good news because if we believe that he is a substitute, we also will be resurrected," Jason said. He sees the relationship between Jesus and Allah as a very close one, and said that Jesus has a divine and a human nature. He realizes that the phrase *the Son of God* is a stumbling block for Muslims and describes it to them as a spiritual relationship. "It is the divine relationship between the two, but that does not mean that they are two gods, with one being the older and one being the younger," Jason said.

On the topic of religions, Jason said that they are a problem if we use our religion as a way to become righteous before God, to earn our salvation. He commented on religions being man-made. "Religion is man's perspective. People made religions, not God. I see salvation [as] from God and religion [as] from man."

When I asked about the doctrine of the Trinity, Jason shared two testimonies of Muslims coming to faith. "When Muslims come to faith here, they immediately understand that Jesus is not just a prophet but that he is God. It is a religion of the Holy Spirit." He concluded, "So, we don't have much discussion on that [the Trinity]."

## Africa M-Framework Plots

### Arnold

Arnold described Allah as the Creator, the Supreme God, the gracious one, the merciful one, and the one who takes care of us every day. He thinks that Allah created us for relationship. "His original plan was messed up by human beings," Arnold said, "So here is Plan B. Because of the love Allah has for us he could not just let us be destroyed like that and be wiped out from the earth, so he provided a solution." Isa al Masih is that solution, according to Arnold. I asked whether the solution is for individuals to be saved to go to heaven or for all of creation to be restored. Arnold said that the blood of Jesus is to redeem man, but all of nature also will be restored. "Yes, I can say that the restoration will be for everything, for the whole creation including man, animals, and trees. Everything will become perfect." In addition, Arnold believes that Allah is interested in each of us being just and righteous, but ultimately he is interested in entire societies here on earth being righteous. He followed this up by saying, "That is why he wants to have a righteous people in heaven. Not just one person but everyone being righteous."

| Theology Proper | 1 | 2 | 3 | 4 |
|---|---|---|---|---|
| Essence | | | Ad | |
| The Problem | | Ad | | |
| Satan | Ad | | | |
| Man | | Ad | | |
| Missio Dei | 1 | 2 | 3 | 4 |
| Gospel | | | Ad | |
| This World | | | Ad | |
| Our Mandate | | | Ad | |
| Healthy Societies | | Ad | | |
| Religions | | | | Ad |
| Election | | Ad | | |
| Hell | | | Ad | |
| Heaven | | | Ad | |
| The Bible | | | Ad | |
| The Qur'an | | | Ad | |
| Isa al Masih | 1 | 2 | 3 | 4 |
| Identity | | Ad | | |
| Christology | | Ad | | |
| His Life | | | Ad | |
| On the Cross | | | Ad | |
| The Cross | Ad | | | |
| The Resurrection | | Ad | | |
| The Future | | | Ad | |

**Figure 32:** M-Framework plot for Arnold

Regarding heaven and hell, Arnold believes that God's plan was messed up because sin came, which was introduced by the devil, who was expelled from heaven together with those who followed him. God declared hell to be their last judgment. "So hell and fire has been prepared not for human beings but for the devil and his angels," Arnold said. The problem now is, according to Arnold, that human beings are following this evil here on earth. "If they have chosen to follow the devil here, they will also follow the devil into hell," Arnold concluded. He believes that whoever does not repent and follow God, confessing his sins in the name of Allah and in the name of Isa al Masih, and then dies, there is no more solution for him. "Forgiveness, you have to get it here. If you don't get it here, after death it is finished, it is too late." Man has been given freedom of choice from the beginning, and not choosing also is a choice, according to Arnold. He qualified this statement later via a follow-up correspondence, saying that the fires of hell will not be burning forever and that the suffering is not eternal. The judgment of hell is an event that results in the total annihilation of those being judged. Arnold believes that the effect of hell fire is eternal. "Whoever burns in hell fire will never come to life again ever."

Allah revealed himself through the prophets through thought inspiration. "They wrote in their own language and culture what they thought the inspiration to be," said Arnold. He believes that Allah also reveals himself through the Scriptures, which is a narrative story of God telling us about God's relationship with human beings throughout history. Another way that Allah is revealing himself to man is through nature, Arnold mentioned.

"The Qur'an has some truth in it," shared Arnold, "But I wouldn't speak for the Qur'an and say that the entire Qur'an is truth, because it is not my book. My book is the Bible." Arnold said that he uses the Qur'an to try to help people focus on Isa al Masih as the Savior. He finds many truths in it that help build bridges of understanding for Muslims. "These are bridges that can bear the weight of truth."

Arnold summarized the actions of Isa al Masih as helping those who were desperate have hope. "He fed those who were very hungry, both physically and spiritually. He healed many sick people who did not have hope. He healed them and gave them hope and a future," Arnold said. I asked what the purpose was of these actions, and what does that mean for us today? Arnold mentioned that Satan, the person of darkness, had claimed to be the owner of this world. "When Jesus came, through all these healings and feedings, through all that he did, he came to claim back his kingdom. To redeem this world and to get it back," shared Arnold. He believes that this gives us hope today, knowing that in the end Jesus will claim this whole sinful world. I asked what Isa's message is for us today.

> The clear message that I am seeing that Allah is teaching is, "I am the Alpha and Omega, the first and the last, the beginning and the end. Whatever happens, believe in me and trust me that everything is going to be fine. Have this hope. See beyond what carnal eyes can see. Have this hope that one day everything is going to be restored and we will get back this paradise that was lost right at the time of Adam and Eve."

"Isa al Masih is the appointed one, set aside for a holy purpose," Arnold said. Isa al Masih died because of us, because we sinned, and we should have suffered this penalty, this kind of death, according to Arnold. "But because Allah loves us so much, he died for us, for the entire human race," he said. Arnold believes that Isa al Masih is Allah himself.

On the topic of religions Arnold said that Isa al Masih did not come to plant any church or any mosque or any religion. "He just came as the Savior of the world." Arnold sees religions as human forms and practices and believes that Jesus never intended these things. "The original plan was just to say the good news, to share it with people, and to get people to accept Isa al Masih, and live holy lives," Arnold said.

Arnold shared how his best days are when someone who initially was really against the gospel comes to a different understanding. He recalled one of those moments.

> I remember one of them telling me one day that he had come to understand that Isa al Masih is not just a prophet. He is more than a prophet. And he told me, "You know, I want to tell you, Isa al Masih is God." I never told him that. I asked him, "How do you know?" He said, "You just read the book and you just know that you cannot compare Isa al Masih with any human being, so he must be God himself."

On the term *Son of God* Arnold said that he tries to avoid entering into any debate with anyone about Jesus being the Son of God. He explained how in his language there are expressions such as "son of the road" (a traveler) or "son of Satan," who would be someone who likes to fight, so he explains the term *Son of God* as referring to someone who likes God, who is close to God, and who is always mindful of God's business. "So, that is the meaning and people are okay with that," Arnold said.

He has not faced any serious theological problems yet within the movement. "People are just happy to know that they are saved by Isa al Masih. They live day by day with gratitude towards Isa al Masih," Arnold said. "These people have been raised in an Islamic context where you don't ask questions but just listen to the spiritual leader. They are not that inquisitive." Arnold added that asking questions about God is being disrespectful to God himself, in their viewpoint. They just learn how to obey and how to follow God joyfully and do what he wants people to do without asking any deep theological questions.

## Oliver

Allah is the Creator of the whole universe, according to Oliver. He further described Allah as the Almighty God to whom all humans will submit on judgment day. "There is no other god than Allah. He is the only one." As I probed more about Allah's character, Oliver said, "It is very hard to describe Allah. He is above us and he is very powerful. If we try to study him, it will be very difficult. In my culture we cannot explain him." Oliver said that people know that Allah is very powerful and merciful, and that he must exist, because we see this in nature. Regarding Allah's plans and purposes, Oliver believes that he created Adam and Eve for them to obey him and submit to him. "There is no other thing than to obey Allah and to pray to him. I understand that to be the main purpose of his creation." Oliver explained that in the early stage man fell into sin and that up to today we still are not too obedient to him. "Even today that is happening because we are not listening to what God wants us to do. We're listening to what the devil is saying. I think that is the problem." Oliver continued, "We are still not on the right path. We are trying to be on the right path, but the devil is trapping us out. He is taking us from the right path."

Heaven and hell are real places created by God that will exist forever and ever, according to Oliver. "God created heaven to be inherited by those who are in obedience." On the other hand, Oliver said, "Those who don't obey God, those who don't follow him, those who do evil things, those who shed blood, those who are against God and his people will go to hell." He believes that most are going to hell. "Even the Qur'an says that most of the Jews, Christians, and Muslims are wrong. There are only a few among the Muslims, Christians, and Jews that are right. Those will go to heaven." He mentioned how the Injil, the Tawrat, and the Zabur talk about the few, the righteous people, and he mentioned the people in Noah's day. "I think hell is there, because unrighteous people will go there."

On the question whether the focus of God's mission is populating heaven or restoring and redeeming his creation here on earth, Oliver talked about our obedience and Allah's mercy. "We talk about salvation from the Injil, since Jesus died for our sins and gives salvation, but still we are under the law of Allah. We have to follow what Allah says, to obey the commandments of God." He mentioned that we are all sinners and that Allah forgives who he wants to forgive for heaven. "I mean, we are all sinners, but the majority commit more sins and don't repent to God, so those ones will fall into a bad situation after judgment."

| Theology Proper | 1 | 2 | 3 | 4 |
|---|---|---|---|---|
| Essence | Or | | | |
| The Problem | Or | | | |
| Satan | Or | | | |
| Man | | Or | | |
| **Missio Dei** | **1** | **2** | **3** | **4** |
| Gospel | | Or | | |
| This World | Or | | | |
| Our Mandate | | Or | | |
| Healthy Societies | | Or | | |
| Religions | | | | Or |
| Election | | Or | | |
| Hell | Or | | | |
| Heaven | Or | | | |
| The Bible | | | Or | |
| The Qur'an | | | Or | |
| **Isa al Masih** | **1** | **2** | **3** | **4** |
| Identity | | | | Or |
| Christology | | | | Or |
| His Life | Or | | | |
| On the Cross | | Or | | |
| The Cross | | Or | | |
| The Resurrection | | Or | | |
| The Future | Or | | | |

**Figure 33:** M-Framework plot for Oliver

Oliver affirmed that Allah likes justice and is interested in us living together in righteous societies with justice and dignity, but he sees the problem as mankind having turned God's message into religions. "We want to undermine each other. We want to criticize each other. We want to create politics and religions." He said that God never brought any religion, but that these are human creations. We forget the message and undermine the prophets. "And today in this world this is happening because we worship religion. We read religion, but we do not read the Word of God. We are not listening to God." Oliver asserted that a problem is created when someone claims to be a religious person and insists that only his religion is correct. "That creates problems and conflict." Oliver gave an example from the time when Jesus came. "When he came down, he never said that he was the Son of God, but his people charged him to be the Son of God. They immediately renamed him after God." Oliver said that the priests were saying that Jesus was bringing a new religion, since they had made their own religion from the Tawrat. "Moses brought commandments from God, not a religion. But these guys made the commandments and the Zabur from David into a religion." Oliver believes that Jesus came to tell the Israelites the message to obey God, and not to have this religion, this temple, and the business of obeying the priests. "They did not like this because they wanted to hold onto their power. So they had to kill Jesus, according to the Injil. These were religious issues." Jesus' disciples were sharing the message. "But now the Greeks and the Romans changed it again into Christianity. I do not think the disciples were teaching Christianity, which is not a message but a religion." Oliver added that the same happened in Islam. "The majority of the Islamic scholars say that Islam is not a religion but a message. But after Mohammed died, peace be upon him, his disciples also changed." Oliver lamented that there are new denominations and doctrines in Islam and Christianity every year. "It seems that we are not listening to God. In both the major religions there are right people who want to do righteous things, but they are in the minority," Oliver said.

On the matter of freedom of choice, Oliver described our time here on earth as a test from God, testing our faith. He believes that everyone has a choice. "You can choose to follow the wrong path, and you can choose to follow the right path. That is a personal choice." He thinks it is very clear. "Whoever chooses the right path goes to heaven and whoever chooses the wrong path goes to hell." Oliver also clarified that he believes that the garden of Eden was in heaven, and our goal is to get back there. This earth is God's testing ground for us.

The Scriptures are the message of God as revealed through his actions, Oliver believes. "We try to interpret it in a way that we can understand. So it is the interpretation that we study and seek to learn and know." He talks about the notion among Muslims that the Bible has been corrupted by people who gave it their own understanding, based on their context and culture. "These Muslims say that you don't need to read the Scriptures, from the Christian community and the West, that they call the Bible. It has never been there as a Bible." They are referring to the belief that God revealed himself three times in different centuries, which led to the Tawrat, Zabur, and Injil. How did these three books become one book?

Oliver added that he thinks that the Word of God is not just a written thing, but that it is about faith. "It does not matter whether you read or not, it is faith. Abraham was not reading, but just listening to God in faith. I think our faith is very important over just reading a book or a text or whatever it is."

The Qur'an suffers similar challenges, Oliver said. "Every culture will misinterpret the text in the way they want to understand it." He also commented on the Qur'an being in Arabic. "The message was revealed through Mohammed, Aleh Salam, and he gave it to his people. It implies that you need to know Arabic to understand and to talk to Allah. But that is not the truth. Allah knows all languages."

The actions and miracles of Isa al Masih show that he had the authority of God, according to Oliver. "We know that he was the Word of God among us. He was here in the world because he wanted to see how we behaved, how we lived, and also he came to die." He added some comments about the identity of Isa al Masih. "There is no differentiation between God, his Word, and the Spirit. So there is a lot of confusion even when we say he is the Son of God." He added, "He is not the Son of God—rather, he is not God himself. In my understanding I could say that he was the Word and the Spirit of God." Oliver also said, "The Christians make a mistake. They call Jesus God, but he was not God. He never ever said that he was God. He always said that he was depending on his Father."

"Jesus suffered and died because that was Allah's plan," Oliver said. How is that good news? "It is hard to understand, but it was good news to his followers." He also said, "The purpose was to show to the Jewish community that this man Jesus was different than others. It gives them a witness that he was above all other people and human nature." Oliver referenced the Qur'an and sura 3:55, which mentions that Allah will make the followers of Isa superior. "Jesus was superior to all others." All the other prophets died, and none of them are alive now. "Jesus is the only one, and he is sitting at the right hand of God, as is written also in the Qur'an and the Bible. It qualifies him as having authority." Oliver also said that Isa al Masih is the coming Judge. "Only God can judge people. Jesus is the mediator between God and his people. You can call him a mediator."

I asked about his understanding of how our sins are related to Isa's death. "That is very hard to know," Oliver replied. He mentioned that in the Christian teaching it says that Jesus died for our sins, but he attributes that to mistakes in translation that feed into Christian culture and a desire to reach Muslims.

> Allah says that each individual is responsible for their own life. Each one gives an account for what they did, right or wrong. In my understanding now, Jesus died and rose again and went to heaven as evidence that he was superior to others. He was not like us, but it doesn't qualify that he died for my sins. It qualifies him for me to follow him, but I am accountable for what I do. If he died for my sins, I would not need to keep away from sins. That doesn't make sense. I have to be accountable for what I do. God is mercy and love, and he can forgive the sins that I commit.

Oliver made some additional comments. "In the entire Bible or Injil it never says that Jesus himself said that he was going to die on the cross for our sins." This happened in the translation process. "It is part of the misunderstanding of the Injil to whoever translated it into the Greek language. They interpreted this wrongly. Jesus cannot die for my sins." He further clarified this point. "We sin, we do bad things and we do good things, but still Allah can forgive us. The way we follow him is different from the way we do sin. We can become a follower of Jesus and we can still sin or not sin." He finds the notion of being under grace confusing. "Most of the Christians say that we are under grace, which doesn't make a lot of sense either. As a Muslim I am under the law, which I need to protect. He told me not to kill and all those things in his commandments, which are part of the law." He also pointed out that the law and Jesus tell us to love our neighbor and to be righteous to people. He repeated his belief that Jesus died and rose as evidence that he can defeat death, and that he is superior to all others. Oliver feels very close to Isa al Masih. He prays to Allah, and also to his Word and his Spirit.

Different theological viewpoints may come up, but Oliver emphasized that they are trying to avoid conflict and misunderstanding in the community that could affect the movement. They do not discuss deep theological questions like we were doing in the interview.

> We talk about the truth and about having faith in God, and we ask God to give us understanding and wisdom to know the right path. Usually we don't discuss conflicts and we do not discuss much about God's nature because it is offensive to Muslims to discuss how God is. Now you are trying to study God, who is higher than you. That is something we avoid.

As a final comment, Oliver said that he feels it is important that people understand that insider movements are not a new religion. "It is about seeking the truth and following Jesus without contradiction from any religion."

### Homer

God is the Creator and sustainer, to Homer. "He takes care of my health and what I eat. In general, he is the provider and he is everything to me. I cannot be here without him. He is very caring and merciful to me." God's plans and purposes are to cleanse this world with fire and make it all new. "I teach my Muslim friends with whom I share my faith, that there will come a time when the holy ones will be taken to heaven, and the world will be desolate." Those who stay behind face destruction. "All the sinners will remain here, and God will bring his destruction to all who refuse to believe in him. Therefore, the world will be cleansed by fire." A full restoration follows. "God will make heaven and earth all new, and people will come and be here forevermore."

Homer believes that God has prepared heaven as a good place where all those who are committed to him and faithful to him will go and be with Jesus. However, he does not believe that believers are staying there forever.

> I believe that heaven will not be our eternal place. We will come back to earth and we will inherit the earth. This is heaven coming down to earth. After being in heaven for some time, we will come back to this earth. All that Jesus is preparing for us there, we will have here. But that will be that new earth.

Homer shared that for some people hell is a place associated with evil and eternal torture and suffering for unbelievers. "But from the viewpoint from the Bible, I do not see this hell . . . There is heaven, but there is no hell." Homer believes that unbelievers come to an end. "Those people will remain here while the good people will go to heaven; and God will destroy the earth and those evil people." Homer explained further, "When an evil person dies he stays in the grave waiting for the judgment. At the end of time when God will destroy the earth, they all will wake up, and then they will be destroyed." Regarding man's freedom of choice to follow Isa or not, Homer said, "What I believe is that God does not force people to follow him. He has given everyone the knowledge and capability to make a good decision. He has left the decision with us."

Homer considers the Scriptures to be God's Word through human means. "God inspired people to write, and therefore it may not be 100 percent. There may be some deficiencies because it was written by human beings. But the concept is still there." Regarding the Qur'an, Homer said that he is not treating it the way he used to. "To me it has no value. But for the cause of teaching others about Christ, teaching others about God, I use it as a means to reach Muslims." He realizes that there are verses in the Qur'an that can lead a person to know Christ, and when he is with a Muslim who is not a believer, he treats the book the way they treat it. "I cannot just take it the way I like it and share with them. I give it maximum respect, but not from the heart but because of them, so that they may know Jesus." Homer acknowledged that all truth is God's truth, so it was God's work to have the truth in the Qur'an that leads to the knowledge of God. With regard to the prophet Mohammed, Homer said, "God might have used Mohammed in whatever he preached to his people. He might have used him."

| Theology Proper | 1 | 2 | 3 | 4 |
|---|---|---|---|---|
| Essence | | | Hr | |
| The Problem | | Hr | | |
| Satan | | Hr | | |
| Man | | | Hr | |
| **Missio Dei** | **1** | **2** | **3** | **4** |
| Gospel | Hr | | | |
| This World | | Hr | | |
| Our Mandate | | Hr | | |
| Healthy Societies | | Hr | | |
| Religions | | Hr | | |
| Election | | Hr | | |
| Hell | | | Hr | |
| Heaven | | Hr | | |
| The Bible | | Hr | | |
| The Qur'an | | Hr | | |
| **Isa al Masih** | **1** | **2** | **3** | **4** |
| Identity | | Hr | | |
| Christology | | Hr | | |
| His Life | Hr | | | |
| On the Cross | Hr | | | |
| The Cross | Hr | | | |
| The Resurrection | | Hr | | |
| The Future | | | | Hr |

**Figure 34:** M-Framework plot for Homer

The actions of Isa al Masih show God's power. "When Jesus came to the world, the Qur'an says that he treated the sick and he raised some of the people who were dead. He did miracles which were leading us to see Jesus as a Savior," Homer said. "People were amazed and said, 'He must have God's power.'" Homer believes that Jesus came to solve the sin problem that came to the world. "He solved the sin problem through his act of accepting to be hung on the cross." Homer further explained the sin problem the way he sees it. "Sin brought death; through one man the world fell into sin; Jesus had to die, on our behalf, in order to conquer death. It was God's plan that he would die."

Homer explained how he had many questions about the Scriptures and the identity of Jesus. "I looked at the Scriptures and the contradictions, and there was the question about the Son of God and Jesus being God. That was disturbing me so much." Homer wondered, "What will I do when I follow Christ? I cannot say that he is the Son of God, nor say that he is God. I continued in my mind that Jesus was just a prophet like the others, but that God had chosen him to save mankind." In the end God gave him answers. "People could not explain it to me, but they were still insisting that Jesus was the Son of God and God. But it was God who revealed it to me, and I got satisfied, and it has never troubled me." Homer applies a similar reliance on God when he witnesses in Muslim communities. "When I am among Muslims, I do not tell them everything. I tell them to where I can convince them. Other things, I leave to God to work on." He said how he sometimes would ask them questions, and how he would marvel, because the answers they would give him clearly did not come from him. Homer said that one of those difficult topics is baptism.

> Sometimes there are things that are hard, that we think we cannot do, but God goes ahead and prepares the way. And there are things that we may fear to tell those Muslims, but God tells them. There are things that I cannot explain to them, but God can.

When I asked whether God is interested in righteous societies, Homer talked about the need for us individually to be righteous. "We have been called to become righteous, and to be different from what we knew before." He gave some examples of helping people. "So whenever I see injustice or bad things happening, it is my duty to intervene. I don't like seeing people crying or being treated unjustly. I just like to see people living in peace."

Regarding religions and God's plans and purposes, Homer mentioned the similarities between Islam and Christianity because they have the same origin. "Both religions come from one God who is the God of Abraham." He added, "The only thing is that there is a veil on the side of the Muslims which does not allow them to see God in all fullness." Homer also mentioned the Scriptures. "The Qur'an says that you have to believe in all Scriptures, the Tawrat, Zabur, and Injil." He concluded, "There is enmity that is brought by people from both religions."

## Brad

Brad described Allah as the Supreme God who has manifested himself through his Son, Isa al Masih, and through his Spirit, the Holy Spirit. "I know him as a loving God who goes out of his way to look for the lost sheep." Brad said that God wants to save his people regardless of their background, regardless of their ethnicity, regardless even of their religious background. Brad believes that Allah has good intentions for his creation. "Allah wants to restore this world and his creatures in this world to the state where Adam and Eve used to live." Brad added, "Allah wants to restore his relationship with them and also wants to take them to heaven, so that they can enjoy eternal life."

| Theology Proper | 1 | 2 | 3 | 4 |
|---|---|---|---|---|
| Essence | | | Bd | |
| The Problem | | Bd | | |
| Satan | | Bd | | |
| Man | | Bd | | |
| **Missio Dei** | **1** | **2** | **3** | **4** |
| Gospel | | Bd | | |
| This World | | Bd | | |
| Our Mandate | | Bd | | |
| Healthy Societies | | Bd | | |
| Religions | | Bd | | |
| Election | | Bd | | |
| Hell | | | Bd | |
| Heaven | Bd | | | |
| The Bible | | Bd | | |
| The Qur'an | | | Bd | |
| **Isa al Masih** | **1** | **2** | **3** | **4** |
| Identity | | Bd | | |
| Christology | | Bd | | |
| His Life | Bd | | | |
| On the Cross | | Bd | | |
| The Cross | Bd | | | |
| The Resurrection | | Bd | | |
| The Future | | | Bd | |

**Figure 35:** M-Framework plot for Brad

To the question about God's plans and purpose being focused on this world, people, societies, nature, etc., or on saving people away from this world for heaven, Brad responded that he had heard about this topic of salvation on this earth particularly from Jehovah's Witnesses, but not within the church. He said, "My view is that Isa al Masih will come back soon to this earth to take the saved ones, those who believe in him, to heaven." He also believes that after 1,000 years the earth will be cleansed with fire and that the saints will live on this new earth forever.

Is Allah interested in healthy and righteous cultures and societies? Brad said, "Of course Allah wants people or mankind to live righteous lives while they live on this earth. He doesn't save us with sin. He wants to save us from sin." Brad added that once we decide to dedicate our lives to Allah and his ways, to the right path, Allah wants us to do the right things before him.

Brad sees heaven as a place where God lives, and where he wants to take his children after the Second Advent, or the second coming of Isa al Masih. Regarding hell, Brad said that it is not something that burns forever.

> It is the kind of punishment that Allah uses at the end of the world to cleanse this earth from sin. Satan and his followers will be burned and they will turn to ash, and that is it. They don't burn forever and ever, because Allah does not get any pleasure in letting people suffer forever and ever. Hell does not exist.

Brad mentioned that this view on heaven and hell is what he shares with others, particularly with insider believers. Will most people be receiving this hell-punishment? Brad answered, "Most people will be part of that, and fewer people will be part of heaven, according to my understanding of the Scriptures." Brad believes that everyone is free to choose. "Allah does not force anybody to join his kingdom, but he invites every single person to come into his kingdom and to be saved through the path that he prepared, which is through believing in Isa al Masih."

"The Holy Scripture, meaning the Bible, is the true Word of God that guides us," Brad said. He believes that the words were not dictated, but that the prophets understood the message from Allah and wrote it down, guided by the Holy Spirit. Brad also said, "For me, this is God's narrative story of salvation." On the topic of the Qur'an, Brad shared that he is using it as a window or entering wedge, helping people who read the Qur'an to the Scriptures.

Regarding religions, Brad mentioned that many people may have the whole truth as revealed in Scripture while others do not, but as long as they are faithful to the truth that has been revealed to them and they worship Allah as much as they know, he believes that Allah considers their worship and will lead them to more understanding of his truth, as is revealed in Isa al Masih. Brad supports the idea of people coming together to worship Allah. "It is not wrong to worship Allah in an organized way, in the form of a *jamaat*, or a group of believers. They may call that a religion, as long as they follow the truth." He added his support for structure.

> I prefer to have an organized form of religion. This means in our case that as insider believers we have our own structure, and we lead the fellowships in a structure that can help to advance the cause of Allah and also nurture the believers. I think that having an organized form is better.

Brad explained that believers in these *jamaats* call themselves Muslims. "But they know that they are special Muslims. They believe in Isa al Masih." There also is an awareness of the church. "Even though they don't have any direct relationships, they know that there are believers from the Christian background who are following this path too."

Isa al Masih performed many miracles. Brad shared that insider believers see the power of Allah himself in Isa al Masih through these miracles. "In fact, insider believers believe that he is divine. He was performing those miracles from his divine attributes." Brad added, "He is the Word of Allah that came and took flesh." He suffered and died because of our sin. "For the remission of sin there is a need for the shedding of blood. Isa al Masih shed his blood in our stead to reconcile us back to Allah." Brad made an additional comment about the seriousness of sin.

> That is why he had to suffer, because Allah cannot just simply say, "Sin is a simple matter, and I forgive." Sin is not a simple matter for Allah. It is a deadly thing and a very serious matter for Allah, and it needs the sacrifice of humans and the shedding of blood. That is why Isa al Masih had to do that.

I asked Brad where he sees God in the scene on Good Friday. "It is a complicated thing and very difficult to understand," Brad said. "We believe that the Word of Allah was suffering, but Allah also is the Holy Spirit, and Allah himself was in heaven looking at it." He added,

"He was in a way sacrificing himself, because it was his Word that was being sacrificed."

The term *Son of God* shows a very intimate relationship between Allah and Isa al Masih, according to Brad. "It also indicates his divinity, because no one else has been given that title in the Scriptures." Brad further confirmed Isa's divinity. "Isa al Masih is Allah himself, but it is a relational title to be called the Son of God." Brad also mentioned Isa in relation to the love of God. "Isa al Masih is the revealed love of God. He came to die for us without any force behind him except love, except pure love, except yearning to save us." Brad expressed the need for everyone to understand that love and benefit from it. "Second, there is a responsibility laid on me by Allah to share that love."

### Melvin

Melvin is an alongsider who is connected with insider movements in various parts of the world, but especially with the ones in Africa. He introduced me to and connected me with Arnold, Oliver, Homer, and Brad.

To Melvin, Allah is the Creator God who created the earth in six days. "He gave himself for his world and his children. He loves us immensely." Allah's plans and purposes are for his creation to live in peace, harmony, and happiness. "I think his plan and purpose was somewhat derailed when Adam and Eve sinned, and he has been in the process of restoring mankind," said Melvin. He sees a cosmic conflict between good and evil.

> There is a conflict between good and evil, and at this time God's main aim and purpose is to bring good back to earth. That will only happen through extreme goodness, and he wins the conflict between good and evil through goodness. I would say that is the main metanarrative of what his purpose is, how he brings that about in creation, and with mankind, as we finally fully submit to his will, learn to live a life of full submission to him, and understand the principles laid out in Matthew 5–7, and to a greater extent across the Bible.

After sin came into the world, the main purpose is to restore creation back to what it was, according to Melvin. He added, "Personally I don't see this happening on this side of eternity. We can live close to it, but I see a restoration after a Second Coming." To him it is not about populating heaven but about restoring relationships. On the question whether Allah is interested in healthy societies Melvin commented, "Absolutely. I would say that is the main goal. I see an eschatological salvation and a salvation here and now."

Regarding heaven and hell, Melvin said that fear of judgment and desire for rewards are not good motivators. "The real and first motivator should be a heartfelt submission to God and a heartfelt love for God. Our goal should be to live with God and to love him, and as a consequence we will go to heaven." He sees hell as a consequence for those who choose not to live by the Golden Rule, who choose not to live within the kingdom of God, who choose to live a self-centered life. He believes that heaven is forever and that there is total annihilation in hell. "I don't see an eternal hellfire being consistent with the love of God." Melvin treats references to eternal fires metaphorically. "If you look at Revelation and the fire and torment going forever and ever, this is metaphorical language saying that sin is no more, evil is no more. There is a triumph of God's love." He believes that God will come to a place where he says, "Enough is enough," and he will burn and destroy the world in the hellfire and then there will be a new heaven and earth. Melvin does not know whether most people will go to heaven, but commented, "Those who live to the light that they know, whether you have heard of the name of Christ or not, will be saved." Regarding man's free choice or God's election, Melvin said, "There is absolute free choice, and we all have the choice to follow that quiet calling in our hearts." He sees free choice as probably the biggest value in the kingdom of heaven. "God values free choice so much that he only wins us back by evidence. I see that this is how God works, and I also think that is how we work." Melvin was referring to the evidence of God's all-encompassing mercy and compassion.

"God has revealed himself through prophets using visions, dreams, and inspiration," Melvin said. The Scriptures came about in a similar way, according to Melvin. "I believe that God inspired the thoughts of the prophets. They had visions and dreams, and they put all this in their own words." He sees the Scriptures mostly as a casebook from which we draw principles. "We see how God has interacted in the past and from that we draw lessons for how to live in the present." In addition, Melvin shared that he sees the Bible as authoritative for his life, and it holds every other book, such as the Qur'an, to its authority. Melvin thinks that there is a lot more similarity between the Bible and the Qur'an than current translations lead you to believe. "That does not mean that I hold the Qur'an at the level of the Bible, but I do see what you might call diamonds of truth in the Qur'an, or the footprints of God." He sees the Qur'an as a puzzle with strong evidence towards the true nature of Christ and the plan of salvation.

Melvin described various aspects of the actions of Isa al Masih. "I see that his actions are following the full will of his Father in heaven, and that they are revelatory of how the people in his kingdom should live." He believes that the legitimacy of Christ was validated at the cross, but mostly Melvin sees the law of love in action, as he considers that the plan of salvation was being acted out throughout Jesus' life and ministry and not just in one period at the end of his life.

> The big issues of this cosmic conflict were laid to rest at the cross in the minds of the unfallen angels—namely, that God can keep his own law, that he can in the most extreme circumstances live and love by his law of love. It was proven that God indeed is a God of justice as he deals with the penalty of sin when he died a second death, the death that the sinner dies, but also that he can keep his own law of love in the most extreme of circumstances.

Who made Jesus die? Melvin mentioned that Satan and his servants were used, but Isa al Masih decided to lay down his own life. "He wins the battle over all odds, but he dies of a broken heart. He lays down his life for his people." Melvin also said, "The Son actually does not see beyond the grave, but he is so committed to his mission and his love for his people is so great that he decides to lay it down, and he dies of a broken heart." This is good news because we see the amazing love of God. Melvin referred to the basic atonement theories as metaphors. In contrast he highlighted the practical interpretation by insiders. "I see a very practical reaction among Muslims. 'Wow, he did this for me, there's this much love? I want to serve him. He is now my Lord and Master.'" Another part of the good news Melvin brought out is about the kingdom. "It is good news that God's kingdom has been established." Melvin shared that the biggest part of this good news is that Christ in his death has overpowered the powers of evil.

He referred to the link between Islam and folk Islam practices and its related demonic presence. "When they come to Christ, they are free of this demonic oppression." Melvin mentioned the need for explaining the good news in a way that fits in a shame-honor culture. "Once we have really cracked it well how to explain the atonement theory in a shame-honor paradigm, the gospel will go viral within the Islamic people groups." I mentioned that the Hebrew culture seems to be based on shame-honor values. Melvin fully agreed. "And I think that a better understanding of first-century followers of the Way, within a Judaic experience, will be extremely beneficial to an Islamic context."

Regarding the relationship between Isa al Masih and Allah, Melvin summarized it as Isa al Masih being the Word of Allah. He talked about how the Aramaic word *debar*, which means "word," can also mean the Shekinah glory. "We have found about fourteen little mini-steps to help Muslims understand the divinity of Christ, and this story about the word *debar* helps significantly." Melvin sees the phrase *Son of God* in Jewish tradition referring to the son with the birthright that was passed down from Adam but broken up in parts by Isaac to his sons. The Messiah regains the full birthright, according to Melvin. "This is how a first-century Jew would have understood the phrase *Son of God*. They would not have put divinity to the term *Son of God*."

| Theology Proper | 1 | 2 | 3 | 4 |
|---|---|---|---|---|
| Essence | | | Mn | |
| The Problem | | | Mn | |
| Satan | Mn | | | |
| Man | | Mn | | |
| **Missio Dei** | **1** | **2** | **3** | **4** |
| Gospel | | | | Mn |
| This World | | | Mn | |
| Our Mandate | | | | Mn |
| Healthy Societies | | | | Mn |
| Religions | | | Mn | |
| Election | | Mn | | |
| Hell | | | Mn | |
| Heaven | | | Mn | |
| The Bible | | Mn | | |
| The Qur'an | | | Mn | |
| **Isa al Masih** | **1** | **2** | **3** | **4** |
| Identity | | | | Mn |
| Christology | | Mn | | |
| His Life | | | Mn | |
| On the Cross | | | | Mn |
| The Cross | | | | Mn |
| The Resurrection | | Mn | | |
| The Future | | | Mn | |

**Figure 36:** M-Framework plot for Melvin

Theologizing is an increasing interest among movement leaders, according to Melvin. He shared that there are a few keen minds among them that have focused on theology, but in general this has not happened on a large scale. Melvin said, "We have seen a lot of practical things. Each one has attached onto different metaphors of the atonement.

They all seem to use a shame-honor perspective, but they have taken different aspects." He shared that in their last gathering of national movement leaders, there was an expressed desire for more theologizing. In the beginning it was just sharing about each other's ministry, but that is changing. "They don't want to do that anymore. They want to theologize. They want to study the Scriptures; how can we explain these things better." Melvin recalled that when this insider work started it was mostly about transformational forms. "I don't think anyone saw themselves as reformulating theological thoughts." He believes that as the movement goes deeper in the communities, we will see more of a move from ecclesiology to Christology and theology.

> Now that the forms of the expression of faith have been defined and the identity of the believer has pretty much been settled, there is this emerging area about what it means to root the gospel within not just the forms but the meanings of these cultures where God has put us.

Melvin added that rooting the gospel in the culture includes a social context, some of which is repressive because Islamic fundamentalists are controlling society. Some fundamentalists are questioning insider believers, claiming that they just sound like Christians. "Out of that whole questioning, the insider leaders are starting to say, 'If we are truly insiders, we should not sound like Christians. We should sound like we are Muslims.'"

Is there a felt need that everyone stays united theologically? Melvin thinks that a wide variety is acceptable. He said, "I think they are influenced more by the Islamic way of thought. As long as you have five practices and five pillars, you can have a wide variance of thought within Islam." Melvin also noted that quite a few of the people whom they come alongside have gone through a Christian experience and then returned to their people, and then emerged as leaders as they started national movements. They have been affected theologically by the denomination from where they came. Melvin has not seen this emerging as a problem. "I think they are quite open to each other, more than we might be in the West, working across different thought-beliefs." He feels that there are some core beliefs that are shared across all of them. "One is the Bible, that the Bible is authoritative and the ultimate authority over the Qur'an. Some use the Qur'an to a greater or lesser degree." Melvin mentioned that another big core belief is that salvation is in Christ alone. "Those are the two biggies." I asked whether the various atonement theories or views on eschatology might be outside the core. Melvin affirmed that assumption.

Is the doctrine of the Trinity talked about or accepted? Melvin talked about how the type of questions about the ontology of God that we are asking in the West and in the Greco-Roman tradition are different from what most Muslims are asking. "The questions for them are, 'How does this relate to me, and how do I relate to God? What is God asking me to do?' I have seen this in insider movements." He further said that asking questions about the nature of God is irreverent to the Eastern mind. "The articulation of the Trinity is in a sense ontological Christology. It is not writing from a Muslim context." Melvin said that Muslims approach the pursuit of knowing God by looking at how he relates to creation, not how he is separate from creation. "God does not reveal himself to us outside of creation." Melvin added, "And this is what we see with a new believer. He now understands God through the face of Jesus."

Melvin closed with the firm belief that God is putting something incredible into play with insider movements, and that it eventually will go viral.

> God is preparing for something very big to happen, as we better and better understand this paradigm of how to really reestablish the first-century apostolic church in an Islamic context. This community-building is also the heart longing of Muslims. This insider community that is forming is positioned to help restore the *ummah* [the global community of all Muslims] that they feel has been broken.

## Summary Plots by Region

A summary plot is one plot per interviewee. I took the scatter plot for each individual and summarized the 21 plots for each of the 21 frames as one plot that falls in the middle of the scatter. The figure below shows Monty's summary plot, which is not quantified in the figure and does not reflect the spread of my 21 plots for Monty, but it represents and summarizes where Monty fits among the four paradigms. As such, this plot is a summary indication of Monty's theological and missional understanding.

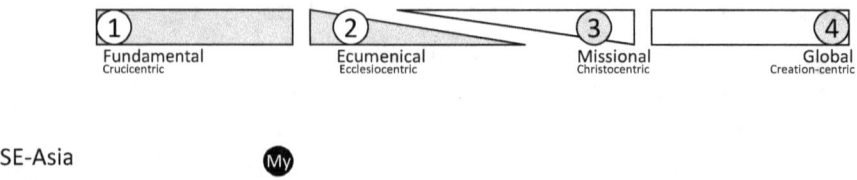

**Figure 37:** The summary plot of Monty's theological and missional understanding

After summarizing the plots for each interviewee I placed them together by region. Figure 38 depicts in summary the theological and missional understandings of the 26 IM leaders and the five alongsiders.

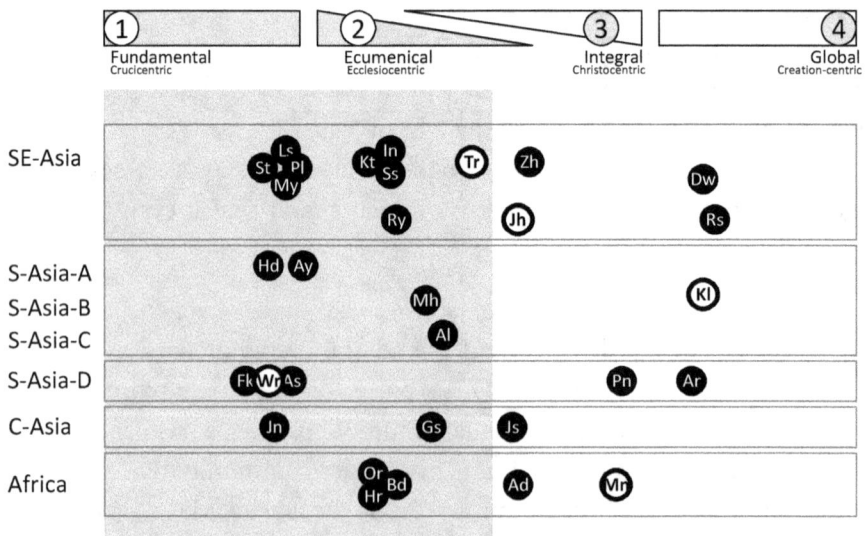

**Figure 38:** The summary plots of the theological and missional understandings of 26 IM leaders and five alongsiders

The first important finding is that most of the IM leaders solidly belong to the Fundamental and Ecumenical paradigms, which form camp A (the shaded box in Figure 38). The theological and missional understandings of 19 of the 26 IM leaders align with paradigms 1 and 2. This is significant because those who publically oppose IM also align with these same paradigms, according to the literature review.

A second general observation is that the alongsider summary plots have a wide range, and the alongsider in most cases leans towards a higher paradigm than his associated IM leaders.

In SE Asia the alongsider Tyler associates with seven IM leaders. This cluster of plots is fairly tight, with most IM leaders having more fundamental views than Tyler, with the exception of Zach. Tyler lives in this region and has frequent face-to-face contact with these IM leaders. This may explain the general closeness of these summary plots. Josh is an alongsider who does not live in the region anymore, but who used to associate closely with Ray, who falls by and large in paradigm 2. Josh's connections with Ross are less direct. Ross aligns with camp B, while Josh's views straddle A and B. Josh is a public voice as an IM proponent and as such has an indirect influence on all IM leaders. Drew's plot is second furthest to the right. This is based on his own feedback. He is not connected to an alongsider or a large movement and as such is somewhat isolated.

The situation in S-Asia-A is most intriguing in that Kevin, as the alongsider, is solidly in paradigms 3 and 4, while Howard and Andy are almost on the opposite side of the spectrum. Kevin does not live in the region anymore, and he admitted to not being involved or even aware anymore of the details of the movements in region A, which may explain the large theological and missional gap. The IM leaders in regions B (Mitch) and C (Axel) are slightly closer to Kevin's viewpoints, but they also are still in camp A.

Another very interesting situation is occurring in S-Asia region D. This is a case where the alongsider (Wilbur) has strong Fundamental and some Ecumenical paradigm views, while two of the IM leaders (Arthur and Paxton) are solidly in paradigms 3 and 4. Wilbur's views are closely aligned with those of the other two IM leaders in this region—namely, Frank and Angus. It appears that Wilbur is protecting these two from, in his words, "reckless theologizing" by Arthur or Paxton, or by both. Referring to one of them, alongsider Wilbur spoke of his mediation role.

> He will forget who he is talking to and get into metaphysical discussions that the people listening to him cannot begin to understand, so their impulse is going to be,

"This guy has totally taken leave of any moorings or any reference points." He is just what we call a communist freethinker. Other people like me who interface between him and the sort of simpler disciples mediate the effects of that kind of reckless theologizing.

I observe that if Arthur or Paxton would be relating with alongsider Kevin or Melvin, they would be very likeminded and no mediation of so-called reckless theologizing would take place.

The final general finding is that in Africa the IM leaders are more conservative than the alongsider Melvin, but the gap is not as wide as in S-Asia region A. I noticed Melvin's possible direct influence on Arnold, Homer, and Brad, since all four hold to the view that Satan and his followers, including unbelievers, will be annihilated with God's judgment of them in hell. This is part of the Seventh-day Adventist Church theology.

## Outlier Frames: Religions and The Qur'an

The 26 individual M-Framework plots for the IM leaders show that there are two outlier frames: Religions and The Qur'an. These are outliers because the theological and missional views on these two frames are consistently from a higher paradigm than the average of the rest of the frames. For the Religions frame, paradigm 1 represents the conflict-of-religions model in which Christianity is the one true religion in every aspect and is in conflict with all other religions. Conversion to Christianity is the goal. The paradigm 2 view is that Christianity is the one true religion and conversion is the goal, but that there are some truths in other religions that can be used as bridges towards that conversion. In paradigm 3 the conflict-of-religions model is not used, but rather, the objective is interfaith dialogue and understanding towards harmony and peace. Individuals who hold to paradigm 4 find religions irrelevant and sometimes even an obstruction to the message of God and to following Jesus Christ.

I summarized the Religions plot for each of the regions and for clusters within a region where suitable, and I did not include any of the plots for alongsiders. Figure 39 shows these summary Religions plots in comparison to the individual summary plots, by region. It is immediately clear that the Religions plot is always to the right of the summary plots, and as such it is an outlier. Most IM leaders view religion as irrelevant or, worse, as a hindrance to following Isa al Masih. For insiders this refers to both Islam and Christianity. They are living in the context of Islam and are not interested in Christianity as it is known to them, so they deconstruct their need for any religion in their pursuit of God and Jesus.

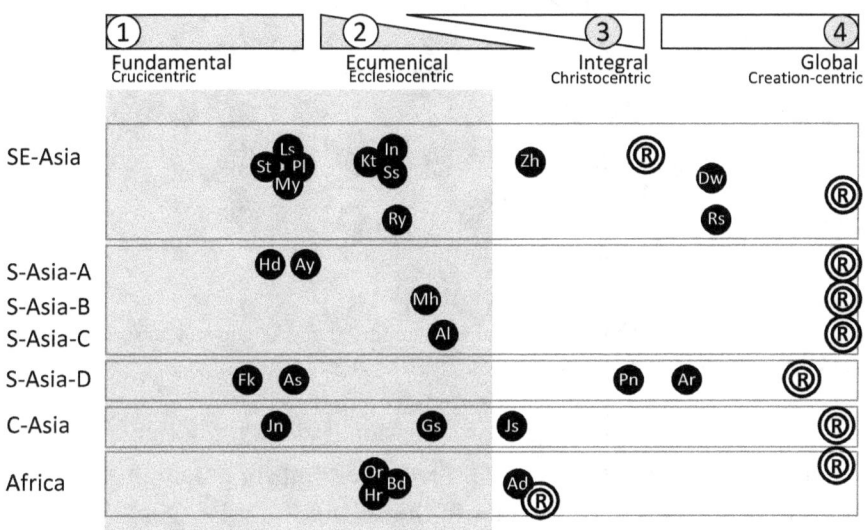

**Figure 39:** Showing regional plots for the frame Religions and 26 IM leader plots, indicating Religions as an outlier frame

The second clear outlier in the M-Framework for IM leaders is the frame titled The Quran. The view in paradigm 1 is that the Qur'an is a satanic book. Paradigm 2 looks at the Qur'an as a dangerous book that should only be used with Muslims as a one-way bridge to the Bible and Christ. In paradigm 3 the opinion is that the Qur'an contains many truths from God, whereas in paradigm 4 the Qur'an is on par with the Bible in the sense that it records part of an ongoing communication between God and man.

As with the Religions plots, I summarized the views expressed by the IM leaders about the Qur'an and plotted those views by region and by usable cluster within a region. Figure 40 shows those plots. In each case the summary plot for the Qur'an is further to the right than the individual summary plots.

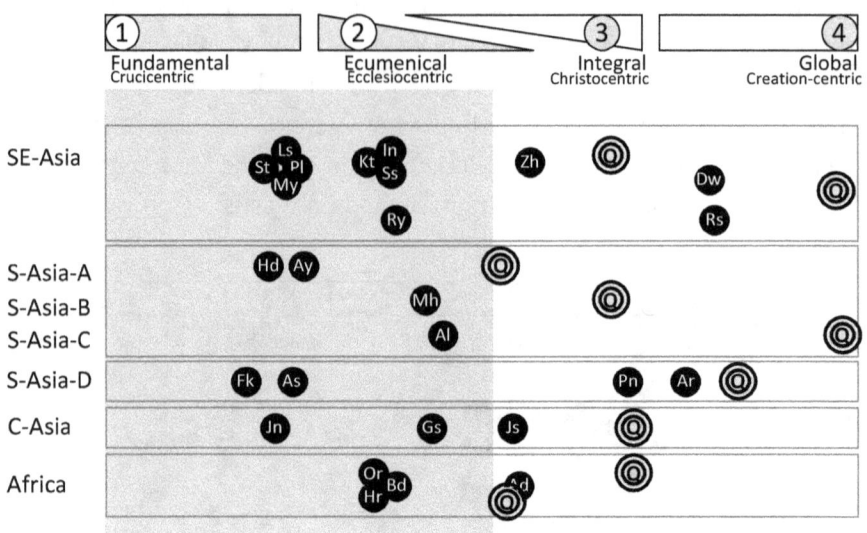

**Figure 40:** Showing regional plots for the frame The Qur'an and 26 IM leader plots, indicating The Qur'an as an outlier frame

IM leaders have theological and missional views for both of these outlier frames that correspond by and large to camp B: paradigms 3 and 4. This is a significant finding, since in the debate about IM these two topics are sensitive to IM opponents, who have a camp A set of views about religions and the Qur'an. Most opponents of IM are likely unaware that many IM leaders have very similar theological and missional views to theirs, with the exception of these two outlier frames, because these often are the two topics being debated. By definition, a Muslim insider looks at the religions of Islam and Christianity differently than an IM opponent. Likewise, an insider has respect for the Qur'an, whereas an IM opponent tends to considers this a satanic book. On the other 19 frames, however, most IM leaders have conservative theological and missional views similar to those of a typical IM opponent.

## Isa al Masih Identity and Christology

In addition to the topics of religions and the Qur'an, the topic of the identity of Jesus and of Christology in general is often a point of contention in the IM debate. Do insiders deny the divinity of Christ? Muslims believe that Isa al Masih is a highly respected prophet who is still alive and will come back to finish his ministry as Judge, but nothing more. Have Muslim insiders moved to high Christology? Do they acknowledge that Jesus is God? Those are the questions that opponents of IM use as a litmus test. If the answer does not fit within their own vocabulary of doctrine and beliefs, the person answering is a heretic.

In the initial observations I grouped responses from IM leaders into five sections: high Christology, other, low Christology, al Masih, and Son of God. This grouping reflects the vocabulary the interviewees used to express their theological and missional understanding of Isa al Masih. The M-Framework allows for further analysis of these expressions since it has two frames that directly address this challenging topic—namely, the Identity of Isa al Masih, and Christology. The M-Framework puts these two frames in the larger context of all 21 frames and the four paradigms. Table 40 shows my plots for each IM leader for the two frames, Identity and Christology. I bolded and italicized the names of the seven IM leaders who adhere to views on Christology from paradigms 3 and 4, since those views may be of concern to IM critics.

**Table 40:** Identity and Christology frames

| Name | Identity 1 | 2 | 3 | 4 | Christology 1 | 2 | 3 | 4 | Comments |
|---|---|---|---|---|---|---|---|---|---|
| Lucas |  | x |  |  |  | x |  |  | Oneness of God; the Anointed One; the Son of God |
| Zach |  |  | x |  |  |  | x |  | Oneness of God; Messiah, Savior; human and divine |
| Ian | x |  |  |  | x |  |  |  | Born of the Spirit of God |
| Phil | x |  |  |  | x |  |  |  | Incarnation |
| Monty | x |  |  |  |  | x |  |  | From heaven; incarnation |
| Silas | x |  |  |  |  | x |  |  | Incarnation; Lord God; the promised one |
| Kent |  |  | x |  |  |  | x |  | The Word of God; al Masih; anointed; Lord God |
| Stuart |  |  | x |  | x |  |  |  | Word of God; al Masih; God |
| Ross |  |  |  | x |  |  |  | x | Word of God; King; Son, not Father; represents God |

| Name | Identity 1 | 2 | 3 | 4 | Christology 1 | 2 | 3 | 4 | Comments |
|---|---|---|---|---|---|---|---|---|---|
| Ray | | | | x | | | | x | Word of God made visible; human mediator; not Allah |
| Drew | | | | x | | x | | | God as human; personal; Savior; above Mohammed |
| Andy | x | | | | x | | | | Trinity, the Son of God |
| Howard | x | | | | x | | | | One with God; the Son of God |
| Mitch | | | x | | | x | | | Word of God; with God before creation |
| Axel | | x | | | | | | x | Mediator; a man close to Allah but not Allah |
| Angus | | x | | | | x | | | Incarnation; God with us |
| Frank | x | | | | x | | | | Son of the divine unity; God |
| Arthur | | | x | | x | | | | Word of God; uncreated; not separate from God |
| Paxton | | | x | | | x | | | Word of God; the eternal beloved |
| Julius | | | x | | | | | x | Word of God; submissive servant; highest prophet |
| Gus | | | x | | | x | | | Word of God; equal with the Father |
| Jason | x | | | | | x | | | Trinity; Son of God; two natures |
| Arnold | | x | | | | x | | | Incarnation; the appointed one |
| Oliver | | | x | | | | | x | Word of God; Spirit of God; Savior; not God |
| Homer | | x | | | | x | | | Savior; Son of God; God |
| Brad | | x | | | | x | | | Incarnation; Son of God; divine |

The first observation is that almost half of the interviewees prefer to identify Isa al Masih as the Word of God. Looking at this group more closely, half of them still hold to high Christology. This indicates that it is not necessary to identify Christ in Trinitarian or incarnational terms in order to see him as divine and as God. This also underscores again that the M-Framework does not assume that someone exclusively falls in one paradigm for all 21 frames.

The second observation is that the majority of the IM leaders express the identity of Isa al Masih and Christology in ways that fit with paradigms 1 and 2. They believe in the incarnation and they believe that Jesus is God.

The third finding is one of the more challenging ones within the IM debate, since seven of the interviewees hold to a paradigm 3 or 4 Christology and as such could be seen by some as heretics. Paradigm 3 Christology looks for wholistic Christology in which Jesus' divinity and humanity are equally important. Paradigm 4 also has wholistic Christology but puts emphasis on Jesus' humanity as significant to the gospel. Neither paradigm denies the divinity of Christ, but that attribute is just not as exclusively in focus as in high Christology. The M-Framework does not include a paradigm that sees Jesus only as a man, which means that the statements by these seven IM leaders needed further analysis.

Zach, Kent, and Ross adhere to Christology paradigm 3, and none of them seemed to deny Isa's divinity. Zach talked about the Messiah being fully human but then added, "We also see in the theophanies and other revelations of God in the Old Testament that this figure is also seen as divine. He is 100 percent divine within the oneness of God. Like two faces of one coin, these are inseparable." Kent uses a local word for "Lord" that is normally a reference to God. He said, "Isa is Lord, and therefore he is capable of defeating death." Kent also considers Isa to be the Word of God and added, "And he is the same with God." Ross, interestingly, emphasizes the father-son relationship between Allah and Isa al Masih, and he calls Isa "Father-centered." At the same time, he believes that the Son is not lower than the Father. To Ross a statement like "Jesus is God" is confusing. He said, "Jesus does not make a coup d'état. He does not say, 'Father is nothing and I am greater than the Father.'" It is clear from their comments that Zach, Kent, and Ross see Isa al Masih as equal to God in some way.

This leaves four IM leaders who are in paradigm 4 with regard to Christology. These are Ray, Axel, Julius, and Oliver. I quoted them in the earlier section in this chapter titled "Isa al Masih—Theology-Christology." All four say that Isa is not God, but what do they mean by that statement? Ray calls Isa the Word of God, the Spirit of God, and the mercy of God. He emphasizes the oneness of God and finds the doctrine of the Trinity confusing and not based on the Bible. He believes that the Word of God was in eternity past in the form of God, which we cannot see, because God is spirit. Isa al Masih is the seen and physical part of the Word of God, sent by God to redeem and save humankind. "He will be reigning in the kingdom of God, but eventually he will give the kingdom back to

God," Ray added. He holds that the Bible does not explain the ontological relationship between Isa and Allah, and as such he keeps that a mystery. To Ray, both Isa al Masih and Allah have distinct functions, and they are not the same. I observe that Ray approaches this topic from a functional or *economic Trinity* perspective. He only relies on what God has revealed and refuses to speculate beyond that point in metaphysical terms towards ontology, or an *immanent Trinity*.

Axel believes in the oneness of God and rejects the idea that a human can be God. He said, "The Isa that came to earth is not Allah. That is *shirk*. We would be making someone the same as Allah. He was human, and you cannot say that a human is Allah." Like Ray, Axel has no problem believing that the Word of God is eternal and indeed God, but the human expression of that Word in Isa cannot be God. He said, "So when the Word became flesh, is this another god? It looks to me that Allah is sitting on the throne and he is sending another god to the world. That is saying that there is another God." Axel rejects this notion, but he believes that Isa is very close to Allah and is the one who can reconcile us. "He deserves high honor," Axel added. He considers the phrase *Son of God* to be a metaphor for belovedness and closeness, and he does not believe in the Christian explanation of the Trinity. "Understanding Allah is a mystery. I would not use this explanation or method to teach others," shared Axel.

Julius said, "Isa al Masih reveals Allah and embodies Allah but is not Allah." He believes that Isa came to this earth as God's Word and Spirit, being cast into Mary, fulfilling the prophecies about al Masih. He was the highest prophet and our perfect example of a submissive servant, dependent on Allah to defeat temptations.

Oliver repeated several times that Isa is the Word of God, and that he is the Messiah and the Savior who saves his people. He noted, "He had authority to give life to a dead person, to give sight to a blind person, to cast out demons, and to do many other things that only God can do." In Oliver's understanding, Isa was not God himself, but he did have the authority to do these miracles because God was there. He added, "There is no differentiation between God, his Word, and the Spirit." Oliver sees Isa as the mediator between God and his people. He concluded this topic by saying that it is offensive to discuss the nature of God. "You cannot study God.

God is above everything. We don't talk too much about God. He is our Creator, the Almighty," said Oliver.

I observe that this last statement by Oliver about the transcendence of God undergirds the caution by him, Julius, Axel, and Ray to call the human Isa "God." This is the unthinkable. It is a disrespectful notion towards the Almighty God. All four place Isa in a special and honored category by himself as the Messiah, the Word of God, the Spirit of God, the one closest to God, the mercy of God that saves mankind, etc. They also have no problem seeing the foreshadowing of Isa as eternal and divine, but they simply cannot say that the human expression of these attributes and functions is God himself. They do not philosophize about the essence of God, which somehow includes the human Jesus. Rather than studying God's essence, they stay at the pragmatic and functional level of God's revelation to his creation. At that level they see a distinction between Isa and God, based on the biblical record.

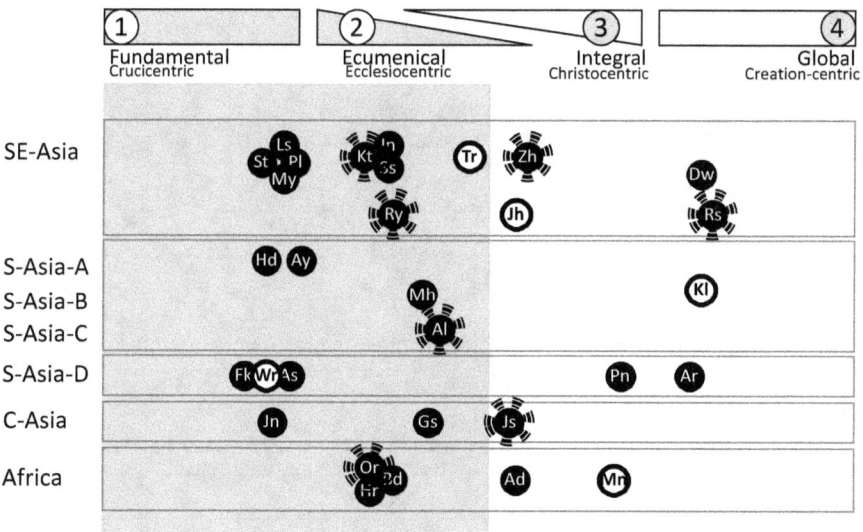

**Figure 41:** Seven IM leaders who adhere to Christology paradigm 3 or 4

My final observation regarding paradigm 3 and 4 Christology is that the seven interviewees who hold those views are not all consistently scoring in those paradigms for other frames. Figure 41 shows the summary plots for all 26 IM leaders and highlights the plots associated with the seven interviewees who adhere to Christology paradigm 3 or 4.

These seven spread across paradigms 2, 3, and 4, and the majority fall in camp A. Even the four interviewees with Christology paradigm 4 have summary plots divided between camps A and B. This indicates that the views of an IM leader on Christology are not indicative of his overall theological and missional understanding. Instead, the whole M-Framework with its 21 frames indicates this understanding.

## Correlation with IM Leader Background and Movement Size

Theological and missional understanding develops within a context. I collected basic context information for each IM leader: namely, their religious background, their connection to the traditional church, their formal religious education, and the size of the IM that they are connected with. Table 41 and Table 42 show this basic context data for each of the 26 IM leader interviewees.

**Table 41:** IM Leaders' background and connection to traditional church

| Name | Background | | Connection to traditional church | | |
|---|---|---|---|---|---|
| | Islam | Christianity | Never been connected | Was connected | Still connected |
| Lucas | | x | | | x |
| Zach | x | | | x | |
| Ian | x | | x | | |
| Phil | | x | | x | |
| Monty | | x | | x | |
| Silas | x | | x | | |
| Kent | x | | x | | |
| Stuart | x | | x | | |
| Ross | x | x | | x | |
| Ray | x | | | x | |
| Drew | x | | | x | |
| Andy | x | | | x | |
| Howard | x | | x | | |
| Mitch | x | | | x | x |
| Axel | x | | | x | |

| Name | Background | | Connection to traditional church | | |
|---|---|---|---|---|---|
| | Islam | Christianity | Never been connected | Was connected | Still connected |
| Angus | x | | x | | |
| Frank | x | | | x | |
| Arthur | x | | x | | |
| Paxton | x | | | x | x |
| Julius | x | | | x | |
| Gus | x | | | x | |
| Jason | x | | | | x |
| Arnold | x | | | x | |
| Oliver | x | | x | | |
| Homer | x | | | | x |
| Brad | | x | | | x |

**Table 42:** IM Leaders' religious education and movement size

| Name | Religious formal education | | | Movement size | | |
|---|---|---|---|---|---|---|
| | Christian | Islamic | None | < 100 | 100 < X < 1,000 | > 1,000 |
| Lucas | x | | | | | x |
| Zach | x | | | | | x |
| Ian | | x | | | | x |
| Phil | x | | | | | x |
| Monty | x | x | | | x | |
| Silas | | | x | x | | |
| Kent | | | x | x | | |
| Stuart | | | x | x | | |
| Ross | | | x | x | | |
| Ray | x | x | | | | x |
| Drew | x | x | | x | | |
| Andy | | | x | | | x |

| Name | Religious formal education | | | Movement size | | |
|---|---|---|---|---|---|---|
| | Christian | Islamic | None | < 100 | 100 < X < 1,000 | > 1,000 |
| Howard | | x | | | | x |
| Mitch | | | x | | | x |
| Axel | | x | | x | | |
| Angus | | x | | | x | |
| Frank | x | x | | | x | |
| Arthur | x | x | | | x | |
| Paxton | | x | | | x | |
| Julius | | | x | x | | |
| Gus | | | x | x | | |
| Jason | x | | | x | | |
| Arnold | x | | | | | x |
| Oliver | | x | | x | | |
| Homer | x | x | | | | x |
| Brad | x | | | | x | |

The context data indicates a significant general connectedness to Christianity for quite a few IM leaders. Most, but not all, have a Muslim background. I show Ross as having a Muslim and Christian background because he grew up in a "mixed" home. Many IM leaders had connections with the traditional church, and some still do. Twelve of them have had formal Christian education. This general connectedness to Christianity is understandable, since at this stage of these movements many of the top leaders are cross-overs—i.e., believers who have crossed back over from a Christian context to their natural Muslim context in order to make a difference in their communities for Christ. These are the type of individuals who are still able and comfortable, in the right setting, to meet with a trusted outsider like myself. Second- and third-generation IM leaders such as Silas, Kent, and Stuart do not have that ability or interest. They were interviewed by Phil.

In order to see the relationship between the theological and missional understandings of IM leaders and their context, I created summary M-Framework plots for the following context characteristics:

1. Christian background
2. Never been connected to a traditional church
3. Still connected to a traditional church
4. Christian religious education
5. Only Christian religious education
6. Islamic religious education
7. Both Christian and Islamic religious education
8. No formal religious education
9. Part of a movement < 100
10. Part of a movement between 100 and 1,000
11. Part of a movement > 1,000

Appendix B summarizes M-Framework plots for these eleven characteristics. I observe that these characteristics do not seem to have a specific influence on the theological and missional understandings of the IM leaders. I realize that I am only using a sample of 26 IM leaders and that further research may demonstrate some influence. I was especially curious about the influence of past formal religious education on current theological and missional understandings of IM leaders. Figure 42 and Figure 43 show the summary M-Framework plots for those who have had formal Christian education and Islamic education, respectively.

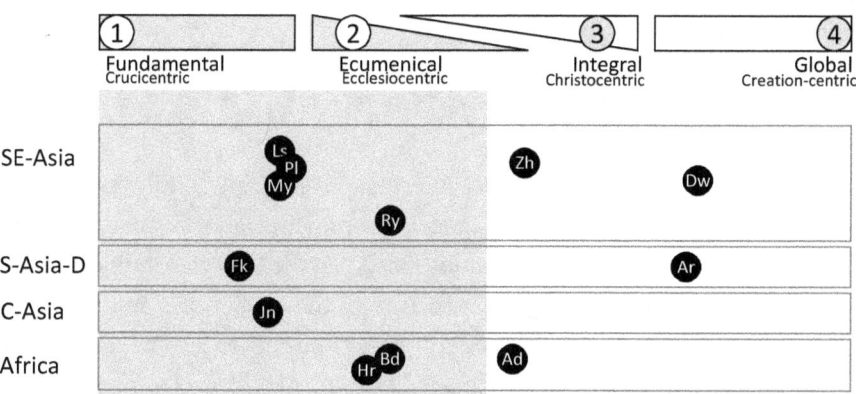

**Figure 42**: M-Framework summary plots of IM leaders with Christian religious education

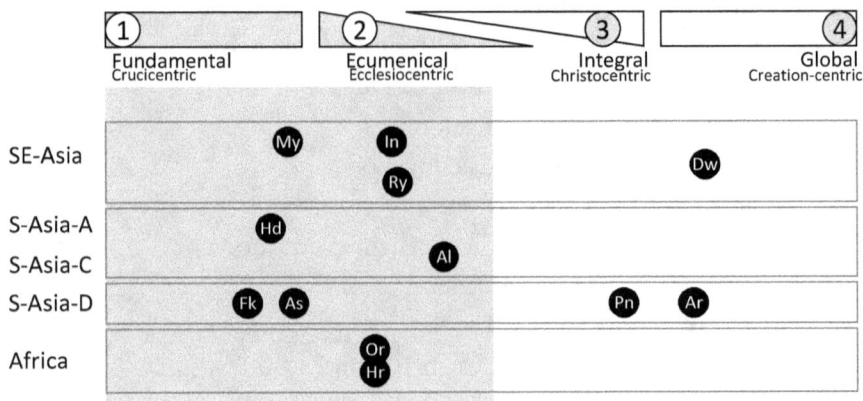

**Figure 43:** M-Framework summary plots of IM leaders with Islamic religious education

There is not much difference between the two plots in Figure 42 and Figure 43. Appendix B shows that plots for other context characteristics also do not indicate a specific influence on an IM leader's theological and missional understandings. I conclude that for those who already have decided to be part of an IM, their theological and missional understanding has a range between paradigms 1 and 4 of the M-Framework, and this range is not specifically influenced by the person's religious background, past or present connection to a traditional church, religious education, or size of the associated movement.

## OVERVIEW OF FINDINGS

After analyzing and coding the interview transcripts, I developed the M-Framework to capture the range of comments and responses, using the central research question, the sub-questions, the interview guide, and the final set of codes as input for the structure of the framework. In addition to the references cited herein and the responses from the IM leaders, I consulted the works listed in appendix C during the M-Framework development process.

Figure 44 shows the connection between my central research question, the first two sub-questions, and the M-Framework with its 21 frames (rows) and four paradigms (columns). The central research question is, What are the theological and missional frames of IM leaders? My research shows that the answer to that question is the set of individual M-Framework plots of the 26 IM leaders in chapter 4. I summarized those plots in Figure 38.

| What are the theological and missional frames of IM leaders? | | | | | | | |
|---|---|---|---|---|---|---|---|
| Allah—Theology | 1 | 2 | 3 | 4 | Allah | How do Muslim insider leaders understand Allah and his plans and purposes? | Theological |
| 1. Essence | | | | | | | |
| 2. The Problem | | | | | | | |
| 3. Satan | | | | | | | |
| 4. Man | | | | | | | |
| Allah—*Missio Dei* | 1 | 2 | 3 | 4 | His Plans and Purposes | | Missional |
| 5. The Gospel | | | | | | | |
| 6. This World | | | | | | | |
| 7. Our Mandate | | | | | | | |
| 8. Healthy Societies | | | | | | | |
| 9. Religions | | | | | | | |
| 10. Election | | | | | | | |
| 11. Hell | | | | | | | |
| 12. Heaven | | | | | | | |
| 13. The Bible | | | | | | | |
| 14. The Qu'ran | | | | | | | |
| Isa al Masih—Christology | 1 | 2 | 3 | 4 | Isa | How do Muslim insider leaders understand Isa al Masih and his role and identity? | Theological |
| 15. Identity | | | | | | | |
| 16. Christology | | | | | | | |
| Isa al Masih—*Missio Christi* | 1 | 2 | 3 | 4 | His Role and Identity | | Missional |
| 17. His Life | | | | | | | |
| 18. On the Cross | | | | | | | |
| 19. The Cross | | | | | | | |
| 20. The Resurrection | | | | | | | |
| 21. The Future | | | | | | | |

**Figure 44:** The connection between the M-Framework and the main research question and sub-questions 1 and 2

The first finding is that the M-Framework is a very helpful communication tool to express complex and multi-faceted theological and missional understandings. The M-Framework only includes topics, or frames, that belong in the theology-proper domain, but those are foundational to more expanded theological and missional expressions. I went from 236,000 words of transcribed interviews to a set of 655 codes, to a 21 x 4 M-Framework, which then allowed me to analyze the original data by plotting each interviewee in this framework. I derived the central understanding, or grounded theory, as presented in these findings, from my analyses of these M-Framework plots.

The second finding is that the individual plots for each of the 21 frames in the M-Framework have some spread across the four paradigms, but for most there is a distinct center or alignment with only one or two paradigms. This being the case, a significant finding is that most IM leaders adhere to paradigms 1 and 2, which is camp A. This is an important finding because the literature review shows that opponents of IM by and large seem to belong in camp A as well, based on their theological comments in the IM debate.

A third finding is that there is a wide range in theological and missional understanding among alongsiders and that their influence on IM leaders varies. For example, in S-Asia region A the IM leaders Howard and Andy have paradigm 1 and 2 beliefs, while alongsider Kevin, who does not live in the region, adheres to paradigms 3 and 4. Kevin's influence on Howard and Andy appears to be minimal. On the other hand, alongsider Tyler, who lives in the SE Asia region, has similar theological and missional understandings as the IM leaders in that region. In S-Asia region D alongsider Wilbur's summary plot between paradigms 1 and 2 is very close to those of IM leaders Frank and Angus, indicating possible high influence. I also observed that Wilbur protects Frank and Angus from the views of Arthur and Paxton, who fit within paradigms 3 and 4. In Africa, alongsider Melvin, who does not reside in the region, aligns with paradigm 3, while most IM leaders align with paradigm 2, indicating a limited influence.

As a fourth finding, I noticed that frames 9 and 14 (Religions and The Qur'an) are outliers in that IM leaders consistently expressed views on religions and the Qur'an that fit with a higher paradigm than their summary plot. The overall plots for Religions and The Qur'an were in camp B for all regions.

My fifth finding is that most IM leaders prefer and hold to high Christology compatible with paradigms 1 and 2. Four IM leaders align with paradigm 4 Christology, which adheres to wholistic Christology that emphasizes Jesus' humanity while not denying his divinity. These four IM leaders expressed the identity of Isa al Masih at the functional or economic level and therefore made a distinction between Allah and Isa al Masih, not equating the latter with God. They were not comfortable describing the essence or "being" of God, which they consider a mystery. I observe that church doctrines and creeds that express high Christology are ontological statements. I also note that of these four IM leaders, three align with camp A and one with camp B, indicating that there is not a strong link between their summary M-Framework plot, or their general theological and missional understandings, and their views on Christology.

The final main finding is that an IM leader's context characteristics such as his religious background, education, connection to the traditional church, and the size of the associated movement have no specific influence on his theological and missional understanding.

In chapter 6, "Conclusions and Recommendations," I integrate these six findings with those in chapter 5 and expand on the implications for IM, the IM debate, and mission strategies.

# CHAPTER FIVE
# INSIDER MOVEMENTS AND THE THEOLOGIZING PROCESS

## INTRODUCTION

The central research question is, What are the theological and missional frames of IM leaders? The third and fourth sub-questions are:
1. How do Muslim insiders study the Tawrat, Zabur, and Injil and apply insights gained within IM?
2. How do IM leaders develop theological and missional frames within their communal context?

This chapter documents the analysis of the interview data related to these two sub-questions. The fourth sub-question is naturally in focus, because it relates directly to the central research question. The third question is representative of several questions in the interview guide that help describe the general setting of the movement in which the topic of the fourth question takes place.

With regard to the third question, in addition to the Scripture study and application question, I also asked about the structure of the movement, its leadership, how it grows, and secrecy. Towards the end of each interview I asked about what internal and external challenges to the movement the interviewee sees, and how they are addressing these challenges. The answers to these questions provide a general description of a movement. In the code set I labeled the top code related to the third question "Movement."

The fourth question looked for the processes in a movement that developed an IM leader's theological and missional understanding. I asked about their general approach, any challenges, and how different views were handled within the movement. The topic of the Trinity came up several times in the interviews. I named the top code for this set of information "Theologizing."

Based on my final code set for research sub-questions 3 and 4 I used the following topics to analyze each of the movements represented by the interviewees:

Movement
    Structure and Growth
    Strategies
    Challenges
Theologizing
    General Approach
    Differences
    Trinity
    Challenges

The "General Observations on Movements" section of this chapter relates to the third research sub-question and covers the movements' structure, growth, and strategies, by region. I also present the challenges the movements face from Islam and the church. The "Communal Processes for Theological and Missional Frame Development" section addresses the fourth research sub-question and looks at the general approach in the theologizing process, how differences in viewpoints are handled, views on the doctrine of the Trinity, and process challenges.

Chapter 3 includes the list of the IM leaders and alongsiders by region and describes the interview process. I used an interview guide that had some open-ended questions, but I also asked additional questions during the interviews depending on the comments and responses from the interviewees. This partially structured format proved especially helpful when talking about insider movements in general and about the communal processes for their theological and missional frame development, since each movement seems to be unique. Chapter 4 documents the summaries of the sections of all interviews that relate to the theological and missional views of the interviewees.

I used MAXQDA to analyze my qualitative data. Table 43 indicates the number of codes in my initial and final code set for research sub-questions 3 (Movement) and 4 (Theologizing).

**Table 43:** Number of codes for "Movement" and "Theologizing"

|  | Initial Set | Final Set |
|---|---|---|
| Movement | 15 | 179 |
| Theologizing | 09 | 93 |
| Total: | 24 | 272 |

# GENERAL OBSERVATIONS ON MOVEMENTS

## Introduction

This study is narrowly focused with regard to topic but wide in respect to region. I did not study one movement in detail but several movements, and then exclusively focused on *theology proper*. These general observations on insider movements are in themselves not the focus of my research, but they are of interest because they allow for some comparison of different movements and set the stage for further study of my research topic. I limited myself to only documenting general observations that were indirectly relevant to my main research question.

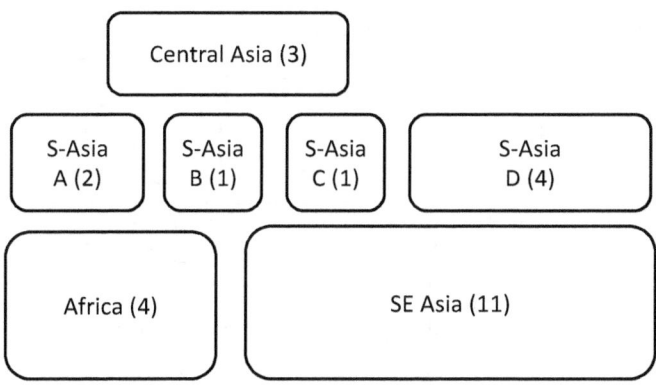

**Figure 45:** The 26 IM leaders came from seven regions

The 26 interviewed IM leaders came from the seven regions depicted in Figure 45.

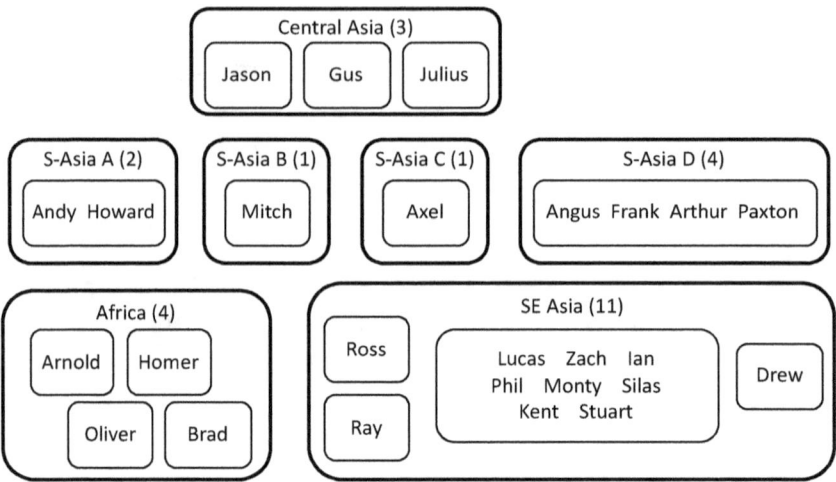

**Figure 46:** The 26 IM leaders came from 15 groupings

Some of the 26 IM leaders are fairly closely associated with each other in the same region, whereas others are from distinctly different areas within a given region. This reality creates 15 IM groupings, as shown in Figure 46.

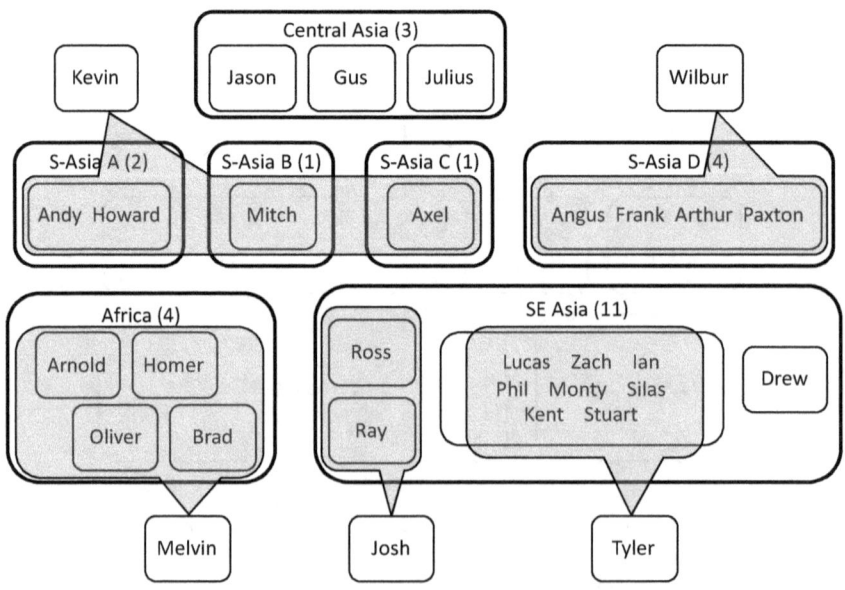

**Figure 47:** Five alongsiders in seven regions

Even within these 15 groupings, each IM leader represents a unique movement in which he is involved, which means that this research looked at 26 different insider movements, all at different stages and of different sizes. Figure 47 shows where the five alongsiders link within the seven overall regions.

Each of these IM leaders has personal testimonies and many stories to tell, and each of these IMs has a history and a distinct beginning. My research is not to investigate the *why* of IM, as I take it as a given that these movements exist, but to the extent that the personal stories told by the interviewees relate to their theological and missional motivations and convictions, I share here a mere sample of their many stories. The main catalyst for IMs was, for many, the desire to share Isa al Masih with their own communities and to bless those communities. Mitch shared his amazing testimony with me one evening, telling me how he as a Muslim teenager was seeking some answers from his imam on the identity of the Qur'an as the Word of Allah and on Isa being called the Word of Allah as well. Over the years this led to him talking with Christian missionaries, putting his faith in Christ, being baptized, and needing to leave his family and community. He got involved in church ministries as a respected teacher and lived on a church compound. He had a burden to reach Muslims with the gospel, but over time his idiom and vocabulary had christianized, and Muslims rejected him outright. One day a missionary sent a group of young men to Mitch for him to check their faith. They had come to the missionary to be baptized. The missionary told Mitch that he would be ready to baptize them if Mitch approved. Mitch recalled this time.

> I found that they believe the same things that I do. They are believers. They are not Christians [as public identity] because we had not baptized them yet, but they believe. At the end of our week together I told them that my advice to them was not to become Christians. I told them what happened to me, why I am sitting there and who I am, and how the Muslim villages and people are rejecting me because of what I did. They see me as a betrayer. They say that I brought shame to the whole *ummah*, the whole community. So I said, "Go back home and don't try

to become a Christian, but remain in your faith quietly, pray to Jesus, worship him, and tell him your problems. If you openly pronounce that you are Christian, you are going to get killed or rejected by your family, and you will end up here on the compound. This is maybe thirty acres of land. How many people can come and live here? If we want our whole country, then this compound is not ours. Remain there. Your parents will notice the change in your life. If there is no change, your faith is not active. But there will be change and they will ask you what happened. Then you can share and tell them what happened. At the same time, if you are burning inside to tell someone, go to a very close friend who will not betray you and tell him." Everybody was happy. We prayed and they left.

The missionary was upset and told Mitch that he had probably lost his last chance to bring Muslims to faith. A month later these young men came back to Mitch together with sixteen older men who were heads of families. The young men told Mitch that they had followed his advice, praying every day and sharing with trusted family members, and now these sixteen men had accepted Isa and had come to be taught. This went on, month after month for several years, as groups of Muslim men came to be taught. Mitch shared with me, "The missionaries were noticing all these things and said, 'Maybe we should not include these people in the church, because the church will not be able to accept this. By now they are already bigger in number than the church itself.'" This small local church did, however, support the training of these groups of Muslim followers of Jesus. Mitch reflected and said, "This way it continued for several years, and this has become a movement now. It started on its own. It was not intentional."

Each IM leader I interviewed had a story to tell. Table 44 shares a portion of five more stories that indicate how IMs come from the missional conviction of followers of Jesus to make a difference in their own communities.

**Table 44:** Why insider movements?

| IM Leader | Direct Quote |
|---|---|
| S-Asia-C\Axel | I was thinking and thinking, I had been praying for a long time for my family. I can go there. If I say that I'm a Muslim, nothing is wrong. I can go and reach my people. It was like a vision for me. I want to be an insider. I don't want to be an outsider. I will put myself in the place of my family and friends, to come to them. If at that time some Christian will come, I will hide him. Who will talk to my friends and family? |
| C-Asia\Julius | Just two years ago, after getting married, I made a decision to return to live among my family, which I had left six years ago, to live close to them and my extended family. I came to a clear condition that I needed to share the gospel with my people. I started from the beginning to share the gospel with my family and friends. I would call this a calling that I believe I received from God. As I did this, I naturally started to learn some of the principles about insider movements. I considered Islamic culture and the way my people think. |
| Africa\Arnold | It took me 10 years to finally catch that vision and to understand what it really means to remain in one's context, to be able to reach out to others. From then on, I began to reach out to my own people. I went back to my people. They accepted me back, but they saw many changes in me that made them say, "He has something to offer." Once a believer takes a Christian identity, I know that this will not help. Perhaps it will help the church, but it will not help the community and society as a whole. |
| SE Asia\Drew | When I got baptized in 2006 I did not consider myself a Christian. I simply considered myself to be a Muslim who had accepted Jesus. I had a desire to bring Jesus to my Muslim friends, and I had never heard about insider movements. After I got baptized and got home from church, I did the regular *salat*, as my expression of thankfulness to God. My mother [a Christian] was very angry with me. "What are you doing that for? God will be very confused with you!" This is what my mother said, and I still remember it until now. I told her that I had accepted Jesus, but that I was still a Muslim, and that I wanted to bring Jesus to my Muslim friends. Yes, there are some Muslims who convert to Christianity and who hate Mohammed, but for me, I want to serve my friends and I want to respect their beliefs, and a central figure of Islam is Mohammed. I don't find that this goes against the teachings of Jesus. |

| IM Leader | Direct Quote |
|---|---|
| SE Asia\Ray | As a Muslim it is easy for me to share the gospel, because when I talk about Isa as a Muslim with other Muslims they know that I am not trying to convert them. That is not a problem. It is a very different story when a Christian talks to a Muslim about Jesus. He would say, "Be careful, you cannot convert me." When I initially discussed this idea with my wife she told me that I could do it, but that she could not, since she is from a Christian background. Over time she saw and understood what was happening in the ministry, and she decided to become a Muslim convert to Islam. I did not force her, but she personally understood that this was needed for the kingdom of God. |

I close this brief look at the *why* of IM with an observation from Paxton. He finds IM completely natural and nothing new, as he recalled how the first Jewish believers had to find a way to talk about Jesus and the only language available to them was the Old Testament and rabbinical theology, which is what they used to express their faith.

> So it was an insider movement. It always has been an insider movement. This insider movement is actually a movement of those people who take their religion very seriously, and who want to express their faith in a way they express any other experience in their lives, in their own language and within their context.

## Structure and Growth

### SE Asia

The main structure for the IMs in SE Asia is the *jamaat*, or fellowship. Alongsider Josh commented on the high level of commitment he has noticed members having to attend weekly *jamaat* meetings. These gatherings are modeled after a type of meeting generally held in homes, where they read or chant Holy Scripture in segregated groups between men and women. The *jamaat* gatherings are also social in nature. They eat something together and pray for each other. Alongsider Tyler mentioned that most of the *jamaats* he is familiar with are fairly small in size, with anywhere between four and six members. "This creates a bit more safety for people that are used to being beaten down," he said. IM leaders from SE

Asia confirmed the use of the *jamaat* structure in their movements. These groups meet in homes or more public places. For example, Ray regularly meets with a group of students at the university where he is studying for his PhD.

The *jamaat* structure does not replace the existing macro structure but fits within it. Normal mosque life continues as a macrocultural community structure. Monty said that they do not want to change the existing macro structure because it would trigger disorder. "We want to build a believer community inside the mosque. We want to build a Bible college within the Islamic boarding house," he shared. Monty's personal ministry is within an Islamic boarding school. He said that their *jamaats* in this school were relatively hidden in the first five years of meeting and learning together, but after that the students and leaders in these *jamaats* were ready to be more open about the fact that they were studying the Gospels and Jesus. This school is now known in the community for doing so, and the *jamaat* members have their answers ready to questions about why they study the Injil and Isa, from a qur'anic viewpoint. As Muslims they can explain these studies and continue their *jamaat* movement. The macro structure forms the setting for ministry. Monty mentioned, "Insider movements are moving so quickly because there are no walls as obstacles keeping it from happening." They are using the former ways to make new changes. He did admit that sometimes these old structures need some modification if part of them is in conflict with the Word of God.

IMs have multiple so-called generations, which are clusters of spiritual *offspring*. A first-generation insider is someone who was led to faith in Christ by an outsider. A second-generation insider is someone who came to faith through a first-generation insider, etc. The *jamaats* within a movement are associated with a certain generation. You have second-generation *jamaats*, third-generation *jamaats*, and so forth. Each *jamaat* has a formal or informal leader, which means that there is a structure of IM leaders within an IM that is used as a venue for communication and training. In SE Asia there is a quarterly multi-day meeting of the top 20 leaders in the various movements in the region. Much of this time is spent in Bible study. There is also a biannual gathering of multiple leaders from various national organizations who are involved in contextual Muslim work, to share best practices and to encourage one another. The formats of these top-level leadership meetings are duplicated among the leaders down into the lower-level generations. As such, the connections between the leaders in an IM are part of the IM structure.

A leader of a *jamaat* emerges naturally within a group setting, but there is always consensus building. Phil said, "It could be a younger person. It is a consensus discussion. It will take some time, but there always is one person who is chosen to be the most senior." A group of leaders within a certain area follows the same process to choose leaders among themselves. Monty shared that they are planning to send out 500 leaders within the next five years, to start movements in unreached areas. He explained the reason for the five-year timeframe. "The idea of five years is that there have to be children and grandchildren leaders behind them, prior to them being sent." He was referring to IM generations.

Growth in the IMs in SE Asia happens through social networks. These are existing networks of contacts within the existing macro structure. Phil recalled his change in approach towards natural networks.

> At the beginning when I started doing evangelism I worked from a map, and my thoughts and plans were mostly based on areas I wanted to go. As time went by, and especially after I started meeting with others with the same passion some seven years ago, there is more of a principle of following the Spirit. What are the natural flows of relationships of a person? He has friends over there, so that is how faith spreads. This is more a natural style away from the command-center approach. It is much cheaper and more efficient to follow whatever God opens.

Lucas mentioned that within his movement they encourage individuals who come to faith in Jesus to stay in their own context so that they can invite others from that same context and background to form a community or *jamaat*. Silas also stressed using a network of personal contacts that already exists and infusing the gospel into that network rather than trying to create a new network around the gospel that is not natural.

Several of the IM leaders in SE Asia mentioned that growth indeed happens through existing social networks, but that the *engine* behind the growth is a transformed life. People observe changed lives. Silas mentioned that growth is a heart thing and not based on thoughts but actions. "Faith spreads from community to community in a very similar way, from the heart," he said. Stuart also stressed the need for followers of Isa al Masih to be involved in social action in the community, for the sake of the community and the growth of the movement.

## South and Central Asia

The IMs in S-Asia region A are structured around small fellowships or *jamaats*, but alongsider Kevin mentioned that there is all kinds of variety in terms of how often a group meets, where they meet, and what they do when people meet. "There's much more variety in it than what people are probably looking for or hoping for in the West, when we talk about movements," he said. Kevin also shared that Howard likes structure and is intentionally organizing the movement into *jamaat* clusters with leaders for each *jamaat* and cluster. Leadership training events played a big role in seeing a movement start, and these events are still the fundamental core structure, according to Kevin. There could be anywhere between 10 to 70 people at any given event. Howard and Andy also designed a four-year leadership training program in which they function as the teachers. The program has a cycle of one-week training followed by forty days back into the community. This discipleship program includes the study of much of the New Testament, parts of the Old Testament, and topics such as spiritual warfare, building bridges between Muslim and Christian worldviews, comparative studies between the Qur'an and the Bible, Christ through the prophets, and church planting.

The *jamaat* members select their own leaders, with some involvement by Andy or Howard. "We pray for someone who looks like a leader according to 1 Timothy and Philippians, and then we try to encourage him and ask others to pray for him, if he can be their leader," Andy said.

The growth of the movements in S-Asia region A happens via existing relationships. Howard shared, "Friend to friend, brother to brother. This is how it goes, like a river; it keeps going that way, tribe to tribe." He also said that by now he does not know the exact size of the movement anymore. The movement expands over into other language communities based on the cultural rules of intermarrying, which are natural bridges that assist the spread of the gospel.

In S-Asia region B there is a fair bit of interest in *organizing the work* by the main alongsider, according to Kevin, even though the start of the movement was very unintentional per Mitch's testimony. The leaders of the overall movement in the region have organized it around geographical districts, intentionally establishing *jamaats* in districts that still need fellowships and following up and establishing local leadership in districts where *jamaats* have been established.

Axel is involved in some *jamaats* in region C, but the movement he is connected with is still in its infancy. He reaches out to friends and family members in the mosque communities in this region. His background as imam helps to give him credibility and makes him uniquely suited to introducing the gospel from the inside of a Muslim's frame of mind.

Frank shared that in S-Asia region D the *jamaats* typically meet on Friday afternoons. A usual place would be the special guest sitting room in a house, where it is very cultural for male guests to gather. These meetings are not closed, and groups come together along general exposure lines in families and neighborhoods. These *jamaats* may recite the Tawrat, Zabur, and Injil in the Arabic version, but they study and interpret the text in the vernacular language. The structure of this movement is built around these semi-open *jamaat* meetings as well as around fully public and open events. The insiders hold open events in the courtyards of a mosque or other public places. These events could be a one-on-one conversation or a larger gathering of maybe 100 people. The topic of these open events is evangelistic and apocalyptic, proclaiming that the return of Christ is imminent. Alongsider Wilbur explained that these are the entry-level broad appeal events, encouraging people to attach themselves to Isa and to repent and believe in him. The Qur'an has an equal place at the table in these fully open events that engage with the broadest section of society.

Angus and Frank are involved in the selection of *jamaat* leaders. They look for someone who is well respected, married, and a good husband and father. "The two of us, in consultation with the group in question, we'll talk and pray and decide," Frank said. Interestingly, they also look for leaders who are literate. "These are people who can read and write, and we give them the responsibility to teach their children and people in the neighborhood. We have several books," commented Angus. *Jamaat* leaders have a teaching role.

In Central Asia, Julius, Gus, and Jason are all three in very different settings, but each one is involved in the very beginnings of an IM. Julius has moved back into his own community as an insider and is meeting contacts one-on-one at this time. They study the Qur'an and the earlier books together, and he is already planning on bringing these contacts together in *jamaats* when they are stronger in their faith.

Gus mentioned that in his setting the movement is still small but that it is growing through relationships. "Nothing happens without relationships," he said. In describing the general *jamaat* system, Gus interestingly mentioned freedom and made a reference to communism. "A leader gives much freedom to people. We function more like a Soviet society: no bosses."

Jason is on staff with a fairly large local traditional church. He tries to introduce more contextualized ministries and new initiatives but encounters much resistance from the church elders. For now he is trying to stay connected to this church and make some changes from within. Jason organizes insider home groups following local cultural norms, using the local language, and being sensitive to everyone's Muslim background.

## Africa

In the Africa region Arnold, Oliver, Homer, and Brad represent four different IMs. Arnold forms groups or *jamaats*, but he first meets with people whom he would like to place in a group on an individual basis to talk and study with them, "lest they cause some disturbance in a group," Arnold said. "There are some people that have really advanced and have come to understand that Isa al Masih is not just a prophet." Arnold groups these people together. He also shared that when they connect with a new family, one of the leaders of the movement approaches the head of the family first to see if there is openness and support on his part. Arnold avoids open gatherings with a group of people. "In groups everyone wants to ask questions, and then they will be stronger than you and they unite against you," he said.

Arnold referred to himself as an overseer within the IM for a certain territory, and within that area he appoints the leaders for each *jamaat*. He is controlling the structure and direction of growth of the movement quite directly in his personal realm of influence, but this overall movement has grown to over 1,000 insiders, which means that much growth is happening without his direct involvement. He added, "Once someone gets to understand this he gets so excited, and because he's remaining in context, he is not afraid of anything. This makes a kind of network, and it goes very fast and smoothly, without much opposition. This is how it grows."

Oliver is connected to a large movement across a wide region in Africa, but in his own setting the movement is still in its infancy. He had several visions of Isa several years ago when he was a teenager, and he is still very much part of his Muslim community and people. Melvin explained that in this large movement the structure of the groupings is the *oikos*, or household. The leader of a *jamaat* is the head of the household. He explained that the patron-client system is the way movements form and grow, from households to tribes. "Those with the most patronage become bigger and bigger leaders within the movement."

Homer is a leader in a large movement. He is still very much involved at the grassroots as well and loves to meet with people one-on-one, "until they are ready to consider that the Bible is not corrupted," Homer said. He starts with the Qur'an and shows them how it confirms and points to these other books. "You don't reveal that you have a Bible in the initial meeting," he noted. When they get deeper and deeper into the Scriptures, "then they come into the light from the darkness, and then I can introduce him to other believers," Homer shared. Within this movement the *jamaats* are grouped along the mosque structure, which forms natural communities. Homer said that a *jamaat* leader is chosen democratically by the group members. He was clearly excited during the interview when he explained how the movement is growing. He gave an example of an insider with whom they had lost contact for a while since he had moved closer to where his extended family was living. When Homer met up again with this man, he learned that the latter had been sharing with his family members and that 40 people now are ready for baptism. Homer mentioned other examples of people moving within their wider language tribe but across country borders and spreading the movement that way. "It is spreading just as you see with the trees. When the wind comes the seeds spread, and wherever they fall they start germinating. This work is growing that way."

Brad's situation is somewhat unique in that he is the national leader for his church denomination for the ministry of IMs. He employs several so-called change agents who guide the local outreach ministries. Brad shared how they are encouraging believers to reach out to others, and to study the Scriptures with someone initially one-on-one before putting this person in contact with a *jamaat* or cell group. They are keeping these groups as small as possible to avoid exposure. Most *jamaats* have five to ten people, according to Brad. "When a new person reaches a certain level of understanding and interest, one of the change agents will do more in-depth Bible studies with him," Brad explained. One change agent may service anywhere between one to three *jamaats*. In areas where the movement is growing in numbers they establish a committee led by someone who volunteers for that role. The local change agent is part of this committee as well, and the committee leader reports plans and progress to Brad.

## Observations

Small local fellowships, or *jamaats*, are the building blocks of all IMs represented by the 26 interviewed IM leaders. These groups form naturally within family, tribal, and mosque communities. The movements grow via existing relationships, as people share with friends, colleagues, and family members. The movements move from one area to another when believers move around.

Leaders in a movement either appoint new leaders or guide a community process of selecting new leaders as new *jamaats* form. In some cases the *jamaat* leader role falls naturally to the community leader, such as in a family or tribe, if this person has become a believer. The generations of believers within an IM seem to create levels of isolation and protection in that most believers only know other believers from their own *jamaat*, and the *jamaat* leader only knows his leader one generation up from his own. This creates a very flexible IM structure and also makes the network between IM leaders a vital part of an IM's support and learning structure. IMs use leadership training programs rather than hierarchical leadership structures to enable and empower all believers and *jamaat* leaders within the movement.

## Strategies

In this section I discuss IM strategies related to identity, the local mosque system, and *jamaats* in the local community, as they apply to each of the regions.

## SE Asia

One of the IM strategies is choosing the proper identity. Within the wider Muslim context all insiders have a Muslim identity, but what is their identity when they are among themselves as believers? This research is not an identity study, but it is worth making a few observations on this topic, as it creates the general environment in which the processes for the development of theological and missional understanding take place. Alongsider Tyler talked about a double identity.

> We find that we are getting a lot of followers of Jesus who still have some allegiance to Islam, having a double identity of being followers of the way of Jesus while also in some broader cultural sense a part of the cultural majority of their surroundings. They are trying to work out their identity as some kind of combination of this double identity. They don't necessarily say that they are other than Islam, but if pressed by Christians they might not also say they are other than Christian. They are creating for themselves a collective identity that is strong in allegiance to Jesus and the Word, and they are trying to work out what that means in their context.

Alongsider Tyler refers to their "Jesus follower" identity as a sub-identity that is layered underneath their public Muslim identity. He has noticed that when insiders get together with other believers they go deep in talking about the Bible, praying for each other, and applying what they are learning. "I think they do far more than believers in a christianized context," he said.

Ross promotes the idea of insiders taking on the identity of reformers of their Muslim communities, reforming their societies from the inside out in respectful and non-aggressive ways. He reminds those who would rather extract themselves from their community because they do not agree with its leaders and teachers that they also were once like those authorities. He said, "After we listen to the stories of the Tawrat, Zabur, and Injil, our attitudes become different. We become reformers. Reformers in a nice way. Reformers who are not afraid. Like a deer who desires cool water."

Some general strategy principles that relate to the wider mosque system are that you should never insult the prophet Mohammed, discard your Qur'an, or change your place of worship, according to Monty. Ross referred to the mosque as the house of God, where you remove your sandals and come into his holy presence. He mentioned that many evangelists in his language community tell people who accept Jesus to stop going to the mosque.

"That is bad news," Ross said. "Stop going to the house of God? Where should I go? To their secret house, to their secret training center? That is what these evangelists say, to come to their Christianity club."

Alongsider Tyler mentioned that using the Islamic calendar has been a helpful strategy to gather large numbers of believers together. For example, they use the Eid festival as a gospel object lesson. "We buy some goats to be killed as a way to gather Muslim believers together, sharing the illustration of the killing of the goat as an aspect of the gospel. It is told symbolically at a religious event." They also use the Christian calendar as they gather large numbers of up to 600 for the celebration of the birth of the prophet Isa. Tyler explained how they start with a reading from the Qur'an to legitimize the Scripture and then have a reading from the Gospels. Their hope and prayer is that from these large gatherings, some individuals may become more open to learning about Isa and eventually join a *jamaat*.

A leader in the mosque system should remain in his position when he becomes a believer. Both Phil and Monty mentioned that strategy. Phil said, "We want to help those religious leaders who have repented or turned so that their teaching begins to take on a flavor that points people into the direction of Isa within their natural influence channels."

The strategy related to secrecy or openness is another interesting element of the general IM dynamic. In SE Asia the strategy is cautious and culturally appropriate openness, not secrecy. Alongsider Josh mentioned that in this culture people have a very inclusive way of being. At any given *jamaat* meeting there are often people attending who are not part of the group, but who are friends or relatives. In the public eye these are gatherings by a strange Muslim group, according to Josh. Alongsider Tyler has observed a layering of openness, from completely open to more restrictive or exclusive layers of relationships, but he acknowledged that no gathering is completely private because people can walk in at any time or can hear a conversation through a wall.

The non-secretive strategy allows nonbelievers to draw closer and listen in. Zach mentioned that this often triggers a renewed interest in the Qur'an, comparing its reading to the Scriptures. Kent shared that openness sometimes means that people oppose you in public. This creates an interest in the community, and he has noticed that on occasion people have come to him quietly after a public event to get more information about Isa. Stuart quoted an interesting local proverb related to secrecy and culturally appropriate behavior. The proverb is, "If you catch fish, don't make the water muddy." He is saying that there is no need to create a disturbance and unnecessary suspicions, but that you need to stay purposeful in catching fish.

*Jamaats* are not only part of the IM structure, but they are also an IM strategy in that much of IM life happens within a *jamaat*. One of the main activities in the *jamaats* is Bible study. Having the appropriate version of the Bible seems important. Alongsider Josh mentioned that having a contextual translation available was a huge factor in the movement. He said, "The churches don't use that Bible, and these Muslims really view it as, 'This is our translation.'" He added that even the pronunciation of names such as *Allah* in audio Bible products like the "JESUS" film can make a big difference. He knows of one case in which a version of the "JESUS" film that includes a pronunciation of *Allah* as used by the local Christians is available in bookstores, but another version with the Muslim pronunciation circulates among *jamaats* in the local IM. Ross noted that they are using the Arabic Sharif Bible in the *jamaats* for chanting and then turn to the local translation to read. Referring to the Bible version published by the national Bible society, Ross said, "They use Christian terms in this Bible, such as going to a Mass. Moses went to a Mass, like a Catholic Mass? So we are very confused. Did Moses go to a Catholic Mass?" This version burdens insiders with foreign stuff, according to Ross, so they are not using it. Phil called the Bible they are using "the translation that uses cousin-friendly terms."

The most-used format for Scripture is a printed product, but audio formats are popular as well, especially for chronological Bible stories. It is common practice to have Scripture read aloud in the *jamaat* meetings, but Scripture memorization is also very popular. Ian stressed the need for believers, including children, to memorize Bible portions. He said, "We need to ask the children to memorize as well, so that when they finish their ritual prayers, they should quote verses." He believes that Scripture memorization raises their functional capacity and authority in the community. Monty shared that two of the IM leaders in the movement that he is connected with have memorized Philippians and Ephesians. It took them five years. They now have decided as a leadership group to memorize the entire New Testament among themselves within the next

10 years. His assignment is Acts, and he is now in chapter 10. "This is our living gospel, our gospel without walls." Monty said. He added that hard experiences, including prison time, have led them to this strategy, so that the evidence of owning a Bible in written format is removed.

The use of the Qur'an in *jamaat* gatherings is normal and expected. The Qur'an leads to the truth, as it points to Isa and the Tawrat, Zabur, and Injil. Zach said, "The Qur'an is not a problem for me or my team, because it is the beginning of a process to help people to understand the grace and mercy of God."

It was interesting to note that most of the IM leaders associated with alongsider Tyler mentioned their use of the Seven-question Model. They use this in each *jamaat* meeting. The model includes some personal questions and then has some basic questions about their understanding and application of any passage under study. The last question is, "What shall we do together as a group application?" This builds a brotherhood among them that sustains them in their context.

Another clear IM strategy in SE Asia is having direct involvement in the community, trying to meet real needs. However, a non-secretive approach with direct engagement in the community can lead to suffering. Ross had an interesting expression. "From Egypt to the Promised Land is a desert. It is a desert here." He also referred to Jacob as the one who struggled with God and then was renamed Israel. We all need to be Israel, according to Ross. He himself spent almost three years in jail. "My crime was glorifying Jesus excessively as a Muslim," he said. Zach stressed the need for mentors in IM to deal with the theme of suffering with everyone. An insider's faith is proven and strengthened through challenges and suffering.

Meeting real needs in the community happens in various ways, such as through microcredit loans and social visitation around important days and events, going to weddings, inviting others to events, participating financially in community needs, and opening fasts. Phil commented, "There is a social legitimization of the carriers of that kind of help, and acceptance of their message."

## South and Central Asia

On the topic of identity, Andy and Howard and insiders in S-Asia region A see themselves as completed Muslims. Their general public identity is Muslim, and their lower-level identity clearly is distinct and separate from that of the Christians in their region. As completed Muslims they welcome interactions with other Muslims. "I can challenge the Muslims by saying that they are not complete Muslims if they don't believe in Jesus," Andy said.

Bible reading, memorization, and study are strategies in region A. Andy mentioned how a Muslim gets up every morning and reads the Qur'an, so in their IMs the believers get up in the morning, wash their face, and study the Bible. "In some places they play audio-recorded Bibles, and in other cases only one in the family can read and he or she reads for the whole family each morning," Howard added. When they meet in *jamaats*, Bible study is their main activity. Memorizing Scripture is popular in this region for security reasons. Their leadership training program includes the assignment in the first year to memorize parts of the Psalms and the Gospel of Luke.

Alongsider Kevin mentioned that both Andy and Howard are involved in relief and community development activities as well, as they seek to make their movements relevant to people in their communities. Suffering is an expected part of this strategy and of being a believer. Howard said, "Jesus himself is saying that if you declare yourself a follower of me in this world, you will have many problems."

In region B the matter of identity is straightforward. Insiders have a Muslim identity. Mitch sees that as a decision made by God. He said, "We are born in a Muslim family. This is a God-given identity. He could have allowed me to be born in a Christian family, and then I would've had a Christian identity. This is God's decision, and I should remain there." When I asked him to what degree he sees people within the movement trying to seek a connection with the church and taking on a Christian identity, he answered, "There is no symptom or understanding yet that one day we will become Christian. There is no feeling like this. Nobody is asking me about that yet."

Regarding mosque attendance, Mitch supports the idea that someone should not change their attendance habits after coming to faith in Isa. "He can worship in the mosque in the name of Jesus." In addition to visiting the mosque, insiders are part of a local *jamaat* in which they study the Scriptures. Portions of the New Testament are available in a contextualized Muslim-idiom translation. Mitch mentioned that they also encourage everyone to read some Scripture at home each evening. The Qur'an is still in use in the *jamaats*, but Mitch noted that most people in his region do not understand Arabic. Some can read the Qur'an in Arabic, but they do not comprehend the actual words. Mitch is not nervous about the use of the Qur'an. He said, "We never ask them not to read the Qur'an, but we know that the Scriptures have more power and will shift the people's attention away from the Qur'an to the Scriptures."

For Axel in region C, his identity is Muslim. He recalled how, early in his faith when he connected with foreigners and a Christian group, he was out in a village to share some materials with Muslims. He still had his beard and his white outfit like a mullah, and the villagers asked him, "Are you a Christian or a Muslim? Are you trying to convert Muslims to Christianity? What are you doing here?" His Christian mentors asked Axel after this trip to remove his beard, which he did. "It was very bad for me," he recalled. Axel has since then left this Christian group and now operates as a Muslim insider, with a beard. He attends the mosque and prays with his friends there. Axel said that he actually prefers praying like that over the way they pray in churches.

Axel studies the Scripture with friends in small *jamaats*. A few years ago he felt the need and the call to get involved in Bible translation, because existing translations are not communicating well to Muslims. He now brings printouts of his own translation to his *jamaat* and friends.

In region D the chosen identity of insiders is "pro-Christ Muslims" or "completed Muslims." Angus referred to himself and other insiders as sheep among wolves. Their strategy regarding the mosque system is to be a Sufi-style group separate from the regular mosques, within which the scrutiny is high and the tolerance low towards variations. Alongsider Wilbur reminded me of this situation and mentioned that this is why some Muslims burn each other's mosques and madrasahs. The IM strategy to take on a Sufi ethos is an attempt to avoid this level of scrutiny.

> Part of it is that these guys are shrewd and they understand that a certain type of avoidance is useful at this stage, and I think the Sufi ethos is a key avoidance strategy, because it gives them a wider berth within the majority community. They are staying away from using the regular house of worship venues in a full-blown C5 paradigm, where they would sort of take over particular houses of worship,

and where the scrutiny is high. So, by avoiding the realm in which that scrutiny is the norm, they can maybe in some cases at least get helpfully dismissed as just mystics who are kind of loosey-goosey about important things, but sort of forgiven for being loosey-goosey mystics.

Avoiding the denominational C5 approach also allows those who are not professional clerics to emerge as leaders. Angus reiterated that with the identity they have they can talk about Jesus with anyone. "People see us as a sect within Islam that observes all holy books and waits for the judgment day when Jesus is coming back," he said. They follow the month of Ramadan and other events in the Islamic calendar. Arthur is in a somewhat different situation in that he is still very much part of the mosque system and its leadership. He preaches from the pulpits in the mosques.

The approach to secrecy is one of the cornerstones of the IM strategies in this region. Their approach is non-secrecy. Alongsider Wilbur believes that a compelling identity solution in the mouths of the first IM leaders is a big part of why it did not start out in secrecy mode. He is convinced that in their context the movement only works when it is in the open. "Otherwise there would be no spread. Everyone would just try to protect the secret and feel threatened by the others, feeling threatened about being ousted by the others especially," he said. Their non-secretive approach has not led to a swallowing of the message. In region D they are using the open-air public appeal events as entries into their *jamaat* system. In both the public appeal events and the *jamaats* they are finding ways to interject the old books and the person of Jesus Christ back into the status quo worldview. Wilbur and others recognize that their non-secretive, para-mosque Sufi venue may be uniquely fitted to their context, which is legally restrictive and does not allow for any kind of pluralism. Their approach, however, requires that they strictly guard one secret: the fact that they have any kind of connection with foreigners. Wilbur is convinced that if the connections that he and a few other foreigners have with less than a handful of IM leaders became known, the whole movement would move underground, become secret, and eventually come to a halt. "This is the trade-off, and we believe it is the right trade-off."

Even baptisms are open-air events. They invite people who will find it meaningful, but anyone can walk up and observe the ceremony. Even when that happens there is no fear, because the insiders are able to completely interpret what is happening there using Sufi meta-language that is quite compelling and understandable to anyone who just happens to walk by, according to alongsider Wilbur.

In Central Asia the movements that Julius, Jason, and Gus are connected with are still in their early stages. Regarding identity, Julius admitted to sometimes being somewhat confused as he meets with Christians one day and with Muslims another. He moved more fully into a Muslim-only context about two years ago. "I have slowly moved from an identity as a Muslim-background believer to one who is a Muslim who follows Jesus," he shared.

Jason is in quite a different situation than Julius and Gus in that he is on staff with a local church, and as such he has a thoroughly Christian identity within the church environment. When he meets with people in the community and in small groups, however, he has a Muslim identity. "They think that I am a Muslim because I greet them like a Muslim. I speak to them in their language," Jason said.

The insiders whom Julius knows attend the mosque and participate in *jamaat* meetings when they are ready for that level of exposure. The believers who attend Jason's *jamaats* do not attend church, but the group identity is Christian, even though Jason tells them that this does not mean that they have to become cultural Christians. His *jamaat* follows the local culture, which is majority Muslim, rather than the culture of the church in his country, which uses an imported foreign culture and language.

Regarding Bible study in the *jamaats*, Julius is using storying, since they do not have a suitable printed Bible in the local language. He is working on a translation, and sometimes he brings printed portions on a piece of paper for discussion in the *jamaat*. Gus is likewise involved in a Bible translation that uses Muslim idiom for his language group.

## Africa

As in the other regions, the general identity of insiders in Africa is also Muslim. Alongsider Melvin mentioned that in some places insiders call themselves Messiah Muslims. Arnold just calls himself a believer in Isa al Masih, and Brad commented that insiders call themselves Muslims but know that they are special Muslims. Both Homer and Melvin mentioned another identity expression for an insider that basically means "a person of the straight path."

The IM strategy towards the mosque system in Africa has several variations but in general seems to be one of looking for transformation from within. Alongsider Melvin has noticed that IM is perceived by regular Muslims as a reform movement within Islam, going back to the previous Scriptures and believing in Christ in a fuller and deeper way than they have done in the past. "It is not perceived as an outside thing or a Christian movement, and most don't know of any connection to Christianity from the second level of leaders down," Melvin said. He also noted that the level of integration into the mosque system is higher in the rural areas than in the urban parts.

In Arnold's area Christians and Muslims live together in the community without problems. "You can find families where half of them are Christian and the other half are Muslim. They are living in the same compound and eating from the same bowl," he explained. Arnold also mentioned that there are many different groupings or subdivisions within Islam in his area, "so when you come with something different they say, 'Okay, still Muslim.' This is not such a big deal, which means that people are not that aggressive."

Brad explained their strategy in regard to the mosque system as continuing what you did before. If insiders attended the mosque before they came to faith in Isa, they encourage them to continue going. "Practically that helps us to remain in context and also to reach out to others," Brad said. He also noted that maybe 60 to 70 percent do not attend the mosque regularly. He did mention one case that appears to be one of discontinuity in that a woman who used to be a women's leader in the mosque now works as a change agent for women believers.

The approach to secrecy of IM in Africa is context-dependent, but in general these are open movements since they are taking place from within the existing Muslim communities. A few examples indicate that for some events insiders use a heightened level of secrecy. Homer said that in his area everyone is baptized as an individual and alone, not in a group event, so that no one knows who is baptized unless someone personally shares that information. He also recalled in the interview that some insiders had left the group and gone back to being "regular" Muslims, and that they had feared a leak of information. "But God has taken care of the ministry," Homer said.

In Brad's area, insiders sometimes worship in secret in a rented house. He also mentioned that they carefully bring insiders who are ready to be baptized to a church building for this event, introducing them to believers from a Christian background. "The church is in support and provides the premises, and they support us however they can, particularly in preparing the baptismal," Brad said.

IMs in the Africa region also follow the strategy of having *jamaats* in which insiders come together, support one another, and study the Scriptures. Alongsider Melvin mentioned that some IMs only have portions of Scripture available to them, and he knows of one movement where the *jamaat* members have no access to any Scripture portion. "It is a qur'anic Jesus movement. They use the Qur'an in the fellowships, but it is seen through biblical eyes," Melvin said. He further explained that this is an oral culture and that the insiders know many of the stories about Jesus. However, he has some reservations about this movement and feels that it is different from the rest. "They do not have the power of the Bible in their movement yet," he stated.

Arnold mentioned that in their *jamaats* they talk and research specific topics, tell and read stories, and do inductive Bible studies. Oliver is involved in translating the Bible for his context. He is currently working on the Gospel of John and is hoping to produce a complete Injil in the near future. Oliver is using the *jamaats* to do community testing of draft translations, and to check for accuracy and naturalness of the text. He has also produced booklets with stories of the prophets, which the *jamaats* are using as well. He shared his vision for the movement that has the Scriptures as their foundation.

> I envision that when the Injil is presented in a way that fits their context, it will be less offensive than when Christians come and try to convert my people to become Christians. A Muslim cannot be a Muslim unless he says that he believes in the Tawrat, Zabur, and Injil. If they don't believe all the Scriptures, they are not Muslims. But how can we present the Injil in the context of the community? We need to show them what it means so they

can follow Jesus within their culture and within their identity. That is how I envision the insider movement will grow more than the other traditional church approaches that are being used in the world.

The IM that Homer is connected to is part of a large regional IM that crosses national borders because it is associated with a regional language spoken by many. He expressed how they are constantly juggling various Arabic Bible versions and one in their own language as they study the Scriptures together in the *jamaats*. They also use solar-powered audio Bibles, and the fact that many have excellent memorizing skills helps in their studies. Homer mentioned that if they could have another version of the Bible in the regional language that uses *Isa al Masih* instead of *Jesus Christos*, and that in general is more widely accepted and understood by Muslims, the impact on mission work in this region would definitely be big.

## Observations

My first observation on IM strategy is that the local cultural context seems to play a direct role in the level of integration an IM has within the local mosque system. For example, in S-Asia region D the cultural context is that there is a high allegiance to a certain mosque system, but also a high scrutiny of everyone within a given system and a pressure to stay with the party line and not show signs of interest in a different strand or mosque system. This being the case, the IM leaders have chosen to form their own strand, but in the form of a Sufi-style para-mosque movement, outside the existing local mosque system. They are still part of the larger Muslim community and participate in community life, but they do not try to "take over" a mosque or transform it from the inside out. This strategy stands in contrast to that of most of the other IMs represented in this study, which seek to be reformers and transformers of their communities and the local mosque systems. The local cultural context for Arnold in Africa is almost the opposite of the highly divisive one in S-Asia region D. In Arnold's community, Christians and Muslims tolerate each other and sometimes even live together. This allows the IM that he is associated with to be fully integrated in the local mosque system, since it seems to be more tolerant of some variation.

The matter of identity is interesting. Some talk about a dual or layered identity, whereas others only have one identity: Muslim. I observe that there is a connection between the identity of insiders and the relationship the IM has with the local church. Personal convictions about "who you are" also play a role, of course, in selecting an identity. In addition, the level of secrecy seems to be directly related to identity as well. For example, in SE Asia there is a reasonably healthy connection between elements of the local church and IM leaders. The latter speak of dual or layered identity, seeing themselves as an extension of or extraction from the church that is uniquely positioned to make an impact for Christ in Muslim communities. They are open, semi-open and cautious, or secretive in their approach, depending on which layer of IM is operating at any given time. In contrast, the IM in S-Asia region D has no connection to the local church, uses a Muslim identity, and is fully open, even practicing open-air baptisms. In S-Asia region B the Muslim identity is seen as God-given, and there is no indication that insiders are moving along the identity scale towards a Christian one. Likewise, Axel in region C has a full Muslim identity, enjoys the prayer style in the mosque, and shows no signs of a dual identity. In contrast, Brad coordinates the church ministry to IM in his area in Africa, which means that there is a close link between the church and this IM, to the point that group baptisms are done in local church buildings. Brad mentioned that they have to be fairly secretive about these events, bringing the insiders into the building one at a time through the back. He also shared that some insiders show an interest in joining the local church. Figure 48 shows the identity scale and secrecy scale and the factors that tend to move the identity and levels of secrecy to the right or the left.

There are, of course, some exceptions to the general alignment of the identity and secrecy scales in Figure 48. Homer in Africa talked about a fully Muslim identity, yet there is strict secrecy about who is baptized, which indicates that baptism is seen in the local context as a Christian event and that the local IM has not been able to contextualize it within a Muslim setting. Also, Andy and Howard in S-Asia region A are critical of the local church and do not seek a connection, which would drive their identity to Muslim and their secrecy to fully open. However, they invite foreign partners to fund their operation and development work, which requires more secrecy. They hold IM training events in rural areas away from the public eye.

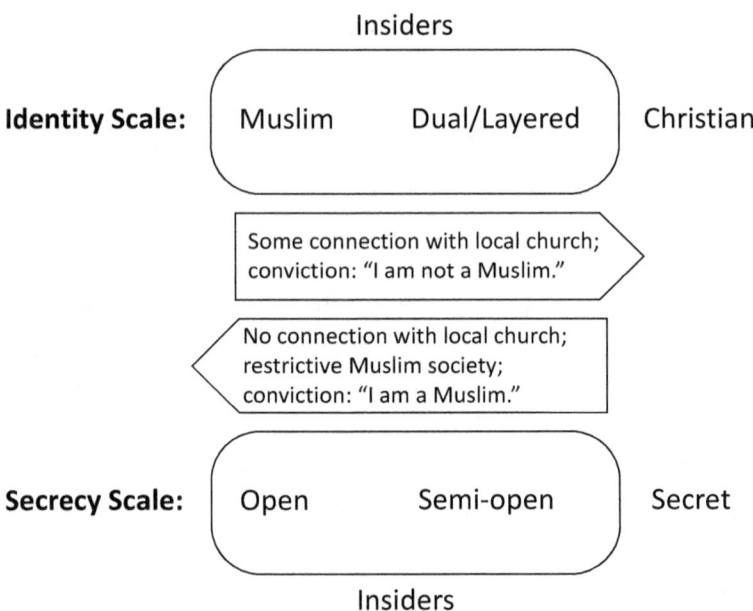

**Figure 48:** Relationship between insider identity and movement secrecy levels, and influencing factors.

My last observation on strategies is that in many cases the *jamaats* in these IMs desperately need a Muslim-idiom Bible translation. Many have one available or are involved in the process of producing one. This seems like such an obvious reality and need, but it is good to confirm from my interviews that this indeed is the case.

## Challenges

IMs face many challenges. Some are internal challenges, but most are externally imposed. My final code set shows a multitude and variety of challenges that IMs face. Since this study focuses on theological and missional understandings of IM leaders, and on the processes by which they arrived at these understandings, I am limiting my analyses of IM challenges to two categories that are closely related to theology: challenges from Islam and challenges from the church.

## From Islam

Muslim insider followers of Isa al Masih face many challenges in their immediate context that often lead to persecution. This research does not focus on persecution within IM, or on the claim by IM critics that insiders avoid persecution by staying on the inside with a Muslim public identity, but interviewees often mentioned the reality of suffering. Maybe it was alongsider Tyler who was the most articulate in addressing this criticism. After sharing about the many deaths that had occurred among the circle of family and friends of the top leaders in their movements, he responded to the common critique of insiders being risk averse with some emotion.

> They [insiders] go to deep levels talking about what the Bible says, praying for each other, applying it. They are far braver, far more ready to suffer than those in a christianized context. That is my experience. How many people have to be killed for us to be seen as brave enough? Let me introduce you to some of the people who are grieving and suffering, and let's see if you are asking that question again. I think if anything, it is the traditional model that is more fearful. They don't even really engage with anyone, and certainly not with Muslims. That is being very risk averse.

In general, some opposition comes from within the Islamic setting and is rooted in the spiritual experiences and convictions of the community members, cultural traditions, and the power and influence of community and religious leaders. From SE Asia, Phil reported that the kind of Islam in his region is not just the Arabian version but is blended with local cultural traditions. Alongsider Tyler added that there are many different blends of Islam in the SE Asia region because of the rich and wide range of culture and folklore among the many language communities in this region. Regardless of the blend of Islam, the expectation is that if the parents are Muslim, the children must be Muslim as well, according to Phil. "There is the assumption that the only true religion is Islam, and there are no alternatives to that," he said.

Monty noted that one of the challenges from Islam related to theology is its low Christology, in that Islam does not teach anything other than a human identity of Christ. He traced this back to the Jewish rejection of the Messiah. "God could not come as a man. And the second thing is that this man who came was not the kind of Messiah they were waiting for," Monty said. He believes that this misconception of the Jews influenced Mohammed, and Monty recognizes these two objections as the biggest obstacles still today when he shares the story of Jesus with a Muslim.

Insiders face the challenge from Islam with the charge of being heretical. They have learned to respond to these challenges by starting from the Qur'an and the Hadith. "We have to remain calm and in prayer while we answer these challenges. We never run from the problem," Monty said. Intimidation and pressure by powerful and influential religious and community leaders are an obstacle to the progress of the movement, according to Kent. He also said that within their honor-shame culture, the striving by leaders to climb the social prestige ladder is a challenge to the progress of the gospel.

From S-Asia region A, Andy and Howard mostly mentioned practical social behavior questions that Islam poses for IM. Can you have multiple wives? What do you do when someone is caught in adultery? Which Sharia are you following? Islam is challenging insiders in daily social behavior, and that would be an interesting research topic by itself, but it is not part of my research. Andy and Howard also mentioned the security threat they are facing from fanatical Islamic groups. "These are very small groups defending Islam against the movement. Sometimes the imam gives them the names [of insiders] and they start working against the ministry of the movement in the village areas," Howard said.

Frank in S-Asia region D mentioned that in general they fit as an IM within the local Islamic setting and continue welcoming others in their midst. They are accepted as just another sect within Islam, even by educated Muslims. He actually finds their identity and teaching more challenging among uneducated Muslims. "They say, 'There are just Allah and Mohammed and nothing else.' That is a difficulty for us," Frank said. He is expecting more problems when the broader society starts to learn more about what they teach about Isa al Masih.

From Africa, Arnold noted that Muslims who have not accepted Isa al Masih as their Lord and Savior pose critical questions to insiders. They use the Qur'an and the teachings from the imam to challenge the beliefs of insiders. "This is a potential external threat to the group, and we need to be aware of that and prepare the people. When I give training to the leaders, I always tell them about that," Arnold said. Oliver reflected on my question about external challenges to IM and concluded that there is suffering because two big religious groups are fighting. He said, "Muslims do not accept us for following Jesus. And the Christians do not want us to remain as a Muslim to follow Jesus. Both are challenges to us." He sees both sides sticking to their traditional teachings and doctrines. Various other IM leaders, including Homer, did not consider Islam to be a major external challenge. "We have done very well, without any opposition from the mosque or from other Muslims. I find them supportive. Whenever we talk to them they say that this is the truth," Homer said.

## From the Church

In many ways the church is posing a bigger challenge to IM than Islam. This challenge appears to be moderate in SE Asia, by and large because of the mediation role alongsiders like Tyler play, and because the local traditional church is simply unaware of the existence of *jamaats* and IMs. Alongsider Josh shared that insiders view Christians as very different from them. There is often an ethnic difference between the groups that is hard to reconcile. Josh explained, "We live in a city of four million people, and a few hundred in some areas are meeting in homes and are reading Bibles. The church is five miles away in the city. They would not know anything about those home meetings." Monty shared that in his setting the separation between the traditional local church and insiders goes beyond ethnic differences. He has not faced major challenges from the traditional church because they have not built relationships with them, and he hopes to keep it that way.

> I feel like they will not be able to understand what we are doing. They have the traditional viewpoint that once a person receives Jesus, this person has to pull out and go to the church. They don't want to receive the idea that a believer can remain in the mosque, or that he keeps the dress code that Muslims use. We hope that they don't know about us, but we consider ourselves having one Lord with them, and one Spirit with them.

Alongsider Tyler noticed that some of the IM leaders who came out of the traditional church were originally seen as the church's poster boys because of their effectiveness among Muslims, but when those IM leaders started baptizing believers themselves and allowed others to do the same, the church heavily criticized those practices. Nevertheless, Tyler said that he and some of these cross-over IM leaders receive invitations left and right from churches to come and train them in outreach among Muslims. The traditional church would still use some of these lessons learned within their own framework, but its leaders are unaware of all the IM details. At least there is some level of interest and tolerance. Tyler quoted one high-level church official as saying that this fledgling movement (i.e., the local IM) needs protection so that they don't get stamped out by the traditional church. Tyler promoted the idea of focusing on the results in the IM discussions, like in Acts 15. We should be asking, "What is God doing?" He questioned the role of outside critics and pointed out the learning opportunities we have as we see God at work.

> I wish they [IM critics] had the starting point of respecting these insiders as brothers, and then realize that they are on a different task than they are. To me there is something that God does in reaching unreached people groups that crystallizes the conversation and can bring about a maturing of the theological discussions.

Howard and Andy from S-Asia region A made it quite clear that their most challenging threats come from the traditional church. They are able to challenge Muslims to become completed Muslims in Christ, but they encounter a firm roadblock when they challenge Christians with their approach to believing in Isa and staying Muslims. "They think that you are riding in two boats. They are looking at it from [the viewpoint of] Christianity and Islam. They are not looking at it by just asking how the Lord Jesus wants us to be saved," Andy said. Both he and Howard are saddened by this treatment from the traditional church. "The Christians are not accepting us as their brothers. They always think about us as half devil, half child; these kinds of threats come from them," Howard shared. They have decided, however, that their ministry is not to convince the traditional church of their approach but to reach their Muslim brothers and sisters.

Mitch from S-Asia region B is keenly aware of the rejection of IM and insiders by the leadership of the traditional churches in his region. Others have investigated and reported atrocities[5] against insiders that church leadership instigated. "Christian leaders openly say that we are not their brothers. They cannot pray for us. We say, 'Okay, you cannot pray, but we can pray for you. We think that you are our brothers,'" Mitch said.

Axel shared some of his bad experiences with Christian brothers. They abandoned him in a time of need and tried to change his vocabulary and the way he dressed. Axel remembered how he was working with some Christians who were working in apologetics, showing how Islam is bad and Christianity is good. "They always needed me to answer their questions. I was not feeling very good in my heart, because I was not reaching Muslims," Axel said.

Alongsider Wilbur reflected on the situation with the traditional church in S-Asia region D. He has observed the church's inactivity in the realm of ministries among Muslims, and as such there has been little direct interference with IM, but he is convinced that if the leaders of the traditional church and even expats were more aware of IM in their region, there would be much more opposition. Wilbur promotes extreme discretion and avoidance when it comes to exposing insiders to the local traditional church.

> I would say that to the extent that those structures [traditional church], expat and national both, knew about people like this [insiders], that their control reflexes would activate immediately and there would be a lot of problems. So I think it is very important for us to be extremely discreet and for those people to be discreet. They have to realize that they can't sort of relate both ways and expect to get away with it. There is an avoidance strategy that I think is very key right now.

Angus shared that he is aware of some criticism by people from a Christian background of certain Muslim-idiom Bible translations. He disagreed with this criticism and pointed out the differences in background between these Christians and insiders, but the commonality in having

---

5. Alleged killings

faith in the same Jesus. "We have translations for them and for us. We don't tell them that they are wrong. We may have different glasses, but the water in it is the same," Angus said. He also expressed fear that atrocities committed against insiders in an adjacent region might spill over to theirs. Frank, who initially was part of the Christian community in the region after coming to faith and before crossing back over to his Muslim context, knows first-hand how Christian pastors are against IM and the idea of insiders having the identity of completed Muslims. He knows that some people see insiders as people on a path that, in appearance, seems like something between Christianity and Islam. "No Christian pastor in this region could accept this, that we consider ourselves completed Muslims," Frank said. Paxton also experiences the opposition from the established church as their main challenge. "They have been brought up in a different way. They think you have to use certain terminology, and we worship only in this way, and therefore if you don't do it, you are not a Christian," Paxton shared.

In Central Asia the circumstances with regard to the traditional church are very different for Julius, Gus, and Jason. Julius was part of that church but crossed over away from it into a Muslim context a few years ago. "Other Christians seem to not really understand what the insider movement is all about, the principles. They often criticize or misunderstand and judge the work," Julius said. He recalled being part of the Christian community in the past. "They had a negative influence on my ability to communicate with my own people, and they actually caused me to dislike the thought patterns, traditions, and practices of my own language group." Julius expressed a desire to see more understanding and tolerance towards IM and a stronger belief in the body of the Messiah as one.

Gus' comment about challenges from the traditional church was short and to the point. He said, "We are not influenced by churches. We don't deal with them." Jason, on the other hand, is on staff with a church and thus deals with it all the time. He said, "The biggest problems are not with unbelievers, unfortunately, but with brothers and sisters in our region who oppose any ministry not done in Western format." Missionaries brought in this format, according to Jason, and the senior national church leaders have been westernized. Jason is trying to transform the ministry into an indigenous one, within a majority Muslim context. He said, "I cannot jump and do whatever. I have to be under the authority of the church leadership."

Jason believes, however, that God called him into this church context to help the leadership see the need for a totally different approach.

As in Central Asia, the church relationship in Africa is unique and different for each of the four interviewed IM leaders. Arnold is trying to keep insiders away from the traditional church as much as possible. "The church has absolutely no clue about what is going on and where these people are," he said. If the church were aware, they would grab all insiders and bring them into the church, cutting their ministry short, according to Arnold. I observe that in this more pluralistic society in which Christians and Muslims live together, the church may actually be able to pull insiders in. This stands in contrast to the societies and circumstances in the other regions, where insiders seem to have no interest in joining a traditional church.

Oliver simply noted that they are facing the challenge that Christians in his region do not want them to remain Muslims and follow Jesus. They want them to join the traditional church and adhere to their teachings and doctrine. Homer shared that in his region the church leaders know of and support the movement, but the church members are completely unaware of it. In Brad's case the situation goes one step further in that he is part of the church staff to support IM in their region. He is part of the church leadership, and members are to some degree aware of the movements that the church supports.

## Observations

It is interesting to see that many IM leaders mention the traditional church as the main challenge to IM and insiders. I use the phrase "traditional church" to allow for the notion that IM and the local *jamaats* are part of the church as well, in an untraditional way. Islam is also an external challenge, and that is understandable, since that is the context in which IM is growing. IM challenges Muslims from within Islam, and as such there will naturally be some friction between traditional Islam and IM. Some face that challenge head-on within the local mosques and boarding schools, like in SE Asia, S-Asia regions A, B, and C, and parts of Central Asia and Africa. Others form parallel Sufi-like sects, as in S-Asia region D, or are somewhat connected to the leadership of the traditional church, as in other parts of Africa. Resistance from the Christian side, however, is less expected and therefore more noteworthy. The literature review shows that voices within Western Christianity critique IM from a distance, but it is worth observing that in many cases the local traditional churches also oppose IM, not from a distance but from within their own region.

The degree to which IM leaders are identifying the local traditional church as an external challenge correlates with their individual paradigms for the Religions frame in the M-Framework, which is an outlier frame, as depicted in Figure 39. Table 45 shows the individual paradigms for the Religions frame, and the comment field gives an indication of the connection between the IM leader and the traditional church, from Table 41.

**Table 45:** Individual religions paradigms

| | | Religions Paradigm | | | | |
|---|---|---|---|---|---|---|
| Name | Region | 1 | 2 | 3 | 4 | Comment |
| Lucas | SE Asia | | x | | | Still connected with church |
| Zach | SE Asia | | | | x | Not connected anymore and critical |
| Ian | SE Asia | | | x | | Never been connected with church |
| Phil | SE Asia | | x | | | Not connected anymore but amicable |
| Monty | SE Asia | | | | x | Not connected anymore and critical |
| Silas | SE Asia | | | | x | Never been connected with church and critical |
| Kent | SE Asia | | | | x | Never been connected with church and critical |
| Stuart | SE Asia | | x | | | Never been connected with church but not critical |
| Ross | SE Asia | | | | x | Not connected anymore and critical |
| Ray | SE Asia | | | | x | Not connected anymore and critical |
| Drew | SE Asia | | | | x | Still connected but critical |
| Andy | S-Asia-A | | | | x | Not connected anymore and critical |
| Howard | S-Asia-A | | | | x | Never been connected with church and critical |
| Mitch | S-Asia-B | | | | x | Still connected but cautious |
| Axel | S-Asia-C | | | | x | Not connected anymore and critical |

| Name | Region | Religions Paradigm 1 | 2 | 3 | 4 | Comment |
|---|---|---|---|---|---|---|
| Angus | S-Asia-D | | | | x | Never been connected with church and critical |
| Frank | S-Asia-D | | | x | | Not connected anymore and cautious |
| Arthur | S-Asia-D | | | x | | Never been connected with church; interfaith focus |
| Paxton | S-Asia-D | | | | x | Still somewhat connected but critical |
| Julius | C-Asia | | | | x | Not connected anymore and critical |
| Gus | C-Asia | | | | x | Not connected anymore and critical |
| Jason | C-Asia | | | | x | Still connected and critical |
| Arnold | Africa | | | | x | Not connected anymore and critical |
| Oliver | Africa | | | | x | Never been connected with church and critical |
| Homer | Africa | | | x | | Still connected and cautious |
| Brad | Africa | | x | | | Still connected and amicable |

There is a connection between the attitude of the traditional church towards IM and the theological and missional views of insiders regarding religions. From the cases represented in the 26 interviews with IM leaders, I conclude that in general cross-over insiders still see members of the traditional churches as their brothers and sisters in Christ, but that the reverse is not true. The traditional church does not recognize IM as an appropriate indigenous expression of following Jesus Christ, and as such, does not recognize insiders as brothers and sisters in Christ. The definition of a paradigm 4 view of religions is that they are irrelevant and sometimes an obstruction to the message of God and to following Jesus Christ. Such a view is undoubtedly the effect of multiple factors, but I surmise that the external challenge the traditional churches pose to IM is one of the major causes of this theological and missional understanding.

# COMMUNAL PROCESSES FOR THEOLOGICAL AND MISSIONAL FRAME DEVELOPMENT

In this last section I review the communal processes for the development of the various theological and missional frames of understanding among IM leaders.

Figure 49 puts this section in the context of the actual frames, which I analyzed in chapter 4, and the IM context within which these processes take place, which I described in the first part of chapter 5.

I first look at the basic or general approach used in IM in the processes towards theological and missional understanding. Next, I present findings on what processes IM leaders use when different understanding starts to develop within an IM. In this part of the interviews IM leaders often mentioned the Trinity as a challenge or a point of difference. I present my analysis of those comments about the Trinity and close with some observation on general challenges in the processes towards the development of the theological and missional frames of IM leaders.

I first look at the basic or general approach used in IM in the processes towards theological and missional understanding. Next, I present findings on what processes IM leaders use when different understanding starts to develop within an IM. In this part of the interviews IM leaders often mentioned the Trinity as a challenge or a point of difference. I present my analysis of those comments about the Trinity and close with some observation on general challenges in the processes towards the development of the theological and missional frames of IM leaders.

## General Approach

The general approach towards theological and missional frames has five elements: *progressive, context-fitted, leadership training, bible-centered application*, and a cluster of other approaches under the heading *other*.

### Progressive

The first general approach in IM towards deeper understanding is *progressive*. Alongsider Melvin talked about using little building blocks that lead to a better understanding of who Jesus is and to a fuller picture of

Insider Movements and the Theologizing Process 277

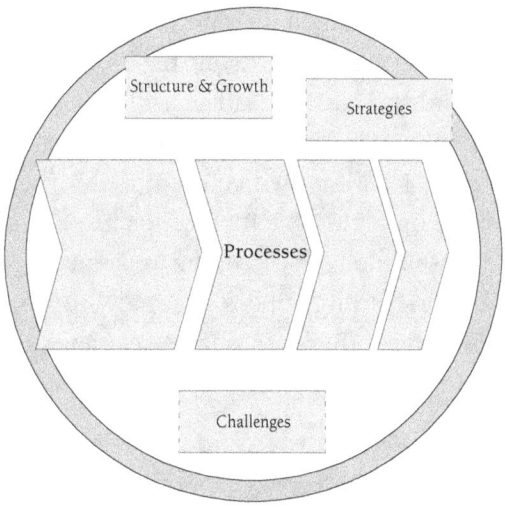

| The theological and missional frames of IM leaders | 1 | 2 | 3 | 4 |
|---|---|---|---|---|
| Allah—Theology | | | | |
| 1. | | | | |
| 2. | | | | |
| 3. | | | | |
| 4. | | | | |
| Allah—*Missio Dei* | | | | |
| 5. | | | | |
| 6. | | | | |
| 7. | | | | |
| 8. | | | | |
| 9. | | | | |
| 10. | | | | |
| 11. | Fundamental | Ecumenical | Integral | Global |
| 12. | | | | |
| 13. | | | | |
| 14. | | | | |
| Isa al Masih—Christology | | | | |
| 15. | | | | |
| 16. | | | | |
| Isa al Masih—*Missio Christi* | | | | |
| 17. | | | | |
| 18. | | | | |
| 19. | | | | |
| 20. | | | | |
| 21. | | | | |

**Figure 49:** Three main aspects of IM as context for the processes that lead to the development of theological and missional frames

the grandeur of God. "His love is so much more encompassing than they ever thought. He is truly the merciful and compassionate," Melvin said.

Mitch mentioned several times that he believes the IM leaders who are coming after him and the current leaders will develop fuller and deeper theological and missional understandings for IM. He is keen on educating the younger generations within their communities. "The second and third generation will come up with some kind of clear understanding. We have to allow time for these kinds of people," he explained.

Progressive understanding applies especially to Christology, according to various IM leaders. Table 46 shows segments of transcripts that promote progressive Christology towards high Christology.

**Table 46:** Progressive Christology

| IM Leader | Direct Quote |
|---|---|
| S-Asia-A\Andy | Many people come from the concept that Jesus is a prophet. We have to give them an introduction from that viewpoint and tell them who Jesus is. And then we let them decide whether Jesus is a prophet or more than a prophet. |
| Africa\Arnold | I remember one of them telling me one day that he had come to understand that Isa al Masih is not just a prophet. He is more than the prophet. And he told me, "You know, I want to tell you, Isa al Masih is God." And I never told him that. And I asked him, "How do you know?" He said, "You just read the book and you just know that you cannot compare Isa al Masih with any human being, so he must be God himself." That was really one of our best days, hearing from someone that you have taught from the beginning, who was really against this, and coming to that understanding. |
| Africa\Arnold | Usually I tell Isa al Masih stories and then they see the works that he did. And because of that, they begin to ask themselves, "He was really great. Who was he?" From there, little by little, I do not rush into getting into his death and sacrifice and all this, but what he did. What should be our response to such a person? We are grateful to him. After they fall in love with him we can go to the next stage, which is the most difficult. Believing in his death as a sacrifice for mankind to be saved is one of the most difficult parts. Once the ground is well prepared in the first part, they love him and trust him, so when we come to the second part, they say, "Why did they kill him?" I always try to show them that they were not the ones, but we are the ones. |

| IM Leader | Direct Quote |
|---|---|
| SE Asia\Monty-2 | When people ask us why we are studying Isa we answer, "One, because Jesus holds the keys to the kingdom of heaven. Two, Jesus is the Judge. Three, Isa will come back again. Four, the name of Isa is what saves us." |
| SE Asia\Lucas | The seven-questions model really brings them into an inductive process to learn from what they are reading. There is a lot of theologizing from the passages that they are reading. They progressively understand the superiority of Jesus. |
| Alongsiders\Josh-2 | If I was getting this in Christian language, I would say they have a simple or primitive Christology. They would see Jesus as Supreme Lord, no question about that. They would see Jesus as worker of all the miracles that he did. The big overarching thing that they see him as is their Savior. In fact, a common thing in the movement that they say is, "Praise God, I now have a Savior!" They see his saving in both this world and the world to come as very important. It helps them in their daily troubles, their financial problems, and their health issues. |
| Alongsiders\Melvin | We have found about 14 little mini-steps to help Muslims understand the divinity of Christ. |
| Alongsiders\Tyler | Mark has some of the lower-level Christology, [Jesus'] powers over Satan and healing and ritual uncleanness, and we have the different stages in the Gospel of Mark that we see the disciples going through as they get to higher levels of embracing who Christ is. One of the highest levels represents these royal scenes. It says that he calls his angels from the four corners of the world, for his people. This is high Christology, an exalted view of Christ as King in the most cosmic sense. In another set of studies we talk about Jesus possessing the unique divine identity of God. That is an inductively derived conclusion, but we don't pop it on people at the beginning. It has to go through these seven phases of Christology. |

Drew had an interesting comment about progressive understanding related to the teachings of Mohammed and Jesus.

> When Christians ask me about what I feel about Mohammed I say, obviously I did not start out being a university student. We all need to go through elementary and secondary school first. I am a university student now and Jesus is my professor, but when I was in elementary school Mohammed was my teacher, yet I don't find any of his teachings contradicting the teachings of Jesus.

> Jesus explains more about what Mohammed is talking about, but they're not contradicting. There's nothing wrong with believing in Mohammed, because it does not affect your salvation. At the same time, there is no obligation for Christians to believe in Mohammed. If you don't want to believe Mohammed, that is okay since you already have Jesus. Yes, there are some Muslims who convert to Christianity and who hate Mohammed, but for me, I want to serve my friends and I want to respect their beliefs, and a central figure of Islam is Mohammed. I don't find that this goes against the teachings of Jesus.

Other elements of the progressive approach, as expressed by IM leaders, are starting with the Qur'an, using the narrative format, pointing out the works of Isa al Masih before presenting Paul, and stressing monotheism from the Old Testament.

### Context-fitted

I labeled another general approach in IM towards understanding *context-fitted*. One of the main aspects of "context-fitted" is that it is indigenous. Mitch from the S-Asia region B is quite keen on indigenous theology and doctrines that are developed locally and without impositions from the outside. "I am totally opposed to importing anything from the outside. I think that taking any book from another country like America and translating it for our leaders will not work," he said. Mitch puts his hopes on the second-generation leaders in the movement to develop Bible-based indigenous theological and missional understandings. He even leaves the decision to retain a Muslim identity to them.

> I am hoping that the second generation will actually clearly define who they are. My responsibility and that of the other leaders—and we have discussed this many times—is to teach our second generation with the Scriptures, without giving them a theology or doctrine. They will discover it. If God wants them to come up with Christianity, they will do it. If God wants them to remain, they will remain. They will have completed master's

degrees, which means they can pick up any Christian book or anything. I don't have to tell them. I will not be upset if the second generation defines theology and doctrine and decides that we don't need to call ourselves Muslims. We can be called something else. I will not be upset, because I am depending totally on God. He will lead them.

Paxton in S-Asia region D also promoted a context-fitted approach. He noted that all the seminaries in this region teach Western Christianity, not biblical Jesus following. "It is about how it was interpreted in the West, and now that has become our model," Paxton said. Referring to the local IM, he added, "This is what is happening: I think people are dissatisfied with the idea that only the West has the right to explain the message of Jesus the way they want to express it."

In SE Asia, Ray said that they are learning from the Bible together without bringing in doctrines from a faraway land. "Usually they read the Bible and discuss one part of it, and they are trying to apply it to their lives. This is building their own theology," Ray said. He questioned anyone's right to judge whether their theology is correct or not. "Even within Christianity there are many different understandings about Jesus and about salvation. There is no one voice within Christianity about the Trinity. Some believe in it and some don't," he noted.

Alongsider Josh has observed that a context-fitted approach includes a non-confrontational way of unlearning and learning, as they openly discuss some of their traditional teachings as Muslims, such as the Bible having been corrupted, Jesus not dying on the cross, and the place of Mohammed and the Qur'an in their overall life of faith. Josh sees IM as a non-confrontational movement. "They reason together sort of like friends, both with the lost and with people in their own movement. They come to some decisions as they go through that," he said. These decisions lead to a rejection, revaluing, or reinterpreting of old truths, according to Josh.

The final aspect of the context-fitted approach is showing respect to all and being bridge builders. Ross challenged himself, as he currently lives in a different culture in order to receive further education, to always see the wonders of God in everyone you meet. "God created them and has been with them, giving them what they need. We must learn from them as God's children," he said. Alongsider Tyler talked about insiders needing a bridge-building heart and peacemaking skills.

> There are almost schisms or earthquakes happening in the land, as they bring Scripture down into the cultural norms. What do you do with violence that is part of fundamentalism? How do you get rid of anger? How do you get rid of bad attitudes of men towards their wives? If the man is the only one being mentored in the Scriptures, what happens to their harmony and how they act together in tandem? We see marital conflicts coming. We find that leaders of the third generation have to be harmonizers. They have to have special peacemaking skills.

Tyler added that because of this context-fitted bridge-building approach, insiders never talk negatively about Mohammed or the Qur'an.

## Leadership Training

The third general approach in IM towards the development of theological and missional frames is *leadership training*. This training is mostly covering how to lead a *jamaat* in discovering new truths rather than passing on doctrinal absolutes. Andy mentioned that part of the content of their training program is based on the felt needs among the people, i.e., on the practical questions insiders are dealing with in their communities. In addition, Andy showed me an outline of their four-year leadership training program that is content specific with a focus on the New Testament. He has a training program for women as well. "In the villages, very few women have a chance to go and learn about Islam. We have created a system for our ladies to come and learn about Isa and then go back and teach all the women in their group," he said.

Alongsider Wilbur in S-Asia region D said that at this point only the leaders in the movement have access to the biblical source text to address and develop indigenous theology proper. Some of them are involved in Scripture translation in the vernacular in order to give more people this ability. Wilbur calls the current "theologizing process" by insiders in the local IM *Scripture-based reflection*.

It is too early, and they don't have the source text. Too few of them have enough of the requisite resources to begin theologizing. It is much more charismatic, it is much more relational, it is much more obedience oriented, it is much more connected to their lives as people who live close to the earth and kind of live hand-to-mouth, and who are very relational and very traditional, very conservative and very oral in their communication approaches. So, what we see is Scripture-based reflection, not theologizing proper, although clearly leaders and those who are coming into it from a much more clerical background are doing that.

Others also mentioned the role of leaders and their training as important aspects of the development of further understanding within the movements. Mitch does inductive Bible studies with the top-level leaders, who in turn do these types of studies in the villages. Arnold uses the same approach. "I gather the leaders from time to time for spiritual nourishment and at the same time also for training, so they are better prepared to help these people in the work," he said.

Several IM leaders in SE Asia mentioned the important role leadership training has for them. They have regular monthly, quarterly, and annual meetings. In general their IM is Scripture-centered and not leader-centered, and their leadership training focuses on mentoring, but Silas noted that there is still an important role for a leader because their culture is hierarchical. The IM he is associated with is organized in clusters. The mentors of cluster leadership provide a measure of checks and balances in the processes. "This person will ensure that this train is on the rails within certain boundaries, and he keeps wrong views from gaining influence," Phil said. The alongsider from this region, Tyler, shared that they recently developed a leader's guide for the study of Mark and Acts, helping them to look inductively at the passages. "We are thinking of those as materials to train leaders on delicate theological issues, especially Christology. This is the first time we start moving in a direction other than them just studying the Bible," Tyler added.

Melvin shared his thoughts and observations about theologizing and the role of IM leaders in these processes. Melvin is the alongsider for Africa for this research but has connections outside Africa as well. He organizes annual leader gatherings.

> This is the sixth year that I tried to bring together as many as we could afford of the national leaders, and there is this growing consensus that we need to study more and more. In the beginning it was just sharing about each other's ministry. They don't want to do that anymore. They want to theologize. They want to study the Scriptures; how can we explain these things better. When this insider work started it was mostly on transformational forms. At the beginning I don't think anyone saw themselves as reformulating theological thoughts. I think that as they go deeper into the community, we will see more of this. They are still struggling with the cross. What is it? This is a big area that is emerging. It is not so much anymore about ecclesiology, but it is Christology now.

## Bible-centered Application

The fourth general approach towards the development of theological and missional frames is being both Bible- and application-focused. All IM leaders that I interviewed view the Bible as central to their movements and to theological and missional understanding, but they also see direct local application and action as foundational. Table 47 is a mere sample of the many statements made by these leaders on the centrality of the Bible.

**Table 47:** Bible-centered

| IM Leader | Direct Quote |
|---|---|
| SE Asia\Phil | One of our innovations is that this system is centered on the Bible rather than on the teacher. There is a tendency in the Muslim context to center everything on the authority of the teacher. |
| SE Asia\Phil | The small groups are not influenced by the outside. Their real focus is the passage that they are reading. There is no real contact even represented by someone else from a foreign group or from a local traditional church. |

| IM Leader | Direct Quote |
|---|---|
| SE Asia\Monty-2 | The most important thing about the way people express their perceptions is that it has to be anchored in the Word of God. They have freedom in the way they express it, but it has to be anchored in the Word. They always have to keep returning to Jesus as the best teacher and mentor. |
| SE Asia\Zach | We always emphasize and say, let's go back and see what the Scriptures are saying. Our objective is not to defend our own convictions and private interpretations. Let's go back to the Scriptures and ask, what is it that Jesus did? What is it that the followers of Jesus did? |
| SE Asia\Ray | One thing to watch for is that we stay in the Word. |
| Alongsiders\Josh-2 | They are very committed to obeying the Word, and the process that we have seen take place is this: when they encounter something in the Bible that is contrary to Islam, they take the Bible over it. |
| Alongsiders\Kevin | We were pretty intentional in trying to develop a process for theologizing using the Scriptures. It was rooted in Hiebert's critical contextualization steps. |

The focus on the local application of the Bible was especially apparent from the comments from the SE Asia region. For example, Phil said, "We empower all the players to take action individually." Lucas mentioned, "We cannot make truth, we can only follow truth." Silas talks about doing what he reads. "I begin every day with the reading of the Word, and then I seek to understand, and then I seek to do what I read. I always pray so that God will give me capacity to do what I understand." Kent was even more to the point when he said, "The Word of God is not just to be read and memorized, but it must be done." Maybe Zach gave a good summary for all of them when he talked about local application and results.

> Let's look at the results of what happened after seeing what Jesus and his followers were doing. So we ask, "If we just sit here and debate the Bible, where is this going?" Instead the focus is, "What should we do according to the Bible? And then after we do and put into application, what is the result of that?" This helps people to realize that the key thing is to put into practice what they are hearing from the Bible.

Bible study in IM happens by and large in community, in a *jamaat* or another gathering of friends. Zach mentioned that this is a very relational process. "No one sits in a room by themselves, discreetly reading the Bible alone." Josh described it as a group hermeneutical process. Brad in Africa also mentioned this communal process and the need to stop at times and pray for the Spirit's guidance when a group process is stuck. Paxton from S-Asia region D noted, "If you are doing certain things on an individual basis, then you do not know what the other fellow is doing. He might have hit upon something which may take you ages to learn." Monty shared what kind of theological and missional topics they discuss in community.

> We discuss these kinds of matters quite frequently, such as God's purposes for his creation, how Jesus is related to God, etc. People need to know that God is the Creator and the Giver, and they need to know what has been given. They need to know why God has given us life. What must we give back to God? Our lives must become the joy of God. Our lives are our perfect sacrifice. We give our lives as a living sacrifice. We cannot make this a secondary topic, but we need to keep talking about it.

Stuart mentioned how they exchange opinions among each other and listen for the ones that gain the most support as they are discussing some problem or spiritual issue. "In the middle of such a discussion, more and more people are gathering and trying to understand the matter, especially if what is being talked about is salvation," he added.

With regard to the Bible-centered approach, IM is known for its promotion of the inductive study method, and my research data confirms this. Mitch mentioned that the inductive Bible study method is the only method they use. Arnold also uses this method. "We dig deep and let them discover by themselves," he said. Tyler prefers the inductive approach because it grabs smaller chunks at a time. He thinks that in cross-cultural work outsiders have the most room for error and difficulty when they use the deductive approach of systematic theology. Zach brings up an interesting benefit of the inductive approach: it levels the playing field for everyone and unifies people around the Bible.

> The unifying factor for all these variances [of Islam] is that when they start to open up the Word of God, they are all beginners. One of the things that helps is if they have this feeling of foolishness as they start, because prior to that they had a sense of pride about what their camp believes in and how well they could express it. They come in as religious people, so they have their lingo and agenda. But if we set the table with, "Let's go to the Word of God and see what it says," we enter on the same page as people that don't know anything yet. That helps.

## *Various*

There are various other general approaches to advance theological and missional understanding that some but not most interviewees mentioned, yet they are worth noting. One is a focus on the first-century church. Zach ties this focus together with being Bible-centered and with looking at what Jesus was doing. "What is it that the followers of Jesus did? What did the people in the first-century church do?" he said. Alongsider Wilbur shared how the IM leaders want to go back to a pre-Constantine expression of faith in Jesus Christ. They want to be part of something less traditional in the sense of what they see in the Western and national church bodies. The New Testament provides them with testimony from that first century. Wilbur added, "If that is what we confine ourselves to, then we won't be doing things like encouraging Easter celebrations and Christmas celebrations on a Roman calendar. There is no basis for that." Alongsider Melvin also mentioned that for us to better understand the first-century followers of the Way within their Judaic experience will be extremely beneficial to an Islamic context. Paxton is the strongest on this point on the first century and links it directly to IM.

> This insider movement actually is about finding first-century Christianity. How did those believers express themselves? They expressed themselves differently in different places, and they used different forms to express their faith.

Another approach that fits in the "various" category is the use of topical materials. For example, in the SE Asia region the IM leaders developed a booklet on baptism for *jamaat* leaders as a discipling tool. They designed this booklet for the more conservative qur'anic segment of the population, as it uses key Arabic terms for main concepts like baptism, which they phrase as "the dipping of God" in the context of surrendering to God. The booklet presents the various baptisms in the New Testament, starting with the baptism of Isa al Masih, and gives details of the actual baptism ceremony. The final question asked of someone who is about to be baptized is, "Do you truly put your faith in Isa al Masih as the divinely exalted one and Savior?" The baptism formula in the standard booklet is, "In the name of the Father, Son, and Spirit, who are one." Alongsider Tyler commented, "These are Arabic terms that not too many people understand, which sanctifies it. The innovation is adding the phrase, 'who are one.'" There is a version of the booklet that presents a slightly different baptism formula. It reads, "In the name of the honored Father, the honored Word of Allah, and the Spirit of Allah, who is very holy." Tyler explained, "We have a limited use for this version. This is one of the rare pieces where we have done some innovation. This booklet was designed for the more fundamentalist people."

Brad in the Africa region also mentioned a pre-baptism product that they are using in their IM with new believers. He called it a manual that has verses from the Qur'an and the Bible, and they use it in the initial pre-baptism discipleship phase. "When they have reached the level of baptism, they have gone through it and understand very well the basic pillars of our faith. After that, they study the Bible," Brad explained.

Lucas and Zach mentioned their use of a topical book series on topics such as fasting and the oneness of God. "People are reading those themselves, and then we discuss them in the *jamaats*," Zach said.

The topic of honor-shame was brought up by two interviewees. Alongsider Melvin believes that once insiders can explain the atonement theory in an honor-shame paradigm, the gospel will go viral within the Islamic people groups. Alongsider Tyler mentioned that he has observed that small discussion groups among IM leaders are reinterpreting the issue of honor. "I feel a significant part of an insider movement is working on reinterpreting honor such that heaven's court is the primary court of appraisal of what is honorable," he said.

The questionnaire for this research was a topical product that some mentioned as being a helpful tool. Tyler said, "This is a good barometer to help diagnose where people are theologically. One of the questions for me is how uniform we are." In general the interviewees found the questions thought provoking and helpful. Andy said, "You are asking us some very deep questions—very simple, but very deep." Howard added, "A common follower of Jesus would not understand your questions and could not answer you very well." Along similar lines, Lucas said at the end of our conversation, "In December I passed my doctoral comprehensive exams, and I feel I just passed another comprehensive exam."

Another general approach from the "various" category is the important role personal experiences play in the development of theological and missional understanding. In my conversion with Monty he talked about the communal process of theologizing, but he said that in the end every individual has the freedom to express their theological perceptions. I asked whether the theologizing process in his IM is more individualistic than communal. Monty linked the process of theologizing directly to personal experience with God.

> The way we theologize has to be primarily individualistic, because what I mean with theologizing is what we experience with God. In our theologizing our objective is not just to know about God, because when will that study ever end? Rather, our objective of theologizing is to know God from an experiential sense. This moves the locus of this activity back to the individual. Our brain cannot fully grasp who God is, because he is the Creator of our brains. This living theologizing is about how we experience God in a more reflective way. This is living theology.

Alongsider Tyler also has observed in the many testimonies he has heard that personal experiences with God are essential to the formation of theological and missional understanding. He said, "The epistemology among these people must include true experiential encounters of a mystical intuitive nature." This especially applies to Christology, according to Tyler. He has seen that simpler people move more quickly up the levels of Christology when they actually experience Jesus' touch in various ways.

"At that point they surrender everything, get involved deeply, and risk even their lives for Isa," Tyler said.

## Processing Differences

One of the questions that I asked in the interviews was, "How are different theological and missional views processed?" I was interested in hearing about the processes but also about their attitude towards differences. Is it acceptable to have different views within a group or movement, or do the IM leaders value unity in theological and missional understanding?

My first observation is that several IM leaders needed a clarification for the question. When I repeated the question and gave an example of two different possible views on a specific topic, they replied by expressing their views on this specific topic.

The opinion I heard the most on having different theological and missional views was that this is completely acceptable and tolerated. Table 48 gives a sample of statements in support of tolerance towards different views within an IM or *jamaat*.

**Table 48:** Different viewpoints are acceptable

| IM Leader | Direct Quote |
|---|---|
| S-Asia-A\Andy | I think that we cannot control people, but as a minimum if they have some misunderstandings, we can help them. But basically, God allows people to come to him, to save them. We are not trying to have everyone be the same. |
| C-Asia\Julius | If a movement grows, which I hope, I think that it is important that everyone within a *jamaat* has a basic understanding of who Allah is, and the importance of Isa al Masih as the true path, but as leaders mature, it is important that as long as beliefs are centered on the holy books, particularly the early books, that there can be differences of theological development. That is not a problem. But it is important that we have something in common as a basic understanding of who Allah is, and the importance of Isa al Masih, to unite us. |
| C-Asia\Gus | There are no restrictions. We want people to think. If some split off, so be it. We are not a controlling community. |

| IM Leader | Direct Quote |
|---|---|
| Africa\Homer | We do not force anything but let the Holy Spirit be at work. He will convince them one day. Even for me, I had many questions in the beginning, but finally they were settled by the Holy Spirit. We give them time. We fellowship together and do other things together. |
| S-Asia-D\Frank | When two people have two different theological viewpoints, that is no problem to me. |
| S-Asia-D\Paxton | I believe in unity and diversity. Different people can express their faith in different manners. |
| SE Asia\Monty-2 | The fruit of their reflective meditation and thoughts will have differences. We are not demanding or expecting that everyone will come up with the same outcome. |
| SE Asia\Ray | Within one group there are different understandings, and that is okay. |
| SE Asia\Silas | We have to protect tolerance. We have to protect religious tolerance, yet we need to use the opportunity that emerges to open the veil, to open up the religious presence or the holy presence of Jesus. |
| SE Asia\Phil | We have the basic principle that we need to respect other people even if they have differences. We don't necessarily judge other people as wrong. We might have to confess that they have different opinions, but it is not certain whether they are wrong. |
| SE Asia\Kent | We respect and value differences, because everything we do is associated with rewards. So, we may have differences, but those who are walking in the way of truth must continue on the way of truth. |
| Alongsiders\Josh-2 | My guess is that they are okay with a lot of ambiguity, or a lot of uncertainty, so long as it is really clear that Jesus is our Savior. After that, they can have lots of different viewpoints and opinions, and it would be okay. |
| Alongsiders\Melvin | I think that they are influenced more by an Islamic way of thought. As long as you have five practices and five pillars, you can have a wide variance of thought within Islam. That probably affects them to a greater or lesser degree. |

Ray gave me a lengthy answer to my question about different theological and missional views within a *jamaat*. He basically framed my question as a typical Christian one and an irrelevant one for IM.

> This is not a big issue in insider movements, because they are mostly uneducated and humble. They discuss things and have their own understanding. That's okay.

> That's no problem. We can still meet together and read the Bible together every week. In this sense this is different than in Christianity. There, if someone has a different opinion even on one verse, the church can be divided. I've never seen this as a big problem. Only an outsider will see this as a big problem. With outsiders I mean Christians here. They will try to make them like Christians. They say, "If they are not like us, this is a big problem." Among insiders, what is the problem? We don't have that problem about theology. The problem is always seen by the outsider. We don't have denominations like Christians. We have freedom to choose everything what we understand.

Alongsider Wilbur pointed out that there are different views but that they all fall in the category of secondary or disputable matters, such as fast observance, attending the mosque, signed gifts, and the taking of a second wife. Ray included in this category the *salat* (prayers), and the use of the *shahada* (Islamic confession of faith). In Mitch's IM the method of baptism is a discussion point, and Homer knows of one group that does not do baptisms. Their reasoning according to Homer is, "We follow the Scriptures, but because the prophet Mohammed also followed all previous Scriptures, but he was not baptized, we don't believe in baptism either."

Phil laid out the process he uses when there is a difference of views. Basically they show respect to all, listen to all, and ask the Spirit of God to guide them forward.

> When there is a difference, the first step in the process is really listening and trying to understand and value, in the sense of respecting, the person's point of view and conveying that respect. We let that be a challenge for us and go home and meditate on the difference that was brought out and pray and ask the Spirit of God to really lead to an illumination of God about that.

Even though there seems to be a general tolerance for different viewpoints, some interviewees expressed that they are seeking unity on a few basics. Table 49 lists what those basics are, according to several IM leaders.

**Table 49:** Unity on basic beliefs

| IM Leader | Direct Quote |
|---|---|
| C-Asia\Julius | I think that it is important that everyone within a *jamaat* has a basic understanding of who Allah is, and the importance of Isa al Masih as the true path. |
| S-Asia-D\Angus | The main things from the Scriptures, such as about Jesus, are one thing, but there are different ways of explaining it. For example, among the believers some come from a Sufi background and some come from a Wahhabi background. They look differently at the outward forms, but the main core of their belief is one. |
| S-Asia-D\Frank | The main thing is that someone understands why they are getting baptized before we do it. If someone understands it within one day or within six months, that is fine. |
| SE Asia\Phil | There are some basic truths that we don't budge on. One is that man has a propensity to sin. Second, there is a promise of a way of salvation. And third, Jesus is the one that has been promised as the sacrifice and solution for this condition as a working out of the promises of God. We have a lot of unity on these three major things. |
| SE Asia\Ray | He is the only way to God. There is no compromise with that. Is there another way? Some say, "Yes, the Torah," but then you have to keep the Torah, but who can keep it? That's why Allah finally sent Isa. |
| SE Asia\Silas | We try not to sharpen the debate, but we look for some common ground. If there is a difference, we try to find a bridge over it to find a solution together. |
| Alongsiders\Melvin | I do feel that there are some core issues that are shared across all of them. These are the core beliefs. One is the Bible. I see that to be key, that the Bible is authoritative and the ultimate authority over the Qur'an. Some use the Qur'an to a greater or lesser degree. Then, salvation in Christ alone is another core belief. Those are the two biggies. |

In addition to holding to some basic truths, there is an indication that in some regions the processes that address different theological and missional views is controlled by the IM leaders and that a level of tolerance for a variety of views only extends to seekers and pre-followers of Isa al Masih. Alongsider Wilbur shared that he has noticed a lot of patience towards people who are in process, but that there is very much a mood that there is a correct interpretation and that anything else is a false interpretation. He commented that people in S-Asia region D don't believe that there is a plurality of correct interpretations of anything. "I think it would be very disturbing to people if they knew, say, the extreme variety that is held within our faith communities in a Western setting," he added. Wilbur mentioned that in this oral society, speculation and inquiry is almost unheard of. He said that the IM leaders with whom he is most closely associated work hard to mitigate there being multiple Christologies in their movement, or multiple canons. He clarified that in his view evangelical Protestants, Catholics, the Orthodox, and everyone in between share the same Christology. In general, people are not asking many theological questions, and questions about God are disrespectful, according to Wilbur. "The majority is satisfied that they are happy and grateful, because they are saved by Isa al Masih," he said.

Arnold from the Africa region also mentioned the important role of the spiritual leader who defines the theological and missional views of the group. He mentioned that these leaders receive much respect and maintain the peace.

> The Muslim community has learned how to live in community and how to respect the spiritual leader's word. I have not experienced or even seen any tension within a group about how we believe or how things should be. I have not yet seen that. I have not experienced that. The leader maintains the peace, and other people also help him maintain the peace. In this society everyone knows who their superiors are and they respect them.

I observe that in some regions the processing of different theological and missional views, and even the development of correct understanding, is more controlled by IM leaders than in other regions. In S-Asia region D, Angus and Frank are controlling this process with input from Wilbur. In S-Asia region A, both Andy and Howard use a four-year leadership training program that they developed to instruct new leaders in theological and missional understandings. Brad shared how IM leaders in his area in Africa use a manual developed by the church to make sure everyone who gets baptized adheres to the tenets of the faith as defined in this manual. These IM leaders all hold to paradigm 1 and 2 views of the M-Framework, whereas those who support tolerance for a variety of views come from the full spectrum of the four paradigms. The regions in which IM leaders intentionally create an environment of indigenous self-theologizing are SE Asia, S-Asia regions B and C, Central Asia, and parts of Africa. These are initial observations. Further research could substantiate, alter, or develop these findings.

## The Trinity

The use of the doctrine of the Trinity to describe God is not common among IM leaders. Even though the vast majority of these leaders affirm that Jesus is divine, only a handful of them support the use of Trinitarian language or doctrine to describe or define God. One who does support it is Andy from the S-Asia region, who mentioned that some people in his movement do not believe in the Trinity. He said, "Then we do not consider them as a believer. We don't want to control them, because we are not extremist Muslims: 'Follow us or be killed.' We allow it, and it's up to them." This implies that Andy allows non-Trinitarians in the *jamaats* but they do not regard them as true believers.

Jason in Central Asia mentioned that the question of the Trinity is challenging even for Christians, but he believes that it is clearly presented in the New Testament. He concluded, "We see it very clearly in the New Testament. There is a close relationship between Allah and Isa, as in a father and son."

The third IM leader who mentioned the Trinity in a positive light was Frank in S-Asia region D. When I asked what he would consider the main attributes of God, he answered, "The first thing is the Trinity, which is like the three pillars on which our whole faith is built."

Besides Andy, Jason, and Frank, all others had some reservations or strong objections regarding the doctrine of the Trinity. Some pointed out that the unity or oneness of God is too much out of focus in this doctrine. From among the alongsiders, Josh observed that the attempts Christians have made to describe that oneness sound to most people more like polytheism. Alongsider Kevin likewise pointed out the oneness of God as primary.

> I am very comfortable talking about God as Father, Son, and Spirit, or Father and Word and Spirit, but I am more and more realizing that the fundamental reality is the unity. The way I was brought up as a Christian and was discipled tended to emphasize the three, and then try to make sense of the unity of the story, and I have probably come to the opposite, which is that I tend to emphasize

the one, and then try to figure out how to talk about the Spirit, and Father, and Son and Word. In fact, ultimately, this is a unity primarily and fundamentally one. Out of that, how do I make sense of these three terms?

Alongsider Tyler also emphasized the oneness of God and sees Isa as the one sharing unique divine roles that belong only to God, without changing his oneness. He pointed out that the IM leaders added the phrase "who are one" at the end of the baptism formula in a booklet they share in several movements in SE Asia.

Arthur believes that when the Qur'an says, "Do not say three," it is referring to those Muslims who interpreted Christianity as a religion with three gods, and by implication maybe some Christians at that time who had slipped into expressions and beliefs of polytheism. Arthur reiterated, "If some Christians say that they worship three different gods, I will take my hands off from them. I will be away from them, because that is really polytheism." He added that if Christian brothers say that they believe in one Almighty God and that the Trinitarian expression is their philosophy and their language to talk about different attributes and aspects of one God, then he believes them and agrees with them. He is convinced, however, that within Islam today the Trinity is seen as polytheism and as such makes Christianity irreconcilable with Islam. His main point and message was that the Qur'an itself refutes today's Muslims when it says, "Do not say three."

Ross rejected the idea that God can be counted as being one, three, eight, or ninety-nine. To him our efforts to count God are an indication of our desire to manage and control God. In addition, he does not like the ranking that comes when we count God as anything more than one. "If we say God is one, it means that Jesus is lower than God. It means that in being sent by God he is lower than the sending Father," Ross said. He dismisses this interpretation and promotes the idea of God being *first* as opposed to one. He clarified by saying, "Jesus does not say that God is one. If he says God is one, that means that he is not God. Jesus only says God is first. 'If you believe that God is first, you respect me.'"

Both Arthur and Ross pointed out that the Trinity is a philosophy that was formulated to bring various parties together on how to understand Jesus Christ. "The First Council of Nicaea decided that since the people were differentiated about the entity of the Lord Jesus Christ, to frame this belief in these words," Arthur said. He sees it as a philosophical statement. "How in the world can you use a philosophical answer to explain to a layman who doesn't even know a complete ABC? You cannot do it. You cannot explain it to him. It is philosophy!" Arthur exclaimed. He reiterated his belief that the attributes of God as addressed in the Trinitarian formula are not God's creation but are God himself.

Ross expressed frustration with those who have joined the traditional Christian church in his community and who now are coming and teaching him about church doctrine like the Trinity.

> For example, Jesus is God. We do not read that in the Bible, but suddenly they teach us that Jesus is God. When you say that Jesus is God, do you tell us about doctrine or not? This is a Christian doctrine. But we are still learning. To learn from people that want me to accept the Trinity and Christian doctrine, to me is difficult. They tell me everything about God as if they know God. They don't want me to read the Bible. They preach to me. It is very difficult.

Ross explained that this difficulty is because he is comparing what people are saying with what they are doing. He wants to see proof in their lives first. "And you say that Jesus is God only by mouth, but you are still stingy, you are still full of worry, you complain about many things, yet you believe that Jesus is God. So it is only a doctrine," he concluded.

Paxton in S-Asia region D admitted that indigenous theologizing is a necessity but that it has not happened much in his region. He is looking forward to the day that more people engage in that process, but added, "When we come to it, we will never use the term 'Trinity.'" Paxton considers this a philosophical term that was invented later to describe an unlimited God who has not revealed that part about himself. "We know only the thing which he has revealed. It does not go beyond that. We can talk about it until doomsday, but we will never come to any conclusion whatsoever," Paxton said. He used an interesting analogy between simple and complex oneness. First, talking about simple oneness, he said, "If you have a stone and you break it into two pieces, then you have two stones." Moving on to more complex oneness, he illustrated, "But if you cut a human being into two pieces, you don't have two human beings." He concluded that the more complex the unity is, the more difficult it is to divide it. "God is complex and therefore cannot be divided," Paxton explained.

Ray believes that the doctrine of the Trinity is not based on the Bible. He believes in the special functions of each of the three Persons in the Trinity. Ray sees Allah, who is called Father by Isa, as the Creator and Provider and as the one who owns heaven and earth. Ray looks at Isa, who is called Son of God and Son of Man, as the Savior and the Messiah. And third, Ray understands the Holy Spirit as our guide and the one who gives us comfort and joy. "What their relationships are ontologically, I do not understand. To say that Isa is the same as Allah, of course I cannot say that," he said. I observe that Ray makes a functional distinction between Isa and Allah, while he refuses to speculate on any possible ontological distinction or unity between them.

Both Axel and Julius find the doctrine of the Trinity incomprehensible and unhelpful. Axel referred to Allah's revelation through other prophets and believes that Isa does not support the notion of three beings. "The [doctrine of the] Trinity says that we believe in one God but there are three. How can that be? I have tried to understand the Trinity, but I cannot," Axel said. Julius was more to the point and said, "I don't believe in the Christian explanation of the Trinity." He finds it a confusing concept and concluded, "Understanding Allah is a mystery. I would not use this explanation or method to teach others."

Wilbur, the alongsider of Frank who called the Trinity the three pillars of their faith, is much more cautious about using the Trinitarian expressions in that context. He is hoping for more meaningful descriptions of how the Godhead has revealed itself in the Scriptures and steers away from so-called divinely sanctioned references to triangles. He was clearly referring to the Trinitarian formula. Wilbur is looking for context-fitted expressions and would be concerned with the wholesale borrowing from Western traditions.

> If I heard Jesus Christ referred to as the Second Person of the Trinity, I would have a great cause for concern, because that would mean that there is an alignment happening with something that is very alien to their own setting, and everything else will likely follow, to their own great detriment. That numbering is meaningful within a world

and a context that is very alien to them. I would rather see them developing all sorts of new language and illustrations to help them meaningfully get their minds around a difficult topic than just sort of wholesale borrowing those that have appeared in the Western tradition.

I close this section on the Trinity by making the observation that alongsiders Tyler and Melvin both referred to writings by Richard Bauckham as very helpful. Melvin specifically noted Bauckham's book published in 1999, titled *God Crucified: Monotheism and Christology in the New Testament*. The thrust of their comments was that God seems to reveal himself in relational terms, as he relates to his creation, and not in ontological terms. "The articulation of the Trinity is in a sense ontological Christology," Melvin said, and then added, "But God does not reveal himself to us outside of creation." We can only know God in terms of relations, which is a Semitic but also a Muslim way of asking and answering questions about who God is, according to Melvin.

## Challenges

I identified general challenges to the movements, such as from Islam and the traditional church, but I also was interested in the specific challenges IM leaders experience in the communal processes towards the development of theological and missional understandings.

Ray and Stuart mentioned folk Islam and animism as a challenge in the attempt to move toward a biblical rather than syncretistic understanding. Ray stressed staying in the Word and said, "In my region, going to a fortune-teller or shaman is acceptable, but we do not want to create syncretism—i.e., believe in Isa and still go to the fortune-teller." Stuart, who is from the same region, identified the fairytales that have been passed on from generation to generation as an obstacle. "People believe in the strengths of objects and in the power of animals, or in the power in big trees," he said. He finds that local people are not brave enough to leave their non-biblical traditions, which have controlled their lives, and their fears. "These fears are great hindrances to the progress of the gospel," Stuart lamented.

Monty expressed an often-heard challenge—that within Islam the Word of God cannot be made the object of debate. Rather, it should be meditated upon. "This means that we do not want these discussions to emerge as a debate. It cannot be debated, but we do have discussions in groups among believers," Monty said. This indicates that the processes towards deeper understanding through inquiry and discussion are sensitive and only happen in restricted groupings.

Four IM leaders shared that the wide range of education levels in the *jamaats* challenges the way they process together towards deeper understandings. Phil mentioned that these different levels of education make it hard to keep moving together. He has also noted that someone with more education may feel smarter than the leader of a *jamaat*, which can upset its power structure. "I am addressing this by saying that it is not most important who is the smartest, but who is applying the Scriptures in their lives and who is bringing about an impact," Phil said. To him the degree to which someone applies the Scriptures in their lives determines their *intelligence* and their right to have influence in a *jamaat*.

Lucas mentioned the range of education levels as a challenge as well. "There are people with great understanding, and people with little understanding. There is a lot of variety, and that makes it challenging," he said. Zach also identified education levels as well as social status levels as factors influencing their processes towards understanding.

Ray noted that the term "theology" has different meanings within Christianity and Islam, and that Islam has less of a systematic approach to understanding God. "For Muslims this is complicated, especially for uneducated Muslims," he said. All they need to know is who God is and who Isa is, and that's all. They don't have to systematize all these things, according to Ray. I observe that Ray is indicating a lack of interest and ability among less educated insiders to develop deeper theological and missional understandings.

The so-called theologizing process in IM is slow. Arnold mentioned that very few ask deeper questions about theology. Asking questions about God is disrespectful to most. "They just learn how to obey and how to follow God joyfully, and they do what he wants people to do without entering into theological questions," Arnold said.

Mitch in S-Asia region B is part of a large movement that was one of the first of its kind, but even he sees things moving slowly when it comes to theology. "Their theology and their thinking are not fully established yet. It is not formulated. We cannot say fully or strongly, 'This is it.' We are not in that situation yet," Mitch shared. He quickly added that he believes that theologizing keeps going and going and should never be established and stagnate.

One last observation I made about the slowness of the processes towards the development of theological and missional frames came from me asking Paxton about emergent theology. I consider Paxton one of the most well-read IM leaders I interviewed, with the possible exception of Arthur. Paxton had not heard of emergent theology and said that it is difficult for him to get access to the vast amount of literature in the West. However, he had heard and read about the New Perspective on Paul, which authors such as N. T. Wright and James Dunn have introduced in more recent times. I equate those perspectives mostly with paradigm 3 in the M-Framework, whereas emergent theology has connections to paradigm 4. These types of new or renewed theological and missional understandings are increasingly developing in the West, and I expect those conversations to enter more into the IM world as well, albeit at a slower pace.

## Overall Assessment

In this second half of chapter 5, I introduced the topic of the processes towards the development of theological and missional frames in the context of IM and the actually M-Framework. Figure 50 depicts the actual main processes that emerged from the analysis.

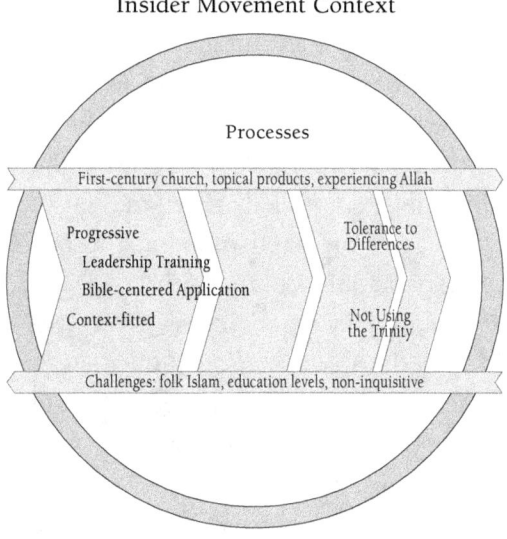

**Figure 50:** The main processes that lead to the development of theological and missional frames

Progressive development of understanding happens from generation to generation, as described by Mitch, and especially applies to Christology, bringing people from a low to a high Christology. This corresponds to the finding in chapter 4 that most IM leaders adhere to a paradigm 2 Christology, which the M-Framework defines as "Process from a low Christology to the goal of high Christology." An overall progressive process towards deeper understanding does not, of course, rule out adherence to wholistic Christology as seen in paradigms 3 and 4.

The context-fitted approach includes the preference for indigenous theology, a non-confrontational way of unlearning and learning, showing respect to all, and being bridge builders and peacemakers.

Leadership training or mentoring is clearly part of developing deeper understandings in all movements represented in this research. My assessment is that such processes are most developed in the SE Asia region, with regular face-to-face mentoring sessions. The training program in S-Asia region A is the most controlled in that it has a four-year program that appears to have an element of specific theology teaching, as seen by Howard and Andy. I label the leadership training program in S-Asia region B the most indigenous, with Mitch protecting the movement from outside influence and completely relying on the second generation to develop the proper theologies. The theologizing in S-Asia region D only happens by a few top IM leaders such as Angus and Frank, and the alongsider Wilbur protects them from reckless freethinkers like Paxton and Arthur. I consider this IM to be the most top-heavy when it comes to developing deeper understanding through leadership training. Lastly, the IM in Africa that Brad is involved in is quite controlled as well in their theological development by the provision of a pre-baptism manual from the leadership that teaches insiders "the basic pillars of the faith."

The Bible-centered application process shows the centrality of the Scriptures in IM and the insistence on immediate application of new understanding in their daily lives. This process includes IM's preference for inductive versus deductive learning. Another aspect worth noting is that this Bible-centered application process is a communal process.

Beyond these four general processes, the research data also show various other processes that were not mentioned by most interviewees but still seem worth noting. They include a focus on the first century, i.e., on how Jesus and his followers in the first century expressed their faith and acted. This process bypasses almost two thousand years of church history, including the church councils and the Reformation, and therefore gets criticism from the traditional churches. I observe that this focus on the first century by some IM leaders would be an outlier in the M-Framework if it were one of the frames, since it aligns with paradigms 3 and 4, while most IM leaders hold to paradigm 1 and 2 views. Two other processes that fit in the "various" category are the use of topical products such as a baptism booklet, and the importance of a personal, intuitive, or almost mystical experience with God before deeper levels of theological and missional understanding can come about. This is not a comfortable notion among people with a Western rational and modern mindset, but the research data includes this process as important. This finding corresponds with other research that indicates how personal visions and dreams play a significant role among Muslims in their coming to Christ.

Regarding the acceptance and processing of different theological and missional views within one IM or *jamaat*, the general approach seems to be one of tolerance and acceptance. I noted, however, that in some regions the IM leadership controls a development towards the correct interpretation and views, as defined by the leadership.

Discussions about the Trinity brought out interesting viewpoints. With the exception of three IM leaders, all others find no use for this doctrine in their IM. I interpret this as the discomfort most Muslim insiders feel in venturing into the realm of God's essence and being. Their understanding and expressions of faith stay at the functional and relational level, which does not have room for the doctrine of the Trinity. I found Arthur's view from the Qur'an on this topic quite interesting, since the Qur'an refutes polytheism rather than a philosophical Trinitarian formula for one Almighty God.

Researching the challenges to the communal theologizing processes revealed a few additional points. Folk Islam and animism appear to be strong and hinder progress in some regions. The notion that holy Scripture can only be meditated upon and not studied is another hurdle. Related to this, any systematization of theology is foreign to most Muslims. Interestingly, different levels of education can hinder progress within some *jamaats*. In addition, a general lack of inquisitiveness about theology proper, out of respect for Allah, and the lack of access to resources on emerging topics has made the theologizing process in IM a slow process to date.

# CHAPTER SIX
## CONCLUSIONS AND RECOMMENDATIONS

In conclusion and in summary, what is the general IM context, and within that context, what are the communal processes towards theological and missional understandings? And to return to the research question, what are the resulting theological and missional frames of IM leaders? The sections below answer those questions and give summary clarifications.

## GENERAL IM CONTEXT

The general IM context and daily life has a missional foundation, because the drive of each movement is the desire of followers of Jesus to reach out to and make an impact in their own community, in an authentic and indigenous way. Insiders take their faith very seriously, which means that they seek to understand and express it in the same context-fitted way as all other important experiences in their lives.

*Jamaats*, or small fellowships, are the foundational IM structure, but they operate within the existing community macro structures and social networks, which is why IMs can grow fast. The engine behind this growth is a transformed life actively engaged in community life through social action. *Jamaat* clusters form naturally in regions, and a *jamaat* leader may connect to leaders from other *jamaats* in the same cluster and to the cluster leader, but in the local setting there is no broad awareness of or connection to the whole movement. A cluster leader connects further up to a regional coordinator and to nearby cluster leaders. In general, the layered connections between leaders in an IM form a venue for communication, sharing, mentoring, and training within a movement.

The basic identity of a Muslim insider Christ follower is Muslim. Some take this as their God-given identity, while others use closely related terms such as "completed Muslim," "pro-Christ Muslim," "a Muslim who follows Jesus," "Messiah Muslim," "believer in Isa al Masih," or a term that means "a person of the straight path." The phrase "Muslim-background believer" is not in use. The level of secrecy or openness insiders apply depends on the general context. In a conservative, legally restrictive Islamic setting the movement tends to be open, combined with a Muslim identity or variant thereof, with no connection to the local traditional church and no visible connection to foreigners. In a general context where there is some connection with a local traditional church, insiders use a layered set of identities, and IM operations are open or semi-secretive depending on the activity.

Having access to Muslim-idiom Bible translations is vital for a movement. Many of the IM leaders who I interviewed are involved in translation projects, because suitable context-fitted Bible products are lacking in their communities. Scripture memorization is one of the IM strategies. Monty called it "the living gospel without walls."

The leaders see IM as a reform movement within Islam, back to previous books and Isa al Masih. Most insiders and even leaders from the second generation down are unaware of a Christian connection. Use of the Qur'an and mosque attendance is normal, and insiders seek to be socially active, meeting real needs in their communities.

IMs face some challenges from Islam, sometimes in the realm of social traditional behavior, but at times also at the level of theology and Christology. Insiders remain intentionally in their local Islamic context, and they are ready to face and meet these challenges. This requires huge personal investments by them to develop and maintain the ability to operate as Christ followers in an Islamic environment. It also requires a high tolerance for risk. Suffering and tragedy are normal realities for insiders, and especially for IM leaders.

The established church is the biggest external challenge to IM. Voices in the global church and in the local traditional churches speak out against IM. They do not consider insiders to be brothers and sisters in Christ, and they reject IM based on their ecclesiology and missiology. In many cases, the local traditional church is completely unaware of these movements happening in their area. There is a correlation between the attitude of the traditional church to IM and the theological and missional views of insiders regarding religions. The more outspoken the local traditional church is against IM, the more the theological and missional views of IM leaders move towards paradigm 4, which considers religions irrelevant or an obstacle to following Isa al Masih.

## COMMUNAL PROCESSES

The processes towards arriving at theological and missional understanding have various characteristics. They are *progressive* in that understanding deepens from generation to generation, as more biblical resources in Muslim idiom become available. "Progressive" also relates to Christology when insiders start seeing Isa al Masih as more than a prophet. Another characteristic of these processes is being *context-fitted*, which promotes non-confrontational indigenous theologizing. *Leadership training and mentoring* are also crucial aspects of the processes towards the development of theological and missional understanding. The fourth characteristic is *Bible-centered application*. Various additional characteristics include a focus on the first century, the use of topical products, and the recognized importance of a personal experience with God.

IM leaders generally accept and tolerate a range of theological and missional views within the movement, but there are indications of direct control by some IM leaders towards the adoption of the *correct* interpretation. These IM leaders adhere to paradigm 1 and 2 views. Most IM leaders are choosing not to use the doctrine of the Trinity, which they see as Western philosophy. Challenges to the theologizing processes, which are communal, are bondages to folk Islam practices; different levels of education within a *jamaat*; and the general attitude by Muslims towards Allah, which is to simply submit and refrain from further inquiry.

## THE THEOLOGICAL AND MISSIONAL FRAMES OF IM LEADERS

Responses by IM leaders to questions such as, "What are Allah's plans and purposes for creation and all of mankind?" brought up topics like the Fall, broken relationships, Satan, this world, the cross, the gospel, and our mandate. Additional questions from the interview guide on Christology, the concepts of heaven and hell, religions, election, the resurrection, the Bible, the Qur'an, and the future (eschatology) complete the list of 21 frames, or topics, in the M-Framework. The IM leader's answers and comments covered a range of views that led to the definition of four distinct paradigms within the M-Framework: Fundamental, Ecumenical,

Integral, and Global. The set of 21 plots in one of those paradigms in the M-Framework for an IM leader represents his theological and missional understandings on these 21 topics.

I used Western and Christian labels for the frames and paradigms in order to communicate meaningfully to a global Christian audience, but it should be understood that these IM leaders did not use words like "ecumenical," "ahistorical," "conciliar," and "integral." The interviewees by and large used Muslim idioms that I interpreted, translated, and contextualized in a framework with Christian idioms in order to make the views of insiders accessible to the global church. My premise is that language and idiom are very important for accuracy and comprehension, and therefore I used Christian idioms for the purpose of accessibility to the global church. Even so, there is always room for misinterpretation. For example, the word "Christian" needs to be understood in context. For some, the word refers to any person who identifies himself with the religion called Christianity. Others more narrowly define a "Christian" as a "true believer" who adheres to their own set of beliefs within Christianity. For others still, the word "Christian" very broadly refers to anyone who follows the teachings of Jesus. Similarly, the word "church" has a range of meanings. Does it refer to only those whose identity is Christian, or to all who follow Jesus? I tried to ensure that the context in this book for each instance of the word "church" or "Christian"—or "Christianity" for that matter—communicates the intended meaning.

One of the building blocks of someone's theological and missional understandings is the view on what God is like. Almost all IM leaders made no distinction between the Allah of the Qur'an and the God of the Bible. They see Allah as the Creator and as merciful. IM leaders also answered the question of what Allah is like indirectly when they shared their views on Allah's plans and purposes, including notions of heaven and hell, and on the identity and role of Isa al Masih and the cross. These indirect answers to what Allah is like correspond directly to several frames in the M-Framework. I incorporated and integrated all frames within a certain paradigm to define the first frame, which describes the essence of Allah, or what he is like. Table 50 shows the summary description of the frame Essence, under Allah—Theology.

**Table 50:** What is Allah like?

| 1–Fundamental | 2–Ecumenical | 3–Integral | 4–Global |
|---|---|---|---|
| Truth; just but also loving; judgment | Teacher; loving but also just; judgment | Merciful; loving, guiding, and correcting; seeking righteousness and justice | Love; enabling, guiding, and correcting; seeking righteousness and justice |

Most IM leaders adhere to paradigm 1 and 2 views that correspond to the Islamic view of Allah's coming judgment followed by paradise or hell.

There is a general affinity among the IM leaders to the notions of obedience, application in daily life, and personal responsibility for one's actions. They talk about *the way* and about *being on the right path* as an expression of faith in action. This affinity also comes out in their views on election. All IM leaders said that man has a free will and choice to submit to Allah and follow Isa al Masih. This view, combined with an overall paradigm 1 or 2 conviction, translates into an Arminian rather than a Calvinistic view on election. Paradigms 3 and 4 represent a different view on election all together.

Most IM leaders refer to Isa al Masih as the Word of God rather than as the Son of God. In S-Asia region D the insiders use the honorific "his peace be upon us" for Isa, as opposed to the regular "peace be upon him," to indicate Isa's exalted status and the fact that he is still alive. All but one IM leader consider the phrase *Son of God* a challenge in their context and a metaphor or figure of speech for a special relationship that remains a mystery. To some, the phrase is widely misunderstood and an offense to Allah, and to others it is an obstacle towards accepting the divinity of Jesus.

The individual and summary plots in the M-Framework for each of the 26 IM leaders shows that 19 fall within paradigms 1 and 2 (Fundamental and Ecumenical), which is camp A. These two paradigms represent basic evangelical viewpoints. Seven IM leaders adhere to paradigms 3 and 4 (Integral and Global), also called camp B. The views in camp B focus on the kingdom of God on earth, new perspectives on Paul, liberation theology, and the emergent church. The M-Framework defines each of the 21 frames and four paradigms in more detail. The finding that most

IM leaders adhere to paradigms 1 and 2 is significant because, based on the literature review, those who speak out against IM also fall in paradigms 1 and 2. This new insight and awareness should temper theology-based criticism of IM and insiders.

The M-Framework is a helpful tool. Each interviewee favored one or two paradigms, with the occasional outlier frame in a different paradigm. This shows that the M-Framework has a workable structure that allows for the effective plotting of someone's basic theological and missional frames, or views. I consider all four paradigms in the M-Framework part of the historic orthodoxy of the church, meaning that each paradigm has been part of the teachings of the church. I personally favor paradigm 4, as mentioned in the Introduction. Paradigm 3 and 4 views (camp B) are fundamentally different from camp A (paradigms 1 and 2), per their definitions in the M-Framework. I consider camp B to be truer to the teachings of Jesus, and I see those views mostly reflected in the early church and in today's emergent church.

The summary plots by region show some clustering, but in general the spread across the four paradigms is similar in all regions, and as such, theological and missional understanding does not seem to be region-dependent.

There are two outlier frames: Religions and The Qur'an. Each IM leader fits in a higher paradigm for these two frames compared to their summary plot. Most hold paradigm 3 and 4 views on religions and the Qur'an, which means that they respect the Qur'an and believe that it holds truths from God. Regarding religions, many IM leaders view them as irrelevant and often as a hindrance to faithfully following Isa al Masih. This is a significant finding in that the role of religions (specifically Christianity and Islam) and the view on the status of the Qur'an are two of the main topics in the IM debate. If opponents and proponents of IM could see the various opinions on those two topics in terms more relative to the local IM context, rather than as representative for someone's overall theological and missional paradigm, the dialogue could improve and continue in a healthy way.

Another main topic in the IM debate is Christology. This research shows that most IM leaders prefer and hold to a high Christology. There are four IM leaders that ascribe to paradigm 4 views on Christology, which highlight the humanity of Christ while embracing a wholistic Christology.

These four IM leaders shared that they do not believe that Isa al Masih is Allah. Further analysis of their transcript shows that they only express the identity of Isa al Masih at the functional level. They are uncomfortable putting any definition to the mystery of the ontology of Allah. They call Isa the Word of God, the Spirit of God, and the mercy of God, which they see as coeternal with God. The summary plots for these four IM leaders are divided between camps A and B, which makes the Christology frame something of an outlier as well. I conclude that the views of these four IM leaders fit within the M-Framework and historic orthodoxy.

The context characteristics of the IM leaders, such as their religious background, education, and connection to the traditional church, and the size of the associated movement, have no specific influence on their theological and missional understandings.

## ADDITIONAL OBSERVATIONS

The theological and missional views of the five expatriate alongsiders form a set of secondary and supplementary data to this emic research, but it is worthwhile to note any correlation with IM leaders and a possible influence of alongsiders on IM leaders. The spread of theological and missional views among the five alongsiders across the four paradigms is almost the same as among the IM leaders, but in general the alongsiders hold to a higher paradigm than the IM leaders. Three of them fall in camp B, one is borderline camp A, and one is solidly in camp A (Fundamental and Ecumenical). The dynamic between the alongsider and the IM leaders is region dependent. The alongsider who lives, or who has recently lived, in the region has more influence on the IM leaders than those who come alongside from a distance.

In S-Asia region D, alongsider Wilbur has paradigm 1 and 2 views, together with two of the IM leaders. Wilbur protects these two leaders from "reckless theologizing" by two other IM leaders in this region who adhere to paradigm 3 and 4 views. This is an example of direct alongsider influence. On the other hand, alongsider Kevin in S-Asia region A does not live in the region and holds paradigm 3 and 4 views, while the two IM leaders in this region have paradigm 1 and 2 views, the opposite of Kevin's. This is an example of minimal direct influence or interference by an alongsider.

The other three alongsiders fall closer to, but by and large to the right of, the IM leaders whom they associate with, as they give support, coordinate resources, and provide mentoring services.

Kevin is the alongsider whose summary plot falls the furthest to the right, between paradigms 3 and 4. Kevin is a published author of many articles in support of IM in various mission journals. It is important to note that while I respect, support, and on the whole agree with Kevin's theological and missional views, they are not representative of the views of the 26 IM leaders whom I interviewed. This research helps the readership of Kevin's articles to put his comments in the context of his theological and missional views and to appreciate them for what they are, while avoiding the assumption that he is the representative spokesperson for IM and insiders.

I consider the picture this research shows of the theological and missional frames of IM leaders to be very healthy. There is a range of views among both the IM leaders and the alongsiders, which can create helpful dialogue and further exploration. The assumption by some IM critics that per their convictions all insiders are heretics, as they allegedly all hold to emerging theology, is not true. At the same time, there are some voices within IM that hold to paradigm 3 and 4 views, which I perceive as healthy, biblical, and constructive. The IM environment allows for the kind of theological and missional creativity, exploration, and indigenous discovery and development that in the past has brought the church forward. My hope is that this environment of freedom and learning will continue and will not be stifled by internal or external control, or by the natural tendency of any movement to settle down, to define the parameters and to stop progress.

IM has mostly been about forms for the local fellowships. The C-scale is an example of that focus as Christ-centered communities take form in a Muslim context. There are indications that IM leaders are ready to shift from ecclesiology to theology, as they consider afresh various atonement theories, non-atonement views, and Christology from and for their context. I encourage them to consider the M-Framework or some derivative as a tool in this new and emerging chapter in IM. The M-Framework can be used as a tool that promotes broad-based exploration and awareness of multiple paradigms. This creates opportunity for learning and development of various Christ-following expressions and an array of deep theological and missional understandings. I encourage the IM leaders who have access to an increasing amount of useful resources in their context to become aware of this range of possible theological and missional viewpoints, including paradigms 3 and 4, and to consider the benefits of these views for themselves and their communities, and of course for the sake of the kingdom of God. I encourage alongsiders to broaden their views as well. It may very well be that God is using IM and its unique environment to bring about new understandings of him that will in turn be a lesson for the global body of Christ. May we have the grace and humility, and indeed the excitement and anticipation, to see this happen.

I have great respect for each of the 26 IM leaders whom I interviewed. I consider them brothers in Christ who take their faith very seriously. They have honorable motivations and make incredible investments and sacrifices to honor God, share Christ, follow the Lord, and expand his kingdom in their communities. I thank them for teaching me.

## RECOMMENDATIONS FOR FUTURE RESEARCH

This study looked at the theological and missional frames of IM leaders in multiple regions. Future research could focus on just one region and go deeper into the various generations of one IM. I also recommend the following research topics:

- How do IMs start? There are indications that some movements have started out of Muslim Christ followers' negative experiences in a Christian context.
- What are the challenges IM faces from Islam and the church? This research shows some aspects of these challenges. Further research can expand on those and provide additional insights.
- How do context variables such as religious education and the degree of connectedness to the traditional church affect the theological and missional frames of insiders? This research has 26 data points and shows no obvious correlation, but further research with more data points may reveal otherwise.

- Which theological and missional paradigms control or restrict indigenous theologizing? There is an indication in this research that paradigms 1 and 2 possibly have this tendency, but further research would have to substantiate or correct that notion.
- How are the theological and missional frames of IM leaders expressed in the local idiom? I translated the views of IM leaders into church idiom and categories, for global accessibility, but how would these views be formulated without limiting the terminology to the range in use in today's church language?

# REFERENCES

AoG World Missions. (2012). *The necessity for retaining father and son terminology in Scripture translations for Muslims*. Retrieved from Assemblies of God: http://www.fatherson.ag.org/

Bradt, K. M. (1997). *Story as a way of knowing*. Kansas City, KS: Sheed & Ward.

Brown, R. (2005). Part 1: Explaining the biblical term 'Son(s) of God' in Muslim context. *International Journal of Frontier Missiology, 22*(3), 91.

Brown, R. (2006). Contextualization without syncretism. *International Journal of Frontier Missiology, 23*(3), 127.

Brown, R. (2007). Biblical Muslims: Insider movements: The conversation continues. *International Journal of Frontier Missiology, 24*(2), 65.

Brown, R., Gray, L., & Gray, A. (2011). A new look at translating familial biblical terms. *International Journal of Frontier Missiology, 28*(3), 105–120.

Carson, D. (2012). *Jesus the Son of God: A Christological title often overlooked, sometimes misunderstood, and currently disputed*. Nottingham, UK: Inter-Varsity Press.

Chandler, P.-G. (2007). *Pilgrims of Christ on the Muslim road: Exploring a new path between two faiths*. Plymouth, UK: Rowman & Littlefield.

Charmaz, K. (2006). *Constructing grounded theory: A practical guide through qualitative analysis*. London, UK: Sage Publications.

Coleman, D. (2011). *A theological analysis of the insider movement paradigm from four perspectives: theology of religions, revelation, soteriology and ecclesiology*. Pasadena, CA: WCIU Press.

Creswell, J. W. (2009). *Research design: Qualitative, quantitative, and mixed methods approaches*. Thousand Oaks, CA: SAGE Publications.

Daniels, G. (2013). Worshiping Jesus in the Mosque: What it's like to follow Christ embedded in Muslim culture. An interview with a Muslim follower of Isa. *Christianity Today, 57*(1), 23–27.

Greer, B. (2011). Book review, A theological analysis of the insider movement, by Doug Coleman. *International Journal of Frontier Missions, 28*(4), 204–209.

Greer, B. (2012, April). Revisiting "Son of God" in translation: Reading Acts, Luke, and Matthew in historical and biblical context. *St. Francis Magazine, 8*(2), 188–212.

Hansen, C. (2011, February). The son and the crescent: Bible translations that avoid the phrase 'Son of God' are bearing dramatic fruit among Muslims. But that translation has some missionaries and scholars dismayed. *Christianity Today, 55*(2), 18–23.

Higgins, K. (2009, August). Inside what?: Church, culture, religion and insider movements in biblical perspective. *St. Francis Magazine, 5*(4), 74–91.

Lausanne Theological Working Group. (2010). *The whole church taking the whole gospel to the whole world.* Retrieved September 9, 2011 from Lausanne Movement: http://www.lausanne.org/en/documents/all/twg/1177-twg-three-wholes.html

Lewis, R. (2007). Promoting movements to Christ within natural communities. *International Journal of Frontier Missiology, 24*(2), 75–76.

Lewis, R. (2009). Insider movements: Honoring God-given identity and community. *International Journal of Frontier Missiology, 26*(1), 16–19.

Lingel, J. (2010, October 11). *Recap of "The insider movement conference: A critical assessment II".* Retrieved December 12, 2010, from Biblical Missiology: http://biblicalmissiology.org/2010/10/11/recap-of-the-insider-movement-conference-a-critical-assessment-ii-2010/

Lingel, J., Morton, J., & Nikides, B. (2011). *Chrislam: How missionaries are promoting an islamized gospel.* Garden Grove, CA: i2 Ministries Publishing.

McDermott, G. (2011, April). Evangelicals divided: The battle between meliorists and traditionalists to define evangelicalism. *First Things.* Retrieved February 16, 2012, from http://www.firstthings.com/article/2011/03/evangelicals-divided

Nikides, B. (2009). A response to Kevin Higgins' 'Inside what? church, culture, religion and insider movements in biblical perspective'. *St. Francis Magazine, 5*(4), 92–113.

Olson, R. E. (2011, March 23). *My letter to First Things (responding to the McDermott article)*. Retrieved February 17, 2012 from Roger E. Olson: My evangelical Arminian theological musings. http://www.patheos.com/blogs/rogereolson/2011/03/my-letter-to-first-things-responding-to-the-mcdermott-article/

Olson, R. E. (2011, March 24). *The New Fundamentalism*. Retrieved February 17, 2012, from Roger E. Olson, My evangelical Arminian theological musings: http://www.patheos.com/blogs/rogereolson/2011/03/the-new-fundamentalism/

Parshall, P. (1998). Danger!: New directions in contextualization. *Evangelical Missions Quarterly, 34*(4), 404–410.

Parshall, P. (2013). How much Muslim context is too much for the gospel? *Christianity Today, 57*(1), 31.

PCA General Assembly. (2012, May 14). *A call to faithful witness: Part one, like father, like son*. Retrieved from Bible Research: http://bible-researcher.com/pca.mit.report1.pdf

Piper, H., & Taylor, J. (2007). *The supremacy of Christ in a postmodern world*. Wheaton, IL: Crossway Books.

Richard, H. L. (2009). Unpacking the insider paradigm: An open discussion on points of diversity. *International Journal of Frontier Missiology, 26*(4), 175–180.

Sanneh, L. (2003). *Whose religion is Christianity?: The Gospel beyond the West*. Cambridge, UK: William B. Eerdmans Publishing Company.

Seale, C. (1999). *The quality of qualitative research*. Thousand Oaks, CA: Sage Publications.

Seidman, I. (1998). *Interviewing as qualitative research: A guide for researchers in education and the social sciences*. New York, NY: Teachers College Press.

SIL International. (2012, April 30). *SIL International Statement of Best Practices for Bible Translation of Divine Familial Terms*. Retrieved from SIL International: http://www.sil.org/sites/default/files/files/divine_familial_terms_commentary_full.pdf

Strauss, A., & Corbin, J. (1998). *Basics of qualitative research: Techniques and procedures for developing grounded theory*. Thousand Oaks, CA: Sage Publications.

Tennent, T. C. (2013). The hidden histiory of insider movements: For generations, Islam and Hinduism have had believers. *Christianity Today*, 57(1), 28–29.

Travis, J. (1998, October). The C1 to C6 spectrum. *Evangelical Missions Quarterly*, 34(4), 407–408. Retrieved September 23, 2010 from http://www.emqonline.com/emq/issue-230/2488

Travis, J. (2013). Why evangelicals should be thankful for Muslim insiders: Insider followers of Jesus may not have changed religions, but their lives have been changed by Christ. *Christianity Today*, 57(1), 30.

WEA. (2013, May 19). *Final report of the WEA independent Bible translation review panel*. Retrieved from World Evangelical Alliance: http://www.worldevangelicals.org/resources/view.htm?id=697

Weiss, R. S. (1994). *Learning from strangers: The art and method of qualitative interview studies*. New York, NY: The Free Press.

# APPENDIX A
## *Interview Guide*

The interview guide is a set of open-ended questions that served as reference points during the interviews. I developed this guide with the research question and sub-questions in mind and tailored the wording to accommodate the Muslim context and mindset of the interviewees. The interviews were guided conversations, and all of them were unique, but the guide helped focus the conversation and data collection.

## THE FINAL INTERVIEW GUIDE

1. How do Muslim insider leaders understand Allah and his plans and purposes?

   How would you describe what Allah is like? What are his main characteristics?

   What are Allah's plans and purposes for his creation and mankind?

   Some say that Allah's plans and purposes are to establish and restore all of his creation to what it should be. The focus is on this world, people, societies, nature, etc. The focus is on the salvation of the world. Others say that Allah's plans and purposes are to save people away from this world for heaven. He gave up on this world and is saving people away from it. Is Allah about populating heaven or about saving all of his creation? What are your views on this?

   How would you describe Allah's interest in righteous or healthy cultures and societies?

   How are Allah's purposes affected by your behavior in this present world?

How does your understanding of heaven and hell fit within the bigger picture of Allah's plans and purposes?

How does an individual's freedom of choice relate to Allah's plans and purposes for that individual?

How does Allah reveal himself through the prophets?

How would you describe the status of the Scriptures?

Are the Scriptures a rule book or God's narrative story, or something else?

What status do you give to the Qur'an and how do you use it?

How does Allah reveal himself to you in this life today?

How do religions (Christianity and Islam) relate to your understanding of Allah and his purposes, and to your relationship with Isa al Masih?

2. How do Muslim insider leaders understand Isa al Masih and his role and identity?

How would you summarize the actions of Isa al Masih?

What does the message that Isa is al Masih mean?

Why did Isa al Masih suffer and die, and who ultimately made him suffer and die?

How is Isa al Masih's death and resurrection good news?

What is the relationship between Isa al Masih and Allah?

How do you understand the term "Son of God"?

How do you experience your relationship with Isa al Masih?

How does your relationship with Isa al Masih affect your relationship with others?

3. How do Muslim insider study the Tawrat, Zabur, and Injil and apply insights gained within IM?

What is the structure of the movement and its leadership?

How does belief in Isa al Masih spread within a community?

How does this belief move from one community to another?

How careful or secretive do you have to be about Isa al Masih?

How do they study the Tawrat, Zabur, and Injil? How often and in what setting?

In which format do they access the Tawrat, Zabur, and Injil?

4. How do IM leaders develop theological and missional frames within their communal context?

How do new insights or enlightenment in theology and missiology come about?

How are different theological and missional views processed?

How is progress in theological and missional understanding made and communicated?

What are the challenges with the IM theologizing process?

How is this process challenged by external factors?

How do you address these challenges?

# APPENDIX B
## Summary M-Framework Plots by Context Variable

This appendix depicts the summary M-Framework plots of IM leaders by the following context variables:
1. Christian background (Figure 51)
2. Never been connected to a traditional church (Figure 52)
3. Still connected to a traditional church (Figure 53)
4. Christian religious education (Figure 54)
5. Only Christian religious education (Figure 55)
6. Islamic religious education (Figure 56)
7. Both Christian and Islamic religious education (Figure 57)
8. No formal religious education (Figure 58)
9. Part of a movement < 100 (Figure 59)
10. Part of a movement between 100 and 1,000 (Figure 60)
11. Part of a movement > 1,000 (Figure 61)

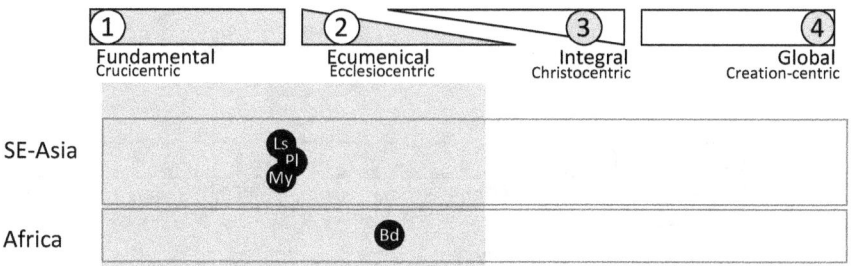

**Figure 51:** IM leaders with Christian background

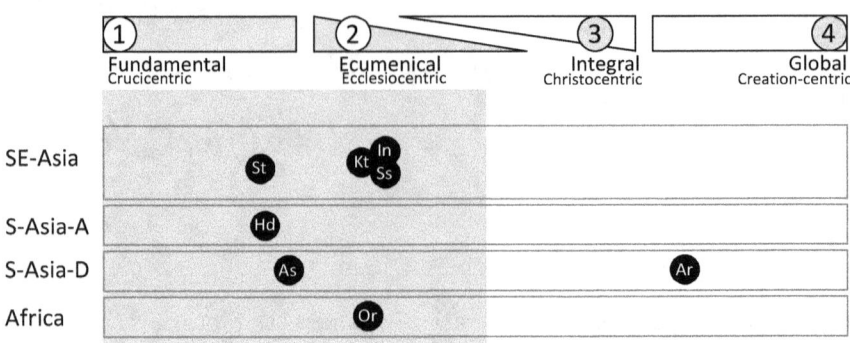

**Figure 52:** IM leaders who never connected with a traditional church

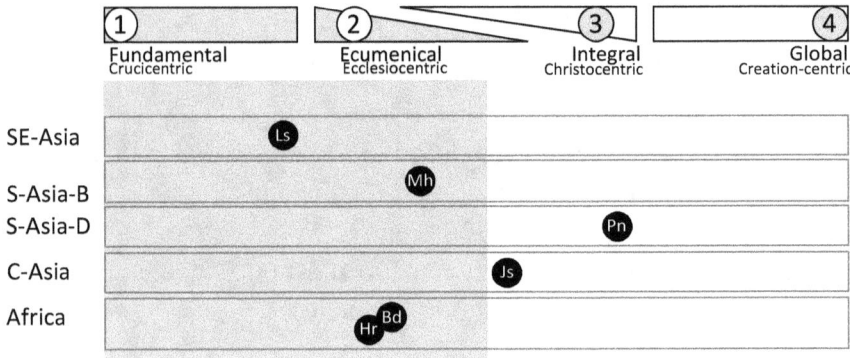

**Figure 53:** IM leaders still connected with a traditional church

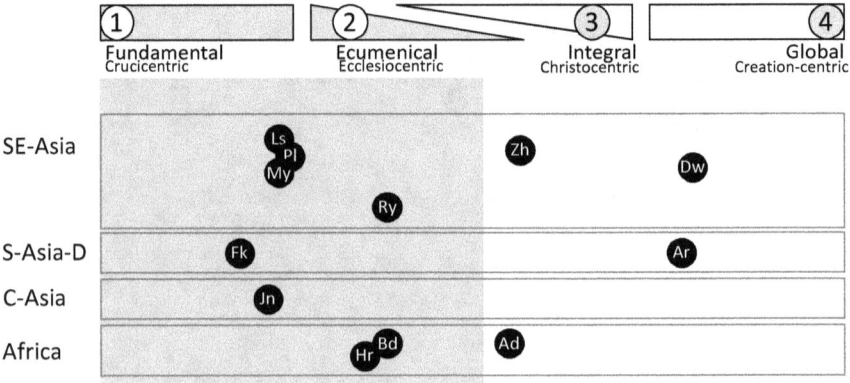

**Figure 54:** IM leaders with Christian religious education

Appendix B 325

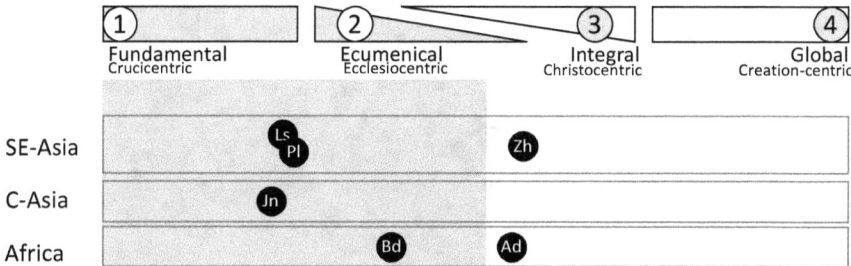

**Figure 55:** IM leaders with only Christian religious education

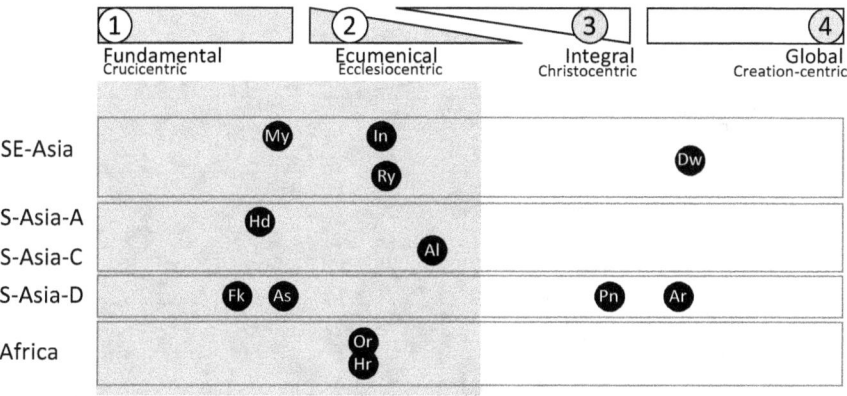

**Figure 56:** IM leaders with Islamic religious education

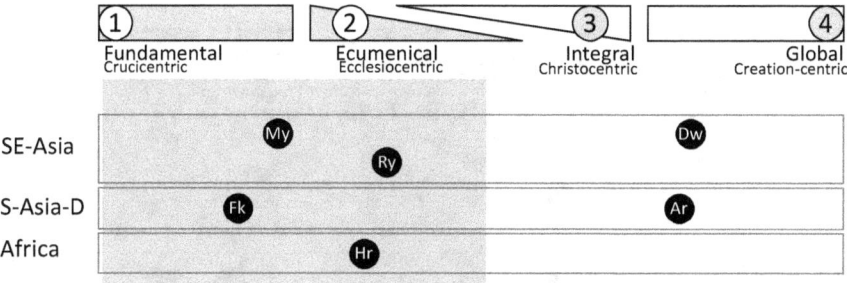

**Figure 57:** IM leaders with both Christian and Islamic religious education

326  Appendix B

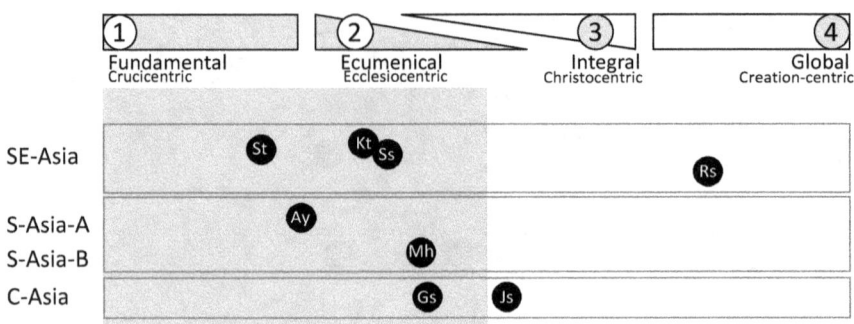

**Figure 58:** IM leaders without formal religious education

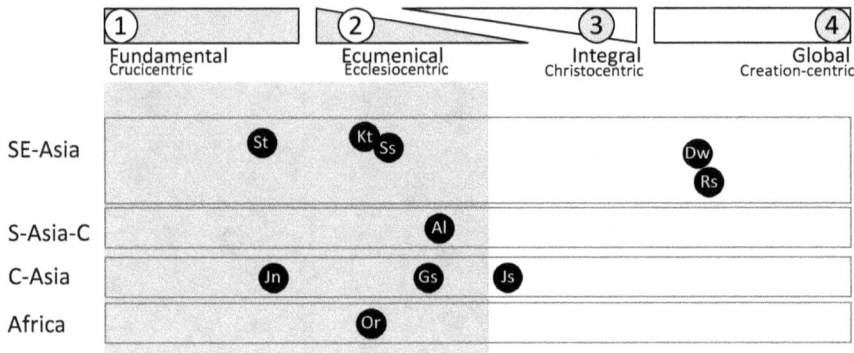

**Figure 59:** IM leaders in a movement < 100

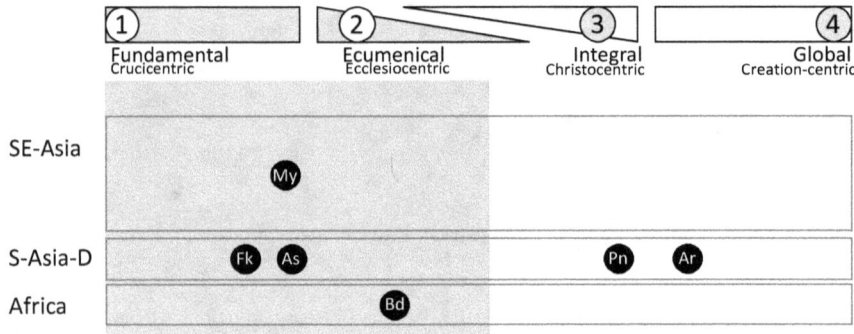

**Figure 60:** IM leaders in movement between 100 and 1,000

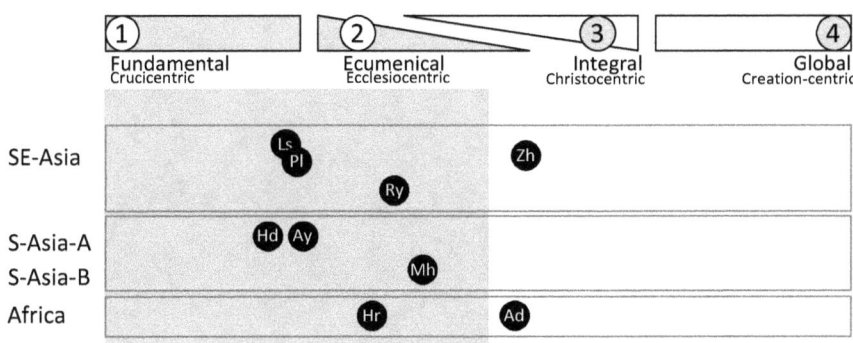

**Figure 61:** IM leaders in movement > 1,000

# APPENDIX C
## Additional works consulted

In addition to the references cited, I consulted the following works.

Augustine. (1945). *The city of God. Everyman's Library* (Vol. 1). (J. Healey, Trans.) London: J. M. Dent & Sons Ltd.
Augustine. (1945). *The city of God. Everyman's Library* (Vol. 2). London: J. M. Dent & Sons Ltd.
Barnard, A. (2000). *History and theory in anthropology.* Cambridge: Cambridge University Press.
Barth, K. (1978). *Church dogmatics I/2.* Edinburgh: T & T Clark.
Beaumont, M. (2011). *Christology in dialogue with Muslims: A critical analysis of Christian presentations of Christ for Muslims from the ninth and twentieth centuries.* Oxford: Regnum Books International.
Bernard, H. R. (2000). *Social research methods: Qualitative and quantitative approaches.* Thousand Oaks: Sage Publications.
Bosch, D. (1995). *Believing in the future: Towards a missiology of Western culture.* Valley Forge: Trinity Press International.
Bosch, D. J. (2008). *Transforming mission: Paradigm shifts in the theology of mission.* Maryknoll: Orbis Books.
Brown, R. (2005). Part II: Translating the biblical term 'Son(s) of God' in Muslim contexts. *International Journal of Frontier Missiology, 22*(4), 135.
Brown, R. (2007). Why Muslims are repelled by the term Son of God. *Evangelical Missions Quarterly, 43*(4).
Cole, N. (2005). *Organic church: Growing faith where life happens.* San Francisco: Jossey-Bass.
Diab, I. (2010, April). Challenges facing Bible translation in the Islamic context of the Middle East. *The Bible Translator, 61*(2).
Dyrness, W. A. (1990). *Learning about theology from the Third World.* Grand Rapids: Zondervan.

Fletcher, R. (1997). *The barbarian conversion: From paganism to Christianity*. New York: Henry Holt and Company.

Fletcher, R. (2003). *The cross and the crescent: The dramatic story of the earliest encounters between Christians and Muslims*. London: Penguin Books.

Frei, H. W. (1993). *Theology and narrative, selected essays*. Oxford: Oxford University Press.

Frost, M., & Hirsch, A. (2003). *The shaping of things to come: Innovation and mission for the 21st-century church*. Peabody: Hendrickson Publishers.

Griffith, S. (2008). *The church in the shadow of the mosque: Christians and Muslims in the world of Islam*. Princeton: Princeton University Press.

Hauerwas, S., & Jones, L. G. (1989). *Why narrative? Readings in narrative theology*. Grand Rapids: Eerdmans.

Hesselgrave, D. (1980). *Planting churches cross-culturally: A guide for home and foreign mission*. Grand Rapids: Baker Books.

Hirsch, A. (2006). *The forgotten ways: Reactivating the missional church*. Grand Rapids: Brazospress.

Holmes, A. F. (1983). *All truth is God's truth*. Downers Grove: InterVarsity Press.

Kee, H. C., Frost, J. W., Albu, E., Lindberg, C., & Robert, D. L. (1998). *Christianity: A social and cultural history*. Upper Saddle River: Prentice Hall.

Keller, T. (2008). The Gospel in All its Forms. *Leadership Journal* (Spring 2008). Retrieved 2013, January 15 from http://www.christianitytoday.com/le/2008/spring/9.74a.html

Kraft, C. (2003). *Anthropology for Christian witness*. Mary Knoll: Orbis Books.

Kraft, K. A. (2012). *Searching for heaven in the real world: A sociological discussion of conversion in the Arab World*. Oxford: Regnum Books International.

Lewis, R. (2011, May–June). Can the kingdom of God break out of Christendom? *MIssion Frontiers, 33*(3), 15.

Lingenfelter, S. (1995). *Transforming culture: A challenge for Christian mission*. Grand Rapids: Baker Books.

McGavran, D. (1965). *Church growth and Christian mission.* New York: Harper & Row.

McGrath, A. (2010). *Christian theology* (5th ed.). West Sussex: Wiley-Blackwell.

McGrath, A. E. (2002). *The future of Christianity.* Oxford: Blackwell Publishers.

McKnight, S. (2010, December 3). Jesus vs. Paul. *Christianity Today,* 54(12), 25. Retrieved 2013, January 15 from http://www.christianitytoday.com/ct/2010/december/9.25.html

McLaren, B. D. (2010). *A new kind of Christianity: Ten questions that are transforming the faith.* New York: Harper One.

McLaren, B. D. (2012). *Why did Jesus, Moses, the Buddha and Mohammad cross the road?: Christian identity in a multi-faith world.* London: Hodder & Stoughton.

Newbigin, L. (1995). *The open secret: An introduction to the theology of mission.* Grand Rapids: Eerdmans Publishing.

Parshall, P. (2003). *Muslim evangelism: Contemporary approach to contextualization.* Downers Grove: InterVarsity Press.

Piper, J. (1993). *Let the nations be glad: The supremacy of God in missions.* Grand Rapids: Baker Books.

Pocock, M., Van Rheenen, G., & McConnel, D. (2005). *The changing face of world missions: Engaging contemporary issues and trends.* Grand Rapids: Baler Academic.

Pope, J. P. (1990). *Redemptoris Missio.* Retrieved 2012, October 2 from http://www.vatican.va/holy_father/john_paul_ii/encyclicals/documents/hf_jp-ii_enc_07121990_redemptoris-missio_en.html

Riggs, H. (1941, April). Shall we try unbeaten paths in working for Moslems? *The Muslim World,* 31(2), 116–126.

Ryken, L. (1979, October). The Bible: God's storybook. *Christianity Today.*

Shenk, D. W., & Stutzman, E. R. (1988). *Creating communities of the kingdom: New Testament models of church planting.* Scottsdale: Herald Press.

Shuster, M. (1987). *Power, pathology, paradox: The dynamics of evil and good.* Grand Rapids: Zondervan.

Smith, D. K. (1992). *Creating understanding.* Grand Rapids: Zondervan Publishing House.

Tilley, T. (1985). *Story theology.* Wilmington: Michael Glazier.

Vander Werff, L. L. (1977). *Christian mission to Muslims: The record*. South Pasadena: William Carey Library.

Weiss, R. S. (1994). *Learning from strangers: The art and method of qualitative interview studies*. New York: The Free Press.

Wiersma, W. (2000). *Research methods in education: An introduction*. Boston: Allyn and Bacon.

Wright, C. J. (2006). *The mission of God: Unlocking the Bible's grand narrative*. Downers Grove: InterVaristy Press.

Wright, N.T. (2003). *The resurrection of the Son of God*. London: Society for Promotion of Christian Knowledge.

Wright, N.T. (2008, June 17). Kingdom come: The public meaning of the Gospels. *Christian Century*.

Wright, N.T. (2009). *Paul: In fresh perspective*. Minneapolis: Fortress Press.

Wright, N. T. (1991). How can the Bible be authoritative? Retrieved 15 September, 2012, from http://ntwrightpage.com/Wright_Bible_Authoritative.htm

# APPENDIX D
## Additional M-Framework figures

The first two figures following depict the M-Framework.

The third figure summarizes the findings of this study. It uses the M-Framework to illustrate the answer to the main research question: What are the theological and missional frames of IM leaders? The scatterplot is the answer. The figure also shows in summary the research findings about the IM context in which these frames develop, and it depicts the communal processes within the IM context that lead to the theological and missional understandings of IM leaders.

| Allah–Theology Frame | Paradigm 1 | 2 | 3 | 4 |
|---|---|---|---|---|
| Essence | Truth; just but also loving; judgment: eternal damnation for most and eternal life for some | Teacher; loving but also just; judgment: eternal damnation for some and eternal life for others | Merciful; loving, guiding, and correcting; seeking righteousness and justice; eternal life for most and eternal damnation for none | Love; enabling, guiding, and correcting; seeking righteousness and justice; eternal life for all |
| The Problem | Satan's rebellion and the Fall; broken relationship between God and man | The Fall and man giving in to Satan's temptations; broken relationship between God and man | Man's forfeit of the Creation Mandate; strife among men and corruption | Man's forfeit of the Creation Mandate; chaos and pollution |

| Allah–Theology Frame | Paradigm 1 | 2 | 3 | 4 |
|---|---|---|---|---|
| Satan | Main figure; responsible for sin and suffering; in a cosmic war with God | Tempts man off the right path | Not a major figure; part of a multiplicity of things that cause man to lose his way | Minor or no figure; man is responsible for sin and sufferings |
| Man | Totally depraved and unable to respond to God | Fully fallen and sinful but able to choose Christ as Savior | Able to follow Christ and impact societies for him | Fully capable of responding to God and doing good in this world |

| Allah–Missio Dei Frame | Paradigm 1 | 2 | 3 | 4 |
|---|---|---|---|---|
| Gospel | God provided a way for your relationship with him to be restored through the substitutionary death of Jesus Christ on the cross and through his resurrection. Believe this and you will go to heaven when you die. | God provided a way for your relationship with him to be restored through the atoning death of Jesus Christ on the cross and through his resurrection. Believe this and you will go to heaven when you die. | God is full of mercy and love for all and is committed to the culmination of creation on earth. Follow Jesus Christ and you will be liberated from bondages and participate in establishing his kingdom on earth. | God is full of mercy and love for all and is committed to the culmination of creation on earth. Follow Jesus Christ and you will be fully human and help bring about his kingdom on earth. |
| This World | Created by God; doomed to total destruction; our testing ground | Created by God but doomed; will be replaced with a new heaven and a new earth | God's good creation being restored and purged from injustice towards the age to come | God's good creation, heading towards the fullness of his shalom over time |

# Appendix D

| Allah-Missio Dei Frame | Paradigm 1 | 2 | 3 | 4 |
|---|---|---|---|---|
| Our Mandate | Evangelism; save people out of this world; Jesus is our Savior away from this world; salvation | Discipleship; save people out of this world and obey God's commandments; impact societies through individual righteous living; sanctification | Missional; meet people's needs; work for systemic justice in societies in this world; liberation | Ubiquitous (omnipresent); manage this world; overcome evil with love; Jesus is our model for saving this world; shalom |
| Healthy Societies | Not in focus and secondary to personal salvation | Come about through individual righteous living | Establish by addressing systemic injustice | The core of man's mandate and the gospel |
| Religions | Christianity is the one true religion and in conflict with all others; conversion to Christianity is the goal | Christianity is the one true religion; there is some truth in other religions that can be used as bridges towards conversion | Seek interfaith dialogue and understanding towards harmony and peace | Irrelevant and sometimes an obstruction to the message of God and to following Jesus Christ |
| Election | Double election: God elects some for heaven and others for hell | A mystery between God's sovereignty and man's free choice that leads to heaven or hell | God's special appointment of certain people to be a blessing to others in this world | God's special appointment of certain people, and in a sense of everyone, to be a blessing to others in this world |

| Allah–Missio Dei Frame | Paradigm 1 | 2 | 3 | 4 |
|---|---|---|---|---|
| Hell | A place created by God for everlasting suffering for Satan, demons and all unbelievers (most people) | A place created by God for everlasting suffering for Satan, demons and all who openly reject God | Not a major theme in God's redemptive history; a man-made experience or a future event created by God to annihilate Satan, demons and all unbelievers | A man-made experience now and later as long as we reject God's love |
| Heaven | A place created by God for everlasting joy in his presence for all true believers (the elected few) | A place created by God for everlasting joy in his presence for all who positively respond to God's revelation to them | Man's joyful experience with God in societies now and in his kingdom on earth in the age to come | Man's joyful experience with God and in all of creation now and in his kingdom on earth over time |
| The Bible | The inerrant Word of God; without error in every domain; our authority; transcultural; truth; teaching; *sola scriptura*; biblicism; for the elect | The infallible Word of God; reveals God and matters of faith without failure; to be read in doctrinal context; our truth; for the church | Inspired record of God's dealings with his creation throughout redemptive history; to be read in historical context; our framework; for all faith communities | A record of communication between God and man; used by God to continue the communication; our guidance; context-shaped; learning; for all of mankind |
| The Qur'an | A satanic book; never use it | A dangerous book; only to be used as a one-way bridge to the Bible and Christ | A book with many truths from God | A record of communication between God and man; used by God to continue the communication |

| Isa al Masih–Christology Frame | Paradigm 1 | 2 | 3 | 4 |
|---|---|---|---|---|
| Identity | The Second Person of the Trinity; the eternal and divine Son of God; our Savior | God incarnate; the mediator between God and man | The promised Messiah and Redeemer of all of creation | The Word of God in human form; our model as the perfect servant, fully submitted to God |
| Christology | High Christology is the only true Christology | Process from low Christology to the goal of high Christology | High and low Christology are both vital elements of a wholistic Christology | Wholistic Christology with some emphasis on low Christology |

| Isa al Masih–Missio Christi Frame | Paradigm 1 | 2 | 3 | 4 |
|---|---|---|---|---|
| His Life | Establishing his divinity through miracles | Establishing his divinity through miracles | The promised Messiah; correcting Judaism, renewing the law, and embracing others; liberating people from bondage | The Son of Man; protecting the weak, liberating people from bondage, exposing injustice |
| On the Cross | The Son of God, carrying the sins of the world | The Lamb of God, atoning for the sins of man | The Messiah, redeeming Israel and showing the way to bless the nations through self-sacrifice and love | The Son of Man, in full submission, reveals and overcomes evil with love |

| Isa al Masih–Missio Christi Frame | Paradigm 1 | 2 | 3 | 4 |
|---|---|---|---|---|
| The Cross | Sin; justice; wrath; penal substitutionary atonement | Sin; justice and love; atonement for mankind | Lostness; love; mercy; solidarity with mankind; the way | Lostness; love; mercy; solidarity with mankind; the way |
| The Resurrection | Proof of his divinity and of God's wrath satisfied | Proof of the atonement accepted and of God's victory over Satan and death | Proof of his Messiahship and God's appointment of him as Lord of all | Proof of his special anointing and of God's commitment to his creation |
| The Future | Second Coming as Judge: destroy the earth; throw Satan, demons, and unbelievers in lake of fire; and bring believers into a new heaven and earth | Second Coming as Judge: destroy the earth; throw Satan, demons, and unbelievers in lake of fire; and bring believers into a new heaven and earth | The coming King, cleansing the earth from injustice and transforming this world into his kingdom for all; or annihilation of Satan, demons, and unbelievers | Presently at work as King towards the culmination of creation on earth |

Appendix D   339

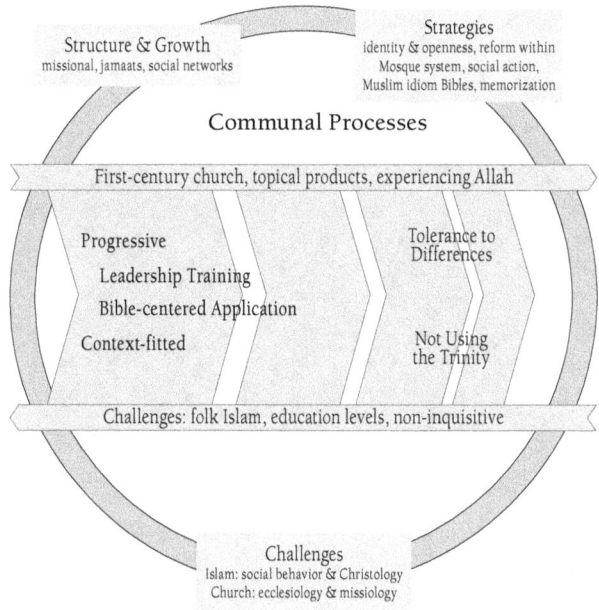

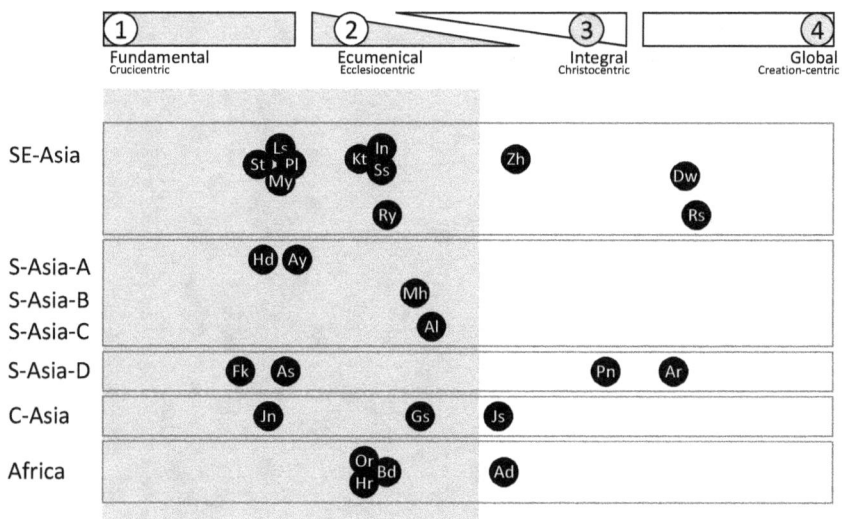

www.ingramcontent.com/pod-product-compliance
Lightning Source LLC
LaVergne TN
LVHW011758060526
838200LV00053B/3622